BLOOD, MONEY, & POWER

BLOOD, MONEY, & POWER

How L.B.J. Killed J.F.K.

Barr McClellan

Skyhorse Publishing

All Rights Reserved. No part of this book may be reproduced in any manner without the express written consent of the publisher, except in the case of brief excerpts in critical reviews or articles. All inquiries should be addressed to Skyhorse Publishing, 307 West 36th Street, 11th Floor, New York, NY 10018.

Skyhorse Publishing books may be purchased in bulk at special discounts for sales promotion, corporate gifts, fund-raising, or educational purposes. Special editions can also be created to specifications. For details, contact the Special Sales Department, Skyhorse Publishing, 307 West 36th Street, 11th Floor, New York, NY 10018 or info@skyhorsepublishing.com.

Skyhorse® and Skyhorse Publishing® are registered trademarks of Skyhorse Publishing, Inc.®, a Delaware corporation.

www.skyhorsepublishing.com

10 9 8 7

Library of Congress Cataloging-in-Publication Data is available on file.

ISBN: 978-1-61608-197-3

Printed in the United States of America

For Cecile, dearly beloved always

Contents

Self-knowledge is the indispensable prelude to self-control; and self-knowledge, for a nation as well as an individual, begins with history.
—Arthur M. Schlesinger Jr.

Introduction

The Texas School Book Depository stands lonely and stark, an ancient red-brick building aside the slope framing Dealey Plaza in Dallas, Texas.[1] Almost one-half million visitors yearly make a pilgrimage to the building's Sixth Floor Museum, retracing the scene of the death of an American president. The Sixth Floor itself is both a historic site and a museum, introducing guests to what happened on November 22, 1963.[2] From the windows on the south side, the overlook shows Elm Street and the boulevard where a man's life was instantly destroyed. To the west, the plaza basin is topped with pergolas along a grassy knoll with trees scattered about. The street itself leads to the triple underpass, constructed in 1936, carrying railroad tracks above the traffic arteries.[3] Some years ago Dallas leaders tried to remove the old building but the public insisted that a memorial remain. Today it is the Sixth Floor Museum. Other floors house municipal offices.

The assassination of President Kennedy in that plaza still remains one of the most tragic events of the twentieth century. At the time, we were shocked that such a charismatic leader could be killed so quickly and so brutally. The sudden, horrific loss remains with us as an emotional attachment that continues to haunt both our individual memories and our history as a nation. Americans remember what they were doing at the time of the assassination on the same level of recall that was experienced with Pearl Harbor, FDR's death, the landing on the moon, Nixon's resignation and flight, and the terrorist attacks on 9-11.

In the ensuing shock, an initial reaction to the killing was fear it was a prelude to a communist attack. The Cold War was at its height. The Cuban Missile Crisis was still fresh in people's minds. Some even preached the gospel, "Better red than dead."[4] In the same way, on November 22, 1963, fear of a nuclear war escalated as our armed forces went on maximum alert. The danger worsened as the "lone nut" was identified as a former "defector" to the Soviet Union and a Cuba sympathizer.

Within two days, a second "lone nut" carried out a mob-like execution of the first "lone nut." Major figures associated with organized crime in America immediately fell under suspicion. In the follow-up, however, the hunt for the assassins ended with Jack Ruby's bullet.

Some conservative elements in Dallas had given Kennedy a very unpleasant welcome, branding him a traitor for negotiating with the Soviets.[5] That vicious political attack fueled suspicion of a conspiracy involving Big Oil in the city and perhaps other right-wing elements in Texas. The doubts even extended to our new president, Lyndon Johnson, a Texas political leader for thirty years.

A "blue-ribbon" commission was appointed to investigate the events in Dallas with Chief Justice Earl Warren named as chair. Within nine months, the members reported there had been only one assassin; there was no conspiracy; and improvements were needed in protecting the president.[6] Although conspiracy theories were downplayed by the Warren Commission as "rumors and speculation," the suspicions and controversies did not end.

In the aftermath of the assassination, politics changed dramatically. In November 1963, Kennedy's progressive programs were mired in congressional infighting. Barry Goldwater, a dedicated conservative, was preparing to run as a traditionalist, promising a showdown over the progressive politics followed since the Great Depression. With the assassination, that equation was gone. Johnson was the moderate-to-conservative against the staunch conservative. With Kennedy dead, Goldwater's anticipated liberal versus conservative showdown for the voters to decide simply did not happen. In addition, in the shock and the spirit of unity that prevailed after the assassination, Goldwater did not have a chance. He lost decisively in the presidential election that November 1964, only six weeks after the Warren Report memorialized the lone assassin theory, created a lasting icon in our lost president, and awarded Johnson the lingering sympathy vote.

Under Johnson's new leadership, important social and civil rights programs were passed. Emboldened by his November 1964 mandate, the new Johnson, now elected in his own right, was driven by the policy of containment to undertake the very controversial Vietnam War. A strange split in American politics resulted. Johnson was hailed by progressive Democrats for his social programs but rejected by the same group for his war leadership. In a similar policy split, conservative Republicans supported the war but opposed Johnson's Great Society programs. At first, Johnson admired his great compromise, having guns and butter; however, he gradually changed, despising any opposition, be they activists, liberals, conservatives, or even long-time supporters.

As this division hardened with continuing civil rights protests and ever-widening antiwar marches, Johnson's sudden elevation to the presidency was subjected to increasing questions. Some never accepted the loss of Kennedy and some would never accept leadership from Johnson as a southerner and a Texan. By the spring of 1968, when Johnson was literally a prisoner in the White House, all these elements surrounded and haunted him. He could not work miracles. He could not have guns for Vietnam and butter for his "Great Society." Acknowledging his overwhelming problems, he abruptly withdrew from any reelection efforts for 1968. On that evening of March 31, 1968, while some Americans were stunned, many rejoiced. There were few political neutrals during 1968.

In the years that followed, Kennedy emerged as a valiant but tragic figure and Johnson a vilified but also tragic character. The former vice president could never be what his president had been. The emotional shock to the nation had never truly gone away. There simply had been no closure because there was no national consensus that justice had been done. In a very subtle way, for a nation united under one leader, the notion that "the king is dead, long live the king" was never accepted. "The president is dead, long live the president" never caught on. It lacked both the personalities and the majesty to gain acceptance. The concept that "JFK is dead, long live LBJ" was simply not acceptable.

As a nation we continued to grieve immensely.[7] Perhaps most tragically, Robert Kennedy was driven into a remorseful seclusion from which there was no escape.[8] Jackie Kennedy showed immense strength but had doubts that remain unanswered.[9] In this overwhelming grief and doubt, most Americans were never able to accept the man identified by the Warren Commission as the only shooter. After all, there were two "lone nuts." The evidence and the conclusions just did not fit together. In addition, we could not balance Johnson with what we had lost and the grief we had suffered.[10] We went through the shock and anger and mourning but there was neither acceptance nor closure.

Emotionally, the initial welcome for Johnson was gradually depleted over the five years that followed. That shock and the ensuing split in our personal assessment of Johnson lingers to this day. We find ourselves divided between Kennedy and Johnson; between a lone nut killer and a conspiracy; between our inability to have both guns and butter; and with a lingering opposition to the Vietnam War or full support for that war for containing communism. This conflict combines to leave us as a nation still searching for an answer to what happened. There is no rational explanation for the assassination and there is no emotional closure for the brutal death. What is needed is to bring these feelings to rest, to undertake an emotional purging, to create a cathar-sis of the will, and, most importantly, to find the solutions to what divides us rationally and emotionally.

The many controversies over the Warren *Report* only make the problem of acceptance more difficult. Using modern techniques for crime scene inves-tigations, numerous researchers have argued every possible theory.

Many center on the bullets. First, there is the "magic bullet" theory, that one bullet hit both the president and Texas governor John Connally and somehow inflicted massive damage with no damage whatsoever to the spent missile. The other controversy centers on the fatal bullet, the one with such horrendous consequences, the one that killed the president instantly. Was that bullet fired from behind, from the "grassy knoll" in front, or from some-where else? From those bullets the controversy has literally exploded into so many contradictory ideas that, when taken together, they prove "everything" or "nothing." Yet as we know only too well and as we cannot forget, the hor-rible and unthinkable did happen.

The ridiculous reach of the controversy has divided the nation into two basic camps. One remains convinced there was a conspiracy, involving at the bare minimum more than one shooter. They tend to deride anyone dis-agreeing with them as an apologist for the Warren Report. The other camp, a shrinking enclave, believes that any person asserting there was more than one assassin is mentally off-balance. For many of them, reference to the "grassy knoll" refers to anyone believing in any conspiracy theories; such ref-erences, this group believes, are cockeyed. They oppose any idea of a con-spiracy in government anywhere.

At the heart of the debate is an issue that has been with us from the beginning of the American Republic. Patrick Henry argued passionately against a federal system, contending that men would always be selfish, serv-ing personal gain at the expense of the general good.[11] That debate was so intense that the Constitution was approved by the several states with only the slimmest majorities. As we shall see, power initiated the tragedy in Dallas on November 22, 1963. Too often, men in power do what they want, not what the law requires. Turning to a solution to this problem, abuse has occurred often enough to warrant a further expansion of our democratic traditions.

Interestingly, what happened in Dealey Plaza remains an event of instant recall. Those remembering that terrible day and the mournful week that fol-lowed remain haunted by the basic events. The same remembrance and recall intrigues our younger generations as they learn what happened and then seek to reach their own conclusions.

George Matthews is a retired Dallas police officer who routinely leads high school students through the Sixth Floor Museum.[12] Despite his careful review of what happened and what he knows of the Warren Report, his group of young visitors remains convinced that there was a conspiracy. Shrugging, he says, "We just never found the evidence." Even though he says he is convinced there was only one shooter, questions linger in his mind. "Just show me," he insists, "or leave it alone."

This book will allow us to take an important step toward a necessary resolution, one that will engage both the mind and the heart. To accept what happened, powerful emotions will have to be overcome. Some of these emotions include strong feelings about what happened, feelings now carved in stone. In addition, the raw exercise of power will have to be understood. For this, some may require a suspension of reason, just to believe that a system of laws can become a system of fiat, a government of might over right. Once the system is understood and accepted, however, what led to Johnson's illegal acquisition of power becomes understandable. The assassination was doomed to happen as the night follows the day. And night did follow day.

Among the many theories about what happened in Dallas, the purpose here is to provide balance, to show how the many interest groups have walked a path that defines the conspiracy. The many researchers who preceded me have made possible the disclosures now made. The issue is not conservative versus liberal, Democrat or Republican, activist or pacifist, reactionary versus radical. The issue is in the nature of power; simply put, power is the heart of the matter.

On the other hand, this book is not a balanced retelling of the life of Lyndon Johnson. There are many excellent biographies about him that restate the public record.[13] Some attempt to provide a "balance," to show his flaws as well as his achievements. Most rely on information readily available from the public record in Washington and scattered throughout many archives. Some attempt to delve deeper into Johnson's personal life and are commendable for revealing what they witnessed. None goes behind the attorney-client privilege to see what really happened, to show the details of Johnson's personal and business life back in Texas that remains outside of the public record and out of sight. In addition, none of the many theories has been able to "follow the money" from the time political contributions started for Johnson to the acquisition of businesses and properties by Johnson to the bonus finally paid to the chief conspirator. No one has followed this "money trail." The assumption by some has been that payoff money was not involved in the assassination. Some apparently assume that many conspirators simply combined to assassinate the president without compensation required. On the other hand, those assuming that the shooters were compensated have never found the money trail.

Behind the attorney-client shield in the deep politics of Texas, the most monstrous crime in the nation was planned, completed, covered up, and paid for with power plays that were in place long before and long after November 22, 1963. The roots of the crime rested in that violent cauldron of cold-blooded murders and atrocious lynchings that permeate Texas history. Lyndon Johnson and his personal attorney Edward Clark were dedicated to an awful objective based on primal emotions of greed for absolute power and, particularly in Johnson's case, of a fear that became a stark necessity for survival. Their crimes against our nation were deemed necessary and sufficient by them to protect their very personal sense of superiority and destiny mixed with a very profound fear of loss of power, one that would be followed by prosecution, by conviction, and by loss of all they had achieved. Particularly for Johnson, for a man in a position to become immortal, the very real threat of eternal condemnation was too much. The combination of these several conflicting motivations proved overwhelming and resulted in the assassination of President Kennedy.

How could lawyers be involved? Today many will chuckle as they consider the obvious answer. In 1963, however, lawyers were deemed bastions of truth. They were above reproach, bulletproof. The specific insights into what so-called superlawyers[14] are capable of doing should confirm the suspicions many have about lawyers at the center of power in our democracy. Still, the facts of what happened behind the privilege are not easily disclosed. The few lawyers who were involved have been well paid and, as participants, had a vested interest in the execution and coverup of the most terrible of crimes. In addition, what the few lawyers who were directly involved actually did was known to only a small group of conspirators. Those lawyers committed the crimes by themselves or participated with as few outsiders as possible. It was common sense to keep the crime "close" and that secrecy and coverup succeeded.

Until now.

The noose around Johnson has gradually tightened. Even today, however, many people remain committed to a belief in Johnson's innocence of any crime and some are still well paid to defend his heritage to the maximum extent possible.[15] In an almost automatic reaction, they protect the LBJ legacy with the best spin possible.

There is also a built-in bias against any conspiracy to the extent that the grassy knoll has become an icon to discredit any disbelief in the fundamental soundness of the American system of democracy. As we shall see, there was a shooter on the grassy knoll or, more precisely, at the fence just beyond it, to the southwest, toward the famous triple underpass for Elm, Main, and Commerce Streets.

A private citizen seeking to be an investigator into the assassination faces many obstacles, not the least of which is government secrecy and self-protection.[16] By and large, that veil over the assassination has been overcome through the help of countless volunteers. Many of these researchers have assisted me personally. My only requirement was that they stick with me in what I knew was a very difficult task. They have. Through their efforts, the story has become more complete than I ever anticipated would be possible. Even though I found myself at the center of the disclosures about the conspiracy, much had to be unearthed to lay out the extended history, one reaching from the founding of Texas to the present day. In addition, the key elements of the assassination had to be corroborated. There is solid evidence thoroughly implicating Johnson, but the critical print evidence, barely one square inch of human sweat, is the final, ultimate corroboration.

Thanks also belong to the many independent researchers into the assassination. Their efforts made possible some of the lines of discovery I was given to follow, and they provided substantive threads to several of the key disclosures at the foundation of this book. More important, despite many trying circumstances and a well-organized opposition that would stop at nothing, they kept the investigation alive.

An assumption is made that readers will have some understanding of the background to both Johnson's political career and of the assassination of John Kennedy. Because of the new disclosures and the interest generated since our key evidence was presented to the Assassination Records Review Board, this book is only an overview for what happened. One future book will explore far more deeply into Edward Clark's involvement by probing into his "Bubba justice"[17] and how it worked in Texas. Dependent on further disclosures by those with the records, perhaps still more detail will emerge about what happened behind the scenes on November 22, 1963. My final volume will suggest the solutions to the government conspiracies that are still possible in Washington, D.C.

There are no videos or tape recordings of what Johnson and Clark did in their conspiracy before, on, and after the assassination. Only a few documents show what actually happened. Of necessity, some scenes for what happened will be the "journalistic novel" with a carefully marked use of "faction."[18] This documentary approach to show the facts will help set out the steps that had to be taken and how and why they were taken. These events are carefully noted in a separate chapter and represent my effort to recapture the events as best as possible based on what I experienced and understood from a unique insider's perspective. In presenting these scenarios, I have also called upon my experience as a trial attorney to present the necessary facts that a jury would hear about what had to have happened.

Finally, and most important, my thanks go to the many friends, fellow researchers, and editors who stood with me in this effort that extended over a seven-year period. These contacts are included in the sources listed in the appendix. Of particular importance, Eric Parkinson has been simply outstanding in his support and encouragement as publisher. Tracey Lee Williams, as agent, provided invaluable support and contacts with both literary and publishing worlds.

During all this time I had the support needed on the home front. My deepest and fondest thanks are to those members of family and friends who persevered with me. Most researchers assisted with useful comments. Outstanding assistance with the necessary editing was by our dear friend, Norma Anderson.

In the overall endeavor, one person stands above all the rest. My wife, Cecile, and I stood together through many trials in a remarkable partnership that is worthy of a book in itself. That book is also being written. And it will be in her honor, for she has provided that utmost support and effort needed for this manuscript to become a published book—and for everything else.

In the final analysis, however, the disclosures and truths revealed in this book are my responsibility—and mine alone.

> The truth which makes men free is for the most part the truth which men prefer not to hear.
> —Herbert Sebastian Agar

> There are many people . . . that have the answers to questions and don't even know the questions exist.
> —J. Harrison, researcher, former Dallas police officer, genealogist

I never saw anything like it. [Johnson] never trusted anyone.
Everybody was after him.
　　　　—Kenneth P. O'Donnell

1

Epiphany

Lyndon Johnson ended his days as president on January 20, 1969. When
Richard Nixon took the oath of office at noon ceremonies in Washington,
D.C., Johnson's reign of power ended. Johnson had lunch with friends that
day, then boarded the helicopter for the ride to Andrews Air Force Base and
the long flight home to Austin.

In the evening darkness, *Air Force One* landed at Bergstrom Air Force
Base southeast of Austin. Only a small crowd was there to welcome the ex-
president. There was no vast turnout of supporting citizens, no parade followed by a dinner banquet, and no welcome-home speeches. He did not
return the conquering hero. With the Vietnam War still going strong and
with the widespread criticism of Johnson, he had few adoring friends left
even in the city where a majority stood behind him no matter what he did.
The small crowd included his key lawyers, a few other diehard supporters,
and those still on his payroll. Austin knew he had failed as president, that the
city would never have the income it realized while he was in office, and that
the new life he was entering would never be the same. After a few perfunctory waves and handshakes at Bergstrom, Johnson got in a limousine, took
the long drive home to his ranch the other side of Johnson City, and began
to settle into what remained of his future.

The change could not have been greater. From days filled with constant
activity and innumerable decisions, from the pressing demands for his time
at a job that was "24 and 7," Johnson suddenly had nothing to do. From the
eye of a driving hurricane to a cold, dry, and very boring ranch, Johnson had
time to think and reminisce, to relive his presidency and all his political years,
and to try to develop a schedule for things to do, one that had some life in
it. In that stark contrast between constant, controlled chaos and a veritable
vacuum, he had no choice but to evaluate his life.

He did not like what he saw.

Soon after the bitter return, Johnson fell into a deep depression.[1] In that combination of melancholy and listlessness marked with outbursts of energy in his continuing delusion of the grandeur that could have been, Johnson's paranoia returned, the fear that had first manifested itself shortly after November 22, 1963, when he had become president in those shocking moments in Dealey Plaza.[2] His depression quickly turned severe and long-lasting, presenting itself in a manner that was life-threatening. As visitors came by to see him, their remarks echoed to the same refrain, that Johnson had become "totally withdrawn" and appeared to have "lost his moorings."[3] One adviser remarked, only half in jest, that Johnson was his "normal, manic-depressive self."[4]

Another development only worsened his melancholy. Johnson was preparing his memoirs. The plan was for three volumes, starting with the presidency, then covering the congressional years, and finally reliving his childhood. Interestingly, the program would be perfect for the psychotherapy he would soon begin.[5]

Johnson could not write; he would only review what others scripted for him, making notes and adding comments. Each event necessarily triggered memories that might have best been suppressed because the ongoing confrontation with his "complex" past only heightened his anxiety, his fear of facing the end of his life—and of having to answer for it.

Johnson became still more depressed, and the combination of pessimism, fatigue, and insomnia heightened the continuing fear of another heart attack. Then, in May 1970, he suffered severe chest pains and was hospitalized. The diagnosis was angina, and, with a heart unable to withstand an operation, nitroglycerine pills were prescribed.[6] He fell still further into a listless state that alternated between grandiosity and paranoia. For the first time, his appearance reflected his condition as his hair grew long, so much so that he was described as a "hippie" in those early morning hours at the ranch when he simply refused to groom himself. One of his lawyers remarked that Johnson had become what he had hated. Always able to compartmentalize what he thought, said, and did—to be "complex," Johnson now expected visitors to at least condone those "complexities" or, more accurately, his "peculiarities." He was clearly psychopathic.[7]

Finally, despite his distaste for "shrinks" and "mind-benders," Johnson agreed to what was needed. Professional help was summoned, and his White House doctor, Admiral George Burkley, began a series of observations and interventions that proved partly successful; at least, he seemed to improve. His condition, however, was far worse than a general practitioner could treat. Any relief was temporary, at best.

Another event then entered Johnson's daily schedule to keep him busy, bringing him a small measure of relief. He had to plan for the dedication of his library in Austin, then nearing completion just east of the University of Texas campus. For the next year he was busy with those plans. With the grandiose plans underway, he seemed to be out of the black hole he had entered.

The library's ceremonies climaxed on May 25, 1971. After several days of greeting the dignitaries as they arrived, the unending parties, and a general feeling of good will from his friends, the formal dedication proved to be a great time had by all. For Austin, the glory days of Johnson's power had returned. The celebrations were short-lived, however, and, when the last visitor left, the vacuum returned.

This time, Johnson's wife determined to try again, and, believing Dr. Burkley could do little, she brought in the best psychiatrist available in Austin. The neuropsychiatrist was schooled in the latest approaches in psychotherapy, and he commenced an intense program of dynamic intervention that winter and spring of 1971–1972.[8] It seemed to work.

Substantial legal questions were presented by the depth of the therapy, however, and Johnson's lawyers intervened once again, to require that the psychiatrist keep what was said secret forever, that he be paid through a standard trust agreement,[9] and that any additional support for Johnson be given, as needed, from his closest and best friends, Ed Clark and Don Thomas; no others. During this time, along with two others, I prepared a memo on the secrecy required, of keeping the disclosures under wraps. We concluded that the attorney-client privilege was needed in addition to the physician's duty of privacy.[10] At the time I had no idea it involved Johnson.

Over the course of three months in 1972, from April through June, Thomas visited Johnson at the ranch on at least three occasions. Key disclosures resulted. First, whatever was told the psychiatrist had to be protected by the attorney-client privilege. This meant the psychiatrist became an employee of the lawyers. Second, as an insurance policy to assure the psychiatrist was kept quiet, he became the beneficiary of a one-million-dollar trust set up through Johnson's money-laundering corporation, Brazos-Tenth, managed by Don Thomas.[11] Finally, because the treatment rested on free association talk sessions and included even hypnosis, Johnson confronted his black hole, faced the demons, and found release. Late in the treatment, he went through a climax that gave him the peace of mind he needed.

Even though Johnson had been helped, he had to talk about his disclosures. For legal reasons, he knew that a necessary step was to tell his lawyers what had been done; that analysis was underway. To complete the catharsis, the cause of his depression had been revealed by the psychiatrist. With all the necessary information, Clark and Thomas could undertake the protective steps needed to assure that what had been said was not revealed. At the time, they did not know what had been revealed.

For Johnson, the dynamic psychotherapy was very demanding and that June, while visiting his daughter in Virginia, he suffered another major heart attack. Despite the severity of the attack, perhaps because Johnson had reached a sort of peace with his life and himself, he survived.

There was still another lingering problem, far deeper in its consequences. Johnson was never a religious man.[12] He was not a member of any formal religion among the nation's Christian faiths. He did belong to a small church near the ranch, but remained essentially agnostic, a religion many men of the Depression accepted. "If I can't touch it, it ain't real," was a typical refrain. Johnson often remarked that his allegiance was to God, then his nation, his party, and his family.[13] Since, in his often-repeated visions of grandeur, he considered himself God, the self-imposed pressure proved to be extraordinarily heavy. In those very personal demands of facing his final days, he developed this need for a sense of confession, apparently seeking absolution. He did not need the hell and damnation, the perdition he came to fear. As the man got religion in those final months, the mental stress was ever more demanding.

Johnson's key lawyers were kept informed of the overall progress during the final four months of Johnson's life, and, through my regular contacts with Thomas in litigation and travels, I later learned about the "climax" and the "release." On looking back, I am convinced that what Thomas confided in me was his own effort to ease the burden he received from Johnson.

There was that one final meeting with Johnson in about mid-December 1972 as Christmas approached, always a time of deep thinking by those facing death. What happened then was that Johnson disclosed his deepest problems and his deepest psychological revelations to Donald Thomas and transferred those demons to the attorney. Of necessity, legal steps were needed to preserve the Johnson legacy. A self-serving affidavit from the psychiatrist was taken.

On January 22, 1973, on another inaugural week four years after leaving the White House, Johnson ended his years. Midafternoon that day, he felt death coming and was initially prepared for it; however, at the last minute, he summoned help. The Secret Service hurried over and tried their best. Too late. Johnson was gone.[14]

On that same day, the legends began as friends and historians attempted to grasp and understand what had happened. Since then, each has placed their unique spin on at least some of the facts, but the underlying realities are fast disappearing into the fog of history.

Over the last thirty years, Johnson has steadily declined in the public esteem. More recently, there has been an effort at rehabilitation. For a deeply conflicted man, his followers have tried to bring balance to his legacy. That is not possible because he was not a good man. The facts of his life conceded by all are not those of a person trying to do the right thing. Johnson was a mean, often bitter man. He would do anything to gain power and to retain power. He was willing to kill. And he did.

Today, Johnson's legend appears to teeter on an edge, looking into the abyss he created while his backers and apologists are trying hard to pull him back. That rehab effort should end, and Johnson should be left to fall into that darkness he brought upon himself so violently, that damnation he feared so desperately in his final months.

Take a look at what happened. He grew up in a background of violence, and his own childhood had all the markers of a psychopath. His career was one of lost elections that were stolen, capped by an agreement with his lawyer in 1949 to maintain the successful conspiracy to obtain that ultimate power—the presidency—that he so recklessly pursued. As the crimes became apparent, Johnson's inbred violence came to the fore. He was deeply involved in several murders and faced political oblivion and imprisonment. So motivated, his criminal career was capped with the assassination of President Kennedy.

Johnson is balanced on the brink. Take a close look at what he did, and then let him fall into that abyss where he belongs.

We need only to end the denial that finds expression on a national basis. For many years, I had the same denial. Surely Johnson could not have assassinated Kennedy. Finally, ten years after parting company with Johnson's lawyers, I faced up to that denial and ended it.

We need to accept what happened and face up to the need for improving our democracy.

In the pages that follow, I will lay out what I know, corroborated wherever possible by the available resources. In a final chapter, I will return to the known facts and go that one step further, to set out what had to have happened but is not of record. For those key events where I was not present, my inside knowledge of how Johnson's lawyers worked will tell the story of what most likely happened. For the demanding reader, ignore the "faction,"[15] as it is called, and concentrate on the known facts. They are enough.

For the reader who wants to know and appreciate how the assassination most likely happened, to see the assassins as they developed their conspiracy, read the scenarios in the chapter on "jury." See how a trial attorney would take the Johnson story to a jury and seek a final verdict.

For example, I was not at that last meeting between Johnson and Thomas in December 1972, but I have a very good insight into what happened. In order clearly to separate what I know personally from what I know most likely happened, I have placed my rendition of that final meeting in the "jury" chapter, one that closes with a final epiphany for Johnson, one that brings a sunset to the darkness he stood for. We can then see the horrific assassination, and its lingering effect on a nation still in denial.

> Madness in great ones must not unwatched go.
> —Shakespeare, *Hamlet*

Power tends to corrupt, and absolute power corrupts absolutely.
     —Lord Acton (1887)

2

Privilege

LBJ killed JFK? Unthinkable! An American vice president would never kill the president. That is impossible.

The perception is to the contrary. According to polls on the assassination, a solid 70 percent of Americans believe there was a conspiracy and that Johnson participated in some way, either knowing in advance or at least assisting in the coverup.[1] Confronted with opinion running against Johnson, historian Robert Dallek was compelled to state, "He [Johnson] had absolutely nothing to do with JFK's assassination."[2] No proof is offered for this assertion. Apparently relying on a personal assessment of the man, Dallek notes that the allegations of several crimes allegedly involving Johnson are inconclusive. At best, this assertion of fact that Johnson was not involved in any crimes has no supporting evidence. If there is evidence, then it must be produced by the historians. Of course, the negative cannot be proven with certainty but the depth of the allegations against Johnson have reached such a low point that they must be denied. The Johnson legacy is so terrible that his apologists are on the defensive as never before.

More revealing is the difference of opinion. In a very subtle way, the American view is that Johnson was involved but apparently not enough for an indictment and conviction. As a nation we seem to be saying, "We know Johnson was in on the assassination but we do not know exactly how." Was he involved only in the coverup? Did he know about the plans in advance? Was he part of the planning? Did he know exactly when and where Kennedy was going to be assassinated? The differences are far more important than mere semantics. Was Johnson "only" an accessory after the fact or was he in on the planning? Was he an assassin? Of course, any participation by the person who would benefit the most makes him criminally responsible to the maximum degree. If Johnson had even the slightest hint but said nothing, he becomes a member of the conspiracy. Stated bluntly, he becomes an assassin.

Many researchers place him there, at least as an accessory.[3] As we shall see, he was deeply involved.

Were the three basic elements to any crime present? Did Johnson have the motive, the means, and the opportunity?

Johnson's motivations included a determination to do anything to become the most powerful person in the world, a fear of total loss of power followed by indictment, and a willingness to go to the edge and beyond. The standard defense for Johnson is that he was "complex," implying that he did many things for many reasons and that there was no single motivation. This clever defense allowed Johnson to point only to good motives and to ignore the bad motives in even a single act. Since some of his complex motives were good, so the logic ran, he could not commit a crime.

Johnson also had the means at his control: a legal system in Texas controlled by his attorney, Edward A. Clark. Johnson and Clark, in turn, had a hired gun on hand for the dirty work.

Finally, when Kennedy, in June 1963, included Texas on his travel agenda, the opportunity was there. Where better to commit the crime than on the home courts or, more appropriately, in the home courts? There, Johnson and Clark could easily control the investigation and the coverup. So, Johnson suggested, urged, and supported the trip to Texas.

The necessary elements for the crime were in Johnson's hands.

Americans are notoriously fair-minded. Whenever criminal charges are involved, we are willing to accord the accused due process. Since the crime was committed two generations ago, distinct problems in due process and, more specifically, in the standard of proof are involved. There are no videos and there are no tape recordings. Documents have been carefully hidden or destroyed. Satisfying due process will not be easy.

On the other hand, the circumstantial evidence is overwhelming. Legally, once a plot is proven, conspiracy law mandates that the conspirators show there was no crime. At this stage, the burden is on the apologists for Johnson to show he did not participate in the assassination. As we shall see, the means are readily available to make the effort. Undoubtedly, some exculpatory disclosures will be made. We need only see the undisclosed "penthouse records."

Here is where the difference of opinion in America reaches a subtle distinction, into a subconscious determination to protect the presidency and the nation that office represents. Perhaps this protection is a form of respect for the nation's highest office but not the person in that office. Therein lies the conflict. We honor and respect the office but may or may not approve of the occupant. A measure of pride also enters our evaluation. We cannot separate the office from the occupant. Denial plays its role. We must, however, confront what happened. Then we need to decide what must be done.

Johnson participated through a few key associates who realized their horrific goals partly through a desperate determination, partly because a few breaks went their way, and mostly because as superlawyers they operated behind the most powerful secrecy allowed in the United States, that of the sacred attorney-client privilege. Far more powerful than the Mafia's *omerta* where an informant cannot tell what he knows, privileged conversations cannot be presented to any court. At one time, the power of the privilege went further, even permitting client and lawyer to plan crimes.[4] Although ethics rules were amended to prohibit plans to murder or injure, the blanket of silence provided by and for attorneys was very complete.

Finally, in the last step of the plan, following the assassination of John Kennedy and the immediate succession of Lyndon Johnson to the White House, the full power of the federal government and its machinery for law enforcement was also in the control of the conspirators.

Interestingly, what follows is what most people believe, but are simply unwilling or unable to confront and accept. While this reluctance is an admirable measure of respect and support for the presidency, of patriotism to our nation and its leaders, the facts must be confronted. For the better we know the truth, the more we are able to enjoy our freedoms. The basic rule remains: we should know the truth because that truth makes us free.

At this point, of necessity, I become an active participant in what happened. As an associate attorney, I became a part of the conspiracy. Later, as a partner, I was deeply involved in the aftermath of the assassination. Fortunately, I pulled out in time. For now, however, I am involved in these disclosures.

As the black Town Car approached a roadside barbecue shanty near Hewitt, Texas, one the most powerful men in the state casually told me that our senior partner had engineered the death of John Kennedy. "Clark handled all of that in Dallas," Don Thomas said, glancing at me. He had already proudly told me he "was the only living witness to what happened at Box 13."[5]

"Dallas," I thought. The center for Texas oil, financial power, and the military-industrial complex. There too we had right-wing politics, the home of the east Texas billionaires, and the money center for most of the political crimes our law firm arranged. But "Dallas" stood for one event over all others, infamous as it would forever be for the assassination of President Kennedy.

Thomas looked at me carefully, always communicating his trial lawyer's experience and his forty years of hard missions for former president Lyndon Johnson, awaiting a reaction to the monstrous evil he had just admitted. He had at the same time confirmed the reports about Ed Clark, our senior partner.

What could be said? The event was acknowledged among the participants and was rumored among the associates; however, by 1973 it was over and done. There was also my abiding friendship with Thomas that dampened any response. Going to the authorities was impossible because of the privilege. At this point it bears noting that only much later would I decide there was no such privilege. In addition, I knew the authorities in Texas would do nothing. The crime had taken place almost ten years earlier. Nothing could be done. I considered the facts virtually "top secret."

I glanced out the passenger window as we crossed the railroad tracks, the tin-roofed shanty there to the right, a thin white smoke trailing from the stovepipe and in that same instant I knew there could be no reaction from me. Strictly speaking, this was law-firm business. As I looked back at Thomas, I conveyed nothing. Appearing disinterested, my expression said, "So what. I knew about it already. Nothing could be done about it." But I said nothing.

By then my seven years with Clark and Thomas had given me all the insights I needed. I knew the stories of murder and coverups, of reckless revenge and personal destruction, of money laundering and payoffs, of all the sordid corruption of Texas power politics and, more specifically, the illegal money machines and the corrupted ballot boxes. After all, we were the best at the power game. I knew from my cases that the only thing that mattered was the ruthless exercise of our power. If scandals were threatened and murder was necessary, "So what?" That was the price of power and power was the firm's business. Besides, what we did was privileged. We only worried about results, about *winning*.

From my first days at Clark's law offices, I was forewarned never to talk about Johnson's business or anything else we did for him. No one outside our walls, outside the attorney-client privilege, the most sacred veil in the law, could know. At the time believing the information was privileged, I fully protected our client. That afternoon in Hewitt, my expression for Thomas conveyed absolute silence and total discretion.

Eyes dancing, his raggedy brow always askew, Thomas grinned. "The hot turkey links are the best," he said as he looked away. I smiled. I had again convinced him I would never violate the secrets, even the most terrible, and that I would keep the trust. Over the years he and I would remain best of friends, he my mentor while I was his choice to work the cases. Despite my deep inner conflict, at the time subconsciously buried and unresolved, I assured him I could be trusted, that I was a loyal partner and discrete attorney. From that point and extending over the next three years, we would talk a great deal more about Johnson and Dallas and everything else during some hard-fought lawsuits and some very long drives.

But there was more.

Partner John Coates had first told me of Johnson's role in the assassination of John Kennedy.[6] I had only been with Clark about six months and, after reviewing an insurance claim, we had retired to Scholz's, the beer parlor of choice in downtown Austin. There, over mugs of beer served under the scattered patterns of a late afternoon sun reaching through the trees and across the outdoor tables, John casually remarked, "If the truth be told, Clark arranged the assassination of Kennedy." When John said it, I shrugged. Surely the admission was not true, just beer and bragging at work. Besides, it was a privileged communication among lawyers; I could tell no one except my associates, except among us, the privileged ones. Seven years later, when Don confirmed it, I knew it was true, and everything else I had learned suddenly came home. Only later, much later, could I sort out what these many confessions meant and how what I knew all fit together.

"Consider that over and done," partner and law firm manager Martin Harris warned when the many subjects of Johnson's past "indiscretions" were mentioned. "It just takes planning." On that first day in Clark's offices, Harris added, "Just be careful. We're paid to protect the president, whether he knows it or not." At the time I had no idea what I was going to learn, but I was certain that I was forever silenced, never to describe what happened. Small wonder Harris could be so candid; nothing I learned could be repeated. His remarks also made it clear that there was no innocence on Johnson's part and that Clark was deeply involved in the ruthless power we exercised.

A few weeks later, riding with Harris to meet "the lobby," the men representing the powers that be in Texas, he had smiled and remarked, "Johnson is nothing more than an Elephadonk, you know, conservative but not a Republican." Clicking off a list of clients, "Oil, ranchers, bankers, utilities, contractors, . . . let's see, truckers, insurance, and so on, you know." He also emphasized, "We do not work with the national 'liberal' democrats, not here and not there." If there was any doubt, I clearly understood my role in lobbying Washington. Shrugging nervously, his thin lips smiling, he added, "That fine little line we travel every day."

As with all my travels in Texas with partners, the return trip with Harris was even more revealing. We drove through property owned by the King Ranch and the home of the infamous precinct for Box 13 in the disputed 1948 Senate election. Johnson won the election with ballots stuffed into Box 13 after the election. Harris reminded me, "Yes sir, always in debt to us. Johnson saved old Kleberg's ass back in the thirties. One of those debts that never can get repaid." Johnson had been congressional aide to one of the Klebergs back in 1932 and he knew them well. Only much later, during a showdown between the King Ranch, Exxon, and Clark did I understand what that remark really meant.

More to the point, when Thomas gave me my first case for Johnson, he warned me to stay low-key but keep the unions out of Johnson's television business, out of his main source of income disclosed to the public, out of his mother lode. Unions were basic to Johnson's election but he hated them. Fine lines like this were everywhere and the patterns of deception could be followed every step of the way. We protected those patterns to the end of the presidential years and thereafter as needed.

Most telling, on the issue of civil rights, another senior partner assured me Johnson had to promote "that legislation" while never for a minute believing in it.

So we walked the Johnson line in dark suits, power ties, and carefully shined shoes, when necessary with big cigars and cowboy hats, as conservative as we could get to keep our clients comfortable while representing a president seen by many as the most liberal ever to serve. The deception was complete.

Whenever push came to shove, we had "the Wall" with us. John Cofer was our criminal attorney, our partner in crime. He told me to come see him if I even guessed the firm or our clients were about to commit a crime, any crime. He was good, especially about saying nothing in public, as silent as we were; leaving no clues, he also did the very important job of keeping the press from ever getting a hint. Our criminal matters went to him, period. The only clue was his presence. Our "Wall" was the most absolute protection against disclosure that any citizen is given and the only true protection Johnson had for his necessarily private criminal matters. Cofer was particularly unique because the crimes of our clients usually went to him even before they were committed.

That beautiful afternoon in October, buying barbecue from a hard-driven and sullen black, there was one big difference. Don Thomas, Edward Clark's right-hand man, knew what he was saying and he wasn't joking. The stocky little man was Johnson's personal attorney for all business and property interests, particularly including the money-laundering operations. The Brazos-Tenth Street Co. was still another veil to corruption where very complex schemes were performed behind both the corporate and attorney-client shields. What I heard from Don was "from the horse's mouth," as solid as the blue-chip corporations we represented who paid us the "quiet money" and the "silent retainers" we needed to prosper.

Edward A. Clark, attorney at law, Johnson's right-hand man and the only man he trusted, was the key man in the scheme that culminated in Dallas on November 22, 1963.[7] He was my senior partner, my boss. He and Don Thomas were my two partners most deeply involved in the deadly serious business of protecting the president's interests in a very proactive way. For us attorneys no joke was ever told about Johnson to others, to outsiders, to "civilians"; of course, among ourselves nothing was sacred. Clark and Thomas had been with Johnson from the beginning and knew never to take those secrets lightly. It was always business, it was always working hours, and it was always Johnson. Whenever he called, they were there.

In a strange mixture of fear and respect, I had once admired Clark. He had this wide-open notion of no law at all, of being the law unto himself. The awe paid him by everyone at our law offices was so powerful as to be intimidating, and as a young attorney confronted with the complexities of the politics mixed in with the law, I was not just impressed; I was overwhelmed. After all, I had to learn how the system worked and Clark showed me. Politics and the law were one and the same. They were not just synonymous; they were identical.

In my first years at the law firm, Clark seemed to work legal magic. A phone call to a judge and the case was won. Get the word out for the final review of legislation and every key member of the lobby showed up in our conference room. Place a phone call to an officer with his bank and get cash on request. Dine in Austin's finest restaurants and bill the client. Enter the dark underside and find whatever is needed to complete the bill of fare—all the nighttime fun and games.

Firm partnership meetings assumed a comical façade; in a word, they were a joke. Twenty lawyers, all men in suits except for one woman, all white, Anglo-Saxon Christians, save one of Jewish faith, would say nothing as Clark entered the conference room. As our mentor and leader, he would then deliver a long monologue. Abruptly concluding, he would leave to our applause. These lawyers were supposed to be litigators? Only a few had ever selected and tried a case to a jury. We were "superlawyers?" By what definition did we earn that title, except by the power we held? My partners lived in awe and fear of the man who was not just their partner but also their boss, the man for whom they would do anything. And we did.

By the sixties, with Johnson in the White House and now wielding all the instruments of power and measures of success, Clark adopted the many *faux* trappings of a Texas gentleman. He was not a cattleman or oilman and he was not a landowner or businessman; he pretended he was now "old money," that he was among the wealthy who called the notes, the "out of sight" gang. His wainscoted office with Texas landscapes in the tradition of Currier and Ives paintings lined the walls, and marble sculptures on the shelves were disingenuously placed next to a very few law books and state statutes, something he never had to read. After all, that was a chore bequeathed to his partners and associates. Of course, in the final analysis under his code of law, the books meant nothing.

Many a crime was planned and committed in his richly paneled and carpeted offices, small and intimate as they were, the necessary setting for doing his illegal work. He didn't need books for he was an influence peddler, a lobbyist, and a rainmaker. He lived by his own rules, serving what he perceived to be the best interests of his clients while taking their money. Cash was the key: corporate and campaign money paid for the reelection campaigns of politicians, legislators, and judges. With that came all the favorable decisions he needed. The results counted for the power, and the power got the results.

Clark had a standard commitment from his cohorts, his minions, and his patsies. The judges agreed to rule in his favor in "close cases" and he knew that, with a little parsing, some doubletalk, a little splitting of infinitives, and a careful distinguishing between commas and semicolons, all cases were close cases. The other commitment was access. If Clark wanted to talk to a judge or a lawmaker, that man had to take the call. At the climax of the decision-making process, a last-minute word, whether true or not, whether related to the case or not, was always decisive. The other side never even heard about the call; they never had a chance.

In addition to getting legislators or judges elected, regular entertainment and favorable loans were routine, a practice Clark promoted with remarkable ease. Starting in the 1950s, Clark simply took over banks in order to invest Johnson's ill-gotten gains. Poker money paid whatever bonuses were needed. All kinds of gifts flowed freely. Family members were rewarded with good jobs. Lawmakers and judges were both rewarded and coddled. If they needed an apartment for a mistress, so be it. Everything was very close, very secret, and very complete.

Clark's personal office was strangely dank, reeking of a mysterious musk-like petroleum, one that spelled power. Located in the northeast corner, he beheld and commanded a powerful vista, a sweeping panorama of the government powers that were in his control. Strangely, given the sweeping majesty he beheld, the louvered panels were always drawn. Clark preferred a dark office while he worked the underside of Johnson's politics and law. But, when he needed it, there remained this glorious view of his kingdom, the capital of Texas, a majestic lookout and a commanding view of Austin that let you know it was, for all practical purposes, his and his alone. The centers of power in Texas were on the other side of his windows—the Governor's Mansion, the State Legislature in the Capitol, the Supreme Court building back to the north, and the Railroad Commission's tall office tower, nearby, closer even than the Governor's Mansion. From that twelfth floor corner of the old Capital National Bank Building, Clark could view them all and call on them whenever necessary.

The corners of the building rounded the power of the firm: Don Thomas in his self-described "brothel" on the northwest corner; Frank Denius was heir to Dallas Big Oil through Wofford Cain, and had his southeast corner decked out in the burnt orange colors of the University of Texas football team; and, finally, completely opposite from Clark on the southwest side, I had the remaining corner office.

Johnson had a distinct political agenda and many personal and business ambitions, but during his political era, he stood for one of the most powerful cartels in America: Texas oil. By 1960, the new billionaires in Dallas were the Texas cowboys taking on the established interests of the old money held by northeastern Yankees. There was a significant role for heavy construction and the related military-industrial conglomerates, but most of those businesses could be traced to either Big Oil or the supportive hand of Lyndon Johnson or both.

Earlier, at the end of the 1930s, the Texas oil industry was firmly entrenched as the real bread and butter for Texas, replacing cotton and cattle. The oilmen only profited and grew stronger during and after the war when the foundation for Dallas and its Big Oil was set in place and when the skyscrapers of "Big D" arose from that flat, dry prairie. With Johnson's political help and power, Big Oil would be during the fifties and into the sixties what the OPEC oil cartel was to the United States in the seventies and beyond.

A fawning allegiance to Dallas and its billionaire leaders was something that would never change throughout Johnson's political career. The true Texas oilmen were not the wild Glenn McCarthys of Houston or the corporate managers of the great oil companies, the "majors." Big Oil was in Dallas, and the most prominent members were conservative businessmen like Clint Murchison, H. L. Hunt, Wofford Cain,[8] and D. H. "Dry Hole" Byrd.[9] The wilder, less-inhibited Sid Richardson of nearby Fort Worth was also a member. These men went to work when oil was first discovered in the early part of the twentieth century, and, when the "black giant" was discovered in their back yards in 1931, they moved in. In an area of east Texas extending over five counties, large tracts of land over the black giant were up for grabs, and anyone with the guns and muscle could have the oil leases. They only had to get onto the property, fight off the other squatters and resist buyout overtures from the majors. Following remarkable success stories in those wild and woolly days, the new rich had the uniquely Texas right to brag nonstop, to fly their jets wherever, to gamble whenever they felt lucky, to own football teams, and, generally, to do whatever they damned well pleased. They did what billionaires did—whatever they wanted to do—and, as the new cash machines, they set the pattern for Texas culture for many yet to come.

During these early years, a strange relationship developed between Big Oil and Washington on three separate fronts plus a notable deference on the fourth. First, the federal government had allowed Texas oil higher tax deductions than any other industry in America. A strange compromise cut in 1923 with the IRS benefited the oil business as no other. Depletion was one of three main government subsidies to the business, and this one was as sacred as the Alamo, saving oilmen millions by reducing their taxes up to 27.5 percent. Specifically, this was an expense deduction for depletion of resources and was allowed as a reduction of taxable income.

Another intervention by government into oil was a continuing problem from 1938 until 1971: the regulation of natural gas prices by the Federal Power Commission. Not only would that agency attempt to set prices based on costs; it would also require disclosure of the actual costs of finding and producing oil and gas. For Big Oil, the nonexistent gamble of the wildcat would be both exposed and then derided. Worst of all, even oil prices might someday be controlled. In addition, there would be no secrets for a business that survived on sensitive geological data locked in vaults and viewed only in guarded rooms.

Imports were another problem. Texas wanted less oil imported so domestic prices would stay high. Keep out that cheap oil from the Middle East. The quota system helped solve this need.

The final benefit was one of inaction. Over the years the federal government had deferred to state regulation. In Texas, this meant the Railroad Commission.[10] In practice, this meant the oil companies established production controls for their product, a process virtually unheard of in other industries. Thus, "spacing" by the Railroad Commission determined how many wells could be drilled on a lease and "proration" dictated how much oil could be produced. Then the MER, the "maximum efficient rate of production," was set, keeping the final controls on production and supply. Supply, of course, determined the price that could be charged. Low supplies kept the price up. The monthly allowable did its job.

The complexities of the process of production and pricing led the Supreme Court to throw up its hands and leave the regulation of oil production to the state of Texas. In practice, this meant the oil industry regulated itself by proposing the allowables for the month. The Railroad Commission issued the permits to drill the wells and set the production levels for the oil to be produced as requested by the "nominations" from the majors. By 1947 it was recognized to be the most powerful government agency in the world. Until production controls ended twenty-five years later, that power remained in place.

The complexity of the oil business leaves most observers in a vortex of matrices. Most people simply let their eyes glass over, roll up, and get wally. In part, the complexity explains how the secrets of Dallas, such as the all-important money trail following Kennedy's assassination, could be buried. No one outside the industry ever understood the basic processes involved, but it was really very simple: the Railroad Commission kept production down, the price of oil went up, and the millionaires became billionaires.

Consider the oil business like the neighborhood filling station. The gasoline is in a big tank underground. The price is determined by how often people fill up. The fewer the buyers, the lower the price. Lots of buyers, raise the price. In addition, there is the gas underground. If there is a lot, the price is lower. Less gas available meant prices would rise. When the number of gallons pumped out can be controlled, as the majors were able to do in Texas, the price would go up or down. When access to the underground tank is controlled by determining how many pumps can run a pipe into it, the price is again controlled. Like straws in a soda, the more pumping out, the lower the price and vice versa. As we shall see, appreciating these basic market forces and understanding the complex production regulations will be keys to understanding what happened in 1963 and, later, in 1974, when the assassin got his bonus.

Some see Texas as cowboys, oilmen, and cotton farmers. The history is far more complex, based in the beginning on men on the run, fugitives with a natural antipathy to law and lawmen. The state of Texas was founded in an important way by bandits and debtors who enacted strong laws to protect themselves from creditors and lawmen and, after the Civil War, from federal troops and from the newly freed slaves. By 1876, the state was basically populist with a constitution designed to weaken any politician's power to the maximum extent possible.

Politics reflected the economy. While Big Oil was the ruling stud horse in 1960, cattlemen and agriculture still had important roles to play in the state's basic industries. The King Ranch, a huge cattle empire extending across south Texas and sitting over one of the great oil fields of the state, best exemplified that role. From the very beginning of Johnson's public life, he and the overseers of the King Ranch had an intimate relationship, one that would survive any disagreement and would always pay off.

Another big business was cotton, at first centered in east Texas, based on the old slave plantations in that part of the state, and then extended throughout the state as migrants from Mexico provided cheap labor. Oil, cattle, and cotton were king during the Johnson era, and they defined the politics of both the time and the place.

Responsibility for this very favorable business climate belonged to Johnson, Clark, and the Texas government led by Lieutenant Governor Ben Ramsey. Ramsey was the man in charge of the Texas Senate and he was uniquely placed to control state politics because he controlled all appointments and all spending. One third of the Texas Senate, just ten men and Ramsey, could control all state action. Clark just happened to be a Ramsey friend from their childhood days in San Augustine. That meant my senior partner played an important role in the overall development of friendly government spending, decision making, and regulation. Big business was a very happy coalition in Texas, and no member of the coalition was happier than Big Oil.

The contrast between the law and the lawmakers—those people who create, interpret, and enforce the law—is all the more remarkable in the early beginnings of the Johnson and Clark conspiracy. During the heights of the Depression in the early 1930s, both came to Austin, one obsessed with obtaining political power, the other craving the untold wealth of the great east Texas oil field.

Clark and Johnson first politicked together on the streets of Austin in 1935, looking important, trying to see who was doing what. In today's idiom, they were just wandering around and hanging out. Clark, a big, robust man, preferred distinct apparel. Johnson was similarly concerned about his appearance but was less flashy, more a tall bumpkin. The two would walk down Congress Avenue, Clark in a bright red vest with a checkered suit and food on his tie, Johnson tagging along, almost "wagging his tail" as some remarked, stepping where Clark stepped, all the time reaching into a hip pocket to get a comb and run it through his hair.[11] They tried to be two of the most dapper men in Austin, the coolest dudes around. Clark was the leader, large and rotund, a great bulk of a man, missing two digits from the fingers of his right hand, speaking with a lisp, physically big but otherwise unimpressive, literally bear-faced. On the other hand, Johnson was a tall scarecrow, lean and lanky, always smiling and outwardly ingratiating but inwardly forever hating the necessity for it. Johnson thought he had to fawn for others in power. When he would later get that power and control, he would turn the tables completely.

Johnson and Clark literally became inseparable, twins in character and conduct who were perfect foils to each other. Johnson was described as complex early on, to cover his many indiscretions. Clark was similarly complex to the extent any action he took might have many motivations but he always had one ultimate objective . . . a favorable result, no matter what. In that one sense he was the perfect lawyer.

The two took their covert steps for many reasons. Johnson always tried to serve as many purposes as possible. Like a coyote, he roamed the country-side, learning what was going on, serving everyone and everything. Clark was aware of those many motivations but he always kept one key consideration in mind. He knew where he was going, and, like a bear heading into winter hibernation, he was always focused, a perfect control for Johnson and a perfect balance. They were the perfect pair.

In those early years, Clark guided Johnson out of his hard beginnings. In 1935, Johnson was a talkative man with nowhere to go but up, from a failed effort at law and no license, from getting a teaching degree from a small Texas college, from being a penniless congressional assistant needing to take care of a wife. Johnson also lived with the embarrassment of a father who was a failure, all the time pushed by a mother seeking for her son the social standing her husband lacked, and fawning over men twice his age for an opportunity to earn the big money.

When, in 1937, Clark rescued Johnson from a failed election campaign, the die was cast. In Clark, Johnson found his kingmaker and his mastermind, and Clark found his first key patsy in Johnson. In the deepest sense, neither truly controlled the other. They knew what they wanted and acted together, twins at the heart of that illegal conspiracy that too often exists between lawyer and client.

In 1937, winning less than 28 percent of the vote in a winner-take-all special election, Johnson became what he considered to be an "exalted" member of Congress.[12] As we shall see, thanks solely to Clark, Johnson was launched on his political career. By this paradigm for corruption, this pattern for crime, Johnson remained in office, steadily moving from congressman in 1937 to senator in 1948 and then to the vice presidency in 1961. Finally, on November 22, 1963, after the greatest crime an ongoing conspiracy could possibly generate, he became president.

Like Johnson, Clark could never get enough of anything resembling power. He was always grabbing for whatever advantage he could, typically by controlling men in political office. By 1950, Clark had it all, through his control of Senator Johnson as well as Lieutenant Governor Ben Ramsey. He was recognized and acknowledged as the most powerful man in Texas and was called the state's "secret boss" by *Reader's Digest*. By 1960, Clark was in charge of the secret "round table" that ran the state.[13] Following Johnson's ascension to the presidency, Clark had it made. He was the powerful person *behind* the most powerful person in the world. Clark was the big gun.

Then, in 1968, after a two-year stint as ambassador to Australia and with Johnson falling out of sight in the polls, Clark toyed with the idea of running for governor. A careful planner, he could foresee the need for power after Johnson was gone. Based on his personal records now filed at Southwestern University in Georgetown, Texas, he received only one letter of support, from a relative. Along with Johnson, Clark's political power was also broken. As the twins rose together so, too, did they fall together. He could save the president in Texas and even in America but not on the world scene.

Especially not in Vietnam.

I personally never had to get too deeply into the sordid operations. By 1966, when I joined the firm, most of the damage had been done and was over. Respectability was Clark's order of the day. After all, Johnson was president. The objective had been achieved. The old days were over, much was to be forgotten, and it was good riddance to that awful past. The crimes had been covered up. The time had arrived to act presidential. Thirty years of deceit had yielded their dividends.

I had originally gone to Washington to do for my country as Kennedy had asked America. I accepted his call for a new generation to take up the torch of leadership. For me, John Kennedy was a ray of light on the national and international scene in stark contrast to the gloomy, brooding political atmosphere of Texas that I knew only too well. When Johnson "shot" his way into the presidency, I instantly knew those traditions would continue. Committed to a career in our nation's capital, I went there for a two-year stay that provided insights far beyond anything I had expected.

I began work for the Johnson administration in 1964, taking a position as attorney-law clerk for the National Labor Relations Board. I was there for six months and then served two years as an attorney for a member of the Federal Power Commission. At the FPC, through my employer, I represented Johnson's interests at this very heart of the ongoing wars over gas controls and utility regulation, not unlike the earlier battles in the 1930s over the oil fields.

While at the Power Commission, I came to Clark's attention. On recommendation of a friend, I wrote him. He offered me a position as an associate with his law firm, part of the revolving-door policy between government and business that exists to this day.

I took the job with Clark for a good salary and the opportunity to return to Austin and its famous amenities, its laid-back lifestyle. Instead, in this heart of urban innocence, I found myself in the inner chambers of a darkness that rivaled any Machiavellian despot. I also saw deep into the vital center of Washington corruption during many visits to the national capital, working for the electric utilities and for Big Oil as a lobbyist and as an attorney. During those years, I discovered Johnson was the president who was never meant to be president. I also learned how the system worked and, respecting the sacred attorney-client privilege of secrecy, fell victim to the system's vicious ways.

Later, when Johnson was out of power, I would follow other money, the cash trail by Clark as he pursued his payoff, his bonus for the assassination. Money does motivate and that was always the case for Clark. Out of national political power in 1969, Clark demanded great wealth in return for the exorbitant profits he had provided Big Oil. He knew what his efforts had done for his clients but he had not received all he considered himself to be owed. So, in that same year of 1969 that Johnson lost power, Clark laid claim to a small percent, to a bonus, for the benefits he had provided. After a Herculean effort that included some brilliant legal maneuvers and some plain and simple power plays in a truly high-stakes gamble with Exxon, he got his two-million-dollar, net after taxes, cash bonus.

When I parted company with Clark, I was forced to leave Austin in a super-heated battle for pride and for secrecy. From the top of the super-lawyers' world to the bottom, I confronted Clark in litigation extending over a thirteen-year period that left his bank broken and in FDIC hands and with him finally out of time; he died in 1992.

In 1984, I had first set out what I knew, but ten years had to pass before I accumulated the solid evidence that Johnson's political operatives left enough tracks to hang themselves. Because my records remained with Clark when I resigned from his partnership, I had to rebuild documents from extensive personal recollection and public files. After several years of slow research and lots of help, I had the hard evidence. My advantage had been in knowing where to dig and in getting a little luck.

Fingerprint evidence was the ultimate connection between Dallas and Johnson.[14] Through the identification of the print, I could tie Mac Wallace to joining forces with shooter Lee Harvey Oswald at the Texas School Book Depository, a building owned by Murchison associate D. H. Byrd, a member of the military-industrial complex and part of Big Oil in Dallas. Clark also brought in two other participants, one a backup shooter and the other a guard disguised as a Secret Service agent. When I had completed my research, the ties were complete. Everything I knew from so many scattered sources could be tied together.

Many seemingly loose ends surrounded the deep politics of the Johnson regime, but there was enough evidence for any experienced investigator to know that crimes had been committed. Weaving the many threads together shows both that Johnson was motivated by many complex issues that were criminal and that all those problems were brought together through Clark for resolution. Behind every power broker rests the political power essential to make things happen and to get paid. This is deep politics at its very worst. The main requirement is understanding how that system really works and then placing your chosen representatives at the key locations, those few cross-roads that control the entire grid, those key interconnections that control the system, that matrix that is power. We can then bring the loose ends together. As the details appear and then fit together, Clark's complex system will be exposed. Ultimately, to see what deep politics really means in action, we will meet and understand Mac Wallace, the key assassin.

Throughout my participation in this corrupt system, there was the abiding question of lawyer's ethics. A layperson would never understand the sense of justice drilled into law students. The law is a beautiful but jealous mistress, demanding, unforgiving, requiring the dedication of your life true to the law. Since I learned about the law in the particularly compelling circumstances of a powerful admiration for and tutelage by Page Keeton, the renowned University of Texas Law School Dean and my then father-in-law, honest legal work seemed to be second nature. The lawyer's business was doing the right thing.

With Clark, I found myself in an irreconcilable conflict. The law insisted I protect my clients' deepest secrets even when it meant concealing the single most terrible crime in American history. The conflict was fundamental. As a committed political activist, I had to replace my admiration for Kennedy, his ideas, and his administration, with the venal ideas and dark politics Johnson represented. I found myself attorney and partner with the man who had killed Kennedy. The effect, predictably, was personally debilitating. Ultimately, I could not do it. Over constant denial, I took eleven years to learn the facts and to drop out of the system.

With Clark, my admiration for Kennedy's ideas, his style and so-called grace, his Camelot existence, was buried under the ethical prohibitions of the attorney-client privilege. In all this experience, there was a subtle influence: a visceral pleasure in exercising a superlawyer's power. For a time this motivation superseded all things, for I was part of an organization more powerful than the law itself; we were the law unto ourselves, playing by our own rules. No one truly served that powerful mistress, the one called "justice." We simply subverted the system, always taking care of ourselves first and our clients second. The mistress always lost. Until completing this personal, inner review, I never reconciled Keeton and Kennedy with Johnson and Clark.

The conflict within me has taken years to sort out. After Clark tried to do to me what he had done to others, I cleared the decks and fired back. After getting devastating threats of my own from Clark, some subtle and some blatant, an entirely different appreciation came to me. With "fear and trembling" and in appreciation for what I was doing, I knew it was time to tell what I knew and could prove. I determined to shatter the myth that a vice president could never murder his president. Based on what I knew, I would show that an ambitious, corrupt, and thrill-seeking American vice president, caught up in the dynamics of personal evil and corruption and determined to become a historic figure of great power and wealth, would not just consider masterminding the personal replacement of the president of the United States.

He would do it.

Today most people accept that fact that there was a conspiracy surrounding Kennedy's death, but there is no consensus on who engineered it. Hypotheses keep surfacing of new and different plots and counterplots. As the multiplicity of unproven scenarios have each collapsed over the years, many Americans have had to embrace the Warren Commission's conclusion all over again. "After all," they shrug, "what else is there?" Even though disavowed by key members, the Warren *Report* serves as a security blanket despite its Alice in Wonderland explanation of strange and magically empowered bullets. Then there were the two "lone nuts," a unique contradiction in terms in its own right. Today, everything is questioned; nothing is believed; we are left having to fall back on the Warren *Report* which we know is not correct. We know justice has yet to be done.

Still overly comfortable in a world where America is the main power, there is perhaps this mystic tranquility surrounding the Kennedy presidency and his successor that is more acceptable to us as a nation. After all, in a very subtle way, we are dedicated to our leaders as an extension of ourselves. The alternative is the obvious national nightmare of facing the telltale frames of the Zapruder film, of acknowledging the altered medical evidence, of accepting the carefully identified fingerprint, and of probing still further, into the fugitive assassins, to that better understanding that results from accepting and embracing what happened and why it happened. Once that *denouement* occurs, we can take the steps needed to make it far more difficult for political destruction to ever happen again.

Having looked into the dark abyss and seen the problems, the time for solutions has arrived. Some obvious improvements are proposed to end the secrecy, to control the public trust, to supervise the officers of our courts, and to dilute the power of the politicians, to take still more control from them and place it with the people. After all, that is what a democracy is supposed to do. And, in a very fundamental sense, we will also right the wrongs.

Like the site dedicated to Kennedy's death, there are similar sites in Texas dedicated to Johnson. At the LBJ Library in Austin, there is a duplicate of the oval office (although slightly smaller than the "oval" itself). In nearby Stonewall, Texas, the LBJ home is a national historic site. Unlike the half million who make an annual pilgrimage to the Sixth Floor in Dallas, only a few thousand feel any compulsion to visit LBJ's memorials.[15] Perhaps we Americans, in our uncanny sense of knowing what is right, also understand that Johnson was an evil man, not deserving of our respect or reverence.

Lyndon Johnson is held in the lowest esteem of any president. There are good reasons.

> The fox knows many things, but the hedgehog knows one big thing.
> —Archilopus

The childhood shows the man,
As morning shows the day.
—John Milton

3

Roots

Different things have different meanings to different people, particularly when viewed over long periods of time. Almost two hundred years ago Bowie meant a large and very brutal knife to Texans. The more recent generation views "Bowie" as a singer at the forefront of music. The differences between Johnson as a child and our children is perhaps exemplified by these differing views of Bowie. Johnson and Clark grew up in a very different time, their times had a significant influence on them, and their learned motivations were very distinct from Texas today. To understand their basic motivations and character, an appreciation of that upbringing is necessary.

Texas was founded during a time of very real dangers, of exploring new lands, taming the wilderness, bringing law and order to the frontier, and building and expanding an economy based, first, on cattle, then cotton, and, by the 1930s, oil. Today the state has a mature, international economy with very different benefits, challenges, rules, and dangers.

Johnson and Clark were products of that lawless era of rough justice and nonproductive land that too often required ruthless action with little concern for the consequences except one, that of personal survival. The elements of the frontier, of war and vigilante justice, were present at the founding of Texas and continued throughout the childhoods of Johnson and Clark. Their same lawlessness would then span that era in Texas from the frontier to the boardroom.

Edward Aubrey Clark was from the small east Texas town of San Augustine, only a few miles from the old Neutral Ground in Louisiana, a short-lived territory where Spain and France had divided their land claims, leaving that area alone and neutral.[1] In the absence of any pretense of law *or* order, the area attracted every form of desperado on the run from either the

United States or Mexico, leaving that area a no man's land with a tradition for lawlessness that would dominate the area for a long time. San Augustine, one of the oldest settlements in Texas, was on the outskirts of that unclaimed land and was populated by its desperate fugitives.

Although bypassed by settlers seeking better farmland than San Augustine's red dirt and big thickets of pine trees offered, the little town was on the old Camino Real, the King's Highway that led to San Antonio. The road brought most travelers through San Augustine and, as the American settlers moved into the area, they paused and then passed through, heading for the better lands extending west over a vast expanse for almost four hundred miles to San Antonio.

With the growth of settlements in Texas, conflict with Mexico inevitably arose, and revolution with its demands for independence soon followed. Sam Houston, originally a delegate from San Augustine to the constitutional convention in 1835, was chosen to lead the American settlers' charge for Texas independence. That war was exceptionally violent, with the eerie trumpet sounds of no quarter the standard for dictator Santa Anna's forces at the Alamo. Time and again as his troops moved eastward, there was no quarter. Rallied by General Sam Houston on April 26, 1836, at San Jacinto, just east of the present-day metropolis bearing his name, troops captured Santa Anna and could finally celebrate the independence its delegates had declared two months earlier.

Although born of violence that would leave a hard-earned but bitter legacy, settlers poured in during the period of the Texas Republic from 1836 to 1846. For a decade, the United States Congress refused admission to Texas primarily because of the slavery issue. This isolation only reinforced the ideas of a violent and lawless independence that would become uniquely Texan.

More specifically, that attitude came home to San Augustine during the five-year Regulator-Moderator war in Shelby County, just north of San Augustine. In 1841, Shelby welcomed a fugitive from Louisiana who was determined to take control of the community by force, to rule by might, not law and order. Opposed by the settlers already there, Charles W. Jackson ruthlessly attacked and killed several old-timers, including one person he shot in cold blood. Jackson was in turn killed by Eph Daggett, a man allied with Charles Moorman, who was on the run from Mississippi. As they said about Jackson, "He deserved to die." In the so-called trial that followed, there would be no punishment for Daggett. The residents were glad to see Jackson gone.[2]

A five-year war of roving militia bands and vigilantes followed that early rash of killings. Jackson had labeled himself a "regulator," a person committed to regulating by the gun where might is right. Enforcing that "right," he and his followers staged many a kangaroo court. The "moderators" sought to ease or moderate the violence and follow the law but, as was often necessary, they too had to respond with power, living behind the gun. Sam Houston, then president of the Republic of Texas, at first decided nothing need be done, declaring the counties "free and independent governments so let them fight it out."[3]

Following this official declaration that allowed anarchy to prevail, raids were common throughout Shelby County and the surrounding areas, representing a classic example in American history of the lawless fugitives fighting citizens supporting law and order. This war was uniquely "Texican" as Texans were called then, because of its devotion to personal independence, to the gun, and to a remarkable, almost inbred contempt for the law.

After five years, with a major confrontation underway near Center, the county seat of Shelby County, Houston finally relented and sent in the militia, seven hundred strong. The Regulator forces laying siege to the Moderators were in turn surrounded, and, in an unusual exercise of good judgment, the warring groups waved the white flag. After a brief and inconclusive trial, an uneasy peace settled over Shelby County. In short, law and order was finally brought to the heart of east Texas.

Ed Clark admired this history and would later prepare a short paper on the subject.[4] Interestingly, although he was a lawyer, he condoned the benefits of lawlessness. The idea that might was right and that power rules would remain a tradition of the frontier that would both fascinate and be actively practiced by Clark.

That same year, Mexico, now recovered from the 1836 war, attempted again to reassert its power with a series of border disputes that led directly to the 1845 war between the United States and Mexico. American success there led to the annexation of Texas. The state was finally admitted to the Union.

There were two interesting features to the Texas treaty of annexation by the United States. One was that public lands were kept by the state rather than becoming federal lands. Income from land sales belonged to Texas. Several decades later, oil under those lands belonged to Texas, giving the state a strong interest in the business. Second, recognizing the vastness of the state, the right was reserved to split into five states. These features were further subtle measures of an independence no other state had.

The annexation of Texas, part of the continuing series of compromises in Congress on the slave issue, meant an even greater migration of plantations and their enslaved workers. Most plantations would be located in the east Texas area, then the population center of the state.

Nationally, of course, slave-related issues led directly to the Civil War. In Texas, then-governor Sam Houston refused to secede and was promptly impeached. He was succeeded by then-lieutenant-governor Ed Clark (no relation to Johnson's Ed Clark), who led the state into what was known in the South as the War for Southern Independence. With the exception of Galveston Island, there were no successful invasions of Texas; however, the shortages brought on by the Union blockade came home early and, following the Confederate surrender, Reconstruction and its very limited civil rights for blacks led to still further hardships for Texas. San Augustine's economy declined and would not recover its prewar production levels for forty years. In addition, it would become a center for Ku Klux Klan activity as lynching became a very private, very criminal means of enforcing and continuing slavery.[5]

Reconstruction and Yankee occupation officially ended in Texas in 1873, but it meant little for the economic well-being of the state's leaders in business and government, accustomed as they were to the obscene privileges of plantation life before the Civil War. The new constitution adopted in 1876 to replace the federally imposed one was dedicated to limited government, to keeping not just the federal government but all government at a minimum. Now well over one hundred years old, that document, having resisted several serious efforts to change it, remains in effect to this day. Texas was, and still is, against the "federales" as well as "gu'mint" in general, in particular, and in principle.

As the wealth of the rest of the United States came to Texas through railroads, the farmers responded with populism and a dedication to the Democratic Party that would be passed as a talisman from father to son. The massacre of many Native Americans and deportation of the rest, a series of successful cattle drives, and then a booming demand for cotton did not pull most Texans out of an abject poverty. In east Texas, cotton meant reinstating the old plantation system along with sharecropping and its continued peonage for blacks. Even the beginnings of the oil boom in 1901 with the discovery of Spindletop to the east of Houston meant little for most Texans.

San Augustine began to recover by the turn of the twentieth century, and Clark's parents opened a general store, which would slowly prosper. Three years later, on July 15, 1906, Ed Clark was born. Since the father had married into the Downs family, it also meant Colonel Edward Downs of nearby Newton would move back with them. Young Clark would come to admire his grandfather as his mentor even in place of his own father.

Downs had been sheriff of Newton County just south of San Augustine where he had been widely recognized for imposing and enforcing a much-needed law and order. The most memorable event during his tenure, however, was the lynching of eight blacks in 1908. A horrific photo of five of the young men was widely circulated on a handbill with a poetic warning about "the dogwood tree."[6] A copy of the handbill remained with Clark to his death as a treasured personal memento. More important, it reflects his unwavering racism and his murderous prejudice against blacks, accurately depicting his character and revealing his capabilities and determination to kill brutally in order to protect a way of life, a belief in white supremacy, particularly his brand of Texas white supremacy. And a belief in violence.

After this atrocity in nearby Sabine County and faced with little opportunity in Newton County, Downs left to join the family's merchant business in San Augustine as Clark and Downs. He also operated a sawmill in nearby Trotti that closed after a few years. In San Augustine he was elected a state representative three times and was recognized as a town leader. Idolized by the young Clark, he left his grandson a small inheritance.

Clark was never a good student, but, for a town with limited economic opportunity, he was fortunate to have parents able to send him to the private Morgan Academy in nearby Bryan, Texas, and then to Southwestern University in Georgetown, Texas, just forty miles north of Austin.

While attending these two institutions in the early to mid-1920s, Clark experienced an important lesson in politics and power. He witnessed both the remarkable success of the reborn Ku Klux Klan and the beginnings of its demise. The growth to statewide control and then to its virtual prohibition would occur over a five-year period, starting with the arrival in September 1920 of Kleagle R. Upchurch in Bellaire, a subdivision of Houston. After several public "tar parties" where objects of the Klan's hate were literally tarred, feathered, and carried out of town on a wooden rail, the citizens accepted the KKK. Soon, the Klan was powerful throughout Texas, with a majority in the Texas Legislature and with "Kluxer" Earl Mayfield elected to the United States Senate in 1922.[7]

For Clark the education process began in Austin where a white rancher was accidentally killed during a secret Klan meeting.[8] Since the sheriff and police chief were Kluxers, no indictments were made. In protest, the district attorney resigned, allowing the governor to choose a successor. Dan Moody, the prosecutor in nearby Georgetown, was named district attorney for Austin's Travis County.

When the next tar party took place, Moody acted. The Georgetown "klavern," the name for local Klan committees, had warned an alleged adulterer to behave, and the man had told them to leave him alone. When the man next met his lady friend, the Klan trapped him, whipped him, and tarred and feathered him in the Taylor town square, a small community just northeast of Austin. The Klan leader was promptly indicted and the case set for trial.

For Dan Moody, the key question was whether the judge would allow klansmen on the jury. When the judge ruled they could be excluded, a conviction with prison time was promptly returned.

Statewide, the Klan reacted with protest marches. At the State Fair in Dallas, more than 75,000 attended and the membership swelled. In Austin, 500 marched. Attention then centered on the 1924 Democratic primary election. Although Felix Robertson, the Klan's candidate for governor, led the ballot on the first primary, he was defeated in the runoff by almost 100,000 votes. Miriam "Ma" Ferguson, standing in for her impeached husband, former governor Jim Ferguson, went on to be nominated for governor in the fall primary. In Texas one-party politics, it meant she was elected in November of that year. Dan Moody was elected attorney general. The Klan was effectively removed from statewide politics and power. The legal end came the following year with a statutory prohibition on wearing masks, meaning the hoods worn by klansmen.

Deep-seated prejudices remained.

From watching the Klan activities and what happened, Clark learned firsthand how law enforcement can control criminal indictments, he saw how important judges were in the legal process, and he understood how their discretion could win or lose a case. Internalizing these object lessons, Ed Clark would later transform them into his *modus operandi*.

After participating in both the rapid success and sudden collapse of the Klan, Clark transferred to Tulane University in New Orleans to complete his college degree. While there during the 1927 holiday season for a friend's wedding, he met his future wife. Following a whirlwind courtship, he married Anne Metcalfe of the Glenbar Plantation in Greenville, Mississippi, and an heir to the largest cotton plantation system in the South. As described in those days, Clark "married over his head."

Moving then to Austin to attend law school, he returned to San Augustine in 1928 to run for and be elected county attorney, a largely administrative task handling misdemeanors and advising the county commissioners on legal matters. He did not win reelection. The office of county attorney for San Augustine was combined with the same office in neighboring Shelby County. His pitch, "Give a home boy a chance," was not successful with the expanded electorate.[9]

The loss would have a profound effect on Clark. He would later assert, "If you ain't been elected, you ain't squat." On the other hand, getting elected was never easy. With the loss, Clark decided to take the back seat, to let others seek election while he worked behind the scenes. His motivation, especially as business opportunities presented themselves, became that of supporting others willing to risk the election process while making money for himself, win or lose. After all, he knew how much, and in some cases how little, power any elected official had.

So, as the Depression was deepening, Clark had a wife and no job and was without prospects in San Augustine. He turned to the place that would pay his way for the rest of his life, the state's government in Austin.

Landing a job as an assistant attorney general in 1931, Clark did some initial legwork in a controversy then arising in nearby counties—the discovery of an oil field that would create the Dallas billionaires of Big Oil. In April, Dad Joiner punched the first well into the "great east Texas field," the only oil "giant" in the contiguous forty-eight states. Within a few months the mammoth size of the field was defined across five counties and was named the "black giant."[10]

One town, Athens, was to become famous as the place where every resident was a millionaire and it was over a small field adjacent to the giant. Athens was also the boyhood home of Clint Murchison and Wofford Cain, both of whom would soon move to Dallas as founders of Big Oil. Sid Richardson, a neighbor in Athens, moved to Fort Worth. D. H. Byrd, long a wildcatter in Texas known as "Dry Hole" for his lack of success, also moved into the great oil field and, for the first time, put together sizable holdings. He then moved to Dallas where he was active in rockets and the military-industrial complex. In 1936, he would purchase the building later known as the Texas School Book Depository and now home of the Sixth Floor Museum. H. L. Hunt, a gambler from Louisiana, also bought into the east Texas oil play with some poker winnings and also became a Dallas multi-billionaire. These men would remain friends as Big Oil in Big D, Dallas.

Because oil in the east Texas field was so abundant, lawlessness was rampant. Illegal wells were easy to drill, "like dropping straws in a punch bowl." Stealing oil from holding tanks once it was produced was also commonplace. Overproduction lowered the price of oil to less than ten cents a barrel. The large oil companies and the successful operators in the field demanded protection from the outright theft and from the overproduction that was ruining their income. Of course, when major producers such as Humble (now Exxon) demanded law and order, they got it, particularly when then-Texas-governor Ross Sterling had been a founder of the company. Clark found himself in the middle of the "oil wars" by going into east Texas to enforce production rules. He could only report that nothing would stop the wide-open theft because the citizen juries would simply not convict their friends and neighbors. This powerful act of defiant jury nullification was often repeated. The inevitable consequence was no law at all.

Governor Sterling sent in the militia, but the courts threw that effort out, bound as they were by the 1876 Constitution, a legal relic of Reconstruction days that prevented any abuse of the militia. Tom Connally, the junior senator in Washington, D.C., then led the fight for the federal Hot Oil Act. Supposedly opposed to intervention from Washington, whenever Texas business needed government help, the future billionaires asked for it, and they received it. Government was good and government was bad, depending on their needs.

Federal enforcement started with the capture of an illegal shipment of Texas oil in Idaho. The jury trial that followed included jurors who would convict, and they did. Wide-open crime came to an end; however, a tradition in east Texas was only reinforced and would continue into the illegal slant hole wells of 1961 and then, in 1969, to Clark's effort for a bonus payment after the Kennedy assassination.

Following his brief original foray into east Texas oil, Clark moved to Austin in 1932 where he would continue to reside until his death in 1992. As an assistant attorney general he moved up when his boss, Jimmy Allred, was elected governor in 1934. Allred, the state's last liberal governor (until Ann Richards), would serve two terms during which time Clark served as his secretary and then was appointed secretary of state. In both positions, Clark had unique powers. As secretary, he knew everything the governor knew. As secretary of state, he controlled state incorporations and all elections. He was in the key place for business and for the traditional state power of controlling its elective processes.

In Austin he met Lyndon Johnson.

Five years younger than Clark, Lyndon Johnson was born on August 27, 1908, near Stonewall, Gillespie County, Texas, near Fredericksburg and about twenty miles west of Johnson City. There, the rocky hills marked the geologic fault line between the coastal pastureland and the high, dry plains. That fault line was also the weather line between those arid plains and the fertile coastal farmlands. The land was dry and rocky—a very hard place to make a living.

The son of Sam and Rebekah, Johnson would grow up in a small cabin on a farm with few livestock and without such modern conveniences as electricity, telephones, autos, and the many other aids to modern living we now take for granted. It was a hardscrabble life, often on the edge of starvation. In those days, adult demands were placed on children at an early age. Indeed, the husband welcomed pregnancy because it meant free labor for the farm. Boys like Lyndon Johnson often worked long hours in the fields to help the family get by. Skill with livestock and with guns was a necessity and fighting was an accepted way to settle disagreements. Racism was another precondition of life in those days. As we shall see, these facts of life would influence Johnson in those formative years and would remain with him throughout his life.

The darker details are less well known, and one little-mentioned event was the killing of a domesticated animal. Farmers and ranchers are extraordinarily protective of their animals. Livestock were a source of food, income, and travel. Typically, a cowboy will, after a hard day's work, carefully groom his horse before ever thinking of caring for himself. The civilized treatment of animals was an unwritten law among "people of the land," and breaking it was something so terrible that very little would ever be said about it, particularly not to outsiders.

Johnson would break this law at least twice.

Even before his teenage years, Johnson caused fatal injuries to an animal when he tortured and killed a mule.[11] Allegedly concerned that the mule was thirsty, he had forced it to drink water and then drove it mercilessly. Not surprisingly, the animal collapsed and died. Johnson looked on with a strange amazement that turned to remorse only after his father confronted him.

Later, as a young adult, Johnson committed a series of dangerous pranks, including setting off explosives in the town square. In a destructive spree that centered on blasting dynamite in the town square, Johnson trapped a mongrel dog with the target, again killing a helpless animal.[12]

This wanton destruction of domesticated animals starkly reveals the pathological character of Johnson's personality. Psychologists note that cruelty to animals frequently arises from or leads to and enhances a lack of empathy for people along with a propensity for violence.[13] Simply stated, Johnson's tough-guy childhood made him a juvenile delinquent by today's standards and showed character traits that would be strong signals of trouble yet to come.

Growing up, Johnson had a doting mother who demanded his success and a father he did not respect because of the failed life the man led. As a direct consequence, in order to escape the conflicting expectations, his childhood also featured a habit of running away from home. Family pressures were too great and the attraction of anywhere else was too strong. After a series of escapes, Johnson tried one final, very serious effort to flee the constant turmoil at home. After graduating from high school in 1924, he fled to Hollywood.

Once there, he tried to become a lawyer. Working with a distant uncle who was more intent on chasing starlets seeking divorces and partying with them, Johnson literally practiced law until informal complaints were filed against his uncle. Johnson "headed for the hills," moving to another town. With the heat still on, he headed for the state line, departing California for good. What he learned in Hollywood was not only how to avoid a serious brush with authority but, more instructively, he learned both the importance and the sterility of the law.

After returning to Texas and home, the only job available was as a laborer on a road gang. This work provides another well-documented example, during his pre-college years, of Johnson's cruelty. While working on the road crew, the future author of America's Great Society programs would stand by in silent approval as foremen refused to let African Americans join the road gang. Simply stated, Johnson was not friendly to blacks. Few whites in the Texas hill country would give blacks the time of day. In nearby San Saba, more lynching occurred than anywhere else in that area of central Texas.[14] All were well known in advance by that private communication system that accompanied lynchings. Johnson knew and tacitly tolerated the savagery.

After working on the road gang for only a short time, Johnson concluded that his mother was right, that more education was the necessary road to success. For a better life, he had to go to school. Still the tough guy, however, one more lesson in violence was needed. Taking an interest in a young woman in nearby Fredericksburg during a weekend dance, he got in a fistfight with another suitor and was badly beaten. The next day he made the decision to leave home for college.[15]

So, in 1928, four years after graduating from high school, Johnson enrolled at Southwest Texas State Teachers College in nearby San Marcos. He had an unremarkable academic career, barely an average student in a less-than-demanding state college. While there, however, he began his life in politics, one that would climax at the little college with his winning an election through what he himself later described as "Nazi tactics" and outright stuffing of the ballot box.

While attending college, Johnson worked in a public school in Cotulla, a Hispanic town in south Texas. Following graduation in San Marcos, he taught in the Houston public schools, putting together a winning debate team that brought him favorable publicity. He also had his first taste of real politics, speaking for a candidate at a camp gathering in Blanco, Texas, and then helping Wally Hopkins get elected to the Texas Senate. That support led Hopkins, within a year, to recommend Johnson to Roy Miller, then Corpus Christi mayor and a lobbyist for Texas Gulf Sulphur, an important part of the state's petrochemical industries. Miller was impressed and in turn recommended the young man to Richard Kleberg.

Kleberg had recently won election in the state's largest congressional district, one stretching across most of south Texas. The district had more voters than any other in the state because military retirees in San Antonio preferred Republicans. The Democrats put all the voters they could in that one district. The district was also geographically large, stretching from the Mexican border up to San Antonio and then north, to include Johnson's home county of Blanco. As heir to the massive King Ranch, "larger than Connecticut" Johnson would often brag, Kleberg was truly a Texas character, a practicing cowboy able to ride herd with the best of them. He was, however, a failure as a businessman, having driven the ranch almost to bankruptcy. He was challenged to run for Congress by the King-Kleberg family and be replaced as manager. He reluctantly agreed to the election. His preference, when not ranching, was to be in Mexico. Defeating the incumbent Republican from San Antonio, he proved to be the key member of Congress that would give Democrats a one-vote majority in the House of Representatives.

Kleberg was not a reform-minded Democrat. In that Depression era, while conditions worsened throughout the country, Kleberg was never intent on using government to correct what was not working. He believed the downturn was a result of Prohibition and that a little more drinking was all we needed. He cared little about the terrible living conditions facing so many families. After all, while millions were without work or hope, all the available amenities were still there for Kleberg.

Following a brief interview, Johnson was hired as the new congressman's secretary (equivalent to the modern chief administrative aide) and, within a week he was with Kleberg on the Bluebonnet Express, the luxury passenger train to Washington, D.C.

And, ultimately, to the White House, the one he had to shoot his way into.

On December 7, 1931, ten years to the day before Pearl Harbor, Johnson arrived in Washington for the first time. The city was much smaller. The beltway was forty years in the future. Most of the great federal monuments and buildings were yet to be built. Only the Washington Monument and Lincoln Memorial had been completed.

Republicans still ran the Congress but their grip was failing and would soon vanish altogether. Kleberg, ready to be sworn in and then gain fame as the "Cowboy Congressman," was one of the two key votes later that same day establishing a Democratic Party majority, resulting in political control that would extend almost uninterrupted for the next sixty years, carrying with them the liberal and progressive policies of the soon-to-be-enacted New Deal of President Franklin D. Roosevelt.

A far more important change, on the same scale with Pearl Harbor and America's role in the world, also began that day. The Democrats would be in control, but southerners would control that majority power in a system of leveraging that would exist throughout the ensuing struggles for economic reform and civil justice. With that pyramided control, the southerners brought and maintained those attitudes so foreign and inimical to the traditional political delegates and their advisers from the North and the East. More important, in a further leveraging, that political power was ultimately in the hands of a few men from Texas, men like House Speaker John Nance Garner, soon to be vice president; Sam Rayburn, destined to be Speaker; and, finally, at the top of the control apparatus of Congress as well as Washington, the nation, and the world would be Lyndon Johnson. As alien as Johnson was to Washington on that day he first arrived, so too was the nation unfamiliar with Texas and what it could do. More specifically, we were to learn what that Texan would do over the next four decades.

Union Station was only a few blocks from the Capitol, and, upon arrival, Richard Kleberg hurried to Congress to cast his key vote. He then settled into the elegant Mayflower Hotel with Johnson in tow. As a dissipated cattleman of vast wealth, Kleberg would enjoy the good life in the Capitol and introduce his secretary to luxuries the young man had never seen. Johnson loved that high life, wanted the luxuries for himself, and was ready to use government to enrich himself to the fullest extent possible. After all, if government made this possible for politicians, why not him?

For the new secretary, however, there was no immediate wealth. The day after arriving, his life would be in the basement of a cheap hotel near the Capitol along with a crash-course education regarding the duties of a member of Congress. In those days the main task was correspondence and, with Kleberg representing the largest district in Texas, there were many letters, particularly from veterans living in San Antonio and from ranchers in the surrounding dry plains. Working hard, Johnson quickly became an expert in the subjects most important to those constituents. Kleberg could have cared less. Mainly out on the golf courses and in the country clubs, content to leave the office to anyone, he simply gave his secretary a blank check, *carte blanche.*

Johnson quickly took advantage, for all practical purposes becoming the congressman, signing his name, impersonating him on the phone, and effectively acting in his boss's place. He learned what it was to be a representative except, of course, for the electoral part, the "getting elected" part. He knew nothing about running for office except what he had experienced in stealing an election while in college and then, in the real world of politics, during his one-night campaigning in Blanco County for Hopkins. He did not know the money part of the game, and he did not yet know the reality of counting ballots in Texas.

With Kleberg, the opportunity arose to perform a true service for the man. Kleberg was a "party man" and he soon found himself in trouble with his wife. Johnson skillfully covered for Kleberg and the bond proved unbreakable. Kleberg served another seven terms and Johnson was always in his favor. Johnson made sure that help extended to the King Ranch family and their vast power in south Texas. Many times, the King Ranch would save the day.

Soon after Johnson's arrival in the national capital, something happened that would shape his attitudes toward the presidency. A twist of fate, literally a slip of the hand, saved Franklin Delano Roosevelt and possibly the New

Deal altogether. He and the nation received a shock when Roosevelt, prior to his long-awaited inauguration, narrowly missed assassination by a cheap handgun in a public park in Miami.[16] But there was something else Johnson learned that would, in a mix of subtle, almost subconscious, motivations, play a role in his thinking.

In that one event Johnson realized how assassination could change government dramatically, how easy it was to do, and how just a firearm could improve or terminate a politician's fortunes. He knew Texan Cactus Jack Garner, the man he opposed, had come within inches of being sworn in as president of the United States. He saw that assassinating a president was not something that was investigated with diligence, that the assassin would likely be tagged an anarchist, and that the crime was not even a federal case. Assassination of a president was treated as an oddity, as mysterious as the office itself, and ultimately under the control of local and state authorities. There would be a hasty trial and execution the assassin taking any secrets to the grave. As we shall see this scenario would repeat itself and contribute to the end of Kennedy's life in Texas.

The assassin struck several days after Roosevelt's speech in Montgomery, Alabama, where he promoted the Tennessee Valley Authority, a monumental effort to bring lower-cost power to citizens amid hostile public utilities. FDR then traveled farther south to Florida. On the night of February 15, 1933, at a political rally in Miami's Bayfront Park, Roosevelt and several other politicians addressed a crowd, only minimally protected by the Secret Service. Perched atop the rear seat of an automobile with a small microphone in hand, the president-elect made a short, informal talk similar to his fireside radio chats.

Present in the crowd was Giuseppe Zangara, a bricklayer with a professed hatred of presidents and capitalists, obsessed with the desire to kill one and all. Reportedly, Zangara had earlier planned to assassinate Hoover, but illness and lack of money had prevented him from traveling to Washington.

Milling about Roosevelt's car during the speech, concealed by the crowd of supporters and well-wishers, Zangara suddenly jumped onto a nearby park bench, pulled his revolver, and aimed at Roosevelt. Seeing the danger, a woman pushed his arm, spoiling the shot. He kept firing and bullets hit Chicago mayor Anton Cermak and four others. Cermak's wounds were serious and proved fatal.

Roosevelt was unharmed but, in the fatalistic manner of many great presidents, he shunned improved security, merely asking friend Raymond

Moley, a Barnard College professor and criminologist, to investigate. Moley interviewed Zangara in a Miami jail and determined there was no conspiracy. In the public eye, the assassin was less a criminal and more a curiosity. There was no Warren Commission. Indeed, there was no federal investigation. The subsequent trial and execution took place in Florida as prescribed by state law. Congress, bustling with the Depression and New Deal legislation, took no steps to adopt laws concerning the assassination of presidents and public officials.

Interestingly, FDR's distant cousin, Theodore Roosevelt, had also survived an assassination attempt and had himself come into power in 1901 after the assassination of President McKinley in Buffalo, New York, by anarchist Leon Czolgosz. The ensuing attempt then to make assassinating a president a federal crime ended in typical Washington inaction. The McKinley assassination was followed by a flawless transfer of power to Teddy Roosevelt. There was no need for legislation. Eleven years later, anarchists took a shot at Teddy Roosevelt in Milwaukee during his unsuccessful third-party presidential bid. He survived that attempt.

This apparent lack of interest by presidents and by Congress was an accepted fatalism, as if to say, "I may be killed. So be it." Any future assassin would have to be comforted with the knowledge, however subtle, of this fatalism.

Another tradition also developed, that of the anarchist assassin. The notion remains deeply rooted in the accepted history of assassination in America. Quite to the contrary, in Europe, "anarchists" and assassination are almost always part of something much larger.

Anarchists, by choice not very close knit or powerful, had nonetheless been a danger for public officials for forty years before the attempt on FDR in Miami. The legendary Emma Goldman, anarchist and sometimes communist, had voiced approval of McKinley's assassination in a Chicago newspaper interview, only fanning the public hatred for her sympathies. Anarchists typically received harsh court sentences due to this public perception as well as the related fact that an attack on the president was also an attack on the nation. The very practical result was inadequate counsel for the terrorists.

By 1917, the problem had become so common that the American Civil Liberties Union was formed by a group of lawyers in New York to defend their anarchist clients in court. There was also a perception that anarchists were part of an organized international plot; however, most proved to be laymen when it came to strategies and munitions. Typically, anarchists acted alone or within small, disconnected groups. By definition, of course, anarchists are not well organized.

A further important and very different perspective comes from the assassination of President Abraham Lincoln. Historians traditionally regard John Wilkes Booth as a loner, virtually an anarchist despite the fact several conspirators were involved. Recent research shows, however, that the South had planned the assassination through that same group of conspirators headed by Booth.[17] The plans had ended with the fall of the Confederacy a few days earlier; however, Booth continued the plot and completed the assassination. Despite efforts to mold Booth into an anarchist, the facts are otherwise. The hanging of four co-conspirators in July 1865 is mute testimony to that fact.

When we consider the loss of any president, we must also appreciate the importance surrounding the loss of the policies that president had for the nation. After the failed assassination attempt on FDR in 1933, *Time* reported, "People seem to feel that their faith in the future was also the assassin's target."[18] Had Cactus Jack Garner of Texas become president, he might have curtailed the New Deal and rearmament would have been delayed until Pearl Harbor. The United States could have sunk into further depression, resulting in our entry into World War II in terrible shape. What happened to Lincoln's plans for Reconstruction are similarly clearly of record. Those plans ended with the assassin's bullet. There was no "charity for all" in the federal occupation of the South.

This faith in the future proved, once again, to be a victim following the loss of Kennedy. With great difficulty, we as a nation managed to survive the ensuing trials and conflicts of both civil rights and the Vietnam War. Something vital, however, was lost in the assassination. To this day Americans remember and continue to search for that missing intangible.

Interestingly, there is a remarkable similarity in the background and results surrounding the earlier assassinations and attempts and in the circumstances enmeshed in the Kennedy assassination: anarchists or loners, critical national times, bullets, limited investigations, downplaying the event, poor lawyers, and a fatalistic acceptance of the dangers confronting the president. After all, in another subtle appreciation, the occupant had achieved an important measure of immortality already; fame was only greater in the untimely death.

These traditional elements have surrounded assassinations in America and have become the paradigm to analyze any attack on the presidency. As we shall see, those same elements would dominate the thinking of the Warren

Commission. Until now, for Kennedy, all that has been missing has been the conspiracy, one present with Lincoln and, earlier, Aaron Burr.[19]

For Lyndon Johnson during these times from 1931 to 1935, he was learning not just assassination protocol in Washington; he was also experiencing and taking to heart the rudiments of power and its exercise. In those less hurried days in the Capitol, there was time to do all he needed to advance and to develop his plans. The man worked hard, putting in "24 and 7" workweeks. First, he worked with other secretaries and, through them, got to know the inside of the federal government and how it operated. In addition, as Kleberg's acknowledged voice, he associated with some of the key men of power, including Garner and Rayburn, who would play such important roles in his future. With Franklin Delano Roosevelt's arrival as president in March 1933, Johnson also met and worked closely with the key players in the Democrats' system of power, including such stalwarts as William O. Douglas and Tom Clark, future members of the Supreme Court; Richard Russell, the senator from Georgia and key to Johnson's control of the southern senators and, through them, the Democratic majority and the nation; and countless lobbyists who would successfully ply their trade with him during his many decades in Washington. Russell would later serve on the Warren Commission and find his independent views buried in the final *Report*.

During FDR's ambitious first "Hundred Days," major legislation was proposed and approved to try to get the nation back on its feet. Johnson participated to the fullest extent he could while his goal of getting elected to anything remained his highest priority. In the month following FDR's inauguration, he managed to become chairman of the "Little Congress," an organization for the secretaries of the members of Congress.

Soon after FDR was sworn in, Johnson found himself enmeshed in controversy with John Nance Garner, now vice president, over appointments of postmasters in Texas, as well as control of that key power, then one of the few federal jobs available back home and, in those days, a most important key to patronage and loyalty. Surprisingly, Johnson won the confrontation, and the victory permanently sided him against Garner as the new vice president's power began to fade away. On the other hand, during that same dispute, Johnson ingratiated himself to Sam Rayburn and won the man's allegiance for a span of time approaching thirty years. A character trait emerged for Johnson, that of literally smoozing himself to anyone in power, which could be seen as a pitiful fawning that bordered on begging. However, he would brutally oppose people he perceived to be against him. Even in those early years, Johnson's political enemies became those men in positions he coveted for himself or needed for his friends. Garner was the first major victim.

As an outsider in the nation's power center, where Texas was as alien to the eastern elite as those same elite were alien to his homes in Gillespie and then Blanco Counties, Johnson often found himself in deep waters, well over his head. As the courts began challenging the New Deal, Johnson became all the more perplexed. In September 1934, to improve his understanding of the law and how legislation worked, he enrolled in night school, trying again to get a law license. He gave the effort only a passing try. Never much of a scholar, education simply did not fit into his plans. After attending classes irregularly for only two months, he dropped out.

His concentration remained very directed, that of learning how to become an elected official in his own right. By leaving the law behind, however, he never understood the vagaries that occurred in the courts, and he would soon fall prey to lawyers ready to manipulate and control him. He learned to accept the problem and would later say, "When you got a problem, go see the man in the biggest house atop the highest hill." Ed Clark would prove to be that man, and he would show Johnson how the law did not matter.

On November 22, 1963, Clark would put Johnson in the most powerful house and the highest office in America.

When Johnson dropped out of law school in that fall of 1934, he took another important step. He knew he needed a wife for his political future and the best method was Clark's way: to marry over one's head. Johnson took this route after meeting Claudia Taylor, a recent journalism graduate from the University of Texas and daughter of a man of means, a grocer and landowner in Karnak, deep in east Texas. In San Antonio, after sending a friend to pick out their wedding ring at a nearby Sears and Roebuck store, Johnson married the woman to be known as "Lady Bird," four years his junior and willing to put up with his insulting and overbearing behavior, his sexism, and his affairs. The foresight of marrying a woman with money paid off for Johnson when her family provided some of the money needed for his election in 1937 and for their radio station in 1943. In turn, her father was rewarded with land and military contracts from the federal government that, during and after World War II, made him a millionaire.

Following a brief honeymoon to Mexico, the Johnsons returned to Washington where he remained an ardent FDR supporter. Marriage had added responsibilities for the man and, in the spring of 1935, he began looking around for better employment and income. First, he considered becoming a lobbyist, knowing it would mean the end of elected politics. He also considered becoming a college president even though he had no graduate degree and was a failed student. He ultimately decided that he had to do something that combined income and politics. As events developed, it proved possible to remain wedded to a political future and to make money—a great deal of money.

Ever on the lookout for a way to get into politics in Texas, he would take the opportunity when the National Youth Administration was established. Eleanor Roosevelt had proposed NYA as a necessary means to save a lost generation of youth during the Depression. For Johnson, the opportunity was perfect. He'd be back in Texas, in charge of a statewide program with ample funds to do the job. Calling on Rayburn, Johnson prevailed on the Speaker to enlist Texas senator Tom Connally and then on FDR himself to name Johnson director of NYA in Texas.

On July 25, 1934, Johnson got the job and returned to Austin, temporarily leaving Washington behind.

To some Bowie still means a deadly knife for killing while to others it means a singer of beautiful songs. That difference was starkly in place with Johnson: Texas and the South compared to the far more civilized Northeast. The difference was between reasonable approaches to government in the North and the power-of-the-gun approach still widely used in Texas and in the South.[20] That difference persisted throughout the Johnson era. Violence was built into his system.

> "That boy'll be the next governor or its most wanted criminal," with the rejoinder, "He did both."
> —Old Texas saying

The capital city began boosting itself as a residential city,...
—Texas Handbook Online

4

The Friendly City

Austin, chosen primarily for its central location and natural beauty, was established in 1839 to be the capital for Texas. In its early years, the hamlet formerly known as Waterloo did not flourish. Because of a raid by Mexico on San Antonio in 1842, Sam Houston ordered the Republic's archives moved along with the capital; however, Austin citizens resisted and the records stayed where they were.

Thirty years later a referendum was held and Austin was officially chosen. The great red-granite capitol building was completed in 1888 and the little town seemed ready to grow. For forty years after 1880, however, the population of Texas increased threefold but the town lagged behind, falling in size among other Texas cities from fourth to tenth. The oil boom did not come to Austin and, since the community served only government and higher education, it made little economic progress. Coupled with disasters in municipal spending and a hydroelectric dam that collapsed, Austin retreated from boosting commerce and industry, becoming instead a "residential city." Growth virtually ceased.

When the Depression hit, people turned to government in a big way and Austin witnessed its largest population increase before the 1990s, growing some 66 percent. The university also expanded, doubling its enrollment. With that stage set by 1935, Austin saw the arrival of its political spokesmen for the next thirty-four years, Lyndon Johnson and Edward Clark.

On arriving in Austin in 1935, Johnson went to work running the National Youth Administration. Because his need for jobs for young men was a statewide issue, he soon came into contact with Governor Allred and, through him, Ed Clark, then secretary to the governor. Johnson said he did not want just busy work for unemployed young men, digging holes and filling them up again; he wanted meaningful jobs and, when the idea of roadside parks was suggested, he readily agreed. The early official meetings with

Clark centered on the business of parks alongside state roads and highways. Before long, a nervous Johnson was following the more relaxed Clark wherever he went. Between the two, Clark was the leader then and he would remain the leader, becoming a shrewd politician and power broker who was in charge.[1]

Because the NYA programs were statewide, Johnson had to travel, and Clark was not in daily contact with the youthful director. They remained in contact, however, because of the power both were generating toward their greater mutual ambitions. After all, Johnson had money and jobs that were powers in themselves; as secretary to the governor, Clark had political power on a statewide basis.

From the beginning, their bonding seemed heaven-sent, but their long conspiracy against the public interest was straight from unlimited ambition and craven power.

In his new position, Johnson was in the middle of the most pressing problem of the Depression. Desperate for work, many of the job seekers in the state's capital would be considered obedient camp followers. They almost had to be. Political operatives, today's wannabes, men seeking government work, young men seeking power and influence, friends and neighbors, and, most importantly, family, all showed up for work. The ties that bound in those days in Texas were primarily family and friends, and many appeared at Johnson's NYA headquarters in Austin looking for work. For many people during the Depression, life was not complicated; most were very poor and survival was very difficult. Many simply craved a stable job with steady income, no matter how many the hours or how little the pay. They knew fear in a most fundamental way, that fear of not having a job and of being unable to feed and house a family. At the time, welfare as we know it today simply did not exist.

Like America, Texas knew the fear that FDR had identified when he said, "The only thing we have to fear is fear itself." Out of fear, the downtrodden and impoverished turned to men of wealth and power and, in turn, committed and even enslaved themselves to those leaders out of sheer blind necessity. To them, Johnson was a savior and many of those early employees stayed with him throughout his long career. With so many petitioning him for help during his twenty months as NYA director, Johnson worked hard to put together a solid team of followers and supporters and to get results.[2]

All that effort was never fulfilled, however, because of a sudden change in circumstances for Johnson. On February 22, 1937, Buck Buchanan, the incumbent congressman from Austin, unexpectedly died. An election was called where the winner would be decided by a mere plurality, by whoever gained the most votes. A majority was not required. This attracted a crowded field of candidates, including Johnson. Early polling indicated Johnson was only in the middle of the field, clearly not high enough in the polls to win. At that point Clark provided the winning margin by convincing Governor Allred to send a letter to state employees, encouraging them to vote for Johnson. The endorsement worked. Although Johnson was elected with only 27 percent of the total vote, the citizens in Austin were the margin of victory. The friendship between Johnson and Clark was forever sealed.

The Austin that elected Johnson was very different from the Austin of today. Now an expanding metropolis with a powerful foundation in technology, Austin in 1937 had fewer than 50,000 people and was, except when the legislature arrived once every two years, a "hard candy" town.[3] Even as late as the 1960s, there was no true industrial or commercial base. Making a living was very difficult. It was changing from a residential city to a city of industry and commerce, but only very slowly.

Most view Austin as having two parts, education and government. In fact there were then, and still are, three essential parts to Austin: the downtown business section from Town Lake to Eleventh Street; the government offices just to the north of Eleventh; and next, starting at then Nineteenth Street (now Martin Luther King Boulevard), the university community of faculty, administrators, and students. There was no great wealth anywhere, and survival was too often a day-to-day problem.

This was particularly true for lawyers. The law school cranked them out, and most loved the university and the town, laid back then as now. Many stayed. Only a few could survive on the very limited resource: clients who could afford legal protections. Lawyers with business clients would prosper. Those outside the business community were typically employed in government or at the law school itself. Of course, in the thirties, the demand for lawyers mushroomed as laws had to be written for the New Deal and for the state's lawyers to respond to the new national laws and to represent the state's interests.

The many new laws in turn attracted lobbyists, and with them came the corruption necessary to serve their clients. Despite the dramatic growth in business, most lawyers struggled to get by. Knowing this, Clark took the special steps needed to assure himself a good living. He worked to control the legal system, "to own a judge."[4]

By the time Johnson was elected to Congress, Austin was "wild and woolly" as people flocked there for relief only to find the government did not have enough jobs. Many simply enrolled in the University of Texas, struggling to improve their situation while barely getting by. As the Depression slowly worsened, temporarily improved, and then slumped again before December 7, 1941, more and more of the displaced or unemployed arrived there, turning to government for help. The legislature remained busier than ever, at first trying to give relief, then opposing the longer-term efforts by Governor Allred and fighting FDR's New Deal.

For those in power there was the nightlife. Austin had been wide open for many years with saloons and bordellos located near the downtown railroad tracks. A cleanup had been attempted when Prohibition arrived, but the booze and the broads simply moved to other locations, mainly near Sixth Street. At night, as the lobbyists plied their dark trade, "booze, blondes, and beefsteaks" were the call to fun and games.[5] Business had a strong presence and a ready voice, and, with lobbyists and lawmakers mutually committed to spending entertainment money freely, corruption was rampant. Despite the Depression, plenty of cash was available to the lobbyists and their chosen few, particularly as the east Texas oil boom stabilized. As supply was controlled, the price of oil shot up, and huge sums were available to lobby and control the government of Texas.

By then in key positions with the state, Johnson and Clark were ready clients, prepared to listen to any lobbyist, eager to join any party. For Clark, the process became very simple, a means of gaining a man's allegiance, of bonding with him forever. To him, the bond from sharing a prostitute was perfect, of having done something immoral and illegal, particularly by the standards then in effect, with neither participant able to tell on the other, like schoolboys sharing a naughty little secret. For Clark the system worked many times to his satisfaction. He and Johnson found that common bond, they "shared a whore."

Their bond of corruption applied to these indiscretions and to every other corrupt deal. After all, if both sides agreed to an illegal transaction, who would complain? Clark's corruption would prove to be an even stronger tie than the mob's code of *omerta*. If both sides to the deal were involved and if both were guilty, then both would go to jail if the silence were broken. The bond was complete and the silence was deafening.

There was one exception. The privilege would protect the lawyer, no matter what. After all, he was an officer of the court. In a deal gone sour, only the nonlawyer, the "civilian," would be implicated, and this was important if the code was broken, particularly by a government employee. Not only could an oral agreement be denied; further inquiry would be barred by the privileges lawyers had, and still have. There were many times when Clark could assure Johnson that many a man in power, like a judge, had been paid off and was "hitched," "owned," or "bought."

The abuse practiced by these men in power was clear at all levels. Blacks had no chance. The Klan or men with its racist attitudes were always ready to "defend" themselves from the former slaves and keep them "in their place." Women were similarly mistreated, both as wives and as employees. In that tough era women had few rights. For many unwanted sex was simply a part of the job, and that so-called right for the men was regularly abused by Johnson and Clark. Religion was similarly a point for prejudice. Catholics and Jews were treated prejudicially and were excluded from the "good old boys" club. The only "right" was with white Protestant men. Finally, the poor were largely ignored, suffering the abuse made possible in a system run by men in power like Johnson and Clark. The finishing touch was in politics. There were no Republicans. Texas was a one-party state and, with so many voting groups already excluded, democracy did not have a chance. Small wonder that abuses of the system occurred. There were no checks and balances.

During the late thirties, Johnson and Clark moved ever higher in the power structure that governed Texas. The big change in the Johnson history was underway, that remarkable dichotomy between what occurred on the record nationally and what went on behind closed doors between the "good ole boys" in the smoke-filled rooms in Austin. Johnson was in Washington, where the loyal party out of power and a sophisticated press corps could keep an eye on the men in power. In Austin, there were no such protections accorded the public interest.

For Clark, his term as secretary of state ended in 1939, and he went into business, "hanging out his shingle" as an attorney. He had great expectations because, in representing his clients, he knew he could enlist Johnson's help. The main money issue then was the Lower Colorado River Authority. LCRA was proposed to build the dams that would bring a TVA-like program to central Texas. That plan for electricity, of getting lights to the rural areas, presented a perceived threat to the electric utility companies in Texas.

The compromise Johnson and Clark developed between the two interests was perfect. Johnson set up the LCRA and Clark represented the private utilities in a dispute that was surface only. Both sides would win. For

Clark, the old Insull utility empire kept the lights burning for his newly opened law offices as he represented the private companies with money. After all, they had a direct interest in government regulation. The LCRA was simply accepted as a necessary evil.

The reason was simple. In addition to the LCRA, the electric utilities had a serious problem. Following national investigations, Congress had ordered a "death penalty" for electric utility holding companies. At the time most were owned by holding companies that made government oversight impossible. They distorted revenues and put the owner of the leading holding company in control of the others in a leveraged system of power that avoided all responsibility for serving the public by delivering electricity. The required breakup of pyramided utility companies like Insull was ordered. Congress declared that the stacked electric companies be consolidated until there was only one holding company for its operating companies. Central Power, a survivor of the holding company system, turned to Clark as the natural conduit to Johnson and to a vote in Congress. The two would negotiate an acceptable living arrangement with the LCRA. In addition, over the next fifteen years, Clark would negotiate the survival of the Central and Southwest system at the Securities and Exchange Commission in Washington, again with Johnson's help.[6]

In this same scheme of getting clients needing government help, Clark also found business with Brown & Root, a construction company that was building the dams for the LCRA. Since Johnson was the key to the LCRA in Congress, Clark's access gave Brown & Root the contracts they needed. Then, as war preparedness escalated, it would grow into a military-industrial complex and become a dominant Houston-based business power. Through it all their full support went to Johnson's political campaigns and to Clark's law practice.

While building a solid political base, Johnson also learned how to accumulate wealth through government with Clark as his conduit and protector. The first step was innocent enough. Johnson began moving into homes owned by others and picking up an interest in the real estate. He was beginning to reap the indirect and carefully hidden benefits of political corruption. The deal was as old as politics itself. Business knows that support for a politician means influence and, in return, the politician learns that business helps him. In the thirties it was tolerated. Over the next twenty years, the business of getting rich while in government would become subject to increasing controls and prohibitions.

A new issue was emerging, however, one that Johnson and Clark could not avoid. As 1939 approached, the war climate in Europe and the Far East was clearly worsening. Clark joined the Texas Guard and Johnson obtained a commission in the Naval Reserve. Soon, both would find themselves unsuited for serving their country.

Politics rode the storm as America converted to war preparedness. Johnson and Clark centered their attention on two key elections before Pearl Harbor.

The year 1940 featured a presidential election, one highlighted by an interesting change in Johnson's politics. By the end of 1930s, Johnson was changing his tune on the New Deal, becoming ever more critical and taking new steps to keep the federal government out of Texas business, to protect Texas from "the federales." On the other hand, for federal money Johnson would do anything. Johnson's ambiguous reactions echo those of another person in the Roosevelt administration he steamrollered before, fellow Texan and then vice president John Nance "Cactus Jack" Garner.

In 1940 this personal conflict between more government and less government came to a head for Garner, the hard-drinking antilabor Texan from a state where newspapers had become decidedly anti-Roosevelt, much as they were later anti-Kennedy and for all the same reasons. Garner had signed on with FDR in 1932 and stayed with him for the 1936 campaign. For Garner, however, the vice presidency proved to be "not worth a bucket of warm spit."[7] He complained often, providing Johnson a very clear insider's view of what "the second highest office in the land" really meant. To be vice president meant nothing, except waiting for the president to die.

Because of his political impotence and his basic policy conflict between big government and Texas money, Garner decided to run against Roosevelt in 1940 for the Democratic Party nomination. Evoking the strong Texas spirit of pro-business praise and anti-government vitriol, he became the conservative Democratic candidate. After FDR's eight years of running the nation contrary to the views of Texas business and frontier individualism, the New Deal programs were just too much, too "socialist," and too "communist." Similarly, Johnson would later be very displeased with Kennedy's policies toward his state.

Garner's constituents were a fiercely independent group with a powerful distaste for government meddling into their affairs, except when assistance was needed. The crisis between president and vice president reached a breaking point when Garner refused to see Roosevelt on a visit to

Texas. Soon after, he challenged Roosevelt's bid for a third term, seeking the Democratic nomination himself. He lost. Johnson and Clark were delegates to the national convention that nominated FDR for the controversial third term. Garner was replaced by Henry Wallace.

Roosevelt went on to win the presidential election, soundly defeating Wendell Willkie.

In the 1940 congressional elections, Johnson managed the funds for Democratic candidates nationwide, and he would successfully deliver to FDR a continued majority in the House of Representatives.

Then, with FDR reelected, the stage was set for Johnson's first Senate race. On April 9, 1941, Morris Sheppard, Texas's senior senator, passed away. An election was called for June 28, 1941, and Johnson promptly entered the crowded field of twenty-seven candidates. Running on a ticket backing FDR, Johnson became an early favorite against the incumbent governor, Pappy Lee O'Daniel, a formidable candidate in his own right. A unique southern and Texas character, O'Daniel was a gospel-preaching evangelist with a dulcet voice to accompany his hillbilly band. The combination was always popular with the voters. Ever the competitor Johnson put together his own band and sent it out to fight the governor, song for song. As the campaign deepened, O'Daniel proved to be the candidate for Johnson to beat.

Based on voter reporting the day after the election, Johnson won by 5,000 votes; however, in east Texas, two other candidates kept their rural votes under cover until the Johnson total was announced. As it turned out, O'Daniel held some 15,000 votes as proxies. The votes were already cast for two other candidates, but the governor kept them in reserve until his team knew how many votes were needed to win. Once Johnson's totals were in, O'Daniel made the changes needed and announced a victory by 1,009 votes. No question the process was dirty politics; however, it was a standard election tactic in Texas Democratic primaries in those days.[8] The important rule was that all stealing of votes had to be done on Election Day. Once the polls closed, there could be no padding.

The practice was simple. Reliable precinct chairs simply voted their lists for the candidate that chair favored. Voters were not even required. Money routinely changed hands for the chair's "expenses" in "getting out the vote." The only rule that applied to these "dirty" and very illegal tactics was that the votes had to be cast on the day of the election or before as absentee, not after.

O'Daniel won the "buy the vote" drive.

A federal investigation was demanded and obtained by the unhappy Johnson, but it soon fizzled. When the final results were announced, the election was set in the public mind. Because of the monumental time required just for a recount then, there was, as a very practical matter, very little that could be done. Johnson and Clark learned the hard way, but they learned the fine art of voter theft to add to their repertoire of tricks and crimes. When Johnson ran his next statewide race, Clark would maximize those tricks. Then, as he so often did, he would carry the corruption just a little bit further, or as he put it, "do a little bit better."

This first statewide race for Johnson was marked by one unique feature. Financial records were not reported on any regular basis, and cash contributions were kept only for private use by the candidate and his supporters, primarily for "thank you" letters and for future mailing lists. In 1941, even those internal records were deliberately destroyed. Substantial contributions were needed for statewide races and Johnson's bookkeeper was maintaining a black book, listing all supporters and their contributions. When shown the records, Johnson attorney Alvin Wirtz grabbed the book and tore it apart.[9] There would be no records: not then and not in the future. To this day, the LBJ Library denies there are any records of contributions to the statewide campaigns Johnson ran in 1941, 1948, and 1954.[10]

An important dichotomy was established. Congress would have excellent records for its members' public service in Washington. For the all-important election records in Texas, however, there was next to nothing. The elections, the businesses, and the private activities by Johnson back home in Texas would remain a mystery. If they ever did exist, such records were forever sealed in the old penthouse records kept in Clark's law firm.

Within six months of the failed 1941 Senate election, the United States was at war and our nation's "greatest generation" turned its attention to defeating fascism.

Johnson made a show of serving his country, activating his reserve status in the U.S. Navy and getting sent to the Pacific to develop a progress report for FDR on military organization and supply. In Australia, after convincing General Douglas MacArthur to send him near a combat zone, he flew in a B-25 on a bombing raid to Lae in northeast New Guinea. The fighting was fierce with Japanese Zeroes allegedly attacking the bomber repeatedly. Somehow the plane survived and returned Johnson to safety. Some airmen that flew on the bombing run sharply dispute the account,

stating unequivocally that Johnson's bomber turned back before the formation ever got near the target, protecting Johnson from enemy fire. Despite
the controversy, Johnson became a war hero. Although no other airmen in
that specific combat mission received any meritorious recognition,
MacArthur awarded Johnson a Silver Star.[11]

Johnson was never near combat action again. Early in July 1942 FDR
issued an order requiring all members of Congress to stay in office and continue to do their work for the country. Johnson happily returned to
Washington.

Clark despised the military. Although the facts have been successfully
suppressed until now, his wartime service would prove to be something that
would forever be kept secret. Two years into the war, he had risen to the rank
of captain in the quartermaster corps when his career suddenly ended in disgrace. He had stolen two vehicles and, while the charges were reduced to mis-
handling funds, he was summarily kicked out of the army.[12] Reimbursement
of a token sum was required. The limited record still available claims that he
had a medical condition and was discharged because his eyesight was defective. As part of the military investigation, a separate formal hearing was also
convened to be certain he could never receive benefits as a veteran. On
January 16, 1943, Clark was formally expelled from the service. In disgrace,
he was booted out in as final and secret a separation as was possible.

An interesting record was made. Clark's wife, Anne, attended the discharge hearing to testify that her husband had vision problems, that those
problems were preexisting, and that they were not related to his military service.[13] The facts of Clark's theft and dishonorable discharge were carefully
concealed from everyone, including his law partners. These facts had to be
covered up because his law license was threatened and, with that, his future.

One long-term advantage came out of his military service. Clark had
under his command a soldier named Clifton "Beau" Carter of Bryan, Texas.
In the years ahead, Carter would participate in many significant ways to
advance Johnson and Clark's illegal activities and, by extension, their political careers.

Once out of the army, Clark returned to Austin to resume his law practice in earnest. On the home front, competition with other lawyers was neg-
ligible. The more qualified men were serving in the military. For Clark,
business was booming. The war was finally bringing America out of the
Depression with giant industrial strides. Clark took every advantage of the

opportunity. Looking back, he readily acknowledged that the foundations for his corrupt power were laid during the war years and immediately following.

Although Johnson lost the 1941 Senate election, he remained ready and available for any political advancement. No other races for the Senate opened up during the war, however, so he held on to his congressional seat. He was not interested in the governor's office or any other statewide office. There were far more significant and profitable politics at the national level. He also had to keep the more liberal Austin voters behind him while attracting new voters statewide who were relatively conservative. Simply stated, he was interested in the presidency and the Senate seemed to be the best way to get there. He would do anything to get that result.

In addition to becoming more conservative, his other problem was getting some income. After all, his supporters were all getting wealthy. He was not.

The money issue arose in a classic way The first serious threat to expose his illegal election efforts centered on the 1941 Senate race. An Internal Revenue Service audit of Brown & Root's illegal contributions of corporate money through individuals had commenced. The criminal charges against Brown & Root were serious and necessarily involved Johnson. Despite an all-out legal battle, the IRS refused to drop the charges. Finally, after much internal maneuvering, the claim was killed in 1944. A private request to the White House got the vital help needed. FDR himself ordered the case dropped.[14] Johnson, of course, learned another important lesson, that the White House controlled the criminal justice system. He also had a far better understanding of the power exercised by the IRS.

Clark learned an equally important lesson: control of the IRS was essential. He set out to get it.

During the war, several key Johnson supporters were working to find a solid source of income for him. Influence peddling went to work. The Federal Communications Commission became the key as attorney Alvin Wirtz worked with Johnson and Clark to bring a fledging Austin radio station under Johnson's control. The owner was not making money and, through Johnson, Wirtz arranged for FCC delays of license amendments necessary to increase broadcast power. The delays effectively destroyed what little worth the station had. This was easy since Wirtz was also attorney for the station's owner. This blatant conflict of interest was no problem for the lawyer. As the value of the radio station continued to decline in 1943, the owner had to sell to Johnson for a small payment. Soon after, FCC increased KTBC's broadcast rights, substantially enhancing the income and the value of the business. Johnson added government largesse to his political vocabulary, important this time because it was also personal enrichment.

In 1944, Clark hired Don Thomas as an associate. The young lawyer was from Bogota, a small town in north Texas in Sam Rayburn's congressional district. Thomas had been deferred from military service because he had three brothers already serving. After finishing law school in Austin, Thomas went to work for Clark and for Johnson. Clark assigned Thomas to work as a libel attorney for Johnson and to review all political statements aired on KTBC, both by Johnson and by any and all opponents. The spin on news to the Austin and central Texas electorate was carefully controlled.

Clark also participated in setting up a new radio station, KVET, to improve Johnson's control of information to Austin voters. During this time, an interesting long-term power struggle was underway. Although Wirtz remained a Johnson attorney until 1948, Clark was the most trusted political adviser on the local scene. Ever the aggressor, he was moving into position to take everything from Wirtz.

Again through friends, Johnson acquired still more comfortable living quarters in Austin for his growing family, now including Lynda Bird, the first of his two daughters.

Also in 1944, Clark was selected a delegate to the Democratic National Convention. Johnson attended as an automatic member. The so-called stalwarts in the Texas delegation, conservatives led by Senator O'Daniel and Governor Coke Stevenson, tried to take over the state convention but failed. At the national convention, Johnson and Clark supported FDR. The president was renominated for his fourth term.

Of direct interest to Johnson, however, was the selection of FDR's running mate. The incumbent vice president, Henry Wallace, had been secretary of agriculture and every bit as much an FDR supporter as Johnson was during the Depression and World War II. In addition, Wallace had been a farmer and plant geneticist who authored highly controversial portions of the New Deal for rural aid. His program called on farmers to destroy surplus crops to keep agricultural prices up while opposing giving that same food away to the hungry during the Depression. During Roosevelt's third term, Wallace was perceived to have become too radical and unstable to succeed the ailing president. In a controversial move during the 1944 convention, the Democratic Party replaced Wallace. FDR turned to Senator Harry Truman.

Interestingly, Henry Wallace had been a friend and active supporter during Johnson's failed Senate race in 1941, providing him the services of his chief aide as a northern fund-raiser. Then, at the 1944 convention, Johnson saw his former mentor pulled from the presidential ticket by FDR. The fate of a vice president, he learned, depended on the whim of the president.

One further note on wartime politicking. As the war was ending, Johnson's key position heading up the War Committee in Congress enabled him to help favored soldiers return home quickly, ahead of the many men awaiting return under a complex point system. One such preference was provided in 1946. An early release was arranged for Clint Murchison's son, giving Johnson another important future connection.[15]

Now very careful about long-term planning, Clark realized the time was ripe to get a stranglehold on the legal system and, through it, the state's laws. After all, most of the able-bodied men were at war. Some would view Clark as doing what any good attorney would do, simply planning ahead. Like a good contract, a successful law business will cover as many possible future problems as possible. Clark went further. He made sure the judges and lawmakers were in the key places that he needed, in order to be sure his contracts were enforced and his clients' needs were served. Having learned the hard way through the Klan, through jury nullification in east Texas, and through the military about what the law really was, Clark went to work "to own a judge."

In Clark's legal philosophy by 1945, the law was little more than a process where the judge was the key to winning. Knowing that every case could be framed to go either way, Clark set out to get full control of the legal system and the decision makers. Jack Roberts proved to be the first key man for an "owned" judge.

In 1946, literally picking the hopeless drunk out of the gutter, Clark rehabilitated Roberts enough to get him elected district attorney of Travis County and then district judge. The deal with Roberts, and all future judges Clark supported, was simple: in close cases, you rule for me. Since all cases could be close cases, he had the key to success.

In addition, Clark had the right to call the case a close case. In this game of superlawyers and their version of law as a business, results were the only thing that counted. In business you had to show a profit; in the law you had to win to show a profit. With a judge in place, Clark could not lose.

Another control of the judges was access. The deal was simple: "You will return my calls immediately." This seemingly innocent agreement meant calls at critical moments to tell the judge things that were usually not relevant and too often not correct. If nothing else, the secret calls reminded the judge of his obligation on close cases.[16] For Clark, if he wanted to win, and sometimes he did not, the case was always "close." The judge had no choice. Clark's client wins. His business succeeds. He makes money.

Clark would get the last word, and, whether true or not, whether related to the case or not, the impact was decisive. This was possible despite the fact that such *ex parte*, off-the-record and secret conversations were illegal. As Clark abused the law, new rules were adopted to place ever more restrictions on secret calls. Clark continued using the old rules throughout his career.

With Roberts in place, Clark had control of the court system, and that control was not just in Austin and Travis County. Since all cases under state law were tried in Travis County, it also meant power throughout the state. "Texas justice" was "Clark justice." This was power not only over corporations litigating with the state; it was also a hold on every elected legislator. During their stay in Austin the "boys in the Lege," as members of the Texas Legislature were known to the media, would commit crimes and misdemeanors while enjoying the after-hours games. Since Clark knew what went on behind closed doors and what happened after dark, he was in a unique position of control. Threats of criminal charges were often all he needed. He could subtly extort from the men in power all the benefits he needed whenever he needed them. Since there was always a need for benefits from the state, Clark was in a unique position to control the companies, the representatives, and the citizens of Texas.

After the Brown & Root tax fiasco, another important step by Clark was to bring the IRS under control. This was done by promoting Frank Scofield, an attorney and accountant for Johnson's radio station, to IRS district director.[17] Again, Clark thought he had the standard understanding. This would prove not to be the case. At best, Clark had only an implied agreement to the effect that, "Because we got you the job, tax cases would not be brought against the Johnson interests." Scofield proved to be independent or, more accurately, both honest and forthright.

This system of cronyism and of widespread abuse of the law and of political power was changing. Johnson and Clark would prove fortunate during the coming decades to stay one step ahead of the law as it changed.

One part of the dismal record was the failure to challenge Clark's practices. The other key lawyers in private practice knew what was happening, but the perceptive ones were making money through Johnson's pork-barreling gifts of federal money for Austin; they stayed quiet. Those who were not rewarded suffered the price for opposing Johnson, for working against Clark, or for simply being Republican.

The Austin voters also knew what was happening, but were rewarded enough for a majority to continue supporting Johnson, to "stay hitched" to him. Perhaps we see a hidden wisdom with voters. They will tolerate a certain level of corruption so long as it does not get out of hand, so long as indictments were not returned, and so long as the elected official is serving the majority. By Clark's control through agreement with key members of the courts and the district attorney's office, he prevented the very unacceptable eventuality of indictment and trial. He had control and he exercised it carefully.

The main challenge after the war for the members of Congress who stayed home was at the ballot box. Returning veterans presented the first real opportunity in five years to remove incumbents. The phenomenon was nationwide. In the 1946 elections, John F. Kennedy would be elected in Massachusetts and Richard Nixon would win in California. As the incumbent, Johnson also had serious competition from a war veteran, Nuremberg prosecutor, and attorney. Hardy Hollers took on Johnson in 1946. In a bitter race that featured substantive charges by Hollers about Johnson's corruption, the new homes, his radio station, and his liberal FDR views, Johnson was still reelected. Austin voters stayed hitched.

With the success of the 1946 election, Johnson and Clark had the raw elements of political control in place. The stage was set for the key 1948 election and the converging of all these loose ends into one well-oiled political machine to gain still more power, to expand that power, and to get very rich.

For a majority in Texas, this was all well and good. The Democratic Party ran the state. Key people were rewarded. The real problem was the impact of this corrupt system on the nation. That problem would only continue and worsen in the years ahead.

The Civil War ended slavery and ruined the southern economy, but it did not end either the southern or the Texas state of mind. Johnson would make the ongoing merger between the South and the nation work, but only reluctantly and always protective of his political base and his personal heritage. In fact, as his record reveals, Johnson could never and would never escape his upbringing, his experiences, and his biases.

In the end, his limited outlook left him isolated from the state as well as the nation as he found himself between the Scylla and the Charybdis or as they said back on the ranch, between a rock and a hard place. With Johnson, the politician, joined as he was with Clark, the power broker, subtle but important ideas from Texas's frontier years were added to the national discourse that became policy and law, determining our future in a way that few to this day understand and appreciate. Stated otherwise, Washington was cultural shock for Johnson and Johnson was cultural shock for the United States. These shocks, quakes, and aftershocks would occur repeatedly over the next twenty years and would climax on November 22, 1963. They would then continue to the end of Johnson's term.

For the most part Johnson and Clark were products of the frontier in Texas when violence was still acceptable and law and order was only reluctantly accepted and enforced. A ruthless violence was also their heritage and they never lost that frame of mind. In the final analysis for Johnson and Clark, violence was, stated quite simply, okay. Stated otherwise, as the twig was bent, so the tree was inclined. The two would carry that old proverb to an ultimate, horrific conclusion.

On a personal note, I followed Kennedy's call to Washington during the Cold War much as others had accepted Roosevelt's call during the Depression. Both leaders witnessed exciting times when our government experienced a transfer of power to new leaders chosen by our democracy. Without FDR's vision the nation may have never embarked on many compelling and progressive steps forward. Without Kennedy, the nation would not achieve the full measure of his visions. Johnson had wholly different visions: those of war, big oil, and personal enrichment.

Until now, a subtle mental twist has prevented these understandings. Just as Washington and Johnson were always alien to each other, assassinations were also misunderstood and too often prejudged. Traditional advisers to presidents understood assassination to be by loners. In Europe, the view was a power conspiracy did it.

On the other hand, the emerging wisdom now is that Lincoln was assassinated as the result of a Confederate plot. In times of great national turmoil, powerful interests act to protect themselves. The South tried in 1865. Again in 1963, the South, acting through consummate Texans, moved to protect itself from John Kennedy and the northeast liberals.

Only after understanding where Johnson and Clark came from and the experiences they had can we fully appreciate their conspiracy. We have to see how their respective states of mind emerged and then came together. We can then understand how the wellsprings in Texas history produced their mind-sets, how Johnson and Clark could be corrupted and corrupted again and again, until they were corrupted absolutely.

During the Clark era a bank expanded into a new building and included a black rock at its entrance, supposedly representing stability. The popular name for the rock, however, became "the banker's heart." Removal soon followed.

Clark was not just a lawyer; he was also a banker.

Similarly, Johnson was not just a politician; he was also deeply involved in business with Clark, including banks.

Similarly, Austin was a friendly city except at its heart: the power conspiracy that was Johnson and Clark, a true darkness at the heart of the capital of Texas.

> Everyone knew that if something wasn't straight it was Lyndon Johnson who had done it.
> —Robert Caro

> ... unless a people are educated and enlightened it is idle to expect
> the continuance of civil liberty or the capacity for self-government.
> —Texas Declaration of Independence, 1836

5

Assassin

So much in the Johnson history is not what it seems to be. Mount Pleasant, Texas, is no exception. The most populated town in Titus County remains small but well traveled on the main highway to points leading east from Dallas, another going south into the great east Texas oil field. There is no "mount." The area is rolling hills and good rivers that were excellent, first, for cotton, then dairy farming, and, today, for poultry processing.

"Pleasant" was also a misnomer. For most of the community's history, the few wealthy residents were surrounded by a crushing poverty so typical of Texas at the turn of the century: very poor, staunchly democratic (against Yankees), populist (anti-railroad), racially divided, and very family dependent. Success depended on knowing the right people, and the best tie-in to access successful friends was through the extended family. Mount Pleasant was a typical community.

Early in the 1920s, oil proved a boom but it soon faded. President Calvin Coolidge's road-building program during the twenties also brought some improvements to the life of the poor white community. But the crushing poverty did not begin to lift until World War II. Postwar America also brought improvements as economic expansion and civil rights were gradually extended into ever-greater parts of the population. Basically, however, the local economy and the living standards for the residents did not change until civil rights lent a necessary assist to the impoverished blacks, requiring fair treatment and better jobs. Power plants were built in the 1970s, offering excellent new jobs. Today, the American demand for chicken brings important production to Mount Pleasant as a major poultry-processing center.

The key hitman for Johnson was born into this small community on a cool October day in 1921, and he would grow up in much of the same cultural and social environment that Johnson and Clark experienced.[1] Malcolm

Everett "Mac" Wallace was his name. The boy's father was a farmer and handyman and his mother did the household chores, a demanding task in those days. They lived along a stretch of sandy loam at the northern edge of that forty-county area known as east Texas, extending south to Houston and east to Louisiana. Originally east Texas was for the early settlers and then it was taken over by the plantations. Many residents would never forgive the Yankees for taking over their land and ending their slave-based livelihood. Even in the 1920s that legacy was still cherished.

Just south of Mount Pleasant, in the Kilgore-Tyler-Longview area, America's largest oil reservoir was discovered in 1931, bringing widespread lawlessness to most and untold wealth for a few. Those new rich soon left, settling in Dallas. Mount Pleasant received only small benefits from that great oil play to the south.

Mac Wallace was the first of six children. A second child was born in Mount Pleasant but the baby died after only eight months. The last four siblings were born in Dallas.

Wallace's early life in Mount Pleasant was the hardest for him and his parents. His home would become the storage place for drilling equipment, and his early life would be as transient as the changing political spectrum of the 1920s. When oil was discovered, tenants were evacuated so a handful of landowners could develop and keep the petroleum millions for themselves. There was no sharecropping in oil.

The boy's father, Alvin, got a job on the road crews to support his wife, Alice Riddle, and baby Mac. To accommodate an emerging automobile industry, road building extended across the open plains and through the pine belt of east Texas, reaching from Mount Pleasant south to the Big Thicket, that impassable growth of pine and wilderness that was home to the desperados of early Texas. In those days, any concern for trees and natural beauty was lost when hungry mouths were waiting at home. Road building was backbreaking pick-and-shovel work then, resembling chain-gang labor more than construction work.

America was on the move, the boom times of the 1920s were underway, and economic growth would last until the stock market crash of 1929. For Alvin Wallace, the introduction to highway construction would expand into bridges and, in the 1950s, into a bridge construction company that prospered with President Dwight Eisenhower's interstate highway program. But that was yet to come. Mac's life during the twenties remained one of poverty, what was then very low middle income, barely a step above the impoverished blacks.

In sharp contrast to Lyndon Johnson's brand of disgraced yet genteel poverty, Mac's parents had never been of particular means or social reputation. Nobody joked about who Mac's father was or had been. Sam Johnson, Lyndon's father, had the family connections that Alvin did not. Still, like Wallace's father, the future president also worked the roads. Unlike Clark, Wallace did not have a family business to provide him with the better things in the Roaring Twenties. He did have a determination to get an education and would at least finish that undertaking at a major university. Unlike Johnson and Clark, Wallace would compile a good academic record.

The early era of the automobile meant greater mobility and improved expectations for whites everywhere in the boom of the 1920s, of the affordable Model T, and an expanding railroad industry to connect rural areas in lesser-developed Texas to its bustling cities. The times were good for some and, as part of that change from rural to urban, the Wallaces had to migrate. In 1925, Alvin Wallace moved the family one hundred miles west to electrified Dallas, seeking better opportunities and wages in the newly emerging construction industries. The new home was in east Dallas near the Fairgrounds and the Cotton Bowl was only two miles east of downtown and only a block from the high school Mac would attend. There would be better schools for Alvin and Alice's children there and better neighborhoods for whites. Still, Dallas was very much like Mount Pleasant and its small-town traditions.

In Dallas, the suburb the Wallaces called home was a stable lower-middle-class area of new tract houses with modern conveniences like electricity and gas stoves. But the new home was not far from the environs where Lee Harvey Oswald would later spend some of his time when separated from his wife. The shanty neighborhoods by the time of the Great Depression held grifters and petty thieves who plagued the South and Midwest. At the time, the state also had its folk heroes in bank robbers Bonnie and Clyde. Despite the boom of the post–World War I years, however, cities were exploding in a malaise of poverty due to immigrants from Mexico, the "wetbacks," and the blacks fleeing the hostility and poverty of the countryside. These newer arrivals would gradually take over the areas near Wallace's home.

Many other important changes, today taken for granted, were underway in the twenties. After the loss of the Civil War, the rigors of Reconstruction and recovery meant depressed agriculture and economic hardship. With the discovery of oil, however, Texas entered into a new and violent state of flux.

The most powerful political movement to sweep Texas after William Jennings Bryan's populism of the 1890s epitomized what happened. That new movement was the emergence and growth of the Ku Klux Klan, particularly in Dallas during Johnson's, Clark's, and Wallace's formative years.[2]

Men in white hooded sheets with torches directed public attention to the social changes occurring in the cities and throughout the state. Their message was not just against foreigners and blacks. The Klan also sought to impose a Victorian code on the citizens. The KKK ensured that blacks remained in the background, never hesitating to use lynching and mob violence to keep the former slaves in what the mob considered "their proper place." Texas ranked third behind Georgia and Mississippi in total lynchings, and these grotesque events were a public spectacle for not just the men but for women and children also, as the victim was often brutally tortured prior to a horribly cruel and horrendous killing that was the worst kind of murder. Many lynchings were in Titus County, Texas. The brutal violence of a lynching was an accepted feature of Wallace's early years.

In 1925 the Klan held a 400,000 strong march on Washington, its leader and former preacher William J. Simmons having charmed many members of Congress into believing the Klan was an upright middle-class organization concerned over declining urban morals. The Klan was not just racist; it was also a religious force intent on enforcing its restrictive moral codes. In the 1924 election, finally, a majority of Texans had all they could take and the Klan was defeated. Within two years, the membership had largely disappeared, never again to be so public a political force. The Klan's racism, however, merely faded in a slow demise that would extend well into the modern era in Texas as well as the South.

Within a year of that 1924 election, Alvin Wallace moved his small family to Dallas, at the heart of the Klan and always a center for conservatism.

Early on, Dallas and east Texas fell into the highly polarized rural versus urban conflicts. Area politicians began to imagine what they thought were the former Confederacy's finer days of wealth, slavery, and conformity. They sought to erase social gains made by blacks and to restrict behavior they felt was imported by Mexicans who were deemed useful only for picking cotton and working the fields when black peonage was not available. The resurgent Klan fostered a tradition of vicious racism that young Wallace as well as Johnson and Ed Clark would embrace in one form or another throughout their lives.

During the 1920s, Texas had become so poisoned with racism that any

substantial reform agenda for civil rights was impossible. The political climate would remain that way for many decades. Translating a progressive civil
rights agenda into acceptable politics in Texas was as impossible there as it
was throughout the South. The idea of civil rights did not translate into the
way the system worked, and would have gone no further than a symbol on
the paper. In Texas, until 1926, how could it work when a majority of legislators were Klansmen? As we shall see, racism lingered for a long time.

Growing up in an area where whites routinely killed blacks, Clark was a
Klan sympathizer and had been recruited in the early 1920s. Klan activities
continued into the late twentieth century in east Texas. The 1998 dragging
death in Jasper of James Byrd was murder by "truck lynching" and for no
other reason than the color of his skin. Jasper is less than sixty miles south
of Clark's boyhood home in San Augustine.

Consider Clark's attitude when Johnson was president. Although
Johnson would endorse progressive policies because of his affiliation with
the national Democratic Party, Clark promoted the real agenda, advising
clients that Johnson was disgusted with the new liberal politics.

As Clark remarked with his lisp, "Well, now, we all know the President
had to back civil rights. But we know what to do here. Nossir, it won't happen here."[3] The official agenda in Texas meant not mentioning the Kennedy
programs publicly in order not to offend the Johnson and Clark clients.

On these same lines, Clark's opinions were based on traditions linked to
reactionary organizations, at first violent, then more respectable but ever
more secretive. One was the Sons of the Texas Revolution and the even more
exclusive and highly secretive Knights of San Jacinto. Founded to promote
Texas history, these organizations were centers for conservatism and propaganda endorsing traditional values. They were secret societies for aging patriots who had already fought and won the cultural and business wars, gilded
clubs where the high and mighty could make deals and bestow favors upon
one another and keep others out, dedicated largely to promoting their own
vision of history and to making sure nothing changed. Interestingly, they also
made certain any spin on current developments would be in accord with
their conservatism. As Texas emerged from the twenties, the conservatism
would linger and become reactionary.

On the broader political scene, most Texas politicians were in the strange
position of being conservative Democrats struggling to keep from becoming Republicans. This ambivalence was not difficult when the agenda was
secretive and duplicitous. As we shall see, it was driven by political opera-

tives and lawyers practicing behind the attorney-client privilege, unseen by anyone except their paying clients. And even the clients did not know. They could understand the code words, and they could guess but they did not know the details. They did not need to know. They just paid.

By 1933, when Wallace became a teenager, the Depression had hit Texas savagely. Even the famous oil booms benefited only a few. East Texas remained boom and bust for many families as they came into great wealth and then lost it, often violently. Wallace was well aware of this life under the gun in that area between Dallas and San Augustine.

With the lingering Depression came the opportunity for increased delinquency among teenagers, and Wallace ran with a fast crowd. After all, he was a leader in high school. Still growing, the teenager, now broad-shouldered and olive-skinned, would top out at almost six feet.

In those days, there were new ways to channel the energy growing young men had. Farming had mechanized and work in the fields was not as important, so children had more time on their hands. As education expanded, the school day demanded more time and extracurricular activities gradually developed. This leisure time would be occupied by such things as football for young men. The major cities, including Dallas, took the lead in providing well-organized high school programs.

Guns were also part of the Texas lifestyle. "Guns talk louder than ballots" was the accepted rule as the frontier died a slow, hard death. Weapons appeared regularly on the floor of the Texas Legislature.[4] Even in the cities, hunting remained a favorite escape, for many a means of survival, for all the thrill of the hunt, of the power of the rifle, and of the intoxicating violence of the kill. Wallace enjoyed the hunt in the countryside outside Dallas. Unlike Johnson, however, his wild side in high school was channeled into high school sports. He would pay a high price because of injuries in the game.

People of Johnson's, Clark's, and Wallace's disposition tend to be grandiose and egocentric, having the so-called presidential gene. But they are frequently lacking in self-control and let the passion for power take over. The law means nothing. In his adolescence and as a young adult, Johnson had some pretenses to respectability. After all, his father had been a legislator. Wallace, on the other hand, was on the front lines in booming Dallas, and, because of football, he was more willing and able to confront his competitors directly and cause bodily harm. For him, there were new role models. His father was hard working and a good future loomed; however, he was from the lower middle class, which in those days meant impoverished whites. There was no pretense to respectability. Still, Wallace was elected vice president of his senior class at Woodrow Wilson High School in Dallas. By the time of his graduation in June 1939, he was considered among those most likely to succeed, his rough passions mistaken for the raw material for success, and his tendency to take things to the limit considered leadership.[5]

Certainly others among his classmates had the leadership qualities needed for success and they provided role models. Football stars like the legendary All-State selection Robert Davey O'Brien led Woodrow Wilson High School to the state playoffs six years earlier in 1932 and would win the Heisman Trophy. The golf team produced star tournament golfer and Professional Golf Association hall of famer Ralph Guldahl in 1930. Artist William Lewis Lester graduated in 1929 and started the Texas regional movement in 1932. Graduate Jim Collins became a United States congressman and his brother Carr would become a major force in Dallas politics.

Of greater interest, two of Wallace's close contacts in high school would move into armed security work. Insall B. Hale would go to Convair Industries in Fort Worth and Davie O'Brien would head security for Dallas oilman H. L. Hunt. Both were close friends, and, as top marksmen with the FBI, they helped set up the Quantico firing school.

Another high school classmate was R. D. Matthews, who became a marine, a bondsman, and a gambler. He would later frequent the Redman Club which happened to be in the same building Wallace's father had his business in Dallas. Matthews was a recognized member of organized crime.

In short, Wallace had many contacts in high school that would appear again in the Johnson orbit and in the assassination records. They remain of interest to many researchers.

Wallace's main insights into the real world came on the gridiron. In those early days of high school football, the game was far more violent than today's more carefully padded version. Vicious fights were tolerated as part of growing up in a man's world. A kick in the face on the football field is different from a kick in a bar or a parking lot. One was a part of the game; the other, criminal assault. The players' uniforms were rudimentary: long baggy pants, small shoulder pads, hard boots, and a leather, skin-tight helmet. The competition was tough and the playing field was vicious. Biting and kicking during blocking, tackling, and piling on were routine. A good football game was little more than street fighting, and the use of bent nails, brass knuckles, and even knives was not unknown.

In his senior year, Wallace suffered a debilitating injury in the mortal combat that was Texas high school football and where victory was the only rule. Spinal fusion, then a painful yet necessary surgical procedure, ended his high school football career; in time, he recovered.

Following graduation and with a world war looming on the horizon, Wallace, now recovered from his back injury, joined the U.S. Marines in June of 1939. Japan had already invaded China and Hitler controlled or threatened Europe on many fronts. Vice President Garner refused to support his president's efforts to end the Neutrality Act, to allow the country to sell arms to China, Britain, and France, leaving those nations helpless in the face of the Axis. After completing basic training with a solid record, Wallace received an excellent assignment. He shipped off to the Pacific where he served on the aircraft carrier *USS Lexington* in Hawaii. He was among the select few to serve as guard aboard ship, and his was one of the best ships in the American fleet.[6]

An accident ended Wallace's marine career. He fell from a ladder while aboard the "Lex" in Pearl Harbor, re-injuring his back. On September 25, 1940, he was medically discharged, just fifteen months before the Japanese turned the battleships of our Pacific fleet into a smoking, sunken ruin. The carriers were unharmed and the "Lex" was among those that turned the tide barely eight months later at Midway.

Mac returned to Texas and, in the fall of 1941, enrolled at the University of Texas in Austin.[7] He was not taken into the fraternity ranks; instead, he joined the fiercely independent Tejas Club, the leaders of the anti-fraternity group. The club provided modest, affordable housing so he lived at the organization's off-campus location at 1408 San Antonio Street.

On campus Wallace started as a conservative taking business courses and enjoying the usual patriotic activities of the time. At the University, many opportunities were available for his political and social interests, and he proved to be a joiner. Serving as bookkeeper of *The Cactus*, the student yearbook, he was also a member of the ex-servicemen's association, was on the board of directors of the University Co-op, and participated in the debate club. Due to the shortage of men during the war and despite the back injury and re-injury, Wallace also recklessly played football again. Nothing remarkable emerged from his gridiron efforts, but he pitched in where he could. These efforts earned him membership in the honorary Cowboys organization, then well known for particularly harsh initiation hazing that included severe paddlings.

Capping his college career, Wallace was elected student body president for the 1944–45 school year, a prestigious post attracting the attention of local and state politicians interested in a good contact with potential voters and future leaders in the student population. Several Texas governors along with many politicians had been student presidents and they respected anyone who could get elected, tagging them as potential wonder boys. While Wallace looked impressive to the outside looking in, the then dean of students Arno Nowotny would have a different assessment. The conservative administrator hinted that things were not at all well with the by-then liberal Wallace, making the callous remark that he "came to the university when a majority of old women and cripples were in attendance."[8] The dean was clearly implying that draft dodgers and other men staying at home could look good because there was no real competition. After all, the real men and the true patriots were serving their country fighting for freedom and democracy. In this regard Wallace was not unlike Clark.

Whatever the circumstances, Wallace would reach a position of leadership that would attract Lyndon Johnson's attention. Thoroughly immersed in campus life and, at first insulated from politics, he was well aware of Johnson's first, unsuccessful run for the Senate in 1941 against former Texas governor Pappy Lee O'Daniel and the country-western bands. Wallace's political interests gradually carried him ever closer to the congressman's activities.[9]

By 1944, with the war nearing an end, Wallace appeared on top of the world. Soon enough, however, he would get to test his mettle as a politician.

At this same time Clark hit rock bottom with the military and with his career. He was cashiered out of the army. From that low point, he would begin his recovery, one that would be permanently attached to Wallace's career. Clark would, of course, continue to rise, using Wallace as needed, in the process driving Wallace ever downward. The key steps in that drama between the two men would be played out over the next eighteen years. To his misfortune, Wallace would be swept into the Johnson and Clark web of corruption, to be owned by them for the rest of his life.

Then the university crisis hit. That crisis had its background in the long history of Texas politics and higher education and it remains a part of the Texas state of mind and, as we have seen, of the Johnson and Clark attitude. That state of mind was torn between adopting the more civilized ways of the Northeast or of promoting the Texas ways. While Wallace was in college, the reconciliation and accommodation was proceeding in earnest.

The idea of the university was born as little more than a hope when, in 1839, the Congress of the Texas Republic called for first-class higher education.[10] The expectation was to bring more civilized concepts and education to what was decidedly the wild frontier. For fifty years, however, nothing was done about that hope. When higher education finally started, the relationship between state government and the university began painfully close, too close as would soon appear.

According to the constitution of 1876, the University of Texas was to be a university of the first class. As an over-regulated state college, however, it continually lagged behind the nation's liberal arts universities. Before the university's expansion, classrooms were still located in the capitol building proper, a relationship of metaphorical and geographical significance that would endure for most of the twentieth century. State government would exercise strict control over faculty and curriculum, and, to anchor that supervision, the governor was initially the administrator for the university. Regents would insist new professors be from Texas in an effort to promote regional and ideological understanding. While reaching out to the Yankees, Texas remained mired in its past.

When a weak state government is dominated by the business lobby, the politics and desires of conservatives would usually take precedence over the anticipation of academic excellence. Excessive funds were spent on buildings for the storefront appearance of a progressive center for learning, a so-called oasis in the desert. Cass Gilbert, later famous for designing the Woolworth Building in New York, laid out the university's first building in 1889, an impressive Spanish Renaissance structure suitable for the grandiose ideals of the region and its proximity to Mexico. Philadelphia and Washington architect Paul Cret provided the layout of the campus, as well as most of the remaining buildings in 1933, using what was dubbed Shakeresque architecture.

By 1923, Regents allowed oil drilling on west Texas lands owned by the state and the wells were successful. More money was gradually becoming available; however, constitutional restrictions on use of the income often prevented the expansion needed. Because of scarce public funds during the Depression, temporary wood structures were built. At the same time enrollment doubled. Money ran out because severely limited government and spending was built into the Texas Constitution of 1876. There was simply not enough money for buildings and needed expansion. Texas remained dedicated to a permanent university fund based on commercially operating oil wells. During the oil boom of the 1970s, that endowment became the world's greatest, only to decline with the oil bust of the 1980s.

There was another thread to the political atmosphere in the Depression era of Texas, an explosion of desperation that led inevitably to religious fanaticism. Freedom of thought began to take on strange forms. By then, the Klan's well-organized and public brand of racist-spiked Victorianism was past history. Defeated at the polls, Klansmen were almost irrelevant but the attitudes they represented would dominate politics for many years. By 1933, poverty was crippling the state and the political infrastructure changed dramatically, actually becoming liberal and progressive. The changes lasted only a few years during the 1930s and changed back to business conservatism by 1940.

When it became clear that Roosevelt's economically imaginative programs were not ending the Depression and that the nation had slipped into a second recession, new politicians were speaking to receptive audiences demanding something constructive be done. By 1937 private citizens and public officials had taken to the airwaves and podiums with messages that appealed to the independent and populist Texas. Quasi-socialist governor Huey P. Long in neighboring Louisiana and his Share Our Wealth movement had already called for all fortunes over a million dollars to be confiscated and distributed. Long was murdered in 1937. Radio priest Father Charles E. Coughlin of Detroit turned the Depression into a popular secular religious cause, calling Roosevelt a "great betrayer and liar." The repercussions were felt throughout Texas.

In the midst of all these changes, Homer P. Rainey was appointed the new president of the University of Texas by the board of regents in 1939. The presidential system had been reluctantly adopted in 1895. Before then, chairpersons answering directly to the governor were in charge. Under the circumstances, the office remained little more than a figurehead, a rubber stamp for the good old boy politicians in the capital and always subject directly to the political changes and whims of the governor. Rainey would be the twelfth university president in a succession of short-tenured leaders who were normally permitted to serve an average of three years.[11] Some were there only one year. Only five blocks from the capitol complex, the university's proximity made it ideal for total government control. School presidents would be mired in controversy throughout their service as Texas governors fought to control academic freedom.

A former minister, valedictorian, and baseball pitcher, Homer Rainey had been president of Bucknell University in Pennsylvania and, to the academic community in Austin, appeared a godsend to many freedom-starved Texans with their populist traditions. On hindsight, he was ahead of his time as he brought together a pastoral sense of academic freedom and socialism that would inevitably anger the tradition-minded, business-oriented regents of the university.

Ultimately, Rainey would take his differences to the crisis point as his Yankee ways confronted the cowboy frontier. The dispute worsened when Rainey presented himself as a modern-day prophet, giving speeches to students that rose to a feverish pitch of cries for a socialist revolution and complete academic freedom. He even championed a cause known as the "Eighteen-Year-Old Movement" that was suspected of having subversive ties.

The dispute between Rainey and the regents simmered throughout his term. Initially, he defended the use of the John Dos Passos novel *America* in sophomore English classes. With the threat of a perceived socialism finally brewing in Texas, many politicians began to demand the authority to remove professors directly. Then Governor Coke Stevenson, a solid conservative and the man who would become Johnson's sworn enemy during the 1948 Senate election, changed the board of regents to reflect his more traditional, cowboy values.

The great schism between Rainey and the regents climaxed when they asked him to fire four full-tenured economics professors who espoused New Deal views. When Rainey rejected that request and made an impassioned statement of grievances to the university faculty in October of 1944, he was promptly and summarily fired.

As student body president, Wallace came to the forefront. Quickly allying himself with Rainey, he called a general strike by the students. He then commandeered 8,000 students for a march from the campus to the capitol and then to Governor Coke Stevenson's mansion across the street, a feat that turned heads in Austin political circles. More important, this leadership at the flashpoint between Yankee and Texas values would change Wallace in a very big way, from a conservative to a socialist and then to a Marxist.

Despite the overwhelming support of students and despite reprimands from the American Association of University Professors and Phi Beta Kappa, Rainey was never reinstated.

Conservative critics in Texas would claim Rainey incited faculty and students to riot and had called for an overthrow of the legal governing board of the university. One critic sarcastically called Rainey a "self-styled messiah who would lead students out of the wilderness," further alleging that he "tried from his position of prestige as president to overthrow the prevailing social system and form a new order in society, seeking to further the privileges of students and the oppressed."[12]

Although ejected from office, Rainey went on to become a Texas gubernatorial candidate in 1946. He lost decisively. He then served as president of Stephens College in Missouri and later at the University of Colorado.

While the university crisis ended Rainey's career in Texas, Wallace's connections improved. Johnson was a bitter enemy of Coke Stevenson and wanted allies with the power of the vote of the university students on his side. Any enemy of my enemy is my friend was standard Johnson policy. Wallace was a natural friend. For Wallace, there was a more fundamental change underway. He was becoming ever more liberal.

For his leadership and good academic credentials, Wallace was selected into the Friars' Society, then a secret honorary society limited to twelve senior men per year.[13] This good old boys' organization featured a hooded monk in black, with sandals symbolizing poverty. In the 1940s the Friars bore a force in Texas similar to Yale's Skull & Bones, an important early link in the Texas good old boy or so-called bubba network, a track that reached to the highest offices of state government. Recruitment into the society was clandestine and had to be unanimous among members, a tight group dedicated to furthering one another's careers in the corridors of business and government. After selection, there was an initiation period, then a ritual-driven induction ceremony to which all prior members were invited.

Among those prior members were many legendary Texas politicians, including several governors and Supreme Court judges along with many politicians, state and national. Significantly, during Wallace's seven-year college career, Johnson confidant and future governor John Connally and Johnson business partner and future congressman Jake Pickle were members along with Johnson staffers Horace Busby, Lloyd Hand, and Frank Ikard Sr.

At the induction, Wallace was blindfolded and ushered into the Sunday breakfast meeting at the Driskill, then Austin's finest hotel. After an incantation of ritual secrecy and high purpose closely related to religious orders, he, along with the other initiates, gave short speeches. Here Wallace was clever enough to play the mainstream card for conservative principles rather than his emerging bias for Marxism. In exchange, he got an introduction to some of Johnson's key men. To politicians in that audience, Wallace was a pleasant attraction. Standing before them was a physically strong, intimidating, and attractive man who could command the attentions of thousands of students in a march on the capitol, an unheard of event in Texas. The audience knew politics was changing, and Wallace looked like an emerging new breed that could handle himself in the ongoing battle for political power against puritans like Stevenson.

In a far more subtle way, Wallace was also introduced to power, one connected to a sense of secrecy, something not taught in university classrooms and unknown to the public. An aphrodisiac not only to the beholder but also to the occupant, the effect on Wallace's ego was exhilarating. His ambitions were strengthened. He could be governor, a man of power and success and at the same time able to help the weak and the poor. He would not make the mistake Rainey made. In Wallace's case, however, that ambition proved to be destructive in the poisonous and secretive air of Texas politics.

Seven years after entering the university, Wallace finally completed his studies and graduated.[14] Capping his tumultuous years in college, including a remarkable mix of recognition and ostracism by local politicians, Wallace had his degree. Unlike his first classes in business, Wallace had changed his course of study several times, to law and then to economics. His grades were mixed but good enough. In economics, his ultimate and final discipline, he learned from the same professors Rainey had protected, and, by the time he graduated, he had adopted the socialist brand of economic thought they practiced. Those professors would have a profound and lasting political influence on the man as he struggled with the Yankee-cowboy dichotomy. That same split would have a profound effect on America.

Wallace was also influenced both by the atomic bomb, first introduced to the world at Hiroshima, Japan, and then to the emerging Cold War with the Soviet Union. He also understood the violence of both Nazism and Communism. In his idealism, in his seeking a better way, he decided to make the world safe, not for democracy, but for extreme socialism. As his life circumstances changed, that political philosophy turned into Marxism. From that very basic philosophical decision, he would fall in with the group believing better Red than dead and he would kill to achieve that objective.

Graduation for Wallace finally arrived in June 1947, and, as a student of the socialist economic professors he and Rainey had defended, he had adopted their views but with a strange split in his personality. Loving politics and the power of being student leader, he was also a radical and he knew that would not easily win elections in Texas. A Marxist could never be governor but he would, for a while, try to mix the two.

Wallace also saw the student body change as hardened war veterans returned, bringing with them a no-nonsense business attitude that was completely out of place with the wartime policies of FDR and progressivism, of Rainey's socialism and his economists' perceived socialism, if not Marxism. Further underscoring these splits in Wallace's persona, consider his best friends. He had an established friendship with Joe Schott, a roommate for two years who gave him a Schmeisser automatic pistol in 1946. Schott would become assistant special agent in charge for the Federal Bureau of Investigation in Fort Worth and would later write a book on J. Edgar Hoover. Wallace was also a close friend with radical Elgin Williams, who would later become an economics and sociology professor at Texas State Teachers College in Denton, Texas, and who would be a witness for Wallace in the later murder trial. The two friends showed the remarkable spectrum of associations that Wallace developed and cultivated. This determination to have both political power and at the same time to promote known radical causes would become the foundation of Wallace's willingness to resort to violence to achieve his ends. That frustrated state of mind soon led to murder.

More specifically, Wallace would later meet John Douglas Kinser through drama classes in New York City. Kinser was a friend Wallace would later kill to protect Johnson's interests.

Upon graduation, another step was taken in Wallace's life that would further seal his fate. After a frenzied courtship of two weeks, Wallace married on July 4, 1947. He tied the knot with a woman who by all appearances was an attractive wife for a future politician. Mary André DuBose Barton was the pretty daughter of a Methodist preacher. She would later meet Kinser in New York City at drama classes to set up the fatal connection with her husband.

There is a possible family connection with Clark's family line. They share a common name, that of DuBose, and, while the connection cannot be made, the possibility cannot be excluded.[15]

Although the wedding was not noticed in the society pages, the couple married at the powerful downtown First Methodist Church, designed in the 1920s by the fashionable Texas architect Roy Leonidas Thomas. The congregation included some of the most powerful people in state politics, particularly lawyers and judges. After all, the Texas Capitol was across the street and the Governor's Mansion was two blocks to the south. Because of the connections to power, Clark attended First Methodist from time to time, although, in his usual ambiguous way, he preferred the nearby St. David's Episcopal Church, referred to by many as the gamblers' church.

The Reverend W. Kenneth Pope performed the ceremony. While only a few friends attended on that hot July day, Williams and Schott were there. There was no honeymoon. When the new couple stopped by Schott's home a few hours after the wedding, he gave Mac and Mary André several bottles of scotch whiskey as a wedding gift.

On that day Wallace, now twenty-six and finally graduated, believed he had it made. He had been elected to high office in student politics; he had inspired and led masses of students in a well-publicized revolt; he had been inducted into the secret ranks of future Texas politicians; and he had married into a prominent family. Wallace relished his apparent success and was prepared to advance his radical political views. He would do so carefully, of course, because he needed to appear conservative while believing in very liberal ideas.

Within two days of the marriage, however, his world collapsed almost as dramatically as it had on the football field when he had been injured. The couple separated and, almost overnight, he fell as deeply from his high expectations as his apparent successes had carried him up.

The reasons for his frustrations and anger are clear. In those days divorce was an unacceptable detour on the road to political success. Even more threatening were some of the private activities Mary André practiced. With the separation, another strange feature of the couple's secret life surfaced.

Wallace later explained that he had discovered his wife was "a sex pervert," a term loosely used then to describe anyone involved in anything other than "normal," heterosexual, missionary position sex. He also learned that she frequented known homosexual spots, where as one witness described it, "She danced only with underwear-clad women." She was also, according to the police reports, "surprised in Zilker Park at night with other women in their underclothes, embarrassed."[16]

Here the tie-in to Johnson became unacceptable. Johnson had a sister with ambitions similar to his. Josefa Johnson had been trying to keep up with her famous and powerful brother through the only readily available means a woman then had. While going through two husbands by 1948, she also worked in the "blondes' brigade" for Texas lobbyists and, as a sideline, when the legislators and the lobby were away, she was involved in the sex group centering on the Austin community theater. Because of Mary André's similar involvement, of necessity Johnson and Clark were terrified. As we shall see, in that period immediately after the stolen 1948 Senate election, neither man could afford any scandalous disclosure or even any allegations of political embarrassment. Men's liaisons were carefully ignored but there was no similar allowance for women. Their affairs would fall under the scarlet letter, or worse. With Josefa implicated, Johnson and Clark could become the subjects of a potentially destructive whisper campaign.[17]

In due consideration of these many compelling circumstances, Mac and Mary André reunited and tried to make things work out, at least in the public eye. The result was a very abusive marriage, one that finally ended in charges of rape, child incest, drunkenness, multiple affairs, and repeated violence over a fifteen-year period.[18] They would spend their time apart but, to keep up the pretenses, would stay married.

Wallace sent Mary André to a psychiatrist at the University of Texas for treatment of what he referred to as her perversion. They then moved to New York, where Wallace spent two semesters attending Columbia University for a doctorate while working as a research assistant at City National Bank and teaching at City College and Long Island University. Colleagues describe his work record as exemplary.

By this time Wallace had yet another problem. Mary André was pregnant. She claimed Mac was violently opposed to her having a baby and that he tried to force her to see a midwife for an abortion, which was at that time illegal and unthinkable. She refused that option and, on February 1, 1948, Wallace sent her back to Austin to be with her mother. There Mary André gave birth to their first child, Michael Alvin, born on June 26, 1948, and named after Wallace's father. The next day, she filed her first petition for divorce. Following threats from Wallace, she withdrew it two months later.

The divorce petition recites the routine allegations of separation, abandonment, and cruelty.[19] For Wallace it was a public mark of failure. To try and save the marriage and his career, Wallace returned to Austin and became a teaching assistant in the economics department at the University of Texas. Mary André and the baby would live with her mother, but, maintaining her shadowy life, she would list an address that was a vacant lot. Consistent with her lifestyle, clearly uncertain of who she was and what she was doing, she was "somewhere else." Overwhelmed by these personal events, Wallace was not involved in the critical 1948 Senate election between Johnson and Coke Stevenson.

During the next eighteen months, Wallace would learn more about

Josefa Johnson and Doug Kinser, and he would find out about their involvement with his wife through the community's Little Theater.

On March 1, 1950, Wallace again left Mary André to work a semester as an assistant professor of economics at the University of North Carolina. Mary André wasn't happy. She was pregnant again. The upcoming months would be some of her wildest on the known record. While Wallace was away, her mother had to report to the police that Mary André slept with both men and women that summer, occasionally in public in Zilker Park near Kinser's business.

Alice Meredith was born in Austin on August 1, 1950. Again Mary André filed a divorce petition, this time on August 10. In frustration Wallace filed a no-contest waiver. At the same time he confided in Joseph Schott that he ultimately wanted custody of the children. He also said that he still had bigger things on his mind, plans which, of necessity, excluded Mary André. So, while the divorce could have been held up, he chose not to contest it. He planned to leave her out of his future career. In Wallace's new role, he would be better off single, where the only witness to his actions would be himself.

Those plans became more apparent when, on October 10, 1950, Wallace formally reentered the Johnson camp, this time permanently.[20] The ties through Clark, strained as they were, continued paying off. He accepted a position with the United States Department of Agriculture as a political operative for Johnson, then Texas junior senator, a man still under suspicion after the stolen 1948 election. A new era in Washington would begin soon, one of near total compromise by conservative Democrats, led by Johnson as majority leader working closely with Republican president Eisenhower.

What Johnson could do was what any United States senator was allowed to do: place key workers in government agencies where they would work for the sponsoring politician, helping with his constituents and his reelection plans but paid by that agency.[21] Johnson gave Wallace a good job with better pay than the teaching assistant work, and, for Wallace, it was another step into the elected political life he still coveted. For Johnson, an important post was provided a man who had opposed their common enemy, Coke Stevenson. Johnson could also be comforted because Wallace kept an eye on Josefa, his problem sister in Austin, through his estranged wife whenever he traveled home. Mary André exhibited still more strange behavior and indecisiveness. After discussions with Wallace, she withdrew her second divorce petition on November 1, 1950.

Unknown to anyone at the time, the stage was set for murder. The events leading to that killing center, first, on the infamous Senate election in 1948 or, more correctly, on what happened in the days, weeks, and years following that election and then on Josefa and her connections with Kinser, Mary André, and Wallace.

Wallace both suffered and prospered in the first half of the twentieth century, realizing highs and lows about as far up and down as they could go. As his record shows, his career through college was unique. He achieved some remarkable successes; however, his subconscious dichotomy between conservative and liberal worlds remained inaccessible and unknown to others. He could still be judged on his actions. As we shall see, he was.

Thrown into the turbulent world of the University of Texas, Wallace was similarly torn between two worlds. That uncertainty would prove to be the foundation for the dirty work Clark would bait him to undertake.

Texas was also torn. The university's planners tried to import ideas from the Northeast, from the Yankees, particularly in the form of college leaders and architecture. The governor rejected the leadership efforts. Texas maintained its nineteenth-century roots.

> Education is an admirable thing, but it is well to remember from
> time to time that nothing that is worth knowing can be taught.
> —Oscar Wilde

Later in Austin [Don] Thomas was said to have bragged that he
had been down there disguised in work clothes.
—Ronnie Dugger, editor, *Texas Observer*

6

Lyin' Lyndon

Every Johnson insider knew their man had to win in 1948. For Johnson himself, it was the blind necessity worthy of a Greek tragedy. He demanded a win. No matter what, he had to be elected. His future was up or out, success or suicide.

Those cynics not believing he did whatever was necessary are ignoring the aftermath, and not only what happened on the days following the election and after he was declared winner. They also need to see what happened in Austin in the years following. Johnson did not win the election on Election Day. History knows he stole it after the polls closed. What has been overlooked is how it was stolen again and again in the months and years that followed. It took many years for Johnson to clean up the mess and regain an untouchable status with the Texas voters.

In addition, a certain arrogance is needed to ignore the voting right after the election, the strange deaths in the requisite cover-up, and the enormous wealth Johnson would subsequently accumulate while in the Senate. Few other presidents have a record of deaths occurring and wealth accumulating in such proximity to his career.

Much has been written about the notorious Box 13 scandal because, throughout Johnson's long career, the stolen election was always deemed an important measure of the man. The theft would continue to haunt him until he was reelected to the Senate in 1954. After that election, he was solidly entrenched in Texas, and he took a certain pride in ignoring the theft and then in subtly bragging about how he got away with it.

The stolen election was only the tip of the iceberg. The unseen part was what the attorney-client privilege hid. Those secret conversations and actions were the essence of the events, the explanation of how power is exercised. The abuse of power occurs behind the scenes in the lawyers' offices and in the secret chambers of the courts and the back offices of the Texas Legislature. Nothing made the news and there was no public record. Until now.

To see and understand what happened we have to know what was not known. Who stuffed ballot box 13? How was the theft covered up? How was the election theft kept behind closed doors? What system was set in place to pay the debts? How were the dangers of exposure eliminated? How did Johnson turn power politics into great wealth?

An important character trait emerges, that of Johnson's personal anxiety not over the crimes but simply over the possibility of losing the election. Stated very bluntly, the ends justified the means. When, through Edward Clark, you possess almost absolute power, you cannot help being tempted to abuse that power whenever necessary. Having the power to manipulate the votes of entire precincts, you do so.[1] Having the power to demand a judge enter whatever final order you want, you take control. Assured in advance that you have the protection of Texas justice, you exercise your raw power.

Last but not least, you deal with the details. What do I have to do and how do I do it? With your course of action decided, you exercise some blind faith, hope for a little luck, and press forward. A thorough knowledge of the legal system is necessary to knowing these details and, similarly, the election system must be familiar territory. Then, you assess the risk and do it. Because you control the court system and the result, you are confident in your ability to forecast the result. You take action. There is a certain measure of sheer bravado involved, a willingness to pursue blind necessity with foolishness, but you do it. Then, when all the facts are considered and the system is in place and you have done all you can, take it to court. Let the judges win the election for you. Make it "legal."

The facts are clear. The sabotage of the Senate race occurred in counties where large tracts of land overlay huge oil fields owned by cowboy congressman Richard Kleberg and the King Ranch. When you had solid contacts with the ranch, you had easy entry into their system for control, particularly when Hispanics are an important part of your work force.

Then you send in your representative. One of Johnson's little-known attorneys would play a major role even though his name remains missing from most accounts by journalists and historians. I know, because as my law partner, mentor, and friend, he recounted the events to me. What he said confirmed what others in the firm had related, usually bragging and laughing but always with great pride.[2] In addition, I was told because the legacy I was inheriting as a partner demanded that I know. I was also told because of the sensitive cases I was handling that were directly related to the same power play. And I had to know because I was Clark's personal attorney in his application for an assassination bonus. Of course, all that came later, some twenty-five years later. I had to be told because I had to know what could be done and how it could be done. In short, I learned because I was expected to do the same if the occasion arose. As a partner, I would be a superlawyer, empowered with a form of diplomatic immunity where there would never be any consequences or expulsion for what I would have to do.

Donald S. Thomas was the man who took me under his wing. Short and stocky with an elfin grin and ragged eyebrows that danced when he sized you up, his eyes would take in everything. He missed nothing. He was one of Johnson's two personal lawyers, and he played a major role in the criminal activity. When he told me he was the man behind the theft, the "only living person" who knew what had happened, I understood his role in the legend. We both knew he was referring to the illegal stuffing of Box 13 during the 1948 election, and I knew then that all the stories were true.

Seventeen years younger than Clark, Thomas was beholden to his mentor. Having been taught by Clark, he had also learned simply to obey Clark's orders and never ask questions. Pleasant and easy to work with, Thomas did what he had to do with a quiet confidence and with a quick wit—a country boy who knew more than the city slickers. He knew people and how to deal with them. He trusted his instincts. These qualities made him an exceptional trial lawyer. And he was a perfect balance to the driven Clark.

When I joined the Clark firm, Thomas was Johnson's attorney for all business and personal matters. Over the twenty years of working with Johnson and Clark, he had earned that trust. In addition, giving him that power over a client that the privilege confers—where he knows secrets that have to be kept quiet—he had the keys to the insider knowledge that kept him on retainer and eventually made him wealthy.

When the critical Election Day for the 1948 Texas Senate race initially ended with honest results, Johnson knew all was lost. He and Clark had to do something and Thomas was given the job to get more votes. So, in this sordid world of Texas politics in the 1940s, three days after the polls had closed, three long days while the final vote totaling and reporting was still going on, Thomas added the fraudulent votes Johnson needed to win. Realizing the simple necessity for additional votes, he made up voters and added their names to the poll list and then to the ballot count.

When Thomas finished his ballot stuffing under cover of darkness, he called Clark from Alice, Texas, to warn of an election contest over what he had done. The results were announced, and it was clear that corruption of the ballot box had occurred. As expected, senatorial opponent Coke Stevenson protested. Clark and his team then acted to control any contest by promptly filing litigation with Clark's friendly courts, enjoining the challenge to the ballots.[3] After all, Clark knew going in what was required, and he had the system in place. The issues would be settled in his courts on his terms. When that court order was entered without notice and in the secrecy of the court's private chambers, Johnson had the advantage. With that, the odds were that he would win.

"Don't believe in elections," Clark had remarked, shrugging. "Not for me." His personal experiences as a candidate had been to win and then to lose.[4] Now, as the self-appointed boss and benevolent dictator of the Texas legal system, Clark steered away from those messy, unpredictable events called elections. They required huge investments and had uncertain outcomes. The gamble and the anxiety involved were too high a price to pay, particularly when it could leave the losers heavily in debt. Clark wanted to win, he wanted good results for his client, and his corrupt legal system provided the way. He would be the power behind the throne, not the candidate.

Opponent Coke Stevenson was the man referred to affectionately and with deep respect as "Mr. Texas."[5] Despite the statewide admiration for him, the former governor ultimately lost because, even though he won the majority of votes, the election was stolen from him by the courts. Still unclear are the details of how Johnson got away with it. There were countless confusing legal maneuvers that render any fair assessment nearly impossible. At the height of the recount, the election contest was stopped. Any revelations were blocked. Now we can show how it was done.

The scandal of 1948 occurred over the three-day period following the runoff election for the Senate. The first election was held on July 24, and former governor Coke Stevenson had the lead over Johnson by 71,000 votes. In fact, Stevenson almost won outright. He did not quite have a majority, however, so the runoff was necessary. Unlike the 1941 Senate race when he almost won, this time Johnson made only a modest showing. With just 34 percent of the total vote, he barely forced a runoff. Knowing that if he lost, the 1948 election would end his future in politics and knowing the opportunities for money and power that were possible if he won, he had no choice. Ruthless ambition went to work.

The critical runoff election was on August 28, 1948.

For purposes of the election, Clark knew how and where to find money without leaving a trace, and he put together a complex web of support among conservatives. The industrialists and oilmen were told what they wanted to hear. All the time, large amounts of cash were needed on a daily basis. Clark would get it however possible. In addition, many friendly banks and businesses extended credit, and Clark worried as he watched the debt pile up. He would deal with the debts after the election, knowing that, if Johnson won, the money would come easily. He also knew he would have to pay some of the debt if Johnson lost because his signature was necessary for many of the loans. The mere thought of having to pay for a loss was not acceptable. He had to maintain his cover of trustworthiness. Future elections and his future power would constantly need cash. As the debt for the 1948 election increased so dramatically, he knew Johnson had to win just to pay the debts. Clark also came to be as driven by absolute necessity. He had to win to get the money to pay the debts.

Under these circumstances, the 1948 election became an all-or-nothing event for both Johnson and Clark. The two men would do whatever was necessary.

Political principle was no problem. Johnson had been a committed New Dealer. He changed his politics while leaving enough slack to please everyone, steering a far more conservative path than he had followed in the past. In 1941, he supported FDR but in 1948 any New Deal progressivism was dropped. One joke was, "Johnson's friends were for it and Johnson's friends were against it. Johnson supported his friends." During the final days of the campaign in San Antonio, Johnson even rode in the same car with liberal Maury Maverick and his conservative enemy Sheriff Paul Kilday. Johnson had the liberal record to keep Maverick with him and he had the money to buy Kilday and his voting machine. Clark made his usual promises of favoritism to business supporters. He became the conservative.

Stevenson ran a relatively clean campaign. Leading in the polls, he was not desperate. As a man with many opportunities apart from politics, he was not committed to victory at any cost. Running an issue-oriented race, he simply ignored many of the absurd charges Johnson leveled. Although a committed conservative regarding unions and blacks, he was not much different from Johnson and, as the campaign deepened, Johnson was not much different from Stevenson. The only real issue was what each candidate had done, and Stevenson had the conservative record while Johnson was the liberal turned moderate and then conservative. Only in international affairs had Johnson shown any advantage in the polls. In Texas in 1948 that counted for very little.

Relations between the two candidates were strange. They were never friends, and they were very different in their basic philosophies of government. Stevenson was the principled candidate, loyal to his basic philosophies of government. For Johnson, it was what do I say and do to win. The main difference in the campaign was that Stevenson kept his eye on winning by running a positive campaign as the front-runner. Underdog Johnson tried anything and everything.

Johnson could chip away at Stevenson's lead a little but many Texans were convinced Stevenson represented stability and reliability. Johnson sought to instill fear and uncertainty in the public perception but that message was not successful. Without even mentioning Johnson by name, Stevenson wrote him off as a "prophet of doom and a howler of calamity."

Johnson also attacked Stevenson personally but the name-calling the public heard was minor. The dirty campaigning also backfired. Stevenson was charged with being "calculating," thus inventing the catchy attack phrase, "Calculatin' Coke." In the name-calling, however, Stevenson's forces did much better. Johnson became "Lying' down Lyndon" for his ability to dodge hard issues. Before long, he was simply "Lyin' Lyndon." The tag stuck with Johnson for a year or so, until he moved up in the Senate. He gradually became known as "Landslide Lyndon."

In the final week before the runoff, Clark knew his candidate was in deep trouble. Stevenson was going to win and Johnson's campaign was stalemated. There was only one answer. They needed a massive purchase of votes.

In Texas politics in 1948, of course, most voting was legitimate. There were important exceptions. Several key precincts were available to the highest bidder and there were always enough precincts on the market to buy a close election. Part of any election was to buy first and then hope the chairman delivered, that he stayed bought. There was competition from both sides. Even though promises were made and cash was paid, there was no certainty the votes would be delivered. Stealing votes was really owning the precinct chairmen and paying enough for them to take the time and the effort personally to cast the votes needed.[6] Untraceable cash was required and the bidding was expensive and risky.

In many cases the only limit on a precinct chairman casting votes was the total number of registered voters in the precinct. In some precincts, the voters had to be brought to the polls, but that was handled by the cash, by paying the precinct chairman enough to cover his costs.[7] By August 21 most of those commitments had been made. By the final week of the runoff, most precincts were bought and paid for, with the politicians anxiously awaiting the final count, to see what was actually delivered. Were they dealing with a reliable precinct judge, one who stayed bought? How many votes would actually be delivered?

More was needed in that final week, and Clark knew the best place to add votes for Johnson would be in San Antonio and in south Texas, particularly in counties owned by the King Ranch in what was then known as Parr Country. Parr Country referred to several counties with mostly Hispanic voters who voted the way George Parr told them to vote.

Step one, Clark took care of the San Antonio vote. The trick there was to turn out the voters and this meant paying Sheriff Paul Kilday's political machine even more money. Clark hit the road, raising the cash needed. Step one was to call a fund-raiser who would collect piles of cash, corporate, legal, or illegal. Step two was Clark flying by private plane, usually owned by a corporate supporter, to collect the money and bank it or deliver it. Personal attention was required with each major donor. The supporters always had something they wanted from government. Clark had to do it in person. Step three, delivery of the cash had to be made. With Kilday, there was no credit. Cash had to be paid. It was.[8]

Finally satisfied there were no more votes to buy or steal in San Antonio, Clark turned to his ace in the hole and his only remaining hope, George Parr in south Texas.

In that area nearest to Mexico, the theft of votes was unique because the migrant population could easily vote illegally and return home to Mexico. No witnesses, no crime. The counties of Parr's political machine were ideal for the "vote and slide" where the voters disappeared back into Mexico. The county officials in charge of the precincts had to be bought with bags of cash, some kept by Parr, some dispensed to voters by his deputies, and some kept by the deputies. These armed men, called padrones or pistoleros, were at the polls whenever and wherever Parr needed them.

Now with less than three days to the election, Clark made the necessary calls and collected the money for delivery to Parr's six counties. Known as the Duke of Duval, Parr was paid to get Johnson all the votes the precinct lists in his counties could withstand. Of all those voters and precincts, only precincts in Jim Wells County were a special problem. There, a committee of war veterans had organized to oppose Parr, and the reformers were ready, watching everything. The careful watch on the polls would require special diligence on Thomas's part when he ultimately added the votes that stole the election for Johnson.

The situation in south Texas requires a special understanding. The political machines that existed there were acknowledged by all to be under Parr's control. Because they represent the sort of system Johnson and Clark had developed, a little history is needed.

Another of the most scandalous figures in Texas history, George Parr was born to Yale graduate and county boss Archer Parr, the man who had been in charge of the six counties since 1907.[9] Due to his father's position and influence, many opportunities were available to George. At thirteen he served as his father's pageboy in the Texas Senate. His record in higher education was similar to Clark's, consisting of brief enrollments at several colleges.[10] Over the ensuing years, since his brothers were not interested in politics, George became his father's heir apparent.

In 1926 his father conveniently chose his son to be Duval County judge, and George was installed to control local affairs. Handpicked candidates continued to sweep county elections, and by the time of his father's death in 1942, George had become the undisputed boss of Duval County. Power in those days meant not only legal and political control, but also money right out of the public treasury. Outright theft was okay. Like a feudal land baron controlling the Hispanic workers as serfs, Parr had great economic power, and he used that power to amass a sizable fortune in banking, mercantile, ranching, and oil interests. Raiding the public treasury was easy and public money went to private roads, construction, and other needs for Parr. In short, he got rich from government, just like Johnson and Clark were going to do. They would, of course, do so on a far greater scale.

Because of his success in making money, Parr had to hide the illegal income; however, the resulting income tax evasion got him into serious trouble with the IRS and he was convicted of dodging taxes. In 1946, with Johnson's help, he obtained a full pardon from President Harry Truman. Not surprisingly, he promptly reclaimed the right to public office. Back home in his fiefdom, he was easily reelected.

During the 1948 election scandal, Parr was both county judge and sheriff in Duval County. In the rural counties of Texas, that was often all the power needed to be boss. George Parr was the boss, "El Jefe."

Following the 1948 election, his political career was highlighted by a seemingly endless series of spectacular scandals. He was accused of repeated election fraud, graft on a grand scale, and repeated acts of official violence. Following World War II, returning veterans had formed a Freedom Party to challenge Parr in one of his counties. Three of the men met violent deaths. After the third murder, Governor Allan Shivers and federal authorities launched major criminal investigations to destroy Parr's machine. Investigations in the 1950s produced over 650 indictments against members of the ring. George, however, survived the criminal charges through a complicated series of dismissals and reversals on appeal. Despite all the publicity and litigation, Parr outlived the Box 13 scandal, weathered public outcries over the political murders, and beat down repeated state and federal investigations.

With the start of another legal offensive in the 1970s and this time facing a rebellion within his own organization, Parr was finally caught. Once again, IRS did the job. When all else fails, federal prosecutors turn to the IRS. Since illegal money is involved, so, too, is tax evasion. During an appeal of his five-year sentence for federal income tax evasion, Parr committed suicide at his ranch in 1975. His organization collapsed with his death.

He is still considered just another "LBJ victim."

But he knew how to run a "banana republic."

What Parr did in 1948 shows how political control extended to many Texas precincts. Thereafter, Johnson and Clark routinely borrowed the abuses he practiced. In 1948, however, Parr went a step beyond the limits and Don Thomas was the man who worked with Parr and took care of the necessary details.

Parr's political machines in the six counties he controlled followed the same pattern of operation. The precinct leader manipulated the vote of the Hispanic majority. Few understood English. They simply did as they were told. In exchange for cash payments to vote for Parr's candidate, the precinct chairman would pay the poll taxes, make up the voting list, write the names on a checklist, and vote for the paying candidate. Usually the "voter" would never even have to vote. During an Austin election years later, Thomas laid out the system, "We paid 'em for the number of votes we needed. They called election central and reported the count. That was it." He smiled. "Some came through and," he shrugged, "some cheated."

The polls closed at 7:00 P.M. that August 28 and the precincts across the state began calling the Texas Election Central office in Austin to report their totals. At the end of the first day, Johnson did not have the lead. The totals were close, a difference of less than 1 percent of the total vote, but he trailed behind Stevenson by 854 votes. Over the next two days, more results were reported and, although the Stevenson lead narrowed, Johnson was still losing. The mood in Johnson's camp was desperation. There were not enough precincts left to make up the difference. The election was over and they had lost. Extraordinary steps were needed.

Clark knew what had to be done.

First, it was understood by all that Johnson could not be involved. He was to stay at home, keeping a close eye on the vote and the public. For what needed to be done, Johnson did not need to be a witness. Second, enough votes had to be cast three days after the election to give Johnson the margin of victory. Third, one person had to be in charge and that person had to be totally and completely trustworthy. The protection of the lawyer-client privilege would assure that trust, and the privilege, of course, required a lawyer from Clark's firm. Most lawyers were already busy on the public features of the election, too tied down to be spared as they tracked down results involving almost one million voters. Only young Don Thomas was available, ready, in place, and set to move. He needed only his orders.

In a frenzy that bordered on panic on that third day, Clark called, sending Thomas to the one place where they hoped there were more votes. The young attorney went to see Parr. The two men met and Parr sent Thomas to Alice, Texas. On that night of August 31, 1948, Johnson was 114 votes short.

Thomas went to the one precinct chair that could still do something. Luis Salas was introduced to Thomas as Johnson's man and he learned 200 more votes were needed to overcome the lead and to provide a margin of safety.[11] Afraid of getting in trouble, Salas declined to add the names himself. After some pressure, he agreed to change the tally list if someone else called out the names and wrote them down. Then he would only have to report the totals. Late that night under the cover of deep darkness at the Adams Building in downtown Alice, Texas, Salas was there as Thomas did the dirty work.

Thomas wrote down names, first at random and then, exhausted and with time running out, in alphabetical order. As he forged names, he called out the vote for Johnson. Running short of names on the poll list and dead tired from the drive and the late work, Thomas shrugged and started adding names of the dead. He voted more names than were on the precinct list as qualified voters.

Thomas did not relate all the details to me. He was primarily interested in letting me know that the theft occurred and, with a measure of pride and humor, that he had done the job.[12] I know that he also wanted me to understand the concept, to know that it worked, and that, if ever necessary, he and I could do it for our political friends. I could even do it alone.

Late that night in Alice, Texas, Thomas did what was required. Salas had the votes needed to report the margin of victory. Election Central was called with the new vote total, adding 202 votes to the election night report: 200 for Johnson and 2 for Stevenson.

Thomas was tired and had been hard-pressed to get the job done quickly. He did not do a good job. He knew the ballots would not stand up in any recount. He could not let any court see the slipshod results. They could not be seen by anyone. With the dirty work now done, the incriminating evidence had to be concealed.

For the rest of the week, as the drama of the new vote totals and the startling change in the election results unfolded, Thomas stayed in Alice, carefully watching developments. He remained as the lawyer on the ground, *incognito* in casual clothes, able to tell Clark what was happening. They could then decide what needed to be done. Thomas was then ready to do it. Prompt destruction of the ballots and the voting lists was the unstated mandate.

At Election Central on Friday morning as soon as the doors opened, the new results were called in. Thomas was listening in Alice as Austin was notified of the results for Jim Wells County. The results for each precinct and county in Duval Country were not changed except for that one, Box 13 in Jim Wells County. The total for Johnson had been reported as 765. The formal report advised that, because of an error on the number seven, it needed to be changed to a nine. Thomas had the illegal ballots to back up the new total.

When the final results were in that day, with some minor changes in a few other precincts statewide, Johnson was ahead by eighty-seven votes.

Outrage was immediate and widespread. Everyone knew what had happened. Stevenson took charge and went to work. He just had to prove Johnson's lies.

Like a scene from an old Hollywood western, of armed cowboys with pistols ready marching down dusty streets, Parr was ready, his pistoleros armed and intimidating. Stevenson sent lawyers to Alice to see the ballots. They were denied access by Thomas Donald,[13] the banker in Alice with custody of the metal cans that were ballot boxes. Stevenson's lawyers glanced at the ballots themselves—the Don Thomas votes—but were denied any right to study or copy the names. The lawyers then left, too scared of Parr's armed deputies to press the issue.

Stevenson took the next decisive step, hurrying to Alice himself.[14] This time he had his own hired gun with him: legendary Texas Ranger Frank Hamer, the man who had ambushed bank robbers Bonnie and Clyde in Louisiana. Confronted by Parr's pistoleros, the two did not flinch. They marched into the bank and forced banker Thomas Donald to let them see the ballots. For a moment, he complied, and they were able to see the fraudulent voters listed in alphabetical order, all signed in the same ink and with the same hand. They noted a few of the names and started to write them down. Realizing what was happening and fearing a judge might see the notes, Donald suddenly took the ballots back. Rather than resort to violence, Stevenson left, believing he had enough to go to court, to start proceedings to prove the deception, get a full review of all illegal votes, get them thrown out, and win the election. Stevenson felt a deep duty to the voters who had supported him. After all, stealing the election from him also meant taking the vote and the election from the majority of Texans.

As the action continued in south Texas, the stage was set for the state's Democratic Executive Committee to review the ballots and certify the party's candidate. This was scheduled for Monday, September 13, 1948, at the Blackstone Hotel in Fort Worth.

This time, Stevenson moved first with action in south Texas, calling a meeting of the Jim Wells Democratic Committee to review the ballots. That committee, with its reformers ready, was to meet the Saturday before the executive committee convened. Stevenson was confident he could get Precinct 13 thrown out.

Like players in a chess game, Clark went right to work again. With his team of excellent lawyers, including his partner, trial attorney Everett Looney, the decision was made in Austin to block the county meeting in Alice. Judge Lorenz Broetter was the local judge with jurisdiction over the county committee, but he could not be reached in time to stop the reformers. Clark instead called on an Austin judge, Roy Archer, to enjoin the meeting with an order issued without notice, one that stopped a committee in another distant county from investigating fraudulent votes. Lending weight to the proceeding, Johnson himself signed the affidavit necessary for the order to be issued in secret and without an opportunity for Stevenson's lawyers to present their side of the case. The judge signed the order. The local committee in Jim Wells County was enjoined: it could not review the ballots nor change the results.

Attention returned to the state committee meeting in Fort Worth. Clark, a member of the committee, was holding the votes for Johnson together and trying to add more votes while his partners attacked the canvassing committee report. The subcommittee report favored Stevenson; however, the executive committee had to review that report and accept it or reject it. Working furiously to add more votes, Clark cut a deal with the Texas liberals. He agreed that a vote for Johnson would mean support for Truman in the national election that November. The ability to make this guarantee was just another measure of Clark's power.

The committee vote was agonizing and slow as missing members were located and brought to the meeting room. The pressure was so intense that several members tried not to attend, hoping to avoid the confrontation. Because the committee was so closely divided, however, every member had to be there. Finally, when all had been done that could be done and all members were there, the final vote was taken. Johnson succeeded by one vote: that of Edward Clark.

Still, Stevenson knew he had all the evidence he needed, so he took an unusual step. The court in Jim Wells County had taken over Judge Archer's order, held a hearing, and stopped the local committee. With the first strike already taken by Johnson, the state courts were deemed to be owned by Clark or Parr for all practical purposes. Stevenson decided to take still another dramatic step: he would go to a federal court to protect his civil rights and the rights of the majority who had voted for him to have their votes counted correctly. Represented by Dan Moody, the man who ended the Klan's public career in Texas, Stevenson went to U.S. district judge Whitfield Davidson, who agreed to hear the case. On Friday, September 15, 1948, he entered an order setting a hearing for the following Tuesday in Fort Worth.

At that hearing, Judge Davidson heard from several voters who said they had not voted as recorded on the Box 13 lists. Satisfied Stevenson had shown him enough for a preliminary showing of fraud, the judge concluded more evidence was needed to support a final order. He appointed court masters to conduct hearings in Alice and report back to him by October 2, the day before the ballots in the general election had to be printed. Because of the enormity of the task and the speed needed, the judge used masters who were attorneys appointed by the court to uncover the evidence by talking to witnesses, taking evidence, and reporting back to him.

During a break in the formal hearing, Davidson suggested that the matter might be settled in the upcoming general election. He recommended that Johnson, Stevenson, and the Republican candidate could all be on the ballot, and the winner would be elected by the voters. Not surprisingly, Stevenson readily agreed. Johnson squirmed. He lost the first primary in a three-way race, and he could not allow another election to be left to the whims of voters. He also knew that the perception of his corruption had been revealed during the court battles, and he correctly concluded he had little chance of winning. There would be no settlement. The trial had to proceed. Once again, Johnson had to win in court, not with the voters.

The focus remained on Jim Wells County and Box 13. Everyone in power knew what had happened. The problem was proving it or keeping it from being proven. Controversy and fraud continued to interfere with the court review. The court-appointed masters were taking evidence as quickly as possible; however, the ballots from Box 13 were suddenly declared to be missing. The actual vote would never be revealed. Banker Thomas Donald disappeared into Mexico. Don Thomas remained on the scene, dressed casually, struggling to stay unnoticed. Guarded as he was by the lawyer's privilege, however, it would do no good to subpoena him or to try to get any evidence through him. He had done what was necessary: get rid of the ballots.

In Fort Worth, Johnson had a team of lawyers representing him in federal district court before Judge Whitfield. One was John Cofer, who would become Clark's attorney for all criminal matters. Angry at the order allowing masters to take further evidence, the legal team contacted Abe Fortas, an old friend and later Supreme Court judge, who happened to be at a conference in Dallas. Fortas made an illegal, off-the-record telephone call, to check with his former mentor, Justice Hugo Black of the United States Supreme Court. In that brief conversation, Fortas made certain Black would rule in Johnson's favor.[15]

When Fortas called Black, he did not just request a hearing as it has sometimes been reported. He went much further. He ran the entire case by Black verbally, discussing with him its nature and merits. He also discussed other activities such as getting together socially. He also emphasized the importance of Johnson being in the Senate as a Democrat and a liberal. Fortas made other arguments involving national politics that were irrelevant to the election challenge but important to Black. In short, Fortas relied on politics, friendship, and benefits to make his case. Stevenson and his lawyers never heard the discussions and were never allowed to respond to all these secret inducements. They were denied even the chance to get a fair hearing.

After the conversation with Justice Black, Fortas called Clark and the other lawyers working on Johnson's team, to assure them that, on appeal, the federal court proceedings would be set aside.

Fortas should have called the justice's clerk and requested the hearing, with an opportunity for fairness, for Stevenson's lawyers to be heard. That was not done.

The decision was needed very quickly, before facts showed up at the masters' evidentiary hearings that would be incriminating, even if subsequently barred by the court. The normal appeal would be from the district court in Fort Worth to the court of appeals in New Orleans and then to Justice Black on the Supreme Court in Washington. The final decision was expedited by getting a writ of certiorari to the Supreme Court prior to appeal and review by the court of appeals. Speed was of the essence. Fortas took the case from Fort Worth directly to Black, the "action judge" for the Fifth Circuit.[16]

The problem of Fortas's illegal contact and Judge Black's acceptance of it, infects all *ex parte* communications. To say the contacts are only procedural and that the judge will enforce the law is not an answer. If secret conversations are allowed or even tolerated, anything can and will be said to injure the absent party's case and their chances at a fair hearing. No record was ever made of what Fortas said.

With Johnson's lawyers acting behind the scenes in a series of startling, unprecedented, and illegal court appeals, the end was near for Stevenson's litigation. While the federal court in Fort Worth was moving ahead and the masters in San Antonio and Alice were issuing orders to force the evidence, Fortas arranged for the case to be dismissed in Washington by one judge on the Supreme Court. There, after a perfunctory hearing with Stevenson's attorneys finally present to argue their case, Justice Black threw out the federal judge's order. For all practical purposes, the election fight was over.

Almost every step in the election contest in 1948 has been debated; however, key people have been missing since that time. The men who were there late that night in Alice, Texas, and who contacted Justice Black in Washington had the facts. No one else could know the details.

Until now, there was no evidence, only speculation. Everyone knew something had happened but no one knew what. There simply was no proof. Just like the attorneys, no judge will admit to secret talks. What happened was that Thomas did the illegal voting, Clark convinced Archer to enjoin the first attempted recount, and Fortas convinced Black in secret visits and private telephone calls. Until now, there was no evidence of these secret contacts. Now, Thomas's admissions as set out by affidavit are public.

Despite the Supreme Court decision, Stevenson continued his fight. After conceding the court case, he tried to get the Senate to correct the fraud.

Justice Black had, after all, ruled that the voting fraud was a matter for the Senate, not the federal courts. The Democratic majority in the Senate commenced an effort to investigate; however, when the Committee on Rules and Administration sent investigators with subpoena powers to Parr's counties, the Box 13 ballot box contents had been destroyed and many of the needed witnesses were gone. In addition, the Democrats running the Department of Justice did a little work with the FBI. They took their time and concluded they could do nothing. The case was finally closed in May 1949. Stevenson's efforts officially ended. The Democrats controlled the key decision makers and they decided in favor of their own party, their Democratic senator, the incumbent liberal, not the conservative former governor.

Back in Texas discontent with Johnson was at an all-time high among voters and politicians. In the November general election for the Senate seat, Johnson was assured of a victory in a heavily Democratic state. A Republican had never won a Senate seat in post–Civil War Texas; however, Johnson's win against opponent Jack Porter was low for a Democrat, losing an estimated 320,000 votes because of the Box 13 scandal.[17] Although Texas Republicans would wait more than a decade to become a statewide power, allegiance to the conservatives became ever easier because of election abuse by Texas Democrats, driving voters to the only other political organization, the Republicans.

There is an interesting footnote to the key elections that were essential to Johnson and his political career. In the two that mattered most and would have ended his career permanently had they gone the other way, Johnson won the 1937 election by only a plurality of slightly more that 27 percent of the vote; and, in 1948, he won only by stealing the eighty-seven-vote margin he needed. The consequence of denying democracy to voters is apparent. Johnson's support was minimal, but he obtained the opportunity to take power and then, empowered by his success, to abuse that power to an unprecedented degree.

Ronnie Dugger was editor for the very independent and very liberal *Texas Observer* from its inception in 1950, and he kept a close eye on Johnson. Recalling his career in Austin as a reporter and then as an editor, he wrote a book on Johnson, speculating particularly on what Don Thomas was doing in Alice, Texas. That part of the missing record can now be completed.

In the continuing dispute over the stolen election, reforms were started and the laws were changed to prevent similar fraud. Johnson and Clark were always slow to follow the new rules. They kept on stealing because they had to pay for the victory. Theft was occurring as late as the 1964 presidential election and in the lead up to the 1968 election.

Following the 1948 election, however, Johnson and Clark had one overriding task, to control the scandal. After May 1949, nothing could upset the election. Looking ahead to the next election, any hint of fraud or corruption had to be promptly contested. In time, Johnson and Clark knew that past charges would be old news and could be ignored, but there could be no new scandals.

The courts should have uncovered the obvious fraud. Everyone knew what had happened. Only bought judges stood in the way. In matters of politics, the politicians simply cannot be in charge. No person should be the judge of their own case. Similarly, politicians should not control their cases. Since the government is inevitably involved in election scandals, procedures need to be developed to isolate the decision makers to the maximum extent possible.

Perhaps there is a way.

Most Americans will reject the idea that an election could be stolen and that the political system could become a slave to the winners. In 1964, a member of the Warren Commission went so far as to comment that we did not want America to appear to be a "banana republic." The spin, the early bias for the case, was set. There could be no interest in finding that a conspiracy had killed the president.[18]

By 1948, however, Texas had with Ed Clark's deft touches become just such a system. Fifteen years later, he imposed that "banana republic" system on America.

Clark knew a great deal about elections and corruption before the 1948 election. From George Parr, he learned still more details. So encouraged, Johnson and Clark could not be stopped.

They succeeded in 1948. Within only a few months the elements to cover up their corrupt system of government were also in place and working.

> The voters stayed home because of crooked politicians. The voters may have more to do with crooked politicians than they believe.
> —Ralph Woods, humorist

They'll never embarrass me again.
—Lyndon Johnson

7

Murders

In the wake of the controversy over the 1948 election, most Texas politicians concluded Johnson would be a one-term senator, and many potential candidates began lining up to run even as the litigation was still concluding. Clark would be the person to make sure no one could take the Senate seat from Johnson. Fortunately for Johnson, that next election was six years away, and that period of time would prove to be more than they needed. While mending his image over those next few years, however, he was little more than the laughable Lyin' Lyndon in the back rooms and private clubs of power politics.

Although the term would gradually decline in use, many people developed a long-term loathing of him. A majority of the voters grudgingly supported him, but few respected him. He knew he had to overcome this vague but very negative perception so he set out to consolidate his "victory." Emboldened by his new position of statewide power, determined to do an excellent job in Washington, and holding power with Clark working behind the scenes, Johnson set out to consolidate his position into an impregnable base.

There would be one fundamental problem, almost subconscious, but very real. Johnson would not decline to do anything because he feared the legal or political systems. While few Texans respected him, he had no respect for politics. With Clark to protect him, he had no respect for the law. Why should he? He had beaten the law repeatedly and was forever convinced Clark could weather any challenge. Johnson was invincible.

Consider that game historians play, that of an alternate history. Had the fraud in Box 13 been uncovered, much of the murder and corruption that followed might have been prevented. The assassination of President Kennedy would not have occurred, because JFK, never burdened with a long-forgotten Lyin' Lyndon, would have made a better choice for vice president.

The shame is that Don Thomas, basically a very decent man when I worked with him, could so flagrantly violate the Texas voting laws in 1948, deliberately falsifying 202 votes under cover of darkness. He knew he was breaking the law. Undoubtedly, the false voting was very exciting, a challenge to his devotion to his client, his ability to get results, his aggressiveness, and even, perhaps, his courage. Undoubtedly there was economic motivation simply because he had to have the job. That he could get away with something done so flagrantly and with such enormous consequences only underscores the need to police lawyers far more carefully and to insist on the sanctity of the ballot box. The election system is at the heart of our democracy. We must protect it by improving it.

Following the election, the plan was for Johnson to concentrate on doing an outstanding job representing Texas in Washington. This was the public picture.

Behind closed doors, the process of consolidating power meant solidifying Johnson's voter base in Texas. Clark had this task. More specifically, this consolidation meant taking care of the conservative moneyed interests, and, in 1949, as the postwar recovery boomed, this meant oil. Johnson took care of this clientele in the Senate. Clark handled them at the state level. The key step was to remake Johnson. That part was easy as the new senator moved from the liberal district centering on Austin to a statewide electorate that was relatively conservative. Johnson simply changed his political colors.

Johnson also had to be in the same economic class as the business interests he now represented. By 1949, he was well on the road to developing his own fortune while carefully serving the business interests of Texas. He was changing from a poor country boy to a charter member of the country club, a step he was to take, as he himself remarked, "without becoming a Republican."[1]

The basic process of consolidation was simple. Win your enemies over. Bring them into the camp, do them favors, and serve their interests. These new friends were the constant objects of his benevolence. On the other hand, Johnson moved hard against those friends who turned on him. They became the objects, forever, of his anger. Now more than ever, his new power became a two-edged sword. At the same time, he had to keep himself "clean as a hound's tooth," as Clark would say.[2] For Johnson, it was an ongoing task of fear and threats, of arm-twisting, bribery, and even murder. There was no respect but there was fear.

Clark would take the extraordinary steps needed to improve Johnson's position with the state's electorate in preparation for the next election. Clark's

job involved several steps. He had to lessen any threat of serious opposition
in 1954, prevent any scandal, continue to cover up the 1948 election, raise the
cash needed to pay for the election and its many creditors, and enrich Johnson
and his supporters to the fullest extent possible. By making those supporters
his clients, Clark knew he would also be enriched. As a power broker and a
superlawyer, he knew what had to be done for Johnson and for himself.

In that final analysis of Johnson's Senate career, power always meant cash.
As we shall see, huge sums would be funneled through the Johnson money-
laundering corporation set up by Clark and run by Thomas.

What happened after the theft of the election and the fallout of that election is the true story of Johnson, Clark, and their crimes. The success in such
a high-profile case emboldened the two men. They believed themselves above
the law and unbeatable. Clark's control would prove to be a powerful driving force. The two would commit many more crimes, and, while I learned
about several, there were many more I could only suspect and leave
unmentioned.

A handwritten memo by Clark to Johnson and Johnson's response provide the clearest statements of the continual criminal activity necessary to
keep Johnson scandal-free.[3] This exchange of correspondence lays out the
system that became their *modus operandi* for all illegal acts to be done in the
future. The amazing exchange in writing would never be repeated.[4]

Clark will be the fall guy in their system. In his memo, he agrees to take
the necessary risks for an election payoff.

Even after the court fights ended, cleanup and coverup for the stolen ballots continued, and not just for Box 13. Now in the Senate, Johnson had to
be protected at all costs from the many small acts by supporters during the
election. This support included legal fees, travel and entertainment costs,
private loans, and expenses for helping. This meant more payoffs and still
more money. As investigations widened and continued until May 1949,
minor players demanded still more hush money. The blackmail and extortion could have been reported but Johnson had to keep all possible scandals
deadly quiet. The money meant these false claims could be handled privately.

Most important, Clark was agreeing in the memo to take any criminal
charges that might result from the loan in question. To protect the leader,
Clark was Johnson's chief supporter and protector, standing in the way, the
willing fall guy, the patsy, if the deal goes bad. As might be expected, this type
of personal exposure would permanently commit Johnson to Clark.

Clark's memo, scribbled by hand on his memo stationery, informs Johnson that Herman Brown of Brown & Root has told W. A. Woolsey, Brown & Root vice president, lawyer, and bagman for Houston interests, to have Lucas's friend, an unnamed financier, "taken care of for good." The identity of "Lucas' friend" has proven a dead end unless further research reveals the deceased man's name or someone discloses more about the transaction.[5]

From researchers it appears Lucas's friend was an illegal contributor based not in Houston but in Fort Worth. He was demanding more money than he was owed. He would not agree to accept only what he agreed to be paid, to be "taken care of." That was not enough, so, as Clark states, the man had to be "taken care of for good." For people knowing Clark this was no surprise. He was a violent man capable of carrying out whatever he said. Such threats were important to his control by might, not right. He used physical power, not just persuasion and reason. He often threatened others and he kept doing it during the 1950s. His last public threat to kill an opponent was still down the road, in 1962.[6] In the code words used then, the phrase meant what it said: finality, the end, murder.

Continuing in the memo about another illegal campaign loan, this one through a bank, Clark tells Johnson that he "strongly recommends going along with the payments."

Johnson's similarly candid reply to Clark reveals the details. Walter Bremond was from an old-line Austin family who worked with the Capital National Bank. Delay in a loan repayment had resulted in calling the note. Suing on the note would disclose use of the funds illegally for campaign debts from the 1948 election. After the note was called, Clark got the notice rescinded before it was mailed. The note was then renewed with monthly payments started. Johnson did not want to make the payments but, on Clark's recommendation, agreed to do it. Setting up the loan procedure was not a simple matter. Clark shored up a loan outside proper procedures and without the necessary security.

This very unusual undertaking exposed Clark to personal liability in a big way, both for interfering with the call and for guaranteeing the loan. As might be expected, there were many more of these deals but this remarkable exchange of correspondence is the only public record available. Not a good lawyer with reading the law books or in writing legal documents, Clark was only slowly learning how to conceal incriminatory documents. Why worry? He controlled the courts. At the time he was far more interested in firming up a very solid and exclusive relation with Johnson. Several lawyers had served Johnson well during the election contest. Clark was moving to replace them completely by irrevocably committing himself to Johnson and Johnson to him.

During this time Johnson was selling out to whoever would get him the money to cover the expenses of the 1948 election. The stink did not die with the Supreme Court victory. This payoff of old loans was another step. There were many more.

The memo reads:

> To Lyndon B. Johnson
>
> Enjoyed talking with you today—Brown immediately called Houston and told Woolsey to take care of Lucas friend for good. Bank matter all ~~straightened~~ [strike through in the original] fixed up—though just in time for Walter to retrieve letter from his mail calling the whole thing—this confidential to you—I strongly recommend all going along and making monthly payments—Hope everybody will be happy.
>
> > Always your friend
> > /s/Ed[7]

Johnson's reply to the Clark memo note makes the personal commitment between the two men very clear. The only known letter documenting Johnson's deep involvement with Clark and their constant problems with the law, the letter underscores the threats the new senator faced after the election.

The letter, dated on March 7, 1949, and in direct response to Clark's memo, reads:

> Dear Ed,
> I am grateful for your wire, and thanks much for your memorandum re Brown calling Woolsey and the letter that Walter Bremond was about to send. You may be sure that I deeply appreciate your own personal attitude toward your individual situation. I shall see that you are thoroughly protected and taken care of when we get the picture worked out. Very shortly our friends here will communicate with Walter and I will keep you informed.
> [Second paragraph omitted. See Exhibit 15.]
>
> > Sincerely,
> > /s/Lyndon B. Johnson[8]

What became the standard operating procedure between the two men is laid out for all to see. The relationship between the two would continue in this same way for many years to come. The basic steps were simple: Clark would take care of the money and any unfavorable developments in Texas; Johnson would do a good job with his constituents and would protect Clark; and, if all else failed, Clark would be the person to be indicted.

There was yet another large concern in the fallout from the 1948 election scandal.

Following the stolen election, the Johnson and Clark drive to avoid any scandal resulted in their first publicized murders.

Early in 1952 Sam Smithwick, a deputy sheriff in Parr's team of padrones, wrote to Coke Stevenson informing him that he was ready to testify about the election fraud. He said he could produce the missing ballot box Luis Salas had kept out of court proceedings in Alice three years earlier. Smithwick, however, had a distinct problem.[9] He was in the state prison in Huntsville, convicted of the murder of William H. "Bill" Mason, a local radio talk show announcer who had criticized the Parr regime. In south Texas during the 1950s the gun still ruled, and that sort of free speech was taboo in a banana republic. Smithwick killed the man. Now very unhappy in prison, sick with guilt, and hoping for some kind of reward or parole, Smithwick was ready to tell what he knew. Since nothing was secret in prisons, word was out about his plans to talk to Stevenson.

Not surprisingly, Clark had already taken the steps needed to protect his now-famous client. The careful system of power and its control that Clark set up in the 1940s was ready to go. The steps to be taken involved a tradition in Texas.

Texas had been settled by an unusually large number of fugitives, and many a man was sent to prison as law and order was imposed. The effect could be devastating on families. In those days every possible breadwinner was needed and powerful efforts were made to return the imprisoned husband or son back to the farm. Pardons became an accepted means of rescue in cases of extreme hardship and most were very compelling. In addition to needing help back home, prison conditions were horrible. A family's effort to get the father or son home was not just to have another worker. They needed to save him from a fate worse than death.

During Governor Jim Ferguson's term in 1914–1916, the practice of getting convicts out of jail was raised to a standard operating procedure, a free key to the jailhouse. The liberal governor looked favorably on freeing felons, particularly in return for generous gifts.[10] The legislature finally decided the governor had pardoned too many and that his abuse of power was just not acceptable. He was impeached. In addition, laws were passed severely restricting the governor's powers to pardon and commute criminals. A state prison board was set up to handle the task of pardoning or paroling convicts.

Soon after the 1948 election, Clark had arranged for Hubert Hardison "Pete" Coffield, a man enriching himself on surplus government property following the war, to serve on the state Board of Prisons. With the sponsorship of Clark's boyhood friend and then secretary of state Ben Ramsey, Governor Beauford Jester agreed to name Coffield to the board. Clark again had a key man in a place of power.

Coffield was from Rockdale, Texas, where he ran the county political machine.[11] During the First World War, he had operated a small radio shop while living with his mother. After World War I, he expanded his business into handling surplus war property and became a millionaire, married a woman from Taylor, a small community just northeast of Austin, and continued using the government to make money.

Coffield later met and worked with Jay Puterbaugh, a partner in the deal that brought Alcoa to Rockdale during the Second World War. Interestingly, Puterbaugh's brother later headed the Democratic National Committee and rode in the pilot car when Kennedy was assassinated. But that tie-in came later.

In 1952, through Coffield, Clark had the access needed to get rid of Smithwick for good. Again, a Texas tradition was involved. In the prison system, insiders are necessary to do the dirty work of controlling the convicts, and by tradition that work was done by a few key guards. From time to time, a special guard squad was selected for the particular purpose of controlling or eliminating problem prisoners. The group was carefully selected to include the most-trusted men on the staff. Known among the inmates by various names over the years such as the Death Rangers or the Enforcers or just the Killers, they were called upon to silence Smithwick. Moving quickly, the goon squad cornered Smithwick in his cell and strangled him. The body was then hung from one of the steel bars on his cell's gate by his bed.

The death was reported as suicide.

Stevenson, then halfway to Huntsville, learned what had happened. Smithwick was dead, strangely hanged by the neck at the side of his bunk with his knees on the ground. The prison coroner had already ruled suicide. The case was closed.

According to the few reports on the killing, the death "stunk to high heaven" and "reeked of corruption."[12] No one believed it was a suicide. After an investigation, Governor Allan Shivers was convinced Johnson was behind it and he said so. In those days, however, no one could go behind the guards, no attorneys were interested in any *pro bono* public service work, and the public just did not care. The Clark rule of law prevailed. No proof equals no crime. In the deep politics of Texas power, Coffield proved his worth. He would do so many times in the future.

Over the next few days newspapers covered the case in great detail, and Clark sent Johnson a copy of one of the longer articles on Smithwick's death. The message was clear. We got the job done and Smithwick was no longer a threat. The mistake of exchanging memos on how to commit crime and cover it up was never repeated. Clark learned not to put it in writing, but he still sent a reminder, in this case a news article. Over the long term, he knew it meant money.

In other words, Clark made a mistake by putting the 1949 Lucas memo in writing. He realized that and destroyed the correspondence. There is no evidence of the documents at the Clark Collection in Southwestern University, Georgetown, Texas. The correspondence was obtained from the LBJ Library. As will be seen with Martin Harris's advice to me, Clark insisted that his lawyers put everything in writing. By 1952, Clark knew better when the transaction was incriminating and went outside the secret, privileged files. "No evidence, no crime," sayeth Clark.

Another far greater threat was emerging in the early 1950s. Johnson had a sister who was as aggressive as he was; however, in those days, women could not make money as politicians. Josefa, as hyperactive as her older brother, was soon labeled wild instead of ambitious.[13]

Josefa, younger than Johnson by five years, had married after moving to Austin but had then done the forbidden and the unforgivable. In 1938, she filed for and got a divorce. Living in her more famous brother's house and having no means to make money, she turned to the underside of Austin politics to eke out a living at local madam Hattie Valdez's "private club" that served the lobbyists' underworld. Remarrying during the war, she divorced again in 1949, and returned to her familiar haunts as what was then labeled a "working girl."

During this period, her need for attention coupled with her wild streak put her in contact with the local art group and, considering the abuse she was suffering at the hands of men, she also connected with the lesbian community.

There was another problem. In those days there was neither financial help nor emotional support for a woman in trouble. Josefa had financial problems, and, not liking secretarial work, her compulsion to act (just like Lyndon's compulsion to act) put her in a prime position to cause a scandal for Johnson. Rumors began spreading but, as was typical of reporters then, she was kept out of the newspapers. After all, the press simply did not cover private sexual activity, at least not until the police acted.

Austin's college population naturally included some of the state's most creative personalities, and there was always a place in town for artists and entertainers. In addition, the university provided excellent training for dramatists and had already helped many destined for future renown. The local community theater was a continuation of the college experience. Doug Kinser was an active participant. So too was Mac Wallace. Although Wallace was several years older, he and Kinser had overlapped some of their time in college.

Many with unfulfilled egos in the "real world" have found acting to be a perfect outlet. As an example, Clark often remarked, "Trial lawyers are little more than frustrated actors." Perhaps a family trait, this drive for recognition and fame was also the case for Josefa Johnson.

Mac Wallace's wife became a friend to Josefa. While not enamored of the acting profession, Mary André thoroughly enjoyed the the experiences she had with her friends in the community theater. "Privileged kids cutting up," a senior police investigator later commented, "and Kinser took advantage of that."[14] Under the auspices of thespian participation and expression, Josefa and Mary André were attracted to Kinser. The fatal connections were complete when they formed what the district attorney would later hesitatingly describe as a "sex circle."[15] Wallace knew about it. He had dated Josefa during his college years and he apparently had participated in the group sex.[16]

For Kinser, the contact with Josefa offered another possibility, that of a government loan through Josefa's brother. Kinser had opened a small business, a miniature golf course near Austin's downtown lake and less than a mile east of popular Zilker Park. (The little pitch-and-putt golf course is still there, near Lamar and Barton Springs Road.) With the predecessor program to the Small Business Administration just getting started as one of Johnson's favorite government aids for a startup business, Kinser tried to enlist Josefa's help to get some money. Johnson would not and could not have anything to do with either of them. Long lists of potential opponents were lined up and ready for the 1954 election, including Coke Stevenson, ever gracious and now more popular than ever. Johnson had to have a perfect record, to be, as Clark cautioned, "pure as the driven snow." The need to be scandal-free was never more seriously threatened by this underside of Johnson's life. With the Kinser contact through Josefa made, with Johnson's sister in a compromised position involving a sex ring, and with Johnson still under the scandal of the 1948 election, the threat from Kinser was ominous.

Kinser was interested only in financial help. He did not have the special concern for state and national politics that Johnson and Clark knew only too well. He did not know Josefa would push the issue with Johnson. Kinser needed money, and, because the opportunity was there, he kept pressing for help. Josefa did even better in pushing her brother for help. The situation only worsened. Johnson had to quash a broadening scandal, the sort that would leave the press crying for blood. If the scandal showed up on the public records, the local reporters would destroy Johnson. So, as the situation worsened, the Austin press corps watched and waited, forced to hold back on private conduct that is always difficult to prove, looking for the break they knew had to come.

Clark appreciated the severity of the problem, of underground rumors circulating and worsening, threatening at any moment to go public. Johnson and Clark also realized they could do nothing above board, open for the public to know. Helping Kinser by giving him a loan could only make Johnson part of that circle of friends that would make ever more trouble. While blackmail and extortion could be alleged in Kinser's efforts, that was a dead end. Johnson could not afford to make such payments. The eagerly waiting political competition would promptly label the loan as hush money and denying it would only aggravate the circumstances.

Under either scenario, the sexual undertones would have been permanently fatal in the early 1950s.

The third possibility was that, even with Johnson doing nothing, the entire scandal would become public. Zilker Park was the sex "hot spot." Police surveillance was active, and Josefa and Mary André had been warned. When would the affairs go public? Would Josefa in a moment of anger tell all?

In Johnson's myopic and paranoid view, something had to be done.

In Clark's view, there was only one solution, and that was to take care of the matter "for good."[17] The only man to be trusted for the obvious dirty work was Clark and he agreed the necessary solution fell to him. After all, that was the *modus operandi* of the Johnson-Clark axis. If the necessity ever arose, Clark was the final fall guy. Already a power in local politics and with the district attorney, he could take action behind the scenes with the comfort of knowing Johnson could never be implicated. In this particular case Clark would be seen taking care of a family friend who was having trouble with his marriage. Johnson would not even be involved.

Because of his wife's role, Mac Wallace became the candidate to bring the scandal to permanent closure. While the crisis was developing, Wallace had moved to Washington where he was one of Johnson's men at the Department of Agriculture. As a Johnson political operative, he was making good progress in the Washington bureaucracy. By October 1951, Wallace had even obtained a new position with the State Department. The job was scheduled to commence the following January.

Clark now needed him for something else because he was the natural to provide a solution to the Josefa problem.

Calling Wallace, Clark briefed him on the urgency of the situation, of the impropriety of the prohibited sex Mary André was practicing. He also mentioned Kinser, painting the man as the real problem, insisting that Kinser was after Mary André and was a distinct threat to her and their family. Clark ended the conversation with assurances that he stood behind Wallace, that all Wallace needed to do was to look into the situation and then act to protect his family by getting Kinser out of Mary André's life for good. Wallace was no fool. He knew what was involved, what was expected of him, and what he had to do.

Clark was also ready. After carefully baiting Wallace to take action, Clark had developed the needed scenario, that of an enraged husband acting to vindicate his wife's honor. The cover appeared perfect.

Wallace went right to work. Supposedly enraged, he took a vacation from the Department of Agriculture on October 10, 1951, leaving the Washington area in his car with Virginia tags. Rather than hurrying to Austin, however, he took a longer, slower route because he needed to get to Dallas and then over to Fort Worth, to get a pistol from his friend, FBI special agent and former University of Texas roommate Joe Schott.[18] From there Wallace drove to Austin where he talked with Mary André for several days, finding out what was going on and who was doing what and to whom. There was no rush and there was no emotional burst of anger. One conversation between husband and wife was at the old Broken Spoke dance hall, several blocks south of Kinser's golf course. The couple was overheard reviewing their pressing need for money and a related insurance policy.[19]

Late in the morning of October 22, 1951, supposedly still in an uncontrollable rage after almost two weeks of careful planning and hesitation, Wallace went to Kinser's pitch-and-putt golf course where several people were playing. Inside Kinser's pro shop, the two men argued, described by the witnesses as loud and prolonged. Next, with the stage now carefully set and with the cover needed, Wallace drew his pistol and shot Kinser several times. Quickly stepping out of Kinser's small office, Wallace went to his waiting station wagon and drove off.

For the next hour, Wallace did not panic and flee. He apparently made a few telephone calls and made some visits. Then, needing the murder to appear to be a killing by an enraged husband, he had to look guilty. He had to behave like a fugitive and flee. So, in fact playing the cool-hand throughout and never too concerned about having killed Kinser, Wallace finally headed out of town on the road leading west from Kinser's golf course through Zilker Park to Bee Caves Road. There was a further complication. Had Wallace disappeared, there would have been the pressing need for the police to investigate. That meant seeking leads among Kinser's friends, and such an inquiry could only lead in all the wrong directions. Johnson and Clark viewed it as having the potential for a politically fatal scandal. The suspect needed to be in custody.

Customers at the golf course heard the shots, saw the stocky man leave, and noted the Virginia license plates. The police arrived and, after a delay of almost an hour, a bulletin was finally issued for the suspect's vehicle. Soon after, southwest of Austin on Bee Caves Road where the road crossed the dam and less than ten minutes from Kinser's business, Wallace was stopped and arrested by county deputies.

Once in custody, Wallace gave little information except to inadvertently remark to Marion Lee, the Austin police investigator on the scene, that he "worked for Johnson."[20] That potential news leak was quickly plugged because Clark had the necessary contacts through the district attorney's office and with his clients, the local newspaper and Johnson's radio station, the one then completing a television broadcast license. The request to the media was the standard one. Honor the old presumption of innocence until proven guilty and await any disclosures until the trial. The reporters were assured that everything would come out then. Clark dealt with the owners of the media, and, as usual, they passed the word to their reporters.

Promptly charged and jailed, Wallace waited, knowing his release would not take long. As promised, the Clark forces acted quickly. Two men posted bond for Wallace. M. E. Ruby owned a construction company doing business with Clint Murchison's ready-mix plants in nearby San Marcos; Ruby was a longtime Johnson ally. Bill Carroll also posted bond; he was a close friend to Clark through the state historical society. Carroll's wife, Mary Jo, would soon be hired as an attorney with Clark and would later become a partner. As the final touch, John Cofer, Johnson and Clark's attorney for criminal matters, was announced as Wallace's attorney. The appearance of Cofer in the Johnson crimes confirmed what would be standard operating procedure in the years ahead.

Wallace was promptly released on bond.

The secret plot behind the coverup then thickened in a strange way and introduced a lingering threat to Johnson and his political interests. Because of an ongoing dispute between the county whose deputies had arrested Wallace and the city where the murder was committed, a jurisdictional issue arose. Following standard procedure, the Texas Department of Public Safety got involved, sending Texas Ranger Clint Peoples to handle the task. The already legendary ranger thus made his first contact with Wallace in a running battle that would extend to another murder ten years later and then to an indictment in that case still another fifteen years later. That murder also involved Johnson. Peoples later remarked about the Kinser murder, "The smell of politics hung heavy over the case."[21]

The minor dispute between the police and the deputies was quickly resolved. Since the coverup was in place, Johnson no longer needed to muzzle the local authorities. Only Peoples kept up the vigil. For the next ten years he would look for the still-missing pistol, one that would fit the pattern in several crimes.

Trial was set for February 18, 1952. Cofer said nothing, just waiting for selection of the jury; he would then see what the district attorney would try to prove, knowing that District Attorney Bob Long was in Clark's pocket just like the predecessor district attorney, Jack Roberts, had been owned.

There were a few unusual events. On February 1, less than three weeks before the trial, Wallace suddenly resigned his government job, unnecessarily implying guilt but perfect for Cofer's objectives to get Wallace convicted and to protect Johnson. With Wallace as the killer, there would be no further questions into the sex circle. The loan problem had already ended with Kinser's death, and Josefa had been warned.

Wallace realized that, given his introduction to the secret world of deep politics in Texas and now facing murder charges, he would have a very different future, one without the power he once wanted, now one basically in the hands of his sponsors. As a political operative in Washington, Wallace had learned to work under false pretenses, to all appearances a government employee, but in fact an arranger helping Johnson by doing favors, raising money, getting out the vote, and taking care of farming constituents. Now he would rely on solid guarantees of good work after the trial. He had no reason to be overly concerned. The plan fulfilled his radical Marxist politics. Get along with the people in power and be ready to bring the government down.

In the "real world" defined by Johnson and Clark, Wallace would become another helper—in place. They had a man who could be forced to work deep underground. Forever barred from public office, Wallace would be perfect for dirty work, for doing what they needed. Johnson and Clark owned Wallace and they would never let him break free.

On the day that Wallace resigned from the State Department, he received still more bad news. His mother, Alice Marie Riddle Wallace, was committed, permanently, to the Terrell State Hospital for the mentally incompetent. Whatever emotional forces were working on Wallace, they were far more damaging to his mother.

In advance of the Kinser trial there was still another strange development. District Attorney Long announced that he could find no motive for murder. Everyone knew immediately that the anticipated disclosures would not be forthcoming. Privately, the Johnson forces were very relieved. Much later, in an oral history for the LBJ Library, Long, with his typical passion for wry understatements, said that he assumed the murder had something to do with the sex circle but that was something he could not even mention in court.[22] The reporters were outraged.[23] This strange admission by Long was a solid favor to Johnson, a victory signal in advance, foreshadowing the verdict to come. There would be nothing about an infuriated husband acting out of a jealous rage. There would just be the fact of the murder of Kinser by Wallace. According to the prosecutor, it was a murder without motive.

Nothing would come out.

The trial commenced as scheduled and lasted one week. Nothing dramatic happened. Cofer, ever on the lookout for an inside advantage, enlisted help from an out-of-town attorney. The lawyer happened to be the uncle of a jury member and was in the courtroom for only one day, just enough to send the message. The victim's mother and wife, both sitting on ready, were not called to testify. Wallace did not testify. He and Cofer simply let the jury hear that Wallace walked into the Kinser pro shop, shot him, and fled. As expected, the verdict was guilty; however, there were two more surprises.

First, the jury agreed that the murder was done with malice afore-thought. They disagreed on the sentence. Eleven jurors were for the death penalty. The twelfth held out for life in prison. Deadlocked, the judge intervened. Another friend of Clark, one of the "bought" judges, he took action that shocked everyone. First, he ordered only five years imprisonment. Even more shocking, he suspended the sentence.[24] The necessary orders were promptly signed, and, on February 27, 1952, Wallace was released on bond and walked out, to all appearances a free man.

The murder trial was over and done. The public outrage was soon over as attention focused on other matters. There was no scandal involving Johnson.

There was only one political price to be paid. The citizens of Austin always had mixed feelings toward Johnson, that he undoubtedly helped them financially but that he was dishonest. That was one public perception Johnson would never escape. Many in Austin prospered from the largesse he was able to deliver. They in turn delivered their votes for him. On the other hand they were well aware of Johnson's many excesses, and his willingness to do anything was not always readily accepted. This mixed support for, fear of, and subliminal dislike for Johnson was always there. In this subtle wisdom, Austin citizens strongly suspected what had happened but there was little they could do. They did take the one action that would reflect their displeasure. They did not reelect D.A. Bob Long.

With release papers in hand, Wallace returned to Dallas, his plans now in place. Mary André accompanied him with the two children; however, within two months, on April 29, she left him again. Two days later Mac filed for divorce and custody. Within thirty days, his requests were granted. Mary André returned to the life she had tried to leave behind.

Johnson and Clark arranged for Wallace to take a job with Luscombe Aircraft Corporation, a small aircraft company just east of Dallas, in Garland, Texas, with offices in Oklahoma. Luscombe soon became part of Ling-TEMCO-Vaught or LTV, a conglomerate deeply involved in the military-industrial complex, and well financed with oil and gas money from Big Oil in Dallas. From time to time, Murchison and D. H. Byrd were prominent supporters, and Byrd was, for a time, chief executive officer. With Luscombe, Wallace received top security clearance. When the company went into bankruptcy and was purchased by LTV, the clearance continued.

In Fort Worth, Wallace settled into serving as a lower-level Johnson operative within the powerful military-industrial complex. For all practical purposes, he continued working just as he had at the Department of Agriculture, contacting constituents, raising money, and getting out the vote.[25] He was still a political operative, working to provide support for Johnson and help for his electorate. Wallace was kept carefully under wraps, below any media radar. While under wraps as a low-level operative, he was in place, a cold-blooded "stone killer," in a secure place, well paid, ready when needed.[26]

Understandably, Wallace was not exactly delighted about the turn of events in his career. Within eight months of the conviction, he faced a charge of being drunk in a judge's office in Georgetown, the small community just north of Austin. The next morning, he paid the fine and was released, still drunk. Twice more he would face DWI charges as alcohol became a cover for and temporary escape from his continuing work for Johnson and Clark. In both instances, his parole should have been revoked. It was not.

Then, in his characteristic ambivalence, Wallace again made an attempt to settle into family life, remarrying Mary André on December 15, 1952. The couple took up permanent residence at 2817 Crest Ridge Drive, a modern new home in Dallas. From that time until his death in 1971, he maintained a domicile and phone in Dallas.

Five years to the day after the murder conviction was entered, it was set aside. During this time Wallace was listed as an economist with LTV in various capacities and was given clearance for work at the top-secret plant for military planes at Garland, Texas. While in Texas he did not obtain any needed security clearances. Despite review efforts, he was exempt from the usual rules.

Family problems continued to follow Wallace. His mother died in Terrell State Hospital on September 8, 1959. On November 17, 1960, nine days after Kennedy's election, Mary André again filed for divorce and it was granted on January 30, 1961. Three days later Wallace was arrested in Dallas for public intoxication. A few days later he was assigned to a branch office of Ling Electronics, a division of LTV located in Anaheim, California.

There he would be in place for the next killings but this time with a far better cover. Since security clearance was again needed, the Office of Naval Intelligence began a series of the required reviews. The lengthy reports highlight the numerous problems they had with Wallace. As required, ONI made contact with the Austin police and with Texas Ranger Peoples. Peoples opposed the clearance. Many other reviewers also expressed reservations.

In addition, despite damning testimony from his wife about an incestuous affair with their nine-year-old daughter, despite evidence of his contacts with persons of Marxist leanings, and despite continuing family problems, including drinking, he was granted the secret clearances. The Johnson connection remained out of sight. Peoples understood what was happening but could only say that "higher ups" were involved.

Wallace stayed on the job for Johnson. In that subtle world of surveillance, ONI's continuing reviews were a perfect cover for Wallace's activities and a perfect way for Johnson to keep a watch on him.

Wallace would marry in California and have a daughter. He would have little to do with that family but would build up some property there and in Dallas. His father and brother in Dallas would prosper. He would not again surface in the Johnson underworld until inauguration week in January 1961.

The Office of Naval Intelligence concluded Wallace was either a Dr. Jekyll or Mr. Hyde but they admitted they were unable to decide which one.

More directly to the point, George Reedy, a future press secretary for Johnson, made the same observation in 1952, that Johnson could be a Jekyll or a Hyde.[27] From 1935 through 1973, the friendship and political success between Johnson and Clark also reflected this same determination and savagery, this Dr. Jekyll.

To return to the question asked by ONI and framed by Reedy, Clark was the Jekyll and Johnson was the Hyde. The two men worked together so long and so closely on the state level, however, that they cannot be separated.

The answer to the ONI question about Wallace is a simple one. The fictional character was one person, a Jekyll in private and a Hyde in public, both in one man, always the same person. There was no either one or the other. Wallace was both.

The same answer applies to Johnson and to Clark. The three conspirators had the same curious mix and unique ability to be a Hyde in public and a Jekyll in private. The combination would prove deadly.

Often.

Over time as a partner in Clark's firm, I discovered that meeting someone associated with Johnson's election fraud of 1948 was an everyday occurrence. Many were in the corridors and well-appointed tables of the petroleum clubs in Houston, Dallas, and San Antonio. Many more were in the countryside, the minor campaign supporters and friends who needed Clark's helping hand in beating down the government or getting paid by it. Most exhibited a sense of pride in being part of the election of a powerful and feared candidate. These men were judges, politicians, and businessmen. Some were only interested in voting as good citizens. Many were, of course, in Austin where the voters knew Johnson better than any other electorate.

When some of these helpers would claim that they had helped Johnson and that they were owed something, Clark might have to act. The money was there, as needed.

Clark could also act with a vengeance, to silence claims perceived to be a threat. The murders are an example here.

The stolen election remains a part of the history and the drama of Lyin' Lyndon. Everyone knew what had happened, but a legal system controlled by Clark meant nothing would be done. A viable second party might have helped prevent such abuses, but the Texas Republican Party would not mature for another decade.

In the meantime Johnson and Clark kept on functioning as before. Nothing changed during the 1950s.

By the end of 1952, the stolen election was fading from the voters' attention span. Four years had been required, but Johnson finally won.

What really happened, of course, is that Stevenson won the 1948 election. After election day was over, Johnson and Clark successfully stole it in the ballot box and in the courthouse. The steps they took were the beginning of their life-long criminal conspiracy against the public. Then, once they were secure, they set out to raise all the money that could be wrung from the Texas economy and its corrupt politics.

Money was what was needed and no one has been able to follow that money because it was so well shielded by Clark, Thomas, and their corporation. We can now begin to follow the money trail.

An uninformed electorate is essential to a democracy.
    —Ralph Woods, American humorist

Give a politician a free hand and they will put it in your pocket.
—Anonymous

8

Cash

On Tuesday, September 27, 1948, Supreme Court justice Black entered his order terminating the investigation started when Coke Stevenson filed his petition in Fort Worth. The result was delivered by telephone calls to Judge Davidson, to the court-appointed masters taking evidence in Alice and San Antonio, and to Ed Clark.

Although there were more formal steps, the litigation was over. The ballots could be printed. The election was held on November 2, 1948, between Johnson and Jack Porter, the Republican candidate. On the national level, as Clark had promised the liberal Democrats in Fort Worth, Johnson's forces supported Truman and Truman carried Texas and the nation.

Johnson's celebration began when Davidson ended the case in his court. Despite continuing efforts by Stevenson, there would be no more incriminating evidence. On that day of victory, the celebrations extended throughout Austin and Washington as well-wishers joined in a long-delayed need for relief, for victory at last.

Johnson was beside himself with excitement.[1] He had gone to the edge and beyond, campaigning throughout the long election and legal process, making all-or-nothing decisions that had to be right, and authorizing legal steps that were, even in his untrained legal mind, long shots at best. Clark considered most of the legal steps a sure thing and so did Fortas when he got involved. After all, they talked to the judges before filing their cases with them. There was always doubt in Johnson's mind. The stakes were too big and the conflict was too heated. Johnson still looked at everything, always uncertain. Clark knew the case was in hand once superlawyer Fortas talked to Black. With the signed order by Black, even Johnson was ready to celebrate.

There was one sobering feature of the 1948 election. Johnson knew the costs of the campaign and the lawyers fees from the ballot and court battles had piled up. With the victory, raising money would be no problem. Clark was the man to complete that task, and he decided Johnson needed a victory tour to raise money.

As Johnson traveled across Texas, from city to city enjoying the victory and collecting money, he found one more thing he wanted. In Dallas, he met a young woman who would become an important part of his celebration and of his future private life.

Joining in the victory tour, Clark was pleased to have a very happy client who was soon to be a freshman senator. Clark had more power and that meant still more clients and retainers. At that moment of victory, however, Clark was greatly relieved. He knew that defeat would have meant the near-impossible task of raising the money for a lost cause. In the oil business, a lost election is a proven dry hole. Just as that location is condemned and forgotten, so too is the candidate ruined and forgotten. With the victory a great burden was lifted from his shoulders. He had signed several notes. In addition, he knew the cleanup work had just begun. Many people had helped and they would expect something in return. With a victory, even more was expected to be paid to the winning team—not unlike a bonus.

So, after the celebrations were over, Clark settled down to complete three objectives. One was to raise the money needed to pay off the loans he had obtained for the campaign. There was a huge campaign debt and many claims would have to be reviewed for payment. The problems were handled over the next few months with payment agreements completed and then paid over the next two years.

Second, money had to be raised for the next campaign. Clark expected very large sums could be collected for an incumbent senator. After all, Johnson now had a six-year term. Clark just needed time. His exchange of memos with Johnson on March 7–8, 1949, shows, in addition to a deadly scheme, how he obtained new loans. Primarily, he extended the term of the old loans while renewing them. "Extend and renew" was the policy.

Finally, and most important, he would be paid. The attorneys' fees proved to be staggering. At one time, ten high-priced senior attorneys and their law firms were hard at work. Associates and support staff had worked twenty-four hours a day, seven days a week, sparing no expense. Because of the victory, the fees would be even higher. Payment would be easy, however, because future retainers from clients, old and new, could be arranged to cover the debt. During that payback time and throughout Johnson's career, special treatment for the clients would keep them paying while keeping the lawyers happy and ever more wealthy.

On October 1, 1948, Clark started to collect the funds needed. The standard way to pay for elections was cash. Well aware of the trouble Brown & Root had with checks in 1941, with three years needed to get out from under an IRS criminal investigation, the untraceable medium of cold, hard cash was the standard operating procedure. Even with Scofield in place as the IRS district director, caution was required.

The best source for large contributions was a "Senate party" at the local country club. Receptions were held throughout the state, and the big money flowed in over the next eight months. Fund-raising was conducted everywhere, preferably at business meetings where the members in attendance had the money and knew the importance of cash to politics. Election financing was a two-way street. Contribute the money to the politician and get the government money in return.

Despite the success in the first major fund-raising drive, more cash was required to settle all claims, and it was not until 1950 that the debt was paid in full. Two years were needed to finish paying for the election, but it was finally done. The objective shifted to collecting money for the reelection effort.

The Senate parties became a tradition, however, and the money kept pouring in from everywhere: country clubs, business organizations, trade groups, and any other source where members had money and an interest in politics. A large sum was gradually accumulated.

As the surplus built up, held in ready for an election still four years away, Clark arranged for the money to be held in trust. Don Thomas became the trustee. After all, not only had Thomas proven himself to be trustworthy; he was also keeper of the special secrets, the "super-secrets." He was a key member of the legal team and of the Johnson fortune. Soon, the fund was so large that the interest was siphoned off to invest. Then the principal began to be converted for private investments. The stage was set for the Brazos-Tenth Street Co., Clark's money-laundering corporation for Johnson's political money and private investments.

The income also meant a measure of personal enrichment for the new senator. A member of Congress did not have a large salary in the 1930s and 1940s nor did they have much power. For national economic interests, dealing with one senator who could control the votes was easier and less expensive than dealing with many members of Congress. Payoffs were much better in the upper house.

At the start of 1948, Johnson owned a few homes in Austin and the radio station was making money operating from a small two-room office. There was no obscene display of wealth that some of his supporters practiced as the booming Texas economy entered the 1950s.

Johnson's close supporters, particularly those in Big Oil, were moving into big buildings, using private airplanes, and going home to their mansions with swimming pools. At the start of 1949 this measure of wealth was not in Johnson's grasp, but he knew his limited means relative to his friends would end once the campaign debt was paid.

Similarly, Clark could not afford the great displays of apparent wealth. He was still struggling with a new law business consisting of partner Everett Looney and associate Don Thomas. After the 1948 election, he could expand, taking in two new attorneys. By Austin standards, it was a big firm. By 1950, his sources for power were in place, and the time had arrived to take advantage of his power at the same time that he helped Johnson. It was time for him to "cash his chips."

Both men wanted the same measures of wealth that their patrons and beneficiaries received. They had a strong spirit of competition and a powerful sense of pride. In the final analysis, however, they were greedy. For Johnson, it was also payback time. He had bowed and scraped before the wealthy and seen them benefit. He knew what he did contributed to their wealth. He wanted his share. Similarly, Clark knew what he had done and wanted his fair share.

For Clark, getting paid was slightly different. Billing legal fees and collecting the cash was done in the fashion of gentlemen, very carefully and discreetly. In those days, few fee arrangements were negotiated in advance. Hourly billing was still far in the future. Typically, the lawyer did the work, got the results, discussed his efforts with the client, and accepted what was paid him. Because Clark got results, he was very effective in visiting clients and getting paid. He knew how to equate his fees to a percent of the continuing benefits to the client. The small percent would mean good income.

In the aftermath of the 1948 election and throughout the 1950s, the two men accumulated very large personal estates. Most of the campaign contributions went to Johnson. Clark collected only modest law fees from Johnson, but he also took between 5 and 20 percent of the money he handled for Johnson.[2]

For Johnson, the process of personal enrichment started in the early 1950s when his radio station was granted a television license. For twenty years it would be the only television broadcast station in Austin. The FCC did not grant any other stations access. In 1950, with the election debts paid and with the huge sums of cash still flowing in, Johnson's first big and very obvious step to showing his new wealth was moving the radio station into a six-story building in downtown Austin at Tenth and Brazos Streets. Just one block south of the Texas Capitol, it was topped with a penthouse for Johnson. He had one measure of wealth that his friends had.

Another big step was to buy back the old Johnson family farm. When his father's businesses had failed during the 1920s, the old homestead was sold and the family moved into a small house in Johnson City. The money available in 1952 meant Johnson could buy back the farm, add some acreage, call it a ranch, and keep up with his wealthy friends.

While taking care of Johnson, Clark also looked forward to his personal objectives. He would become very wealthy and do it the same way Johnson did, by and through the state of Texas. In 1949, everything was in place for him to get rich. As a lawyer, he had learned to look ahead, to see what could be done, and he knew his controls were ready. He had key men in the district courts and in the district attorney's office. His boyhood friend Ben Ramsey was lieutenant governor and in charge of the Texas Senate. As such, he was the most powerful official in Texas, and his hold on the legislature was solid. Through Scofield, the IRS was where it needed to be or at least Clark thought it was. He had an important contact into the prison system with H. H. Coffield. There he could help friends just as Governor Ferguson had helped friends, getting convicts out on parole. The convicts were excellent employees because they had to do what they were told to do. After all, men on parole have few rights. They had to follow the rules or go back to the pen. They showed up on time, worked hard, caused no trouble, and were ideal workers. Clark found work for them everywhere starting with an obvious place, as collection specialists for his banks. Repo men lead a dangerous life. Clark had his debt enforcers. These convicts were also available for the dirty work. He kept them busy.

Finally, and most important for Clark, with Johnson in the Senate, the power broker had a man in high office nationally that complemented his statewide control. In banker's terms, Clark would realize the value and capitalize. He did.

Clark celebrated by getting final orders entered in the lawsuits and then making the calls and sending the letters to raise the money needed. The basic pitch was simple:

> We got the results you wanted. Now you have an obligation to see
> that the remaining debts for the campaign are paid. We assure you
> the benefits of good government will be available to you. Senator
> Lyndon Johnson is at your service.[3]

The pressure was there, the promise of help was easy to understand among the sophisticated, and the money poured in. No one said, "Pay Lyndon and get paid back." There was no memo saying this campaign contribution is for one million dollars in government contracts. Plain and simple, however, political money talks. The citizens of Texas who were politically involved knew they had danced to the tune by supporting Johnson. Now they would get paid back.

Collecting the money was no easy matter. Clark just kept asking, by mailing, by meeting, and by speaking, not just statewide now but also nationally. He had to talk to the moneymen personally because they wanted to explain their problems off the record. For example, the problem might be that they needed a government contract. Clark would collect the campaign money along with the problem and then get the message back to Johnson to solve the problem. The money was collected off the record because Clark could solicit contributions behind the privilege. The LBJ Library concedes that there are no records for such fund-raising.[4] Those records are with Clark's private "penthouse" files.

Although the path is not yet complete for Johnson and Clark, the money trail can now begin to be followed. The economic history for Johnson can begin to be revealed.[5] There are no balance sheets and income statements— not yet. There are estimates and procedures to show how it was done. The results of the rich Texas economy paying off its new senator are abundantly clear. The payoff was enhanced by Clark's direct methods behind the privilege.

The payoffs were so great, however, that the IRS finally acted. Relying on apparent wealth (one of its tests then), it had to act. When it did, the IRS director Frank Scofield would learn in one of the most severe ways possible not to cross Johnson and Clark. He was subjected to character assassination, an act only a few steps above murder. For Johnson, it was just another tool for control.

A key feature of Johnson's underside in the Senate would be the corruption that occurred nationally, outside Clark's watchful eye. That money centered on several outstanding men who came to Johnson for jobs or favors, bringing with them money for the political influence they needed to get the government benefits they had to have. There were several of these "wonder boys" and Johnson helped them while they contributed to his wealth. Only a few were ever a public relations problem for Johnson, but the ones that threatened Johnson's future proved to be an important motivation for the assassination of John Kennedy.

High achievers have always been attracted to political power, and those men encircling Johnson during the 1950s included John Connally, Jake Pickle, Clint Murchison Sr., Jim Ling, Fred Korth, Mac Wallace, Billy Sol Estes, Bobby Baker, and many more. Most avoided trouble and prospered. Some faced serious problems and, when they did, their problems became serious problems for Johnson. The nature of the political beast is that the people you help will be your clients, your "interests." Their problems will be your problems. The only safe course is to limit correspondence to patronage letters and to limit contacts to a handshake. In short, the careful politician stays out of the money trail. In two key instances, Johnson did not because he still lived by the old rules.

In Johnson's defense, when he started in politics, he routinely tried to help people in need. In 1935, that was easy. People without jobs and without hope needed income. He provided the jobs. In return, that beneficiary was expected to help Johnson, if by nothing else than making a small contribution to the campaigns or at least helping get out the vote. This was Texas politics in the late 1930s. The notion that politics was a way to enrich a person changed dramatically in the 1950s. Laws were passed to separate political office from material gain, but those laws were not for Johnson. During his Senate terms, he continued to help, expecting help in return. This time, however, his beneficiaries were not seeking jobs but government money in the form of big contracts. The sums were far more than a living wage. After all, he was helping Big Oil, construction, the defense industry, and any other big business that called.

Jim Ling built up the vast Ling-TEMCO-Vaught (LTV) empire using Big Oil money and leadership from men such as D. H. Byrd and Clint Murchison. His companies also hired Mac Wallace and protected him. Ling survived many controversies and built a business empire for the military-industrial complex. He depended, of course, on substantial government contracts and he got them.

Another important Johnson friendship was in the construction business. This special relationship actually started in 1937 with Brown & Root, the contractors who built the dams needed for LCRA in central Texas. During the war, the company would expand mightily for the war effort as military bases were built everywhere in Texas. After the war, from his new position in the Senate reviewing waste and then preparedness, Johnson was in the middle of the armed forces and the military-industrial complex. George Brown and brother Herman Brown remained good friends of Johnson throughout his long political career. Like old money, these old friends were there from beginning to end. Wonder kids from the start, they stayed friends and prospered.

There was another important class of supporters who had entered Johnson's sphere of friends before the 1948 Senate election. This group included the Ling story, but it was more accurately the Murchison story and Big Oil in what was then high-tech business. During the 1950s as money flowed to Big Oil, the huge sums had to be invested somewhere. Construction was a key attraction and major investments went into building, from ready-mix plants to highways and bridges to high-rises. Murchison and his Big Oil friends had the excess profits needed, called "burn money." Like throwing cash in an incinerator, this was the unexpected cash. They used it to invest in apparently hopeless ventures or into business they knew little or nothing about.

D. H. Byrd attracted their interest because he experimented in airplanes and rockets, important keys to the military-industrial complex in the late 1950s. A member of Big Oil, D. H. "Dry Hole" Byrd was well known for his lack of success in the oil business.[6] Finally, when the east Texas field was developed, he bought into it and became wealthy. Through him, the foundations were laid for the military-industrial complex that centered on LTV. With the money flowing everywhere, D. H. Byrd had enough extra to purchase the building that later housed the Texas School Book Depository.[7]

There were notable success stories. John Connally advanced into the Governor's Mansion. Clint Murchison and his Big Oil friends all became the new billionaires and Dallas became Big D. Old friends George and Herman Brown benefited with military construction during the war. After the war they moved into oil. As one example, they helped convert the Big Inch and Little Inch, the emergency wartime oil pipelines, into Texas Eastern and its natural gas pipelines.

There were many others.

There were notable exceptions.

One was Mac Wallace. The man who would be governor in 1945 was by 1952 under a felony conviction and would ultimately become Texas Ranger Clint Peoples's most-wanted man. From the safe place Wallace had with Ling, he would serve Johnson and Clark in many ways. Based on this symbiotic relation, LTV could obtain needed benefits and Johnson had in place a key political operative and gunman in a secure and very private job. Naval Intelligence would oversee Wallace on behalf of Johnson.

Washington lobbyist Fred Korth helped Convair land the huge TFX military fighter contract through unsavory methods. In his case just the accusations of improper influence through gifts, entertainment, and secret contacts were enough. When confronted, he quickly resigned and suffered no further embarrassments for himself or for Johnson.

Billy Sol Estes and Bobby Baker proved to be huge embarrassments for Johnson. Each would pay the price with felony convictions. Both were wonder boys who achieved great things in the 1950s only to see their careers collapse during the Johnson vice presidency. More than any other single cause, the corruption practiced by these two men with Johnson were key parts of the dark side that led to the assassination. One happened by an accident. The other was the final straw.

In terms of total dollars, Estes was the most successful of these wonder boys. Called "wunderkind" by a fawning press, he was an outstanding Jaycee by 1952.[8] Born in 1924 during a blizzard in the Texas Panhandle, his boyhood was spent in Abilene, Texas.[9] Marrying in 1946, he moved to Pecos where he literally made the desert bloom.

When Estes arrived in Pecos, he saw an opportunity that met the needs of the small town. The plan worked so well that most farms in the barren west Texas plains were soon using his product and his plan. Those dry plains started west and north of Austin near the boyhood home of Lyndon Johnson, reached over to San Antonio, and then extended west to New Mexico and north into the Texas Panhandle. During the Depression the Texas so-called staked plains had been the southern edge of the infamous Dust Bowl. The farmers on those dry plains would do anything to prevent a repeat of the bad years. Estes proved to be their savior.

The problems the farmers faced were not just repeated droughts.

Irrigation costs were too high for the value of their cotton crops. Estes did two things. He switched the irrigation pumps from electricity to far less expensive natural gas. The cost of the water problem was solved. Then he discovered the benefits of anhydrous ammonia as fertilizer. Combining the product and the process, he literally brought farming back to life. He turned the dry prairie green.

As Estes grew ever more wealthy, he became, as a natural born salesman, an ever more flamboyant businessman and, as an inspirational speaker, a recognized preacher. The only problem for Estes was the over-sell. Having a good product was never enough. There always had to be more. He had to have the perfect solution to everything. Even early in his remarkable years of success, this optimism instilled a certain skepticism in his audiences. This inherent ability to sell more than he had would lead to his later problems.

With Estes, you could always be sure that in all the blustering big talk, there was at least a little truth, a way to make money, something you could take to the bank. In other words, at least some of what he said was true.

Estes finally said too much and went too far. He believed what he preached. Perhaps it was inevitable but the law finally caught up with him. In 1962, he was facing federal fraud charges.

The problems started during his expansion years because he used the government for enrichment. For the Democrats, and particularly for Johnson, Estes willingly contributed large sums of money. To all appearances, he was a generous man who enjoyed politics. Behind the scenes, he needed help at the Department of Agriculture with cotton allotments. That meant politics and Lyndon Johnson.

The two men had a natural attraction to each other. His relationship with Johnson was strong because he readily contributed large sums to Johnson's campaigns and because he included Johnson in some of these business dealings, all behind the scenes. By 1958, a memo from staff member Lloyd Hand to Johnson recognized Estes as someone the Senate's majority leader was interested in.[10]

The memo is interesting. Never before disclosed, it belies Johnson's later efforts to distance himself from Estes. When criminal charges were filed in 1962, Johnson would only admit he had one personal contact with Estes, inviting him to a party at his Washington home during inaugural week in January 1961. In fact, the relationship was much deeper and involved large sums of cash and other help.

The problem started in the late 1950s. To help farmers and himself, Estes made anhydrous ammonia tanks readily available by setting up financing. Soon, the white tanks dotted the high plains, a very visible signal that the farmers were making money. The complex financing arrangement was in the nature of a leaseback where the tank remained the collateral. The money was easy—too easy.

The main problem was with the federal government. Cotton was the base for the Estes program and federal money depended on cotton allotments. Because of the success of cotton farming during the 1950s, production exceeded market demand. As in the oil business, cotton had to be controlled. Enforcement of cotton production was the job for the Department of Agriculture, and this was done with allotments telling the cotton farmers how much they could and could not plant. Since Estes wanted his farmers to grow more cotton, he needed ever more allotments until they simply ran out. In desperation, he found an unusual niche. Some allotments were available for farmers displaced by the interstate highway program. Estes began acquiring these allotments to help with his financing needs. The practice was prohibited, but Estes used a loophole that allowed the transfer in a complicated exchange program for other land. Farmers in financial trouble were pleased. Estes continued to prosper. Not surprisingly, additional contributions went to Johnson.

The Estes success story would end in 1961 when his debt payments and other expenses exceeded his ability to pay. The cumulative effect of debt added to debt and ever-mounting interest payments along with his extraordinary campaign contributions finally became too much. Estes made his mistake. He tried to get more money by leasing fertilizer tanks that did not exist and by acquiring ever more cotton allotments in violation of existing USDA regulations. The political costs were also too high. One party for Johnson required $145,017.[11] The inevitable result was the collapse of his pyramid, an upside-down one that fell hard. Johnson was nearly engulfed but extraordinary efforts by Clark, Wallace, and Cofer succeeded in saving him, until 1984 when, as we shall see, Johnson himself would be subject to grand jury indictment for murder.

During the 1950s, however, Estes remained a very visible and successful wonder boy in Johnson's camp.

Bobby Baker started in the United States Senate as a pageboy, running errands for the members of the Senate. Known then as the most exclusive men's club in the world, the members of the Senate insisted on the very best perquisites and benefits possible. In the Senate ego was never an issue; it was just there as an accepted fact. Most senators had huge egos and wanted everything. Baker would be in charge of satisfying those egos.

Only eighteen years old and just arrived from South Carolina, Baker had a patronage job equivalent to that of today's intern.[12] The purpose of the job was to introduce him to the Senate and to the American system of government and democracy. Little did those interns know what they were going to learn. In fact, the job was little more than "go-fers" for the senators, errand boys to take care of clerical tasks such as delivering messages around the Capitol. Baker's job was supposed to last only a year. New students were brought in annually to learn how Congress worked and how democracy in America flourished.

Baker would stay fifteen years, and he would rise to the very important position of secretary to the majority leader. His ability to work hard and to remember details endeared him to the exalted members. Every year that he stayed only improved what he knew, and every year also improved his ability to get the job done. Taking care of senators was his basic task, and he took care of that job every way possible, often in a very personal way. In effect, he was there to take care of their whims and their egos. He proved to be a master. After all, he learned directly from Johnson, whose ego in the Senate had become as unlimited as his lust for power. The evolution of power as a corrupting force can be seen in Johnson's rise in the Senate. Compare the national record to the results back home. He got wealthy as he got power.

Baker was already working for the Senate when Johnson was sworn in on January 4, 1949. Baker's abilities soon brought him to the attention of the junior senator from Texas. Both were hard workers so it was inevitable that they would get to know each other. During the 1950s, they worked closely together.

As Johnson rose to power in the Senate, Baker stuck with him and became secretary to Johnson when the senator became Democratic leader. Within ten years, Baker was secretary to the Senate. Scheduling bills to take care of the individual schedules of each senator was an obvious skill. Baker did it. He was able to let senators know when to leave or when to stay so that hearings or votes on key legislation would occur when they were there. He scheduled the hearings, the votes, and the vacation and recess time. He kept track of everything to make ninety-six egos work together. In the process he learned the details of the each senator's personal life. As he got to know their personal interests, he became the man to provide whatever was needed.

A place to park, snuff for their nicotine needs, pens for visitors, guest passes to the Senate balcony, cash for late-night travel, the time to appear at a hearing, copies of favored legislation, and anything else needed for their success was immediately available from the ever-ready Baker.

In 1957, consistent with Johnson's experiences from his early days in Austin, the women began showing up, and the contacts grew until there were standing arrangements in the nearby Congressional Hotel.[13] Just across the street from the Capitol Building, the hotel was a perfect place to meet, with a good restaurant for lunch and the rooms for "quickies" and "nooners."

For having such intimate knowledge about every senator, Baker also had their unqualified support. He knew so much about them, individually and as a group, that they in turn had to give him what he wanted. After all, each was helping take care of the other. It was "you scratch my back and I scratch yours." By 1961, Baker knew about service, about meals, and about hotels. Then he got greedy. He wanted to make the big money, like the men he worked for. After all, he was learning from Johnson. In the early 1960s, he decided to expand.

Johnson needed Baker because the young man had skills that were invaluable to a senator. Looking back, they clearly learned from each other with what they called "the hand-off."[14] What Baker knew about each senator was what Johnson needed to know. And Johnson passed information back to Baker, handing off what he needed to know. The attention to detail was Johnson's big service and his source for inside information. Johnson knew everything about his colleagues and Baker provided that insider information. This necessarily included the private activity, the secrets, the rumors, and the dirt. Baker was the provider and, with the hand-off, Johnson knew. With that information, he could become their leader because he knew what was happening.

By 1957, Baker had grown into a unique position of power in Washington. With Sam Rayburn heading the House of Representatives and Johnson running the Senate, the two Texans controlled Washington's politics of compromise. Considered by Johnson to be "my son," Baker was within the inner circle of that control apparatus.

More to the point, as Johnson's confidant, Baker learned the inner workings of power in the Senate, of special favors for senators, of rewards for friends, of payments to supporters, and of punishment for opponents. Working at the foot of a master legislator, Baker learned to handle the men of power in Washington. In doing his job, Baker expanded his services as he learned to use the tried-and-true devices of lobbyists to keep the senators well served and cooperative, the after-hours accommodations. From an inauspicious start as an intern, he learned how the Senate really worked.

Fully understanding and appreciating the corrupt power Johnson used, in 1961 Baker decided he could expand. Intent on pursuing his dream investments based on the skills in hotels and food service that he had acquired in the Senate, he first expanded into a beach motel in nearby Ocean Springs, Maryland. He also started in vending machines with snack food services through contracts at aerospace companies serving the military-industrial complex. Still secretary of the Senate and doing an excellent job, Baker expanded his abilities into very profitable ventures.

A candle burning on both ends, however, can only last so long. Baker would be consumed by scandal near the end of Johnson's vice presidency.

With the remarkable success of Johnson's friends and with the continuing flow of political help, contributions only increased. Another device had to be put in place to help Johnson enrich himself and stay above suspicion, or at least stay above proof of any wrongdoing. A corporation was set up by Clark, and it proved to be an effective money processor or, more accurately, a money-laundering machine.

The need arose because money had to be collected for the 1954 reelection campaign. The effort started with the payment of the 1948 debts, and a solid war chest was soon in place. With the success of Johnson's many friends, however, the money kept flowing. There was never a thought given to cutting back. Just keep counting. But something had to be done with all that cash. Clark took care of it and by 1960, Johnson was very wealthy. How he did it has never been made public.

First, there were FCC benefits for Johnson's radio-TV station. The issue was first raised by Hardy Hollers during his 1946 election campaign for Congress against Johnson. Hollers failed to convince a majority of Austin voters, but he raised serious questions. After that, Johnson's problem of owning a government-regulated business and getting rich would never end. Clark knew that a system to make Johnson money and keep him clear of any appearance of corruption was needed. This meant Johnson stayed away from money.

The attorney-client privilege was good protection. Through Clark's connections with banks, he also knew where the best deals were to be found for loans and investments. But the money got to be too much. Trying to invest

Johnson's excess money was simply too risky. Something had to be done to keep him in the deep background. He did not need any problems like the radio-TV station proved to be.

The vehicle chosen was the little corporation known as Brazos-Tenth Street. Set up on October 5, 1955, by outside attorneys to conceal any public connection to Clark, the cover was blown just by its name. It was the address for the radio-TV station. The corporation was managed by Don Thomas and was used to channel Johnson's profits into wealth for him.

Brazos-Tenth money-laundering business proved to be very profitable. The basic split was 20-20-40. Forty percent was for campaigns and was spent on a regular basis to keep Johnson before the voters. For him, campaigning never stopped. Twenty percent was for investment in Johnson's portfolio. Twenty percent was for Clark, primarily as fees. The balance of 20 percent was kept for business expenses and to keep the little enterprise solvent. Although Brazos-Tenth was primarily for political contributions, whenever necessary, excess profits from the radio-TV station were also funneled through the corporation.

As the money flowed in over the years, Thomas turned Brazos-Tenth Street into what would later be considered a small business investment company. From time to time Clark and the other beneficiaries would funnel new opportunities through the money machine, the cash cow. From there, net income would be reinvested, as needed. Income was excellent. Under one million in 1955, it grew to four million, then fell to one million, then four million again and again, leading up to the 1960 presidential campaigns. During its existence from 1954 through 1971, the company provided a complete cover.[15]

Of course, Brazos-Tenth Street was just a front. On paper, it owned nothing and had no money.[16] It just covered up everything else by having the money pass through it as trustee. The privilege worked completely. Whenever anyone in the media inquired, Thomas would always decline to discuss the business as a private matter, as a privileged matter, or as a corporate matter not involving Johnson. The issue was never really pursued because it could not be investigated.

The cover was solid, with a double shield: the corporate veil followed by Johnson's personal attorney for the privilege. There was Don Thomas and there was Brazos-Tenth Street. Behind it all was Clark, the moneymaker.

Johnson's acquisitions through the corporation were conservative and very hard to trace on the public record. On Clark's recommendation, banks were a prime target for investment. Clark would buy controlling interest in a bank and then quit paying dividends. The minority shareholders would be forced to sell at book value or less.[17] Whenever there was a protest, Clark covered any media inquiry about the shareholders. Johnson was protected since ownership was not in his name, and he always said he owned no bank stock. In fact, he owned substantial interests in banks.[18]

During the 1950s, Johnson bought several large tracts of land as an investment. Some would be bought and sold over the course of a few weeks. Clark knew where the opportunities were, usually because he knew where the government was going to locate new offices and where highways and other facilities would be built. He would buy the land before the news broke. When the real buyer came along, the land would be sold for a substantial gain. Typically, the buyer was the government. The practice was clearly an abuse of insider information. No one knew, so no one complained.

Finally, and most important, there was KTBC, the small radio station purchased in 1943. It grew enough to support a second station in 1946, and KVET was set up with denials all around that Johnson was involved. That, too, was a lie. Johnson was involved and so was Clark. Then, in 1950, the first television channel in Austin was awarded to Johnson. It would make solid profits. Anyone seeking to do political business with Johnson would be expected to buy advertising. For almost two decades, Johnson's KTBC remained the only television station in town. Only after Johnson left the White House could FCC let another broadcast station operate in the area.

Some have suggested the station earned $10,000 weekly and was the source of Johnson's wealth.[19] This would not by any math explain Johnson's total net worth exceeding twenty million dollars without counting the trusts. The actual value of the money was far greater. To keep it concealed, it was easily spread into other ventures such as cable TV. Johnson's attorneys were very effective. Had the IRS been able to act, this practice might have been disclosed. Even the IRS was barred.

By 1960, all these schemes combined to make Johnson a millionaire many times over. The appearances could not be hidden. He did what politicians in Texas had done since the beginning of the Republic, they enriched themselves through political power. But the times were changing and Johnson and Clark were not men to change. As the law changed, they remained stuck in the past. For Johnson, he might have a building downtown with the penthouse on the top, and he might have a ranch and mansion with a swimming pool and a major landing strip; however, this display of public wealth would catch up with him. The fallout started during his vice presidency.

The money and the apparent wealth did not go unnoticed. Agents with the IRS started an investigation almost at the same time the cash for the 1948 election started arriving. Although the details are not clear, the IRS noticed the apparent wealth accumulating to Johnson and, once again, had questions about where the campaign funds were going.[20]

Frank Scofield had been the man chosen to protect Johnson from any repeat of the 1941 election scandal that required FDR's illegal help. The arrangement had been very informal because Scofield was too ethical to agree to a tradeoff for the job. When the IRS started an informal review, there was, as usual, an advance warning to Clark.

The IRS case against Johnson and Brazos-Tenth was strong. Clark decided the best protection would be a good offense, so he took on the IRS. He attacked the attacker, the man in control at the IRS who did nothing to stop the review. Clark went after Scofield and had him indicted. The director's only crime was to violate an implicit promise not to cause trouble for the man who got him the job. In short, do not bite the hand that feeds you. When Scofield's agents threatened an audit and Scofield did not stop it, he was indicted. He did not even know what was really happening.

The process leading to a federal indictment was and still is relatively simple. First, there are countless laws in the United States Criminal Code that control virtually every type of activity done in America. Then and now, a person can easily be indicted for almost any ordinary activity. For Scofield, the Hatch Act was chosen. That law prohibited campaign contributions and political activity by government employees. Of course, contributions were expected, indeed demanded, by Johnson in 1948. He still lived by the old rules. Once contributions were made, the Hatch Act was then available as a club. In effect, Clark had control.

The second step in a federal persecution is to have a friendly prosecutor. Just by coincident, the United States attorney was Charles Herring. For two years, Herring had been an attorney associate with Clark, and he had been appointed federal prosecutor through Johnson. Clark made the necessary calls and Herring responded. The indictment was returned and the long wait for trial began.

The first benefit of the indictment was to stop the investigation into

Johnson's contributions and investments before they even got started. The IRS audit was on hold.

Then, for eighteen months, the case sat on the docket. There was no rush for Clark to do anything. In the meantime, Thomas was called upon to act.

In a series of mysterious and until now unsolved series of fires in Austin in June 1953, a number of buildings burned. One of the scattered fires was an old Quonset hut that happened to hold the suspicious Johnson records, the ones pending an audit of his campaign contributions.[21]

Thomas later bragged about taking care of an IRS audit without going to court. Under cover of the early morning darkness in the friendly residential city where there was no crime, Thomas set, over a period of one week, several fires in different locations, every other night or so, to give him both the necessary cover and the distraction needed. The official line was that it was just some young arsonist on a spree, one who was never apprehended.

The pattern was clear. Only Thomas was involved. There were no accomplices to inform on him. He was an attorney so he could field any questions, and he could protect any person he represented because of the privilege. He might just have to be the fall guy but that was no more than the same risk Clark had assumed in 1949. It was part of the firm's services for Johnson.

Scofield finally went to trial. He was found innocent on all counts.

The IRS requires that destroyed records be provided again by the taxpayer. The process of rebuilding the tax records, however, is very time consuming in a complex case. Besides, ample time had passed to prevent an audit into some key records. The IRS investigation came to an end.

The audit was dead for another reason. Bob Finney became the new IRS director. Sponsored by Johnson and Clark, Finney knew to be a friend. He never caused a problem for Johnson, the campaign money, or the investments. During the 1950s, while huge sums were accumulated and Johnson grew ever more wealthy, he never again had a serious problem with the IRS. A key part of Johnson's illegal enrichment was again in place. It was possible because of the pattern of control exercised by Clark. The Scofield case is a perfect example of how it worked.

The one remaining part of Johnson's "cash everywhere" benefits and the associated perquisites he received was with women. One met him shortly after the 1948 election had been declared a victory.

Madeleine Duncan Brown was an attractive redhead in the middle of divorce proceedings when she met Johnson in Dallas during his whirlwind celebration tour of Senate parties the week following his victory in the Supreme Court.[22] He invited her to a celebration in Austin three weeks later. A formal invitation from KTBC, the Johnson's radio station, soon arrived for a party on the evening of October 29, 1948.

What was to become a passionate love affair for Brown commenced that night in Austin's Driskill Hotel. The affair would extend over a twenty-year period and would produce one child. Steven Mark Brown was born December 27, 1950, in Dallas. Clark would take care of the financial arrangements through an attorney in Dallas, paid for through Thomas and his Brazos-Tenth Street Corporation. The child was not disclosed publicly until long after Johnson's death.

The son filed a lawsuit against the Johnson interests in 1987. The case was not successful because of the difficulty of proof and the effect of the statute of limitations. Within only a few years, Madeleine's son died under very unusual circumstances. Arrested by military police on strange charges involving drug abuse, he was confined to prison at the Naval Air Station in Corpus Christi. Transferred to Bethesda, he was released, went home to Dallas, and, in 1990, died of cancer.

Johnson's long relationship with Madeleine was based on her continuing attraction to him. The arrangement worked for him and he kept it going with the necessary support for their child. The romance reflects another part of the Johnson legend, of his sexual energy. This part of the Johnson story is now generally accepted.[23]

Johnson's abuse of women as a condition of their employment with him and as an accepted benefit of his political power includes other children born of his affairs. Typically, the child resulted from affairs with office secretaries. Madeleine's child with Johnson is the only one on the public record. There is at least one other.

Until recently, the private life of politicians has been largely ignored. With the rise of women's rights, however, this right of powerful men to privacy in their abuse of power has been limited to a small degree. Under current laws, women have mixed protections from the unequal power that exists with men. In Johnson's heyday, however, there was no easy way for a woman even to begin to prove an affair. The testimony was "he said" and "she said." There was no use of DNA as evidence. Typically, a child was necessary just to consider a claim. Realizing that, when Madeleine had their baby son, Johnson was generous by arranging for a trust to buy the silence and assure the cooperation needed.

This dark underside practiced by the politicians and the lobby was an accepted feature of Austin and Washington nightlife. Now a second look is underway as the position of women and the abuse they suffered has resulted in additional review.[24] Johnson's background of unrestricted sexual activity constitutes an important indication of his character and his recklessness, of his surviving on the edge, and of his almost total lack of respect for women.

Expanded protection in the workplace is needed.

Johnson's attitude toward women would continue throughout his long career. Only after his retirement would he begin to appreciate his wife and show some measure of decency to her and to other women. During his terms in office, however, his sexual demands only contributed to his abuse of power and fed the corruption he practiced.

Women were an accepted feature, a perk available to powerful men. Johnson routinely abused his power with many women. The long-term meaning to be given this practice is still being played out. An interesting correlation may someday result in a better understanding of what this may mean for corruption in high political office.

Following the 1948 election, Johnson finally began to enjoy the full benefit of the corruption available with the new power he had. For him, based on the practices he learned in Texas politics, the corruption was already second nature. In the 1950s, it paid off for Johnson and Clark in a very big way. The success of the many payoffs simply enabled Johnson's ever-increasing demands for more and more power.

> Congress makes for strange bedfellows but they soon get used to the bunk.
> —Will Rogers

> Essential to any politician is the ability to foretell what will happen and then to explain why it did not happen.
> —Ambrose Pierce

9

High-Low

When 1949 opened, Clark had the priorities underway for Johnson to avoid any scandal, pay off debt, accumulate wealth, and become a Texas conservative. The other big objective was in Johnson's hands, to control the Senate as a moderate Democrat.

From the outset of the Senate career, however, the two basic policies Johnson pursued were reactionary, getting a better deal for Big Oil and preventing any progress for blacks. On a key free-speech issue, he was slow to respond. During his career he responded only slowly and reluctantly to the national Democratic agenda.

Johnson succeeded in his basic objective. How he became a national leader is, on hindsight, simply unbelievable until you consider the southern Democrats. The explanation also rests with an extra ingredient, that of providing what his colleagues wanted. The private underside of the Senate was controlled by Johnson and Bobby Baker and we have seen how it worked.

Johnson's public career in the Senate was both quick to move ahead and then straightforward in implementing his agenda. In only four years, he rose from a lowly junior member sitting in the last row of desks in the chamber to minority leader standing just in front of the presiding officer. With changes in party fortunes, he became majority leader, in charge of all legislation considered by Congress. By the end of his Senate career, he was recognized as *de facto* president of the United States.[1] He was on top, almost.

So, by the end of his Senate career, it would be a giant step down to become vice president—but not if seen as the steppingstone to the presidency.

The other side of this public record of success is largely ignored. Basically, he used personal determination to take over a job few senators wanted, that of taking care of the daily business of the Senate, of doing the clerical duties that the secretary of the Senate should do. When Bobby Baker took over that position, he did it in concert with Johnson. Once Johnson had the position of leadership, he kept it through a strange alliance of conservatives and moderates in the Democratic Party. To all appearances, his colleagues let him have the run of the show while they took care of other business. He was the man who put compromises together and was a leader primarily in that sense. He did not undertake policy initiatives. To the contrary, he often obstructed initiatives. As a result, he missed important opportunities to address most of the underlying causes of unrest that surfaced in the 1960s.

The silent generation was the title given the children growing up in the 1950s. Perhaps awed by the achievements of what was later recognized as the greatest generation, Johnson and his fellow senators were also easy-going, willing to sit back and watch or simply ignore the beginnings of those monumental changes that exploded in the 1960s.

Johnson was perfect for the do-nothing 1950s.

His political life in the Senate was supposedly one of moderation but, where he did act, he was dedicated to reactionary issues on oil, civil rights, and free speech. The first two were based on his southern and Texas background. The last was self-inspired and was geared to his conservative supporters in Texas.

As he gained control, his private life in the Senate backrooms ranged from pandering to those in power to petty retribution against those opposing him. Johnson's approach was basically carrot and stick, and that stick could loom ominously.

Meanwhile, back in Texas, Johnson's political life focused on having all things for himself while being all things to everyone. As we have seen, that private life included corrupt campaign cash, continued pursuit of the dark side he had enjoyed in Austin, and business and investment income that was unprecedented.[2] As a "complicated man," Johnson could compartmentalize all these aspects of his life so that observers too often had difficulty appreciating him for what he really was. Any understanding of Johnson and what he would bring about in November 1963 must be based on what he had already done and why, and on what he did during his twelve years in the Senate and why. If what he did after the 1948 election is considered a surprise, it should not be. The complexities of his character are revealed by his conduct in the Senate, an arc of power that reached from low to high and then, as vice president, back to the bottom.

On January 5, 1949, Johnson was sworn in as the junior senator from Texas and he found himself relegated to a back row desk, a small office, and assignments to insignificant committees. He immediately demanded more.

First, he brought John Connally back to organize his office, and he increased his staff significantly to meet the needs of staying in touch with the voters just as he had done for cowboy congressman Kleberg. Then he approached the southern caucus, the senators from the one-time Confederate states, and he adopted their opposition to civil rights. Thus, he opposed blacks on their key issues of voting rights, anti-lynching laws, fair housing, and, most important, cloture. The latter was the key. Cloture was the process for attempting to end filibusters by the southern caucus when they opposed civil rights reforms. The southern senators had the right to debate and could not be stopped unless a super-majority of senators voted to muzzle them. The process was cloture and represented the votes needed to silence the opposition and take a vote. The other issues could not get a vote unless cloture could be approved.

In that caucus, Johnson quickly allied himself with Richard Russell of Georgia. From that friendship, he gained control of the caucus and a major voting bloc on the Democratic side of the aisle. He then worked conservatives in the western mountain states to put together the votes needed to control the Democratic caucus. The main interest out West was building dams and that support was easy to give. In short, he took the Democratic and moderate conservatives and put together enough votes to control the Democratic caucus, then the Senate, and, as we shall see, the nation.

Within two years, he was minority whip. When Eisenhower was elected in 1952, Johnson shared and savored the victory with the more conservative members and became, on January 2, 1953, minority leader for his party. Then, less than two years later, Wayne Morse of Oregon switched out of the Republican Party to become an independent and to vote with the Democrats. The switch allowed Johnson to become majority leader.

The position of majority leader is powerful because that person controls the progress of legislation. Which bills are to be voted on and when the votes are to be taken are very important. For Johnson, the key was not what legislation was passed and what leadership initiative was given the nation. Johnson did not want bills passed. The major issue during the 1950s was civil rights. Nothing significant was done. The Texas issue of protecting and promoting oil was also kept in status quo.

Most of the other legislation was routine and was approved in the spirit of compromise that prevailed during the 1950s. As majority leader, Johnson was also the main contact with the House of Representatives. There Sam Rayburn was a great friend and ally. Johnson was also the main Democrat in touch with the White House, and he worked closely with President Dwight Eisenhower. By 1958, he was national spokesman for his party. The national Democratic party leaders did not like that fact.

In day-to-day housekeeping, the leader's power was important. For the senators, Johnson would help them with their offices and perks, and he controlled their legislation and voting by setting hearings and schedules based on their needs. Working closely with Bobby Baker, the very difficult task was handled. In similar, petty ways, Johnson would also hurt his colleagues, by denying them hearings, giving them poor offices, and keeping them uninformed or out of the loop. For Johnson, "You are either for me or you are against me." He would reward his friends but, if they turned on him, they paid. The old Texas ways of the all-powerful *padrone* system that worked so well in Parr Country also worked in the United States Senate.

We were reduced to leadership of a banana republic.

For Johnson, the process started slowly. As he accumulated power, he helped his colleagues however he could. Once he had the power of the majority leader, he expanded it. As he gained still more power, he actually turned it against his liberal Democratic colleagues. Strangely, his fellow senators accepted his increasingly autocratic rule. Their acquiescence resulted from private favors and from fear. They dared not oppose him.

The moderate picture that Johnson portrayed with the public was belied by his action on key issues. Once he was in the Senate, he embarked on a right-wing course that remains without parallel in American politics. People marvel at his climb to power. His change of politics is far more surprising. As he would explain, "I don't represent just Austin. I got a whole state to worry about." Austin was liberal Democrat; Texas was conservative Democrat and rapidly becoming Republican conservative.

On the national scene, from his position as leader, these Texas and southern attitudes were projected onto the other forty-seven states.

Big Oil provides an excellent insight into Johnson's politics. In Texas, petroleum was the most conservative industry and it contributed more money than any other voting bloc. That was enough for Johnson to change his thinking and voting.[3] The change is all the more interesting because, until he was in the Senate, he had carefully avoided any close identification with

Big Oil. Before 1949, investment opportunities were rejected, even when a gift was proposed, because he had his eye on national office. The only nationally elected office is the presidency.

This concern about his political future changed in the Senate. He knew he had to represent the state's dominant industry. Still fearful after the close 1948 election, he leaned over backward to help, and he did everything possible to cultivate rich oil friends.

To prove his worth to Big Oil, an opportunity arose during his first year in the Senate. The Natural Gas Act of 1938 was considered by some to regulate the price of natural gas at the wellhead. Leland Olds, a member of the Federal Power Commission, believed he had to fix prices on natural gas. This proposal was considered treason by the oil companies. Production in Texas could be controlled to keep prices up; however, the notion of keeping prices down would just not work. In addition, to regulate pricing, the law required that the actual cost of producing natural gas would have to be determined. This meant the accounting records of Big Oil had to be opened up. Oilmen were not about to open their books.

Truman supported regulation of natural gas and proposed Olds for another term at FPC. Johnson saw his chance.[4] Maneuvering the necessary public hearing on the nomination to a subcommittee he chaired, he led a ruthless, unrelenting attack on the nominee. In Johnson's eyes, Olds was an old-time liberal who became a socialist during the Depression. He had to be defeated. With the Cold War already underway and with the renewed specter of nuclear holocaust, Johnson commenced a vicious, unrelenting attack featuring lies, innuendoes, and redbaiting that destroyed Olds's nomination. In his first exercise of power in the Senate, Johnson showed the public another one of his dark sides, that of resorting to character assassination to promote himself. Johnson had done it before and would do it again; however, this is one of the few times he did it in such a public way and on the record.

This type of attack would soon become standard for Joe McCarthy's many unfounded charges of communists everywhere in America.

Johnson also proved Big Oil was his patron and, by the sheer force of his attack, he compelled his Senate colleagues to accept that fact and to lay off the oil industry. Just as he teamed with other southern senators to protect racism to the bitter end, Johnson would protect oil no matter what. The Senate understood and accepted the power of the oil lobby. They also understood that, for all practical purposes, Johnson was the main representative for the powerful petroleum industry. Johnson was Big Oil's lobbyist on the floor of the Senate.

During his first year in the Senate, Johnson was also determined to initiate legislation to amend the Natural Gas Act to stop federal regulation of gas prices. The Senate, then controlled by Republicans, passed the bill. Johnson voted with them just like a Republican. Truman promptly vetoed it.

By allying himself with Republicans, Johnson was also able to defeat the many Democratic proposals to reduce or eliminate the depletion allowance just as he made sure the oil-rich tidelands of Texas returned to state control.

In 1955, one of his first acts as majority leader was to bring up still another bill to deregulate gas pricing. Here, as elsewhere, the oil lobby was starkly revealed to be corrupt. In a blatant attempt at bribery, Elmer Patman of Superior Oil secretly offered Republican senator Francis Case of South Dakota a so-called reward to support the bill.[5] The $2,500 was, of course, nothing less than a bribe. When Johnson heard about it, he scheduled a short hearing into the matter but still pushed the legislation through. Declaring that corruption tainted the entire process behind the bill, Eisenhower promptly vetoed it. He wrote in his diary that it was "the most flagrant kind of lobbying that has been brought to my attention in three years."[6]

Big Oil and its natural gas remained subject to federal control. By implication, of course, Johnson showed that corrupt practices were acceptable to him and that, for his patron and client in Big Oil, its legislative needs justified whatever means were available.

Another key issue during the Johnson years was civil rights. Until becoming president, Johnson never championed causes for African Americans. One example is perhaps most telling. The NAACP was originally formed in 1909 to put an end to the horrific practice of lynching. The Congress was asked to pass legislation prohibiting the widespread killings that occurred in far too many states. Johnson had voted against the legislation in the House of Representatives and would continue to oppose it in the Senate. He reasoned that the states were the proper place to address the matter and that it was not common in Texas. After all, for lynching, Texas ranked "only third" among the southern states. Thus, he opposed the one initiative that was at the heart of NAACP's program: national anti-lynching legislation.

In 1964 Johnson would support major new civil rights for blacks, essentially continuing what Kennedy had proposed the year before; however, during Johnson's twelve years in the Senate he readily acknowledged he was "not a civil rights activist,"[7] and he did little to promote even minimal rights for blacks.

Johnson was from a different time and had a voting base he chose not to educate and lead; however, by 1956 his racist comments were clearly inappropriate, particularly from a national leader. About the only constructive steps he took for blacks during the 1950s was declining to attend a meeting of the southern caucus that adopted the Southern Manifesto. He later explained that he was supporting the NAACP by refusing to sign the statement opposing the 1954 Brown school desegregation case. He also argued that he approved limiting cloture to end filibusters.[8] The latter step came only near the end of his Senate career when his sights were on the national office, and he finally saw the need to fall in line.

Many credit Johnson with doing something for civil rights. During most of the 1950s, the Senate could not do anything to remove the prejudicial practices forced upon blacks. The only effective action in the Senate was to defer to Johnson. Since the cloture majority did not have enough votes to cut off a filibuster by southerners, there was little that could be done. Johnson protected that practice until the bitter end, when he finally had to act. In short, with his moderate to conservative southern attitude, he did nothing to lead the nation toward civil rights for all.

The third big issue was Joe McCarthy. The Republican senator from Wisconsin had learned from Johnson's vicious attack on Leland Olds and had applied the same methods to alleged communists in government and everywhere else. During a three-year period, the Senate stood by while McCarthy attacked the reputations of countless people with charges of being communist infiltrators, charges that were typically without foundation. The victims of his attacks on freedom and civil liberties ranged from church members to army officers. He also made unfounded attacks on President Truman and General George C. Marshall as well as other members of the Senate. Only after three years, when the Senate itself was attacked, did Johnson do something.

Although urged by many to take swift action, Johnson held back. At first, Johnson kept the conservatives happy by supporting McCarthy. After all, McCarthy's attacks and messages fit perfectly with the philosophy of Big Oil. Soon, however, Johnson began changing his tune, but only barely and then very slowly. He did finally say something to the effect that McCarthy was a "Republican party problem";[9] however, he still did nothing. Then, in 1954 after he had won the Democratic primary back in Texas, he finally took steps that extended over a five-month period. He named a special committee and slowly worked the committee's recommendation to a vote. McCarthy was formally censured on December 2, 1954, and his power came to a long-overdue end.

Interestingly, when the time finally arrived to censure McCarthy, money-man Clint Murchison Sr. was still telling Johnson to vote against censure. The right wing in Dallas was not about to quit, roll over, and die.

During his Senate years Johnson used his power to take care of himself and his friends in small, unnoticed, yet important ways. Clark came to town to finish up an SEC hearing on the death penalty for the Central and Southwest electric company system. Johnson cleared the way.[10]

For his radio-TV interests, Johnson made sure his company received all the frequencies and broadcast power needed and that competition was not allowed. He even made certain that Robert T. Bartley, Sam Rayburn's cousin, stayed on the FCC for twenty years to take care of the small matters that arose regarding the station.

When George Parr of Box 13 infamy appealed to the Supreme Court, Johnson arranged for Abe Fortas to help him. A standard part of the Johnson and Clark operating procedure, their *modus operandi*, was to get their lawyers to help their friends.

Perhaps the best measure of his conceit was when he took over twenty hard-to-get offices in the Senate side of the Capitol and adorned them for his pleasure, in the process spending over $200,000 in public money for decorations alone. His offices were aptly dubbed the Taj Mahal of the Senate.

From the beginning of his leadership days, Johnson's method of governing was appreciated by Eisenhower, who preferred working with him rather than dealing with the more conservative Republicans. The Senate's Republican leader was William Knowland of California, and Eisenhower found he was difficult to work with, largely because he was too closely allied with the conservative majority of the party.

Yet there was a far more important development in the overall scheme of American politics. By 1958 Eisenhower relied on Johnson for the moderate to progressive programs favored by the White House. The two men literally decided policy for America. Eisenhower was intent on retiring and was stepping gracefully out of power. Johnson was not planning to retire. He had other plans and moved to fill the vacuum Eisenhower gave him. Johnson took charge. By the end of 1958, Johnson was *de facto* president and the most powerful man in America.[11]

Johnson's friendship with Eisenhower was not acceptable to liberal Democrats who saw no action on their proposed legislation. In the process of working closely with the president, Johnson was turning himself into a national leader while carefully solidifying his Texas power base. By 1958, he was running for president as a moderate. In the process he lost the support of the national Democratic Party leadership. His efforts to please everyone never had a chance.

Johnson knew from early in his career that his lifetime ambition would not be easy to achieve as a senator from a conservative southern state. The reason rested with his friends in the oil business.

To fully understand the vindictiveness of Big Oil, even after all that Johnson did to serve every one of their interests and to listen to their right-wing rhetoric, one early example stands out. Conservative Texas governor Allan Shivers considered running for Johnson's seat in 1954 and was getting help from some of Johnson's favorite patrons in the oil business. Johnson's very limited support for Adlai Stevenson during the 1952 presidential election had given Johnson an instant reputation as a liberal in Texas, and he was having a hard time shaking what was considered a very bad resumé entry.[12] Ultimately, Shivers declined to run for one good reason. He knew how much money Johnson had.

At the same time many national Democratic senators were demanding legislation to reduce the oil depletion allowance. Johnson was in a difficult position with his own political party. The national liberal problem was far more challenging than the Texas conservative problem because it hurt his chances to be nominated for president. After the Democrats won control in the Senate following the November 1954 elections, Johnson became majority leader. He at once followed the easy middle road of getting along with Eisenhower, which solidified his support with Big Oil and gave him the image of a national leader able to compromise the positions of both Republicans and Democrats.

The effort did not work with the eastern "damned Yankee" Democrats. Johnson was, by his own political choices, alienated from the progressive majority in the Democratic Party. When liberal Paul Butler was voted in as chair of the Democratic National Committee, the members prepared a separate legislative agenda.[13] Johnson vigorously opposed those party leaders and none of their proposals were adopted. The Democrats would try again in 1959 and they would fail again. Johnson simply would not and could not promote the proposals of his own party. The abiding sense among national Democrats was frustration over Johnson's refusal to help them. The political fallout around Johnson's refusal to act gave the overall impression of an unmanageable party and called his leadership into question. His hopes for the presidential nomination in 1960 were becoming very slim, and he knew it.[14]

During all this political maneuvering the relationship with Eisenhower remained strong. The president preferred working with Johnson even when the possibility arose of a Republican taking his place as majority leader. During the interim when Texas Democrat Price Daniel was leaving the Senate in 1957 to run for governor, outgoing Texas governor Shivers had the opportunity to appoint a replacement. He considered a Republican, a move that would have cost Johnson the majority leader post and given Shivers a nice piece of revenge. Eisenhower advised against it. He wanted Johnson. Although Shivers was a closet Republican, he agreed and named a Democrat.[15]

Johnson kept working to stay on top of the conflict within his party. Progressive Democrats attacked Johnson in the press, complaining of the lack of leadership in the Senate. On the dilemma of Johnson being attacked by Democratic chairman Paul Butler, a liberal southern senator complained, "We are paying Butler $35,000 a year to try to destroy the Democratic Party while [Republican national chairman] Thurston B. Morton would do it free." For national Democrats located in the Northeast and on the West Coast, the assessment was that Johnson was not helping the policies of the Democratic Party.

The legislation progressives wanted included a civil rights bill, housing funds, and dam construction projects. At the start of 1959, Johnson showed little interest because Eisenhower opposed any increase in public spending. Johnson only passed legislation that helped his clients in Texas. As an example, he tried to pass bills involving construction that would benefit Brown & Root. Late in 1959 Johnson finally tried to push three housing laws and several construction programs. All were watered down to meet Eisenhower's concern over the budget. At the end of that key Senate session before the 1960 elections, a third housing law was substantially reduced to meet presidential approval and was finally approved.

There is one other part of Johnson's public history in the Senate. In 1956, Eisenhower wanted a civil rights bill protecting voting rights for blacks. After the expected battles with the southern senators, Johnson allowed a watered-down version to pass in 1957. The voting rights issue came up again in 1960 and another weak version was passed. That bill was the only controversial action taken in the short session that year as attention centered on the party nominations for president and on the fall election.

Johnson has been heavily praised for one bill or the other; however, in the long history of his service in Congress, very little was done to advance civil rights. The two bills passed in 1957 and 1960 are the sum total of his positive civil rights record in his twenty-three years in Congress. The real story about this record is what he did not pass and what was permitted to continue under his leadership.

By 1960, Johnson had only guided to passage moderate legislation acceptable to Eisenhower. He had also managed the business of the Senate so that, at least on the surface, there was an appearance of harmony. This good will was fast disappearing as the preliminary infighting over the 1960 presidential election accelerated in the public eye. Behind the scenes there was always a war going on. One was a war to protect Johnson, his interests, and his image as the effective leader. On the other hand, with the elections coming up and with the national party complaining, liberal senators joined in the attacks on Johnson, recommending "more open and spontaneous debate."

The fighting went public in a big way. Senator William Proxmire of Wisconsin proposed reducing the depletion allowance. Johnson promptly removed him from the important Finance Committee. After all, depletion was sacred. Proxmire, an independent-minded Yale and Harvard graduate, was one of the new progressives. He was just the sort of intellectual that Johnson did not like. He was a "Yankee," totally unlike Johnson the cowboy.

In dealing with a senator like Richard Russell, Johnson had a man he could understand. In the raw basics of human political behavior, Johnson could analyze and understand or by intuition could at least work with most "good old boys." There was something almost subconscious between men in power, connecting on common interests in a language few could understand. Specific commitments in writing were not needed. A gentleman's agreement was the only requirement, and those agreements were often so ambiguous as to be unintelligible. There were good reasons for saying little. Keep it vague. The agreement would be proven when the vote was taken. If circumstances changed, the senators, all very professional politicians, could vote together and still have room to give different explanations to protect their own positions.

This system worked particularly well during Eisenhower's presidency. Johnson knew when he had the president behind him. Although Eisenhower was not a professional politician like Johnson, he found it easier to hand many policy-making decisions to Johnson in that ambiguity that accompanies legislation. Typically, they reached agreement in private and then let their staffs put the deal into effect. The result wasn't democracy in action but it was Johnson's way because it avoided embarrassing political questions. In his view, the government best functioned like a corporate boardroom where the real decisions were made in private.

Proxmire was something new. He refused to go along with Johnson's dictatorial rules that decreed that senators rubber-stamp policies and positions that were designed and approved by him. Proxmire refused to accept the appearance of agreements among gentlemen. He also saw through Johnson's fawning to Big Oil. The test came when Proxmire vigorously opposed the depletion allowance. Johnson, in charge of all Senate appointments, in turn denied Proxmire his appointment to the Finance Committee. Under the rules of the Senate, Proxmire was entitled to his seat on the committee. Forget it. Johnson acted with his usual vengeance.

Most senators took this sort of reprimand silently because Johnson was a man to be feared. A senator's career would be far more difficult without the friendship of the leader. Proxmire, however, would not sit back and quietly accept the loss of his committee membership. Instead, he turned the rejection into a national scandal. He attacked Johnson publicly as a dictator and accused him of using his power for Big Oil in a way never before used by a senator. He also objected because no legislation could even come up without going through Johnson. Proxmire knew Johnson's inability to take criticism and knew how to deal a heavy blow to Johnson's ambitions. Although Proxmire's supporters in the Senate were forced to avoid him publicly, Johnson was hurt nationally. The gentlemen of the Senate were no longer cooperating with his program of compromise.

Or dictatorship of *padrones*.

Confronted with this criticism, Johnson turned to another controversial piece of legislation. He had other programs to promote and other cards up his sleeve. He passed the Landrum-Griffin Act to further restrict union power. Again, he was not helping himself nationally, particularly with Democratic union leaders, but he was using his power. He handled the bill easily by letting Kennedy work as floor manager while he set up Nixon to cast the decisive vote for approval. Johnson's hope was to come out on top with unions in a fight between Kennedy and Nixon, the two leading contenders for the 1960 presidential election.

Johnson kept trying to sit on the fence, but it was not working. For the 1960 election, he could not have it both ways.

Many of Johnson's friends wondered if he really wanted to seek the presidency in 1960. Some believed he did not have a chance as a southerner and that he knew it. Johnson tried to make Texas a western state, but no one believed it. Another important consideration was that Johnson had an excellent position in the Senate. Why give it up? And there was the health question. Should he take on the stress of the campaign? He had already had a serious heart attack, and Eisenhower had suffered one during his presidency.

Clark knew better. The plan for the presidency was underway and would not be stopped. There was a dilemma. The obstacle Johnson faced was based on his uncertainty between two elected positions. He clearly wanted to be president, but what if he ran and lost? He did not want to be out of office. If he campaigned again for the Senate, how could he be president? In Johnson's view, with his status as *de facto* president, the actual office was all he needed to complete his power.

Once again, it was up or out.

He wanted insurance.

In the fall of 1958, Johnson and Clark agreed that they did not need another all-or-nothing race either for the Senate or for the presidency. Already considered the most powerful man in America, the loss of the presidential election would force him into retirement. He was not ready for that loss of power. The answer was for Johnson to run for the Senate and to run for president. Amendments to the Texas election law would be necessary. For Clark as chairman of the Texas "round table" that governed the state, that part was easy.[16]

The arrangement was unusual and would have probably been very difficult to get approved in a two-party state. But for Clark in a one-party state, there was no challenge. He was such a force in the Texas Legislature that he could walk as freely as a member on the floor of its sacred chamber.[17] He was very effective.

That spring during the legislative session in 1959, Clark did the necessary lobbying to amend Texas law to allow a candidate to run for both offices. With Lieutenant Governor Ben Ramsey's help, Clark pushed the special bill through. Johnson could be elected president and senator, and then choose the office he wanted. The law also covered running for vice president. That office went with the presidency. In short, in the power politics that was Texas, Johnson had nothing to worry about during the 1960 election. He would not lose power.

The stage was set for the 1960 election campaign.

There is an interesting footnote to these presidential ambitions. As early as 1952, there were reports that Johnson was interested in the vice presidency. Aside from glowing articles in magazines that portrayed him as a likely and acceptable candidate, there were reports of a pact made with his close friend and segregationist Georgia senator Richard Russell.[18] Russell's position then was that the only way he could reach the presidency was through the vice presidency. He knew no southerner could be elected president.

Given his political shrewdness, the remarks should be seen as foreshadowing Johnson's decision ultimately to run for vice president if necessity dictated it. The conclusion about southerners was accurate; however, Johnson's discussion with Senator Russell only underscores his ambition to reach the presidency by whatever means were necessary.

Before leaving the instincts and motivations for Johnson during his Senate years, one fundamental, very serious underlying problem surfaced again, seriously threatening his long-term plans.

Health was a recurring problem for Johnson, particularly during times of extreme stress. In 1937, when running for Congress for the first time, he developed appendicitis. In 1948, at the start of the Senate campaign, he was sidelined with kidney stones. In 1953, he had all the early warnings of heart trouble.[19] Carefully concealed from the public, the episode responded to treatment. In 1955, when he was maximizing his leadership, the early warnings of heart trouble were ignored. Johnson had a severe heart attack. Although he recovered and returned to good health by careful attention to weight and quitting cigarettes, he was not in the greatest shape as the 1960 presidential election developed.

When the foundations of life are threatened, many people will change their lifestyles to protect themselves. Not Johnson. There was this remarkable determination, almost suicidal, to do everything—whatever it took—to achieve his goal. If he died trying to fulfill his ambition, that was acceptable. In short, nothing could interfere with his drive to become president.

The heart attack was deadly serious. Trying to ignore the early warning signs for almost a week, Johnson finally had to be rushed to the hospital on July 2, 1955. After a long hospital stay and enforced rest at his Washington home, he would spend the rest of the year at his ranch in Texas.

Johnson had confronted death and survived. He realized he had limits. He knew he had to act. Strangely, he also had this sense that he could not be stopped. He survived the heart attack. Fate was on his side.

In short, he experienced highs and lows in the 1950s, and he also confronted life and death. His determination did not end; it only increased.

For him, the presidency was do or die.

As 1959 ended, Johnson decided the presidency just might be in reach. Any independent outsider would know there was no chance for a man who sold out to Big Oil and to racism. The presidential nomination could not happen, not in the Democratic Party. Nevertheless, in the spring of 1960 and despite heavy obstacles, Johnson started his drive.

Election year 1960 appeared to be an excellent opportunity for whoever was the Democratic candidate. Richard Nixon was being groomed to be the Republican nominee. The Democratic nominee would likely be the next president.

While denying his candidacy throughout the spring of that year, Johnson was running strongly. Kennedy campaigned in the five mandatory state primaries while Johnson remained in the Senate, acting like he was doing his job and taking care of the nation. He was waiting for Kennedy to stumble, expecting him to lose to Hubert Humphrey in one or more of the state battles. Without a clear winner in the primaries, Johnson would formally enter the race as a statesman. He would be the party's salvation and its nominee.

Johnson also believed he had enough support in the South and in the mountain states to keep anyone from getting a first-ballot majority. He knew he had no support in New England or the Midwest. His political support ended at the Mississippi River going east and at the Mason-Dixon line going north. In addition, he did not count on the Pacific states with the possible exception of Washington.

Johnson decided on a "colonnade" campaign, to be the statesman hard at work in the Senate, doing his job for America. Whenever the Senate was in recess, however, Johnson was taking the pulse of the party, making speeches and visiting the professional politicians, to keep his backers fired up and to drum up more support. He was really hoping for a decision at the Democratic convention, complete with party bosses and smoke-filled rooms.

There was another reason to avoid the voters. Johnson could not afford to take a beating in any of the various state primaries. He knew he would lose. By staying hard at work in the Senate, he left the other candidates to run against each other, in the process cutting each other up, and leaving no one with a majority. Although Kennedy was the early leader, he was thought to be too young to win enough votes, and he did not have the power Johnson had with the elected leaders. Finally, having done little more than an adequate job in the Senate, Kennedy had very little record to support his candidacy.

Initially, the delegate count in the primaries seemed to keep anyone from getting a majority, justifying Johnson's campaign. Then Kennedy won a startling victory: Wisconsin. At that point, Humphrey considered withdrawing, but Johnson encouraged him to keep trying. Unaware of his stalking-horse status, Humphrey stayed in the campaign.

West Virginia proved to be a key state. There, however, even with the support of Senator Robert Byrd, the Humphrey and Johnson team was no match for Kennedy. First, Kennedy unmasked Johnson's plan to use Humphrey. In addition, Kennedy's very wealthy father engaged in some of the same tactics Johnson used in 1948 in south Texas. Joe Kennedy deposited large amounts of cash in the hands of local party bosses. Kennedy did not stumble. He carried the state. The victory opened up political territory that Johnson had been certain belonged to him.

The rest is history. For all practical purposes, Kennedy had the momentum needed to win the nomination before the convention even started.

The stage was set for the Democratic convention in Los Angeles, and Johnson did all he could to tarnish Kennedy's reputation. Although the usual dirty tricks were used, the only attack that drew interest was when his supporters questioned Kennedy's health. That issue laid the foundation for Robert Kennedy's long-term loathing of Johnson. The conflict between Kennedy and Johnson worsened during the convention as the two sparred for delegates and editorially debated the issues even though Kennedy had the votes.

The infighting did not last long. Kennedy emerged the nominee on the first ballot. Then he had to confront the big problem ahead, that of getting enough votes to win the national election. A modern progressive, he needed a conservative base, particularly in the South. In short, he needed Johnson. The majority leader was the natural for vice president.

Supposedly, Robert Kennedy actively and viciously opposed Johnson. In fact, this was the Johnson perception, not the reality. Jack Kennedy wanted Johnson from early on, and his brother lent his support.

Edward Clark was a delegate to the convention, and he later claimed to have brokered the basic deal with Joe Kennedy.[20] Johnson agreed to run as vice president, with the understanding that Johnson would be the nominee in 1968, or even in 1964. At best, this implicit agreement was, once again, an understanding between gentlemen. There were no guarantees. Johnson knew that there was nothing he could take to court. When Robert Kennedy veri- fied the proposal, Johnson was more at ease. If the election went to Nixon, Johnson would still be a senator and would have the inside claim to be the nominee for president in 1964 or 1968. In the final analysis, Johnson had no choice. The die was cast. He knew it. He agreed to be vice president.

As time would tell, Johnson could not wait. "Power is where power goes," Lyndon told Robert Kerr of Oklahoma before trading the power of the majority leader for that of the vice presidency.[21] He knew he would have the power he needed, and he knew the vice presidency was worthless. Why did he persist?

The infighting between Johnson and Kennedy did have lingering effects, leaving both sides unhappy with each other. From time to time, it flared in the campaign.[22] Still, the two worked together in a successful national campaign.

In Texas, as expected, two lawsuits were filed by Republicans, trying to force Johnson to run for only one office. Republicans knew that, with Johnson on the ticket, he would keep the key state of Texas in the Democratic camp. Without his name on the ballot twice, however, that opportunity would be far less likely. Voters might choose Johnson for Senate and vice president but might not vote for him just for vice president. Similarly, if Johnson ran only for the Senate, Texas just might not go for Kennedy.

As a result of the court threat, prominent Houston attorney Leon Jaworski joined the Johnson camp.

As Johnson's lawyer, Clark was responsible for the legal challenges, and the litigation was initially referred to him. Because of the obvious political overtones, Clark knew he should not handle the case. What he needed was an outstanding attorney, one with excellent credentials and a sterling repu- tation. As may be obvious by now, that lawyer was clearly not Edward Clark. The attorney of choice was Leon Jaworski, who would play an important role in the assassination investigation. When contacted by Clark, Jaworski did not immediately agree, saying he needed to give it some thought and to confer with his partners.[23] He mulled things over for a day, then reluctantly decided to go ahead. He knew of Clark's unsavory reputation, and he had little use for politicians like Johnson. Unfortunately, by accepting the case, he was for- ever tied to the fortunes of the Johnson-Clark camp.

Clark's problems had always been deep-seated. As a tough power broker in the old sense of pure power, he had little concern for niceties and finesse. He also preferred working in private, meaning behind the backs of the opposition. As a result, Clark had few friends with the media or with the public. He knew he could not take a public role in the campaign. Jaworski was chosen to bolster Johnson's image, not so much in court as in the eyes of the voting public. In addition, he was from Houston. Dallas was as tight as it could be with Johnson. More clout was needed in Houston.

Jaworski was the man for the job. He took charge and the two lawsuits were speedily dismissed. There never had been much of a case in either lawsuit.

With that representation, Johnson, Clark, and Jaworski became solid friends.

During the general election campaign, one crime did threaten to surface. Billy Sol Estes was already in trouble and unhappy. Clark handled it.[24]

In return for these good results, Johnson sent yet another letter of admiration to Clark. He readily acknowledged his complete trust in Clark.[25]

Behind the scenes, Clark worked mightily as finance chairman for the Kennedy-Johnson ticket in Texas. His promotion of the ticket was blunt and direct. Voting for Johnson for the vice presidency would be Johnson's "greatest opportunity to serve our nation and state."[26] Clark stated that the vice presidency was the place with the power although he clearly knew better. The vice president would never have even a fraction of the power of a majority leader. The long-term goal remained the presidency. Kennedy was barely mentioned in these fund-raising letters.

On Election Day 1960, Kennedy was chosen in a close vote that was undecided for several days. Nixon forces finally conceded, and the Kennedy-Johnson ticket was elected. The Boston-Austin axis prevailed. In Texas, Johnson carried both his races. The Senate race was guaranteed. The vice presidential vote in Texas was much closer. The Texas voters were supportive of him in either position, or both.

An interesting dilemma again presented itself. Johnson won both and could hold either office he wanted. He could remain in the powerful office of Senate majority leader or he could be vice president, an office he knew meant nothing. In his long-term drive for the presidency, after private consideration for several days, he made the only choice that truly matched his ambitions. He became vice president.

With that decision, Johnson knew his power as *de facto* president was ended. Within two months Johnson learned exactly how far he had fallen.

When Congress convened in January, Johnson had fallen from the top of the power order to the bottom, from acting president to a figurehead. His only role was to sit quietly, stay out of the way, and do only one of two things: vote in case of a tie in the Senate and be ready to become president.

Because the vice president presides over the Senate, Johnson tried using that office to retain power. When the new session was organized on January 5, 1961, Johnson was determined to run the show, to be head of the Democratic Policy Committee in the Senate. He was rejected by his former colleagues for the simple reason that he was no longer a member of the Senate.

Next, he sent Kennedy a long memo proposing that he be granted substantial new powers. Cautiously and politely, Kennedy rejected the proposal. The new president was sympathetic to Johnson's sense of pride and gave him the space program and, ironically, the civil rights office; however, he had no real power. He was out of the circle he had enjoyed only months before, of running the legislative branch and of telling the executive branch what to do. As he said, "I went from the mansion to the outhouse."[27]

Johnson's ambitions, however, did not end. He sat back and waited, ready to succeed to the presidency. As a man who never read a book while in office, he now had plenty of time to think. He needed it. His world of power was collapsing around him.

There were many problems to ponder.

At the same time that he became vice president, he took extraordinary steps to protect himself from the corruption he had practiced. Even during inauguration week, there was plenty to worry about. Now not only his ambition moved him forward but also a profound fear of failure and disgrace. He soon began to take the steps that would bring him closer to, and then into, the Oval Office. Once again, he had to avoid any scandal.

There is one more note. A Republican was elected to fill Johnson's seat. The new senator was John Tower. His main campaign supporter had been Edward Clark. Seems Tower had been a friend of the family and those ties remained strong.

> ... the love of power is the demon of men ... for the demon waits
> and waits and will be satisfied.
> —Nietzsche

Ask what you can do for your country.
—John Kennedy

10

Inaugurals

Kennedy's inaugural address on January 20, 1961, was a call to service, a signal for a new generation to assume leadership, and his words resonated with America. Tired of Eisenhower, shocked by the Soviet Union's Sputnik, angry and concerned about the Cold War, and determined to bring civil rights to African Americans, the time for action had arrived. The silent generation would be replaced with activists in many areas.

When Johnson was sworn in that same day, the new vice president was nervous, reading his speech poorly. He was unhappy to be out of power, but he had other problems that were far more serious than being inaugurated Vice President of the United States. His true concern that day was that his many schemes with unsavory partners would surface, and one was of particular concern, that of Billy Sol Estes. Trouble loomed ahead, this time threatening to be far more destructive than Doug Kinser had ever been. In 1960, Clark had contained the Estes problem. With the election now over, some very dangerous yet necessary steps would have to be taken to preserve Johnson's personal victory.

Ed Clark had arrived in Washington several days before the inaugural ceremonies were held, ostensibly to help celebrate. Clark never had time for such pleasures; he was always too busy exercising power. Among other things, he was there regarding the ongoing investigation by the Department of Agriculture into Estes's handling of cotton allotments. Although recognized as an asset for Johnson as early as 1958, Estes was by 1960 out of control, enriching himself from government price controls by innovative means. The USDA had been trying to get ahead of him and trap him, but Estes repeatedly changed his financing approaches to deceive them with new schemes.[1] Agriculture officials were doing their best to close the gaps in their regulations and to nail Estes.

Time and again, the successive cash schemes enriched both Estes and Johnson with large sums transferred to the then Senate majority leader's political reelection accounts. Those same sums were later transferred to the Brazos-Tenth administered by my law partner, Don Thomas, for "investment—20/20/40."

Johnson was thoroughly aware of the fact that Estes was the target of an investigation. In those days, word of criminal reviews were routinely reported to top government officials known to be involved with the suspect. Just to keep politics out of the investigation, nothing had been done by the USDA during the 1960 campaign; however, a top USDA inspector, Henry Marshall, had been assigned to see what was going on and his efforts were approaching critical mass. Johnson knew it was only a matter of time.

Two days before taking the oath of office as vice president, at an evening inaugural celebration at his Washington home, Johnson met in the back yard with Estes and Clifton Carter, Johnson's man at the Democratic National Committee and one of Clark's former army buddies.[2] A new snow had moved through Washington and the evening air was freezing. Despite the cold the three met outside because complete privacy was required. For the moment, the visiting dignitaries and well-wishers were forgotten. There was no celebrating.

Johnson was inwardly furious at Estes because the promoter did not know how to enrich himself from government *and* get away with it. Johnson, through Clark, knew how far to take corruption and how to use the attorney-client privilege to protect the money. In Estes's case, however, stolen land already subject to government control is not easily concealed. There was just too much of an audit trail. The problem for Johnson was the fear that Estes would disclose everything, that he would squeal. The soon to be inaugurated vice president of the United States was ready to agree to anything so that Estes would not take him down any further.

At the meeting Johnson was briefed by Carter and the three men then reviewed their options, none promising. Johnson was not yet convinced the final action Carter and Estes were suggesting was necessary. Agent Marshall would have to be "taken care of for good" only if he probed further and could not be deterred. The final decision was ambiguous but final, that Marshall must somehow be stopped.

The three men realized that a scandal like this was political poison; it would mean the end of Johnson's career. Because Johnson had further ambitions, that disaster could not be allowed to happen. Estes was told to get

Wallace to meet with Marshall and try to make the man see reason. If it meant a payoff, okay. Just get him to quit stirring up trouble. Estes was assured he and his family would be protected so long as Johnson was never mentioned.

In those vague terms, those code words used by the politically sophisticated, the three agreed that Estes was empowered to let Wallace take whatever action was necessary. Under that guise, a fatal mistake was made.

A few days later Estes reported back to Johnson that everything was fine as Marshall had assured him there were no problems. Johnson, however, was not as certain as the ever-optimistic Estes. Nervous for his future, he wrote the new USDA secretary Orville Freeman. Johnson got the facts—all was not well with Estes.[3]

Within two weeks, Estes insisted on another meeting. At the time Johnson was back in Texas. Because Estes had to be muzzled, Johnson agreed to fly to Pecos.

Early in the morning on February 19, 1961, Johnson called for his airplane. The day was heavily overcast, not safe for flying. His pilots had stayed in Austin the night before to be with their families, knowing they would have to fly to the Johnson Ranch in the morning; however, on seeing the weather, they did not want to fly in the thick fog.[4]

For further insight into the key event, in an exercise of the journalistic novel and an attorney's right in jury argument to develop a case, the discussion between Johnson and Clark is included in chapter 17 on Desperation at page 245. They ordered the pilots to make the trip and, at the same time, Clark realized the depth of the problems Johnson faced. As events turned out after that morning of deep fog at the ranch, Johnson had over a year before the scandal made the headlines.

The pilots had only a few hours. Flying into the muck, they looked for the ranch's airstrip. No luck. Flying too low as they looked for a landmark, the two pilots crashed and died on a hillside near Johnson's ranch. In the dense and rocky brush, the bodies were not recovered for three days.

Apologists for Johnson assert he was a compassionate man. This first tragedy of the assassination underscores, once again, the obvious fact that he was not. When the pressure was great enough, particularly as it was in this case where criminal disclosures were threatened, Johnson would do anything.

In the resulting investigation, Johnson was appropriately distressed, even traveling to the crash site to show his false concern.[5] The families of the two pilots were paid handsomely, the record was sealed, and the matter was closed. Within the next year, it would be reopened.

The death of the two pilots was a forecast of things to come. Johnson had killed men before. He was now responsible for the death of the two pilots, and he would in his desperation kill again. For him, there was no value to human life when it meant saving his future, his ambitions, his reputation, and his life.

Soon after, Johnson would take a military plane to Abilene, Texas, hoping for secrecy as he went to meet with Estes and his representatives. All went well until after the meeting when the plane went off the runway in Abilene and a report had to be filed. Questions were raised about what had happened, but Johnson simply ignored media inquiries.[6] After all, the necessary peace had been preserved with Estes, in person.

Over the next four months as USDA's investigation dragged back and forth, Wallace prepared for his fateful meeting with Marshall. An important first step had already been taken. Wallace had moved to California, giving him a new cover. His job was with the same group of companies. The move had been made just before the end of January 1961, right after Estes met with Johnson in Washington.

The effort at containing Marshall came to a head when, on June 3, 1961, Wallace arrived at Marshall's small ranch near Bryan, Texas. The confrontation took place in Robertson County, an agricultural area north and west of Bryan. Wallace had driven to the meeting, stopping at a filling station to ask for directions. He then went to the ranch where the two men met in a quiet, isolated place. They had to get to the heart of the matter at a location where they could talk freely, meaning without witnesses.

Wallace was not successful in bringing an end to the investigation. Marshall refused to cooperate. During the heated argument that resulted, acting pursuant to his vague instructions, Wallace attacked.

Angered at an inability to get Marshall to cooperate at all, Wallace viciously hit the man with a pistol. Marshall fell to the ground, the side of his head cut and his eye badly bruised. Since Marshall was unconscious, Wallace felt he had time to stage a suicide. Rigging a plastic liner to the exhaust and starting Marshall's truck, Wallace counted on carbon monoxide poisoning to kill. Marshall inhaled a substantial amount of the exhaust's fumes, almost a fatal dose. While the poisoning was underway, Wallace removed Marshall's personal belongings and placed them on the seat of the pickup.

Then Wallace panicked. The exhaust was taking too long. He reportedly heard a truck driving nearby. Although he saw no one and no one saw the crime, Wallace had to get out of there. There was a bolt-action rifle in Marshall's truck so Wallace used the man's own weapon to shoot him five times in the side of his lower torso. Three of the shots were sufficient to kill him. After the fifth shot, finally convinced Marshall was dead, Wallace left.[7]

At the first phone he could find, Wallace called Carter to let him know what happened. Carter told Wallace to stick around, to see if anything else needed to be done. They had to get word from Clark.

Later that afternoon, Marshall's cousin discovered the body. He was with a man from Cliff Carter's Pepsi Cola bottling company in nearby Bryan. The body was near the exhaust, the rifle nearby. Personal effects were on the seat of the pickup. There was no suicide note.

The next day, the coroner ruled the death was a suicide. Working with Carter, the local authorities took quick action to cover up the crime. There was no need for an investigation. Somehow, it was accepted that a man nearly dead could work a bolt-action rifle several times, to fire bullets into his own body. Only a fix with the justice of the peace could do it, and, as we have seen, that just happened to be Clark's *modus operandi*.

Wallace, believing everything was okay, incredulously went back to the filling station the next morning, to tell the attendant he had not really needed to go to the Marshall ranch and had not gone there. He then returned to California, his perfect cover, out of reach of Texas criminal authorities.

Over twenty years later, a grand jury was again convened to investigate the Marshall death. It concluded murder had been committed and that Johnson, Carter, and Wallace were the co-conspirators in the murder.[8]

Unfortunately, this startling decision by the grand jury was not issued until 1984. Johnson was not charged because he was dead. The other two conspirators had also passed on and escaped justice. Estes had immunity and told what had happened in 1961, from January in Washington to June in Robertson County. The key testimony and evidence was not just from Estes; the jury also heard from Texas Ranger Clint Peoples, who was finally able to obtain Estes's testimony and fit the facts together.

In the history of any event, what happened is usually told chronologically. Since the indictment report was not issued until twenty-four years after the murder, the all-important chronology of Johnson's motivations in 1961 may be difficult to appreciate. The public record is very different when Clark was not there in 1984 to provide the needed defense. By placing the grand jury action where it belongs, the motivations for what followed should be far easier to understand.

Historians will play games called alternate history. One will write the story of what would have happened if the South had won the Civil War. Another will write what life in America would be like if he was living in a nation where the South won and he was trying to figure what it would be like if the Union won. Still another imagines Hitler had conquered England and Russia.

Johnson's history has a similar feature. Events did not happen the way they should have. To avoid guessing, the belated indictment is placed where it belongs. What we have to do is assume that the indictment was returned in the summer of 1961 and that law enforcement acted in a timely and proper way. If so, one of those different worlds historians call alternate history would be still here, one in which John Kennedy remained president and Lyndon Johnson was convicted of murder.

Remarkably, even into the 1990s, apologists for the Warren Commission oppose efforts by Estes to tell his story. Houston attorney Doug Caddy was enlisted to seek immunity for Estes in return for his testimony to the Department of Justice. All was well when the government attorneys arrived to interview Estes. Notice was received, however, that a state district attorney had refused immunity for Estes, and the interview was canceled.[9]

We know what happened with the Marshall murder and with the indictment. The murder plan started with an argument. When Marshall proved intractable, he was killed. This may not have been according to plan and was done out of anger and frustration. Marshall had to be taken care of for good. Clark's agents then moved quickly to cover up. The murder was then buried for over twenty years. Only on distant hindsight do we finally have the benefit of knowing Johnson was behind the murder of Henry Marshall and that Wallace was the gunman. We also see how Clark worked his machinery to control the key legal system.

In 1961, in the real time of Johnson's history, Marshall was ruled a suicide. The local authorities readily accepted the ruling. The death of a federal investigator working on a high-profile political case, however, did not end there. Many eyebrows were raised in Washington, and the USDA was determined to keep looking. Fully appreciating the many political overtones, USDA officials knew a solid case had to be developed. Marshall's death required that his work had to be started over. The new investigators went to work. Robert Kennedy, as attorney general, gave his full support to the effort.

Estes would cooperate because he was sure he could convince them nothing wrong had happened. He could convince anyone, he believed, of anything. With his allotments program under intense review, however, money could not be obtained from the USDA. He turned to his ongoing scheme of leasing fertilizer tanks that did not exist. Again, he hoped to get enough money to pay off his debt. As it turned out, the clock was running on his timetable for financial recovery.

The Department of Agriculture investigation led to another meeting with Estes in October. Johnson was notified in early August 1961 that a meeting was planned. For Johnson, it was a clear warning that Estes still had serious problems. The notice also increased Johnson's suspicions about who was working against him.

Johnson had no choice. He summoned Clark to his ranch because extraordinary help was needed. The two men had to be alone. There could be no witnesses. This was more difficult because Kennedy had ordered Secret Service protection for Johnson, and Johnson did not want witnesses.

This meeting is off the record. In chapter 17, what happened at this critical meeting is set out. Johnson called on Clark for help. The problem was not just corruption by Estes; now it was murder by Wallace. Johnson knew something had to be done. He called upon the only man he trusted, the one he knew could do anything. Johnson asked Clark to take care of his legal problems, and there was only one way: the assassination of President Kennedy.

At the meeting, Johnson gave Clark the Secret Service policy manual for protection of the president, and the basic planning for the assassination commenced.[10]

In that fall of 1961 the Austin skyline was still dominated by only two buildings: the state's capitol and the tower at the University of Texas. Among the cluster of commercial buildings downtown, the Capital National Bank Building stood out.[11] Then among the tallest in Austin, it expressed an architectural power important to Clark and he looked forward to moving there. Still in the old Brown Building across the street, Clark's firm had outgrown the space. Besides, he needed more prestige, and the big building would give him that.

During the move Clark's longtime partner, Everett Looney, suffered a debilitating stroke and never recovered, dying in 1962. As soon as Looney became too ill to work, Clark assumed full power and ownership. He was majority owner of the firm's assets and its capital account, so he owned the business and the lawyers. A real workhorse, Clark demanded total commitment from his senior attorneys, and, now that he was their sole owner, the pace of business escalated. Never relaxed during the 1950s when Johnson had been majority leader and Ramsey had run the Texas Legislature, Clark's demands on his partners only increased during these very trying times for the vice president.

After meeting with Johnson at the ranch in August, Clark requested a memo on the protection to be afforded the vice president. Martin Harris, managing partner and legal technician, prepared one, carefully concluding that the protection was very good and that any assassin would never escape. The most likely review of what happened when Clark and Harris discussed the matter is included in chapter 17 on Memo at page 253.

The background to legal memos will set forth the importance of careful analysis. Lawyers tell you that doctors bury their mistakes but that attorneys' errors are written forever in the court reports. It's true. There is something compulsive about writing it down. Everything is reduced to writing, if for no other reason than to charge clients by the word; the longer the memo, the better the fee.

As wordsmiths who are also skilled in the legal rules of evidence, attorneys know what to record and what not to record. What is not written is not easily admitted as evidence. On the other hand, what is written is very convincing. Even a slip of paper is admissible, and the effect can be devastating. Knowing this, lawyers write it down. The absence of that same slip of paper could become all the more important. The total lack of evidence sometimes proves as convincing as a written record.

There is a more subtle reason to "put it in writing." What is done is written down because, in a suit against the client or in a malpractice suit against the attorney, evidence may be needed. The lawyer, never knowing what may happen in a case, will write it down far more often than he will ignore it. You just never know what the future might hold. Later, as circumstances require, you can use the written word or you can destroy it.

In a bind later? Need evidence? No problem. Write something down, slip it in the file, and cover your tracks. If need be, get rid of it.

There is a feature of interest to historians involved in this elusive question of proof. People tend to record what they do. Clark had this compulsion and so did Johnson.

A final note. The Harris memo on the security of the vice president
would become one of those documents that would never see the light of day.
Stored away safely in the top-secret penthouse records, it was never intended
for the public. Presumably it is protected by privilege. With that memo, the
beginnings of a monstrous crime were planned. Because of the privilege, that
memo and many more are protected as if buried in concrete and dumped in
the ocean.

But, perhaps, there is a way . . .

When Kennedy was inaugurated, Johnson started his drive to become
president. The plan began in a very different way than Johnson ever expected.
He had his ambitions, but of equal importance was the question of how to
stop corruption by Estes. As Johnson was further enmeshed in that effort by
Marshall's death, his only hope to keep from going down and out was to go
up and in.

So, on that inaugural date in 1961, Johnson heard Kennedy's call but
knew only what he had to do for himself and what he had to do to his
country.

> If men as individuals surrender to the call of their elementary
> instincts, avoiding pain and seeking satisfaction only for their own
> selves, the result of them all taken together must be a state of inse-
> curity, of fear, and of promiscuous misery.
> —Albert Einstein

He always remembered the little things, things you didn't even know he knew.

—Bill Wilcox (for Rayburn funeral)

11

Funerals

By late 1961 Clark seldom left his office. In his relatively perfect world, clients came to him, to do homage, to extract some favor, or to avoid some penalty. Seeing Clark was considered the same thing as seeing Johnson, and in most cases it was. In the greater scheme of things, they plotted how to use the courthouse and the legislature for major business advantages over that constant competitor, the public interest. The clients expressed their objectives or problems and let the superlawyer get the results they wanted. Some moves were brilliant and some were brutal power plays. Clark simply waited for the cases and there were many. He decided whether to act first or to wait. Then, counting on the imperfections of the human conscience that were also the imperfections of the law, he set out to win or lose as needed.

One awesome decision weighed on his mind. The assassination of the president was an unthinkable undertaking with unimaginable consequences, yet he had to think about it. The benefits of having Johnson in the White House were exceptional, an unmatched opportunity, and that eased his mind. As he weighed the risks and benefits, Clark was more comfortable. For a person without feelings for anyone, the process was not hard.

As usual, while Clark was busy, he could compartmentalize whatever he had to do and then work "the case" as needed.

Finally, in that first year of the planning, his analysis was still a game. It might never happen. After all, he still had time. The Estes case was well contained; he was still muzzled.

He told no one what was really involved. He analyzed the situation in vague and indirect terms with his partners, like the memo on protecting the vice president. With a legal framework in mind, he began the process of going outside the law firm, outside the lawyer-client privilege, by finding and testing people he would need.

He took his time. To be exact, he would take two years.

Late in October 1961 the perfection Clark enjoyed was suspended when he took those first critical steps outside the privilege.

Late that afternoon, Clark left his offices to see a criminal at the law offices of John Cofer, criminal attorney. Cofer was the Wall, the attorney who appeared in public for Lyndon Johnson during the 1948 election scandal, the attorney who represented Mac Wallace in the 1952 Kinser murder trial, and the attorney who would represent Estes during later trials.

One step in Clark's *modus operandi* was clear. He did business by selecting the attorney for key criminals involved in the Johnson era.

Cofer was an experienced lawyer because he had the ability to say little in public and to know that Clark would take care of things behind the scenes, out of sight, behind closed doors.

On the public record, where the media had access to what was going on, Cofer knew how to work a case. After all, the state had to prove its charges in any criminal proceeding. If the state made a mistake, Cofer caught the error and made it reasonable doubt. Any doubt was more than enough.

Cofer also worked the angles behind any criminal trial. Enlist the relative of a jury member to show up on behalf of his client. Drop an important news item in the jury room. Let the jury read articles slanting the case toward his client's defense. Sometimes, let them read about articles harmful to his client. Sometimes, let his client get a guilty verdict. Use the bailiff to find out what the jury was thinking, to develop his case, not with a so-called ghost or "mirror" jury sitting in the audience to evaluate the case. Find out from the real jury. See what facts he needed to develop or emotions he needed to play. See how the jury was going and, as needed, change their minds or reaffirm their beliefs. Make the case. Always fall back on Clark's special access to the court and the legal system.

Clark had the other needed elements in place for his criminal conspiracy, his racketeering of the courts and the law. There were the special requirements of secrecy, acting first, baiting the enemy, setting up official protection, and having the alibis ready. He had worked some miracles, or so it seemed. Right now, he was still struggling with a plan. How could he arrange an assassination and leave no evidence? How could he be certain that Johnson would not be implicated? Could he develop a plan so that the risks were minimized to the point where they were acceptable?

For this he needed very careful analysis, and then he needed the guts to go ahead.

Somehow, Clark had to set up a plan that would work, and, in return, he had to be sure it would pay him millions of dollars.

In the months ahead, as the "game" developed, it took on a life all by itself. In those two years it would grow into that final shape played out in Dealey Plaza and in the days following.

That afternoon with Cofer and Wallace, Clark developed his case. The details are missing but we know what happened. In chapter 17 on The Wall at page 254, the scenario is presented for this very important step in getting Mac Wallace involved. Wallace would join the game plan but would not know the details for two more years.

What happened that day in the friendly city was that the preeminent power broker in the state sank ever deeper into unlimited evil, toward assassination, a word that hisses with treachery, horror, and the unspeakable.

The first year of Kennedy's administration was the transition he had anticipated in his inaugural address, of a new generation taking over for the old. Much more would happen in the rest of his term. The last year of the Eisenhower years had been a solid preview of things to come. The first sit-ins began in Greensboro, North Carolina, and an American U-2 reconnaissance plane was shot down over the Soviet Union. We backed a rightist group in Laos that took power at the end of the year. Then, seventeen days before Kennedy took office, America severed relations with Cuba.

Kennedy had his problems. That first year was highlighted by failure of the Bay of Pigs invasion on April 17, 1961, his Berlin appearance, and Soviet resumption of nuclear tests in the atmosphere. On the space frontier Alan Shepard made the first brief, suborbital American space flight. The main problem for Kennedy was getting a legislative program underway. Johnson provided no help in the Senate, and Speaker Sam Rayburn could not ease resistance in the House. Then Mr. Sam fell ill and passed away on November 16, 1961.

Interestingly, Rayburn's funeral services highlighted the two years ahead for Kennedy. Many admired Rayburn, and his small hometown of Bonham in north Texas on the border with Oklahoma was the scene of a large gathering of very distinguished guests. Kennedy was there along with Truman. Half the members of Congress attended. Crowds estimated at thirty thousand paid their respects during the short service and burial on November 18, 1961.

Wallace was also in the crowds, sent there by Clark so his sniper would have an insight into presidential protection.[1] Clark also encouraged Wallace to help with a working plan.

Another strange death occurred at the end of 1961. Johnson's sister Josefa attended a Christmas Eve party at the LBJ Ranch, returned to her home in nearby Fredericksburg, and died during the night, supposedly of a cerebral hemorrhage. Despite state law, no autopsy was conducted. Billy Sol Estes later stated that Wallace murdered her.[2]

Within a year of Rayburn's funeral Kennedy would confront the Soviets in the Cuban missile crisis. A year later he would visit Texas. During those two years the plan to make Johnson president would be developed and fall into place.

For Clark, the key steps were made in 1961, and the broad outlines became clear. Keep the conspiracy small. Use people you can trust. A sniper or two would be required. Looking back, we can make the analysis that is routine in any criminal investigation. We can see how what happened would have developed.

> ... the value of motive must be examined ... [crimes] such as
> homicide, arson, and assault have what might be called "particu-
> larized motives," since they often relate victim to criminal. Once
> established, it would be practical to develop a short list of persons
> who might have a particularized motive; ...
> —Charles E. O'Hara and Gregory L. O'Hara, *Fundamentals
> of Criminal Investigations* (Thomas 1994)

Corruption, the most infallible symptom of constitutional liberty.
—Edward Gibbon

12

Bait

In the fourteen years since the fraudulent 1948 election, Clark had success-fully protected Johnson from political death by scandal. There had been sev-eral close calls, but the cover needed had been provided. The task had been easy in Texas. Clark's good-old-boy network and his now entrenched system of Texas justice were solid guardians. Even in 1961 with the murder of Henry Marshall, the Texas death had been contained. In Washington, however, the USDA was not letting Estes off easy. After all, one of their own men was dead. Several investigations were underway behind the scenes. At the same time Estes was complicating the coverup because he was looking for still more money.

The second Washington problem was wonder boy Bobby Baker. He started a vending company and, at the end of 1961, was looking for more money. During 1962, these two major problems for Johnson would worsen and Estes would make the news. Johnson's protection from scandal would begin to fall apart because the corruption was in Washington, not just Texas.

Following Henry Marshall's death, the USDA continued its investiga-tion, necessarily slowed by the loss of the key investigator. A new team had to get started and complete the record.[1] Estes got word of the ongoing audit and on October 18, 1961, he protested the renewed investigation. During the meeting Estes threatened to get help from Johnson and he mentioned Marshall's death.[2] Nine days later an internal USDA report reviewed the Estes problem and his threats. On December 15, the USDA's general counsel rec-ommended that Charles S. Murphy, undersecretary of agriculture, cancel the 1961 allotments for Estes because they were illegal. Murphy agreed and, on December 22, 1961, the allotments were canceled. In a bizarre turn of events, on that same day Murphy reversed an adverse recommendation and named Estes to the Cotton Advisory Council.

Estes responded to the cancellations with another show of force, paying for a dinner honoring Johnson and meeting with the vice president at the event and then at his home. On January 15, 1962, Estes met with Johnson top assistant Walter Jenkins, who called Murphy. At this same time Estes obtained three cashiers' checks totaling $145,015.

One week later on January 25, 1962, Estes met with Murphy again and the original requirement for a higher bond was waived. Three days later, however, Estes was ordered to produce seller certificates on the allotments. There was no deadline for producing the certificates and, as expected, they were never provided. From all appearances, Estes was back in good standing with the USDA.

The beginning of the end arrived for Estes, not from the government, but from a newspaper in Pecos, his hometown. This unraveling of the corruption is an interesting comment on the benefits of a competitive political system, a two-party state.[3] Dr. John Dunn, a dentist in Pecos, had accumulated damaging information on Estes and the public record of his security agreements. Dunn began printing the information in a local newspaper. On February 12, 1962, the newspaper published details of these loans, including allegations of one by Johnson to Estes. In addition, the U.S. attorney in El Paso had been alerted and was investigating Estes's recorded property transactions in Pecos. Federal law officers prepared to act.

Well aware of the problem for him, Johnson went underground and stayed far away from the press. He escaped to the horse races at a track owned by Murchison in California. FBI director J. Edgar Hoover was also present for the weekend. Johnson had to be insulated as fully as possible from the investigation. At the same time, Estes was struggling to raise money and keep the U.S. attorney from acting. On March 17, 1962, he met with Maynard Wheeler, the president of Commercial Solvents, which had financed his fertilizer tank leases. On March 28 Estes talked to Frank Cain of Pacific Finance. On that same day Estes tried to reach Johnson by phone but was not successful. He reached Carter three times, including one call to an unlisted number. Carter denied anything was done to help Estes.[4] In desperation, Estes tried to get a loan from Jimmy Hoffa. Nothing worked. The pyramided schemes collapsed.

On Thursday, March 29, 1962, Estes and three associates were charged with fraud.

When the Estes scandal broke, the public perception about the Kennedy-Johnson administration began to change. Immediately after the indictments,

Johnson denied knowing Estes except to admit having sent a patronage letter and to having met him in a reception line at a political event.[5] The denials were not persuasive and, over the next eighteen months, Johnson's adverse impact on President Kennedy became a primary concern in every political camp in the nation.

Kennedy would be annoyed with and embarrassed by questions about Johnson and his difficulties. The rumors started that Johnson would soon be forced to resign as vice president or that he would be dropped as the vice presidential candidate in 1964. Some Republicans began talking impeachment. On the public record Kennedy backed Johnson, saying the vice president would be on the 1964 ticket, if he chose to run. Johnson steadfastly refused to have any contact with the press. The wall of silence was at work. Behind that wall, Johnson was especially concerned because, once out of power, he was easily subject to criminal charges.

With the talk of scandal and the growing speculation among politicians about Estes, Clark knew Johnson was right—he had to become president. Something had to be done. Clark also knew he had to be paid and, considering the risks he faced and the benefits he foresaw for Texas companies, he intended to be paid a very large sum.

Clark had an interesting insight into the work he did because he knew how to get paid. Representing clients on statewide matters, whether in court or seeking legislation, what he arranged would benefit not just the one client but every company in a similar situation. For example, keeping the depletion allowance at 27.5 percent helped not just a few oil companies. It helped all of them. When cases arose, he would always get a group together to share in the expenses and to pay his ever-growing "group" fees.

With the plan now well underway for Johnson to become president, Clark knew many companies would benefit from less regulation, lower taxes, and a better business climate under Johnson. He also knew his friends in Big Oil would be the best to confront for money. He wanted to be paid because he knew that Johnson as president would mean Big Oil would be enriched the most, and he set out to get the necessary agreements. For most lawyers, this would be impossible. No one could go to their clients and the statewide organizations and say that they would kill Kennedy and that the clients were expected to help pay for the better business conditions that would result. Clark was far more devious or, as some would say, sophisticated. As we shall see, he could let the clients know in very vague terms that something was up and that he expected them to pay if the business situation improved. He would bait them with vague promises, and they would know that good results would flow to them. They would support him.

The top corporate leaders and the billionaires all understood these subtle workings of money and power.

Once the event occurred, and they would know when it did, then they would not only help in payments; they would also become part of the necessary coverup. They would help Clark by staying silent or by actively backing him.

Immediately after Estes was charged with fraud, the efforts at containment became more extreme.[6] George Krutilek was chief accountant for Estes and his many schemes. Krutilek had been questioned by the FBI on April 2, 1962, in El Paso. Two days later, his body was found in the dry sand hills near Clint, Texas, a hose attached to the exhaust pipe of his pickup. An El Paso pathologist said carbon monoxide was not the cause of death, and he called attention to a severe bruise on Krutilek's head. He was ignored. The coroner's ruling was suicide.

The next day, a federal grand jury indicted Estes and three others on fifty-seven counts of fraud. Not surprisingly, Clark's criminal attorney, John Cofer, was named attorney for Estes. Two other men involved with Estes turned up as suicides. Harold Orr committed suicide in Amarillo, Texas, and Coleman Wade died in Chicago. Much later, Estes testified that the killings were by Wallace to protect Johnson.

The Estes scandal continued in Washington. William E. Morris, an employee at the USDA, was fired for accepting gifts from Estes. Orville Freeman, USDA secretary, reported there were no special favors to Estes but that the FBI was investigating. Two days later, fines totaling more than one-half million dollars were levied against Estes. Labor secretary Arthur Goldberg looked into the Estes dinner for Johnson, to see if there were any favors. One month later Assistant Secretary of Labor Jerry Holleman resigned for accepting a loan from Estes.

The most ominous turn of events happened in Texas. On May 21, 1962, Bryan Russ, the Robertson County attorney, ordered a grand jury inquiry into Henry Marshall's death. In sessions extending over the next six weeks, the mysterious circumstances surrounding Marshall's death were examined again.

Texas attorney general Will Wilson, preparing evidence for the grand jury, complained that he had been unable to get any information from the USDA. The agency had prepared a 180-page report into the scandal but declined to make it available. Under the leadership of Texas Ranger Clint Peoples, the Texas Department of Public Safety was investigating. They developed a composite of the man asking directions to Marshall's ranch.[7] Searching the scene of Marshall's death, Peoples found a plastic wrapper in the brush and believed that it could have been used to guide fumes from the exhaust to Marshall's body. The .22 caliber rifle had been recovered on the day of the murder a year before; however, Peoples was developing another connection, back to Wallace and the Kinser murder, back to the weapons Wallace had available to him back in 1951. In June 1962 Peoples reported to the grand jury that Marshall was murdered and that he was still investigating.

The Houston medical examiner was called in to help, and he reported that Marshall was probably murdered, although it was a "possible" suicide.[8] He explained that at least three of the five shots were debilitating. In other words, any one of the three more serious shots could have killed Marshall. No matter how the shots are counted, five rifle shots were impossible.

The family also showed how Marshall could not have fired the bolt-action rifle into his side. The reach was too far and weakness in his right arm made it very unlikely.

On May 24, the FBI finally announced it would let the grand jury see parts of the USDA's internal report on Estes. In fact, less than 15 percent was disclosed. Robert Kennedy was keeping up the pressure while protecting his evidence and his brother.

The very next day Johnson flew into Austin and drove to San Marcos to receive an honorary degree from his old college. At the ceremony, Johnson kept his mouth shut. Even though he was the honoree, he did not give a speech. Just like he clammed up during the 1948 election fraud, he was silent; the less said, the better. After the ceremony in San Marcos, Johnson continued to avoid the press. He returned to Austin where he met with Clark and Estes. At that same time, Estes was also in town to confer with the Texas attorney general. Since Will Wilson had political ambitions that year, he would not cooperate with Estes.

The grand jury was carefully controlled. Despite the testimony from Peoples and the Houston medical examiner, by the end of summer the final decision was still suicide. According to some members of the grand jury, the prior ruling by the coroner had to be shown to be wrong and, in their opinion, that was not done. The prior ruling by Justice of the Peace Lee Farmer was never explained. When asked, he simply mumbled, "I just don't have nothing to say now." In other words he did not defend his suicide ruling. Still, the grand jury stayed with the suicide ruling. Later, a key member of the investigation was elevated to postmistress by Johnson.[9] In those days, a good job was the main reward for political favors.

Finally, as we have noted, over two decades later, Estes's testimony and the evidence Peoples had was presented to still another Robertson County grand jury. They would have indicted Johnson. Texas Ranger Peoples would also testify in proceedings a year later to change the Henry Marshall death certificate from suicide to murder.

The Estes case can only be explained by the terms of the deal he reached with Johnson. There is nothing in writing but the results show the oral arrangement. Estes was provided an attorney and a solid defense. His expectation was that he would be acquitted. Clark and Cofer, however, could not let him off because, just as with Wallace in the Kinser murder, he would be free to talk and he knew too much. If he were convicted, he would learn to keep his mouth shut and do his time. In addition, as a convict, his word would always be doubted. Estes would be able to keep his family together, living in relative comfort. Following any prison term, he could return to his former life and his family. Estes would keep his end of the bargain.

The FBI turned the focus of its investigation toward Johnson. The conflict for FBI director J. Edgar Hoover was between Johnson, his friend and neighbor, and the USDA, an agency he had an overriding duty to represent. The investigation was half-hearted, at best.

The FBI wanted to know about the plane crash in 1961 in the fog and about allegations concerning payoffs to Johnson.[10] Clark selected Thomas to be the witness. The deposition with two FBI agents started innocently enough. Thomas talked about the three separate transfers of ownership that took place in the week following the plane crash. The agents then wanted information on Brazos-Tenth Street Corporation because, after trying to decide where to put the title for ownership of the plane, Thomas had mistakenly run it through the laundering company. The previously undisclosed deposition underscores the problem for Johnson. The investigators were looking into the man at the center of the rumors and allegations, and the man with the motive behind what had happened. The man who should be untouchable was becoming the focus of the investigation.

During the deposition, Thomas successfully denied any connection between the plane's ownership and Estes. He was then stating how there was no money in the company when a phone call conveniently interrupted. The agents were ordered to leave. The testimony was suspended, never to be completed.

Thomas did not have to invoke the privilege and his skills at covering up for his client were dramatically displayed on the record. At various times, he knew nothing, dodged the question, took advantage of loopholes, or just parsed his answer. In other words, like any good lawyer, he knew how to lie successfully, and he did. His testimony was the closest law enforcement ever came to the grand conspiracy headed by Clark for Johnson.

With indictments against Estes and with the grand jury looking into the death of a federal agent, the Democrats knew something had to be done even if it meant looking into one of their own. Senator John McClellan of Arkansas announced that his Permanent Investigations Committee would hold hearings into the Estes case starting June 24, 1962, and promptly subpoenaed Estes to testify. Just before the hearing date, Estes demanded an immediate trial on the indictments against him. This meant he could not be called to appear before McClellan's committee.

The Senate's inquiry extended over the summer with McClellan showing how the rifle could not be used for suicide.[11] On July 27, 1962, one witness testified that some of the Estes money was used to purchase a grain elevator in Hereford, Texas, and that Johnson was to get one-eighth, the standard Texas oil royalty. USDA representative John E. Bagwell reported that Estes talked to Johnson about cotton allotments. That night, Johnson called the witness, supposedly asking for a copy of his memo but having the intended effect of intimidation.

The committee was unable to get Estes to testify and adjourned until he could appear. Johnson followed the testimony every day, and transcripts of the testimony were delivered to him hourly. The cumulative effect of the hearings, suspended until Estes could attend, was that Johnson was slowly sinking with Estes.

During the summer of 1962, Clark decided that Wallace might be too hot for the role of sniper. A new shooter may be needed. Or two shooters might be necessary. The assassination plan he was developing remained flexible.

Deciding to find another insider, Clark called Leon Jaworski for help. The two men had become good friends following the litigation letting

Johnson run for two offices in 1960. The call dealt with what Clark called a private matter. He said he needed a man capable of collecting debts and enforcing security rights for the bank. Big debts were involved and he needed a man who would do anything. As always, Jaworski tried to help his co-counsel and attorney for the vice president. Jaworski had a suggestion. The man recommended is identifiable but there is not enough evidence to make that final determination that he was indeed an assassin. For now, the man will be named "Junior" while we await additional disclosures.[12] Jaworski made the recommendation to Clark with no questions asked. He was never aware of Clark's plan, and Clark did not reveal anything, protecting Jaworski almost as much as he protected Johnson.

Junior would have been a contemporary of Wallace. Clark needed two men who could work together and who shared a common paranoia of government. The two key shooters would have to meet the criteria he needed.

In interviewing for additional shooter candidates that summer, Clark also called Hubert Hardison "Pete" Coffield, his friend on the prison board. Convicts were excellent candidates for dirty work. Released on probation, they had to do what they were told to do or be returned to prison. Men on parole were also good for what Clark needed because they knew the underworld. Coffield checked around and suggested several.[13]

Clark checked the personal records of the men and decided Junior was the best man to work with Wallace. Clark then interviewed his new recruit, and the man was enlisted with the same vague talk Clark had used with Wallace. Clark explained that he needed a capable man to help with some client problems, someone who was familiar with rifles. He needed Junior to work with others planning a protection system. The offer was made and Junior accepted.

Clark then introduced his new man to Wallace. The extreme Marxist and the new man would later find that they had a common interest in bringing the government down.

That fall, Wallace took another step, one Clark had demanded when he first mentioned the need for snipers. Clark wanted cover for a sniper and that called for a patsy. Wallace talked to several men and decided they had to be tested. After meeting Junior, Wallace joined with him to check out the likely prospects, to see if they had a rifle and if they could shoot.

One other problem arose that summer. Clark knew that illegal slant-hole wells had been discovered in the east Texas field. The wells were drilled on property outside the oil reservoir but the drill stem had not gone straight down. It had been deviated so that it penetrated the oil reservoir from the east. When the illegal wells were discovered, the Railroad Commission did nothing. A federal complaint under the old Hot Oil Act convinced the Department of Justice to act. Robert Kennedy's men moved in and indicted the suspects.

The Strouds of Henderson, Texas, were the main suspects and they showed up at Clark's offices for help. Clark sent them to Martin Harris, who recommended they plug the holes, destroying any evidence of illegal wells. The plugging process meant concrete was poured into the hole so that the illegal direction could no longer be traced. Clark and Harris said the commission would let the Strouds keep a few wells.

The Strouds refused this offer and were later indicted, tried, and convicted. Still others showed up for help and took Clark's advice. Working with east Texas attorney Bailey Sheppard and oil producer Harry Lewis, Clark took one tract with Lewis's L&G Oil Company for payment. Most of the thirty-one illegal wells on the land were plugged. Three were allowed to stay on production.

Seven years later, the little company would be the basis for the bonus Clark sought for his arranging for the Kennedy assassination.

During this spring and summer of 1962, John Kennedy was busy. Having weathered the steel crisis in April, he enjoyed "happy birthday" from Marilyn Monroe on May 19 in New York and terminated his contacts with Frank Sinatra on August 3. That fall, when asked by the press, he could say he was enjoying the presidency immensely. He did not mention his only problem: Johnson and his unsavory friends. The public perception of the administration was not good because of the scandals. Something dramatic was needed to improve Kennedy's image, and the benefits of dropping Johnson had growing support among White House staffers.

That fall, the news still centered on Estes. He was indicted several more times. Then his case was set for trial and he made a strange move. In the excitement of the big trial, Estes tried to get rid of Cofer as his attorney.[14] Cofer refused to be fired, saying he had already been paid. The next unpublicized issue between lawyer and client was whether Estes should testify or not. Estes was ready to talk, believing he could still charm anyone. Cofer was just as determined to keep Estes quiet, for the sole purpose of protecting

Johnson. Estes might say too much and make things worse. On the other hand, Estes might convince the jury and get off. Like it was with Wallace in the Kinser case, there was no alternative, Estes had to be found guilty. Then anything he said later could be discredited. Estes grudgingly agreed. Cofer stayed with Estes.

In late October the trial started, Cofer refused to put Estes on the witness stand, and Estes was found guilty of swindling on the mortgage deals. He was sentenced to eight years. Unlike the Kinser trial, Cofer did not request that the judge enter a suspended sentence. Estes would serve time in jail. So, the trial was over, the appearance was that justice had been done, and Johnson had not been involved in any way. By agreement, Estes could say nothing against Johnson; he did not.

During this time, Estes had placed his company in bankruptcy, and the estate had been purchased by Morris Jaffe, a San Antonio attorney closely allied with Johnson. Estes would be protected.

In October, however, all the rumors and scandals were forgotten. The Cuban Missile Crisis started on October 20, 1962, and dominated the news for the next month. As the nation recovered from the threat, Johnson's problems only slowly trickled back into the newspapers. There would be little breaking news until 1963. Johnson himself continued to remain silent and out of sight.

A seemingly minor event occurred in 1962. Arriving in Fort Worth on June 14, Lee Harvey Oswald returned from the Soviet Union, bringing a wife and child with him. With the help of his brother, Oswald found a place to stay. He then got a job and tried to settle into life back in America. He soon met a Russian émigré named George de Mohrenschildt, who befriended Oswald and introduced him to friends in the oil business. One of those contacts was Sam Ballen, a geologist who owned a small natural gas company in the Texas Panhandle. Because Ballen needed help from Clark, he would inadvertently provide the lead for Wallace to enlist Oswald.

While Estes was going from underground to front-page news during 1962, Bobby Baker was starting the business that would be the second major embarrassment for Johnson and, when the news broke, it was the final impetus in the assassination plan. At the end of 1961, Baker and Fred Black, a lobbyist for North American Aviation and a next-door neighbor to Johnson, formed Serv-U Corporation to provide vending-machine services for employees at aerospace conglomerates. Landing all vending machines at the three major companies in the business, they co-signed a $175,000 loan from alleged mob sources.

In July 1962 the secretary to the Senate opened his Carousel Motel six miles north of Ocean City, Maryland. Johnson arrived by limousine. The motel would be immortalized as an entertainment establishment for senators. On October 8, 1962, a friend purchased a condo in Washington for Baker's lady friends and, that same month, Johnson returned to the Carousel by limousine. Ellen Rometsch of East Germany, wife to a military attaché with the German Embassy, attended. She would serve as madam for the women, and she would visit the White House on several occasions.[15]

The pressure of work and new investments would catch up with Baker in 1963. Even the energetic secretary to the Senate could not keep up with the demands he placed on himself. In addition, since Johnson would later deny any contacts with Baker after he became vice president, consider what Baker said in April when he talked to Johnson about help for storm damage to the Carousel: "I went to the best friend I ever had around the Capitol . . . Vice President [Johnson]."[16]

In 1963 Baker's finances and his services system would collapse.

Meanwhile, Clark stayed busy on several fronts. Particularly important was the need to enlist Big Oil and to get them to promise to pay. So, that November 1962, Clark, acting counselor and paid adviser to Delhi Petroleum, a flagship company for Clint Murchison,[17] was dining with Murchison, the owner of the company. The discussion between Clark and Murchison is reviewed in chapter 17 on Bait, at page 261. The proposal was very discreet, very protective of both parties, and seemingly meaningless. Clark's letter raising money for Johnson in 1960 is similar in its mystery, a proposal fully understood only by the sophisticated men in power.[18]

The deal with Big Oil was closed.

In December 1962, just before Christmas, Lee Harvey Oswald was still only one of several contacts Wallace was pursuing. Clark had heard that word was out in the Russian community about a radical Marxist who had recently returned from the Soviet Union. Sam Ballen was the man giving the information.[19] In one of those strange turns of events where two things happen at the same time, Clark also learned about the same discontent from friends in Georgetown. One had attended a party given by George de Mohrenschildt, member of the Dallas expatriates from Russia. Oswald had been there and had been a topic of conversation for several days. A rarity, he was a former marine who had renounced his country and then returned.

The way in which Wallace and Oswald met is not known. We know they did meet and that they were together on the sixth floor of the Texas School Book Depository when Kennedy was shot. The first contact would have been the most important. It had to appeal to Oswald. When that pitch, that first impression, was made, Wallace would know what he needed to bait the man to join him. The scenario is developed in chapter 17, Patsy, at page 264. As time would prove, this most important contact with Oswald was made, and the necessary cover was in place. Wallace's newly discovered Marxist friend would prove to be erratic, hard to control, and dangerous. In the greater scheme of things, however, there was time.

By the end of 1962, the planning had moved forward, lurching, still uncertain, but soon to be irresistible, taking on a life of its own, one that would become more and more impossible to stop, and more and more necessary for Johnson's survival. Perhaps it was a result of the speed with which humans habituate, triggering some instinct that becomes set in the mind. With determined men like Clark, Wallace, and Oswald, that goal-directed set of mind soon admits of no mistakes and of no return. The plot becomes unstoppable, as the conspiratorial machinations take on a life of their own.

So, one year after the Estes problem broke, Clark had the key steps for the conspiracy in place. Two shooters were ready. Several patsies were available to be used as might be needed.

Now detailed planning was needed. Those details depended on events in 1963. Clark remained flexible. The details would be worked out over the next eleven months.

> When rich villains have need of poor ones, poor ones may make
> what price they will.
> —Shakespeare

> The devil is in the details.
> —Anonymous

13

Details

Eleven months before "that day" as Clark would later call it, the foundations for the assassination were in place. Details could now be planned.

Throughout 1963 the pressure to act intensified. Estes was convicted a second time and was unhappy, threatening to talk. Baker was moving deeper into trouble. The TFX fighter controversy was about to explode. The Rometsch sex scandal simmered, involving a communist spy angle that could be devastating. At any moment something might break and Clark would be too late, unable to do anything.

Bobby Baker would prove to be the main new problem. In January he sold the Carousel Motel to Serv-U Corporation. Then, he and Johnson flew to the Dominican Republic to attend the inauguration of the new president there. In April he purchased a home in the Spring Valley area of Washington, D.C., where he lived next door to Johnson and to lobbyist and partner Fred Black. In May, still promoting deals while running the Senate, he lobbied Governor Pat Brown in California in a meeting set up by Johnson.[1]

Murchison owned the Delmar Race Track, a purchase he made partly as a favor to FBI director Hoover. Legislation was being considered regarding competition at the track and Murchison was opposed. He preferred a non-profit organization to run the racetrack and Baker was trying to help. Baker then tried to expand into hotels in the Caribbean, drawing on his experience with the Congressional Hotel in Washington. Clearly overextended, the business ventures began to crumble when a breach of contract lawsuit was filed September 12, 1963. With that public filing, the press got word.[2]

At the same time problems with Estes persisted. The federal court proceeding began March 11, 1963, and ended seventeen days later. Estes was convicted of mail fraud regarding mortgages totaling more than $24 million. A month later he was formally sentenced to fifteen years for fraud and conspiracy. Senator John McClellan announced he would resume hearings so that Estes could testify. Then on July 8, 1963, Estes reported a shot was fired into his home in Pecos. A .22 bullet was recovered but no arrests were made.[3] Estes got the message. He moved his family to Abilene and waited for the outcome of the appeals in his criminal convictions.

The first news about a possible trip by Kennedy to Texas was announced when Johnson, during a meeting with Dallas newspaper editors on April 23, 1963, said the president would visit that summer. Johnson also addressed the heavy criticism in Dallas about Kennedy saying the president was only the pilot for the nation. He added, "At least wait until November before you shoot him down."[4]

Three days later Johnson was at his ranch for United Nations Day. Although all delegates had been invited, only thirty attended. Clark and Murchison were also there, on business that had nothing to do with the UN.

Murchison had called Clark, suggesting he needed to meet with Johnson. Arrangements were made for them to get together at Johnson's UN function.[5] Murchison flew in. He knew change was on the way, he knew it would be good for him, and he knew he would pay. He just wanted to know more. Considering Clark's evasive manner, he knew something big was up, something very big. He could guess some of it, but his curiosity got the best of him. He wanted to know the details. Most importantly, he wanted to know Johnson's involvement. Was the vice president backing Clark? Since he had to know, that meant talking to both personally.

Clark realized the man was intrigued and just had to have the inside story. Johnson, however, told Murchison nothing. In fact, Johnson said very little about anything. Again, the signals were subtle. Only a few words were needed. Then there was a nod here, a glance away there, a fixed stare when something was said—all gestures and words that carried a code all understood, or were willing to accept on a guess. Johnson merely confirmed what Clark had promised, that whatever was done, would be a good thing for Murchison. No one said "assassination" or "kill Kennedy" or anything close. The same general outlines Clark had ambiguously presented were discussed again, making it clear that something very important was going to happen. When Murchison left, he was convinced something very big was in the works, and he agreed that, if it helped him, he would pay, willingly. Murchison liked the approach. Like drilling a wildcat oil well, there was nothing to pay if nothing was produced. He was a gambler and, with Johnson's reassurances, he agreed to the vague plan, a shot in the dark.

A few days later in Houston on April 19, 1963, Edward Clark was recognized by the super-secret Knights of San Jacinto, the blue-ribbon organization of the Sons of the Texas Republic.[6] Clark was granted honorary membership because of his deep ancestral background in Texas and his apparent wealth. He was also a key member of the secret elite power system for Texas. One interesting function of the group was to monitor Texas history carefully. Stories derogatory to the state's accepted heritage as they understood and wanted it would be squelched as heresy; only favorable accounts and reviews were acceptable. The members were masters of the spin before the idea of spin had even been invented. They knew to slant the media reports and history books, and they knew how to keep it slanted. Nothing could question the greatness of the fugitives who founded the state. Old Cactus Jack Garner, the former vice president, was another of the dedicated reactionaries of that former era still being preserved.

Later that same day, Kennedy's trip to Texas was planned among the power brokers of Houston, meeting in Suite 8F of the Lamar Hotel. Clark was a regular visitor and had a standing invitation.[7] Again, he was advising the key power brokers that great things were going to happen. He expected their support, and he intended to be paid. Clark suggested in those vague terms and words of art that few understood, those same code words and gestures, that something very important was about to happen. The group was receptive. Clark had alerted them before of "big things" and had always been right. They also understood that, if something happened to their benefit, they would pay.

Clark also attended to participate in the planning for Kennedy's stay in Houston during the forthcoming trip.

By April of 1963, the plans were still under development. Clark's snipers could act in any one of several cities on the visit. The decision was clear the assassination had best happen during the Kennedy trip to Texas. Any attempt in Washington, D.C., was out of the question. Other states did not have the supporting legal system. The critical preliminary investigation had to be controlled and friendly. The crime had to be in Texas. Dallas was not a foregone conclusion. The assassination could be in any one of the cities on the Kennedy itinerary in Texas.

Oswald had also been busy. He purchased a pistol by mail, which was delivered in early March 1963.[8] He also ordered a 6.5 mm Mannlicher-Carcano rifle. When it was delivered on March 12, 1963, he had the weapons needed for an amateur sniper, for a killer in training. The rifle was for the longer shots, and the pistol was for "personal protection" if there was a need for a shootout during the getaway.

Wallace decided he needed a test shot by Oswald. The future patsy was just not reliable. This time, however, the target was to be real, a part of the still-evolving plan. Once he participated in a crime, he would be a committed member of the team.

Edwin Walker was a former army major general who had resigned following remarks critical of Kennedy's policies. Walker would be an excellent target for Oswald, a Marxist who hated America. If he shot Walker and escaped, his later participation would be perfect. Kennedy would be killed, not by Johnson's right-wing friends but by a dangerous left-wing zealot. Walker would be the test.[9] Oswald agreed and took the shot. What happened is reviewed in chapter 17, in Test, at page 267.

The day after the attempt to kill Walker, Oswald learned his target had not been injured. Apparently, the bullet hit the window frame and was slightly deflected. It missed. A dejected Oswald left for New Orleans. At the time Wallace was pleased to see him gone.

On June 5, 1963, Kennedy, Johnson, and Connally met in El Paso, Texas, and agreed the Texas trip should be in the fall. The objective would be political, to raise money and to get ready for the 1964 election campaign. There was also a hope by Kennedy that the trip would ease the party infighting among Texas Democrats. Johnson, liberal senator Ralph Yarborough, and conservative governor John Connally were fighting bitterly over appointments and everything else. Texas polls showed Kennedy slipping. He needed Texas to vote for him in November 1964. Kennedy committed to the special efforts needed, spending time in a state that, because of Johnson, should have been easy for him and the Democrats. He should not have had to campaign in Texas. Johnson should have been able to take care of the state. Obviously, Johnson was not worth the trouble he was causing.

Clark had two more important meetings that summer of 1963. One was to be sure Johnson did what he would have to do when the shooting occurred. The other was to take care of the details with Wallace.

The sniper shots were the way to do it. Clark was fearful that one or two shots would not be enough. Whatever else happened, Kennedy had to be killed. He decided a front shot might be necessary and would be important insurance. If the sniper from behind did not succeed, the one in front would be ready. Besides, the shot from behind would divert attention from the front. It should work.

The cover had to be perfect. Somehow, no one could get into the building before the snipers shot. Then they would have to have cover for the escape. The real shooters had to get away. They had to move quickly and be in a secure place within seconds of the shooting, before the police could react. To complete the cover, there had to be real suspects. The patsies would fill that requirement, serving as cover and then being killed.

After considering what would be the best cover, Clark decided to use the Secret Service. Not real members of the president's security force but Clark's snipers posing as Secret Service members. The best way was to have men with Secret Service credentials on the scene. From the manual Johnson had provided, Clark had the inside information he needed. He knew how to proceed.

He called his old army buddy and longtime friend, Clifton "Beau" Carter, and asked about the Secret Service. In the course of the conversation, he also arranged to get badges. Carter informed him the members wore lapel pins with a certain color-coding that changed every day. The system provided instant identification that would be hard to duplicate. Clark was promised the badges. He would get them. He also decided that, in the terror following the shooting, "pocket credentials" would do the job. They would do without the lapel pins.

In this and other subtle ways, the Secret Service was injected into the plan and would play a key role in the assassination. The false credentials would provide the necessary protection before and after the shooting. In one of those strange twists of fate, the Secret Service did not do their job for President Kennedy, but their imposters did provide the cover needed for Vice President Johnson to become president.

Johnson was deeply involved in the mounting political criticism and pressure. He was often the target, fast becoming *persona non grata*. On June 18, 1963, Robert Kennedy had publicly embarrassed Johnson. Johnson was chair of the Equal Employment Opportunity Office President Kennedy had set up by executive order. Robert Kennedy attended and openly attacked

Johnson. The message was that the vice president had no future with Kennedy, with the Democratic Party, or in government. The public display underscored the fact that Johnson was not only afraid that he might get caught in the Estes or Baker scandals. He might be dropped from politics. At the time, he simply could not take any more criticism, and his anger toward the Kennedy "boys" worsened.[10] At the time he remarked about how much he enjoyed the vice presidency. Later he admitted the two years and ten months had been "the worst days of my life."[11]

Soon after, there was another private meeting at Johnson's ranch. The vice president was certain he would be dumped, and he had to know what Clark was planning. He needed to know when action would be taken. After all, two years had passed and the politics for Johnson had only worsened. Something had to be done.

Clark was not about to let Johnson know any of the details. The assassination had to be a complete surprise to Johnson. Under no circumstances would he know what was planned. This time, when Johnson called for Clark, the lawyer decided to "woodshed" the vice president. The process was like taking a child out behind the woodshed to paddle him until he learned to do the right thing. In the case of witnesses for lawsuits, the woodshedding was to be sure they said the right thing, that they told the correct story before a jury. What the witness said and did had to be shaded just right. Woodshedding was never perfect. There were always mistakes in controlling the truth. The process usually worked, was standard for trials, and included all public appearances. When it worked, it was very convincing. For purposes of convincing juries, in the conflicting testimony so often presented, there would be just enough slanted testimony to win.

Clark had one more worry detail, a small one in the overall scheme of things but an important one. He knew how pleased, even ecstatic, Johnson would be when the assassination occurred. He wanted Johnson to react with surprise and then express the correct condolences for the Kennedy family with appropriate assurances to the nation. The best approach for Johnson would be the usual one, to say and do nothing. As things turned out, Johnson would react in good form except on three minor but telling occasions. As Clark had feared, Johnson would overreact.

In that last meeting between Johnson and Clark in the late summer of 1963, this type of convincing denial in the form of plausible conduct or body language was another detail. Johnson could not ever be implicated. Even if Clark were discovered to have played a role, he would never implicate

Johnson. Johnson had to be above suspicion. Clark was the perfect fall guy should an investigation ever get that far up the ladder of the conspiracy. After all, that was their working agreement since the two men had written each other in the 1949 memo and letter. The conspiracy that had started twelve years earlier still worked. Johnson trusted Clark, period.

The woodshedding went well. Clark believed Johnson had been made as ready as was possible. Johnson knew there would be an assassination attempt in Texas but he knew none of the details—time, place, plans, execution, escape, coverup. He understood he was to play it dumb, to be the wall, to say and do nothing.

There was another detail. The rifles needed to be the same caliber, easily concealed, and collapsible, like paratroopers' special rifles or long pistols. That, too, was handled.

Finally, there was the detail of the payoff. Clark had to come up with a fee appraisal. What fees could he justify? He decided an acceptable fee was keyed to what Treasury Secretary Robert Anderson had received when he left private business to run the national economy. The payoff was also keyed to the estimated benefits to Big Oil. Those extra breaks included import quotas, natural gas pricing, and the depletion allowance. Just maintaining those benefits was always worth something to the paranoid members of Big Oil. Clark knew his Dallas group could afford it; they had plenty of money and could hide much more.

Clark also considered the fees charged by lawyers in 1963. Standard lobbying fees for top lawyers in Austin were $10,000 monthly. Over Johnson's two terms of eight years, that was $1 million. Anderson had been paid three times that total, with payment made in complex land rights.[12] Clark wanted more. Clearly the risk justified $8 million to be paid over Johnson's expected two terms of eight years. He also knew he would receive better retainers just as the president's lawyer, and there would be the payments outside the law firm.

When Clark arrived at a monetary value, he was pleased. There were many ways to disguise the payments. The details would be worked out later, when the benefits from Johnson's presidency were realized.

The power he exercised let Clark ignore right or wrong. To him, what did it matter? Some consider this detachment amoral. More to the point,

Clark's detached relativity regarding values meant that anything could be rationalized and thus justified. No need to be judgmental. Nothing was relative to any standard of right or wrong. Of course, the assassination plan was certainly not amoral. It was not just immoral. It was a criminal act of the worst kind. To Clark, however, it was just "doing what you gotta do" and then justifying it. He would shrug and add, "Just like any other lawyer, I gotta earn a living."

Johnson had that same moral code. There was no right or wrong to his ethics. Just do what you have to do. Perhaps the pathological qualities of the man will be appreciated. He had no emotional attachments and no empathy. Based on his entire experience, from inheriting the values of the frontier to a childhood of delinquency and running away to years of ignoring large segments of his electorate, there was only one attachment and that was to himself.

In their system of an apparent relativity of values, of nothing absolute, both Johnson and Clark are too often viewed as amoral, not worried about what was right or wrong. They believed themselves above reproach and that any wrong they did was acceptable. For them, the only balancing of moral values was the outside risk of exposure. When the immoral, illegal, and unethical happened, they felt it was "business as usual." They would shrug, "That's all."

The two men had power. They routinely abused that power. As two men facing the legal problems Johnson had, there was never a doubt what to do.

The summer of 1963 proved to be the most dangerous to date for Kennedy in a very personal way. That June in England, the Profumo scandal had angered the House of Commons and had scandalized the nation. John Profumo was the British secretary of war and he had been involved in a sexual relationship with an expensive call girl.[13] He had then lied to the House of Commons about what had happened. The woman, Christine Keeler, also had an active relationship with the naval attaché for the Soviet embassy in London. The attaché was undoubtedly a spy, seeking whatever secrets of state he could find from the British and from their closest ally, the United States. Profumo was forced to resign. A subsequent investigation revealed that several other ministers had been involved. When the investigation finally ended, the ministry of Prime Minister Harold MacMillan was nearly destroyed.

The same type of scandal almost made news in Washington in August of 1963.

Bobby Baker had been able to provide entertainment for the Senate and lobbyists through his accommodations at the Congressional Hotel, the Quorum Club, and the Carousel Motel. The arrangements were handled very carefully. Women were always present and available; however, none provided sex in the sense of payment up front. To the contrary, payment was expected later and included such extra benefits as room and board. In short, the women were not "professionals" in the strict sense of the word. They were semi-pros. They knew that, if they complied, they would be paid.

This uninhibited Washington sex climaxed with the beautiful Elizabeth Taylor look-alike, Ellen Rometsch.[14] Rometsch was from East Germany but had married an officer in the West German army and had come with him to Washington where he was assigned as an attaché to the German embassy. At the height of the Cold War and less than a year after Cuba was freed of missiles, Johnson was delivering the woman to Kennedy.[15] Taken directly to the White House for John Kennedy's open and obvious indiscretions, Rometsch had been a frequent visitor during that summer of 1963.

The rumors inevitably started and, soon after, Kennedy and Johnson were alerted by Hoover. According to the FBI, Rometsch apparently had ties to the Soviets. Hoover brought the information directly to Robert Kennedy and the president promptly ended the relationship.

Both Kennedys also agreed additional, very dramatic but very quiet steps had to be taken. On August 14, 1963, Rometsch was forced to leave the country. The Immigration and Naturalization Service, a division of Robert Kennedy's Department of Justice, stepped in and she became a diplomatic *persona non grata*. Confined by Immigration authorities, she was conveniently kept under wraps and away from the press until, on August 21, 1963, she was deported.

The sex scandal may have been carefully silenced but the Republicans and the media had heard the rumors. Both groups were charged up and ready for anything that might help their respective causes. They just needed witnesses. Rometsch was gone, behind the Iron Curtain. They would not be disappointed, they hoped, when Baker's troubles hit the news. If he fell and started talking, they would have all they needed to win the 1964 election.

After sixty days of dodging bullets and soon after Rometsch disappeared, Baker's business problems were disclosed. Litigation was filed and the press reported it. In the ensuing uproar, the Democrats rose to Baker's defense, saying he was doing a good job as secretary to the Senate; however, when Baker refused to appear before a Senate committee to explain his situation, he was given no alternative. On October 7, he resigned.

One week later, Fred Korth, Johnson's choice as secretary of the navy and the man responsible for the purchase of oil for the American naval fleet, was forced to resign. A clear conflict of interest between his duties and the awarding of the TFX contract to Convair led to his downfall. Interestingly, he had served as attorney in Marguerite Oswald's divorce case, representing the husband.

One week later Kennedy was again asked if he would dump Johnson. Kennedy replied, "The idea is preposterous."

The next day the Senate commenced hearings into the Baker scandal. Johnson denied any connections with Baker but disclosures revealed the many ties between the two men. Fourteen months later, during President Johnson's term, Baker was convicted and imprisoned.

Estes remained quiet. Clark had arranged another payment system. The media noted the convict was doing just fine, was not bankrupt, had a Cadillac and cash in Abilene, and was being taken care of by, no surprise, his attorney. The trust arrangement through Brazos-Tenth was at work. On October 9, 1963, attorney Jack Bryant revealed he made the purchases for Estes's benefit. Again, because of the privilege, no one could discover who paid Bryant.[16]

For the president, his official and unofficial duties in November proved to be demanding. His wife had been away after losing a baby prematurely. She was not happy with her husband's lifestyle in Washington. In Vietnam, the Diem regime had been assassinated, and the new military leaders were not yet proven capable of running the nation and keeping the communists out. On top of it all, Kennedy had "Lyin' Lyndon" to worry about.

The details for the Texas trip were announced on November 3. Kennedy's visit to Houston was for one main purpose, an appreciation dinner for Albert Thomas, a member of Congress. Kennedy would make other visits, announced four days later, to include Fort Worth, Dallas, and Austin. San Antonio would be added a few days later.

The McClellan committee announced the end of its hearings except for one item: the record remained open for Estes. Two days later, on November 11, Estes said he would not testify.

At a press conference three days later, Kennedy urged the press to keep the Baker and Korth problems separate. By then, the problems Johnson posed for Kennedy were clear. As Johnson's standing worsened, he knew Kennedy had once described him as "a riverboat gambler," and had added, "The man is incapable of telling the truth."[17]

A big question has intrigued investigators and historians on the issue of whether Johnson would be dropped from the Democrat's presidential ticket in 1964. Kennedy's secretary noted that, the night before leaving for Texas, the president had said Johnson would be replaced and that Terry Sanford of North Carolina would be the next vice president.[18] No corroboration has been provided. As recently as 1995, the Assassination Records Review Board took up the issue. They were unsuccessful in verifying the remark. The record appears to be that Kennedy did say he was dropping Johnson. The real issue, however, is not whether Kennedy said it or even if he did, did he mean it. The only issue is whether Johnson believed it.

He did.

When Kennedy left for Texas, Johnson's future was clearly in the balance.

Oswald had returned from his excursion to New Orleans and then Mexico City, arriving back in Dallas on October 3, 1963. Separated from his wife, he took a room at the downtown Y and applied for unemployment. Seeking work over the next week, a job was found for him as a warehouse worker at the Texas School Book Depository on October 14. He would not miss a day of work.

When Clark heard about the final trip plans and the best location for the shooting, he had one more thing to do. At the time Kennedy's plans for the Texas trip were moving forward. There had been a limited announcement that the president would be in Dallas. Few knew the details.

Carter provided the information Clark needed. Most important was to be sure the motorcade passed down Elm Street, directly in front of the Book Depository. It did. For Clark, Oswald's return was all he needed.

Kennedy arrived in Fort Worth at 11:15 P.M. on November 21, 1963, and spent the night there. A ninety-minute drive away, at Clint Murchison Jr.'s estate in Dallas, a meeting was underway. Described as an after-hours party, it was in fact a smoker, a time for men to relax, have a few drinks and a good smoke. They would also take care of some business, and then have the fun and games. Privacy was assured and a good time for the good old boys was guaranteed.

Clark's appearance and remarks at that meeting are not of record, but the best rendition of what he said is included in chapter 17, at Fees, page 270, where we take a look into the heart of the conspiracy on that final evening. The men at Murchison's estate were told something would happen, and, when it happened, they knew to keep quiet. Clark's manner of baiting worked this way. When the unknown event happened, they said nothing, becoming part of the coverup. No suggestion was ever made by those silent participants that departed from the Warren Commission conclusions, until now.

For Clark, the stage was set for the assassination.

Strangely, the Kennedy charisma included a muted confidence that inspired a hostile reaction from the men who envied him. Often political opponents complained the president thought he could do anything and that nothing bad could happen to him. The next morning in Dallas, that Kennedy confidence was fully justified by the adoring crowds. But a jealous hostility was also at work among his impassioned opponents, and they had a subconscious but profound determination to prove he was not a superman, that he was not bulletproof.

> Those in possession of absolute power can not only prophesy and
> make their prophecies come true, but they can also lie and make
> their lies come true.
> —Eric Hoffer

... that time may do him justice ...
—from *Profiles in Courage*

14

Assassination

One of the most publicized and researched days in American history began quietly enough, with a cold front that pushed a light rain through Dallas and then cleared, leaving a beautiful morning in its wake.[1] History has since treated the assassination with controversy, surrounding every moment in Dealey Plaza with alternative theories about what happened. Although agreement is hard to find on the varying details, the basics are reasonably clear.

Kennedy arrived with Jackie at Love Field in Dallas at 11:37 in the morning. The politicians waiting for Kennedy included Johnson and Governor John Connally. The planned motorcade through downtown Dallas was to end at the Trade Mart where the president was to address a group of community leaders and businessmen.

Because the skies had cleared, Kennedy's limousine did not use the bubbletop. The motorcade formed with a pilot car one-quarter mile ahead of the main convoy, a lead car that included the Dallas police chief, the president's car with the Kennedys and the Connallys, a follow-up car with eight Secret Service agents, and Johnson's car, which included Mrs. Johnson and Senator Ralph Yarborough. Other vehicles trailed behind.

The motorcade departed at 11:50 and proceeded to Main Street in downtown Dallas. The welcome was very satisfying to Kennedy. He did not carry Dallas in 1960 and had been notified of hostile posters and news ads distributed that morning. There was no overt hate. The crowds provided a warm reception.

Near the end of the motorcade, Main intersected Houston at Dealey Plaza. The cars turned right onto Houston and went one block to Elm where they turned left. The president's limousine was directly beneath the Texas School Book Depository as it proceeded slowly down Elm. The time was 12:30.

Shots were fired after the car had passed the depository. One hit the president from behind and exited through his throat. The shot was not fatal but could have been paralytic. Bullets also hit Connally, penetrating his right shoulder, breaking a rib, emerging to hit his wrist and then lodging in his thigh. Then another shot hit the president, apparently from the front, penetrating his right forehead and causing instant death. The shots were in rapid succession over a period of approximately six seconds.

The president's limousine hurried to Parkland Hospital where Kennedy was pronounced dead at 1:00. Johnson, the new president, then drove to Love Field where he was officially sworn into office aboard *Air Force One* at 2:38. He insisted Jackie Kennedy stand beside him and she did. By that time, the casket with Kennedy's body had been placed on board. Immediately after the swearing in, the plane took off for Washington, D.C.

When the shots were fired, a flock of pigeons had flown from the depository, directing attention to the building. As chaos took over in Dealey Plaza with people running, falling, or just watching in amazement, officers on the ground hurried to search the area; however, the depository itself was not sealed until later. One officer ran around the depository. Another hurried up the slope toward the pergola and the picket fence running along the top of a grassy knoll. One officer, Marrion L. Baker, entered the depository and, with supervisor Roy Truly leading him, the two men went up the stairs, heading for the top of the building.

On the second floor Oswald was confronted by Officer Baker. Truly stated Oswald was an employee so the officer moved on with his search of the building. Oswald left the building and boarded a bus. Because the traffic was heavy, he got off the bus and, four blocks away, reportedly hailed a taxi to take him to his boardinghouse. He arrived there about one that afternoon.[2]

Oswald stayed only a short while, then left. About a mile away he encountered a patrol car, and, after a brief discussion with Officer J. D. Tippit, Oswald shot him. The killer then hurried several blocks and entered a movie theater without buying a ticket. There officers confronted the suspect, and, after a brief struggle, arrested Oswald. He was taken to police headquarters, arriving shortly after two that afternoon.

A search had commenced at the depository. On the sixth floor, three empty cartridge shells were located in the southeast corner by the window overlooking Elm Street. A carton of books was placed there with three cartons stacked by it, providing an apparent resting place for aiming a rifle. A rifle was found behind boxes stacked near the stairwell on the northwest side of the sixth floor.

Oswald proved to be a former marine who had defected to the Soviet Union, only to return with a wife and child. He had held several jobs in the

Dallas area and then had gone to New Orleans for work. In late September, he traveled to Mexico City, returning to Dallas soon after and taking the job at the depository.

After two days in the city jail, arrangements were made to transfer Oswald to the county jail. At 11:20 Sunday morning, as he was being escorted to a waiting police cruiser, a man suddenly approached and fired one shot into Oswald's abdomen. The gunman, Jack Ruby, was immediately arrested. Oswald died at Parkland Hospital.

Ruby was subsequently found guilty of murder on March 14, 1964, and sentenced to death. On appeal, the conviction was reversed. He died of cancer on January 3, 1967, while awaiting a new trial.

The Warren Commission was appointed by Johnson to investigate and report. The members completed their work on September 24, 1964, concluding that Oswald acted alone to kill Kennedy, that Ruby acted alone to kill Oswald, and that there was no evidence of a conspiracy.

There was a conspiracy. The plan carried out on November 22, 1963, started with the conspirators getting in place, taking the shots, and then escaping under cover of false Secret Service credentials. Oswald was a patsy. Over the years, a substantial sum was paid Clark as the chief conspirator. What follows is the Clark plan for Johnson as it was executed in Dallas on November 22, 1963.

Wallace was up early that morning. He had stayed in the back room of his father's home near downtown Dallas, preparing for the biggest day in his life. His gear was ready, a dark business suit, a special rifle with scope, now dissembled and hidden under his suit jacket. His Secret Service badge was in his front coat pocket. He smiled, appreciating how the assassination fit into his theories of government, politics, the economy—everything. He had become the perfect instrument of revolution and chaos. His life was ruined. He was ready to ruin the lives of many more people.

He quickly put on the suit, slipped his pistol in the holster under his arm, got the bullets for his men, and left the room. He looked up the hall, for a moment thinking of his family and then he quickly left the house, got in his station wagon, and drove to meet Clark for one last time. The two men would not meet again until Wallace left California in 1968. The meeting was brief and is recounted in chapter 17 on Cash, at page 271.

When Clark and Wallace parted company, the lead sniper stepped into the windy, drizzling cold morning and into history's darkest pages.

Clark drove back to the hotel to pick up Don Thomas. Clark had driven up for a meeting with Murchison and to make one last contact with Wallace. He had insisted Thomas ride with him to Dallas but stay away from the meetings. Keep it close, he knew. Thomas did not need to participate. Clark just wanted someone to talk to on the drive back to Austin. If need be, Thomas would be someone to drive.

Clark's most trusted partner knew nothing about the assassination plans. Thomas knew something ominous was up but he had no details. By evening, he would suspect Clark's role. Within a week while in Washington to be on top of the investigation, Thomas would know almost exactly what had happened.

As Clark drove south from Dallas through the early morning dawn, he recalled Murchison's meeting earlier that week. He had been pleased with what had been said. Those men knew what they were doing. Nothing more need be said. The die was cast, the stage was set, and the actors were moving into place. Like any court appearance, this "case" would soon be over. Today, the only law was his law.

In Waxahachie, they stopped for breakfast and Thomas took over the driving. When the two attorneys arrived in Austin, Clark was ready with an alibi. He would be in his office the rest of the morning.

"Junior," the second sniper, had not slept. He had shut his eyes and thought he might have dozed but there had been no refreshing sleep. He had the training and the discipline to kill a man, but today's shooting would not be an easy thing. The little man was on edge, wired to shoot. He took comfort in eliminating a left-winger from government, but political cause no longer motivated him. He was a loner and he enjoyed any way of life that would give him obscurity. He wanted to go underground, deep underground. What he had to do today would mean just that, a life in darkness with a solid retirement fund to take care of him.

His uniform for the day was strictly business. A suit and tie, the perfect cover, with pockets inside the jacket for his two-part barrel and the stock, holsters under his arms for the pistol and scope. When his uniform was complete, he would be the perfect Secret Service agent: big chest, arms slightly raised for the weapons under his arms, and the badge ready to use. He was ready. The look was complete, a look of authority to intimidate and convince anyone questioning his presence at the scene.

The room he had in downtown Dallas was only a few blocks from the Dealey Plaza. He would drive there later in the morning and meet up with Wallace. He only had to act like what he was supposed to be, a Secret Service guardian for the president.

An hour away at the Blackstone Hotel in downtown Fort Worth, Johnson awoke from a troubled sleep, one that left him tired and irritable the rest of the morning, a hangover that would keep him miserable until the adrenalin went to work the moment he heard the shots. Exhausted but on the edge, he knew something was going to happen, and he was, as usual, running on nervous energy.

The tall man looked in the mirror, rubbing his whiskers, hoping Clark had the plan underway. He shrugged at the thought. He knew Clark would do the job. He had no details. When would it happen? Would it work? He always knew everything that was going to happen. This time he did not and he was worried. Maybe it would be in Austin, he wondered?

For Johnson, the time had long passed for action, and he was in a deep depression. Baker had resigned because that damned vendor deal had fallen apart. Estes was waffling every which way, making new demands on Johnson. His loyal supporters in Texas, the ones he had so carefully cultivated, were leaving or gone. Most of his friends in Big D were gone. His east Texas supporters were drifting away, and his few remaining political friends in Texas were fighting, arguing like school children when they should be united. In short, his world was falling apart. The depression came first and was soon to be followed by the desperation.

Because these many unknowns had encircled him, he was exhausted, angry, his thoughts muddled and uncertain.

The man knew the politics that entrapped him and he knew the key players that would free him. He knew what was going to happen. He knew it would happen. It had to happen. He just did not know the details. And he had to know. He could not let go. Every detail belonged to him. But he did not know any of them.

He shook his head. Clark was right. He could not know. Tensing the stiff muscles in his shoulders and stretching to ease the pull across his chest, he took a deep breath and began dressing.

The plans for the president included a short speech outside the hotel in Fort Worth followed by a breakfast where he was presented a Stetson cowboy hat. There he commented that it took Mrs. Kennedy a little longer to get ready in the morning. The schedule then called for a quick flight to Dallas Love Field, a motorcade through the downtown, and a luncheon speech. That afternoon, he would fly to Austin and participate in a dinner celebration at the Municipal Auditorium, a big fund-raiser.

With all these activities going on, Kennedy was also trying to make peace between Johnson, Connally, and Yarborough. He had worked with the liberal Yarborough already. Connally he would handle. His biggest problem remained Johnson and he did not know yet what to do.

He looked forward to a campaign against Goldwater, the apparent Republican favorite. Progress versus reaction. He was comfortable because he knew the voters favored his ideas for progress. He grinned. The issues did not matter. The voters just liked him, and that was all he needed.

There was one very real, very personal problem. He had to make peace with Jackie.

After getting the depository job, Oswald had rented a boardinghouse room in southwest Dallas. On the night of November 21, 1963, however, he had stayed with his wife. The next morning, he was up early, hurriedly completed his preparations, and was gone before the others arose. The wife had berated him again but he had not beaten her. There was too much crowding his mind. In his new determination, he was strangely at ease, committed; nothing was in his way. Of all the men, only he and Wallace were truly ready.

Today, he would be natural; it's just another day. The old rifle was folded into the wrapping paper he had taken with him from work. Carrying his package to the home of B. W. Frazier, he was waiting when his co-worker and driver came out. They left for the job, for the depository.

Dallas police sergeant D. V. Harkness arose early. He had to be on the job, to protect the president. He looked forward to the duty and the parade. Waiting for his morning coffee, he noticed it was not a bad day, cold but clearing. Great day for a parade. By noon, it would be sunny and a comfortable sixty-eight degrees.

At the lunch hour, Thomas wanted to go home, but Clark told him to stay. He did.

Despite the influence Clark had, he was careful. He let others know what he could do and he got his way. On the surface, he was always reasonable and always working for his clients. What he did, he believed, was no more and no less than what any other power broker would do. He could live with that appearance of power while being very lonely and very private. No one really knew what he did.

The newspaper was on his desk, its headlines announcing Kennedy's visit scheduled for Austin that evening. He opened the louvered windows and surveyed the majesty of downtown Austin. Then he closed the windows and went to his desk. The morning mail was there. Not interested. A stack of newspapers to read. Not interested. He sat in his judge's chair and leaned back, waiting.

That night he was scheduled to speak at the dinner honoring "JFK/LBJ" and the famous "Boston-Austin Axis." Soon, he anticipated, that celebration would be cancelled. Grimly determined but confident, he smiled. He was where he should be. The doorkeeper. Waiting for the president. A dedicated supporter of Kennedy's reelection. His alibi was complete.

The ringing phone brought him out of his reverie. He did not answer it but leaned forward, to sort through the mail and then to pick up one of the morning newspapers, the *Dallas Morning News,* his favorite.

Wallace drove to the home of "Bill Yates," another conspirator not yet wholly identified, and made sure the man was up and ready to follow him in his car. They drove slowly.[3] It was early. Wallace knew they had plenty of time. Do not arouse suspicion. Act normally. Yates was to secure the site for him, be the Secret Service imposter by the building. The sentry-to-be was a trusted companion, the closest of close friends, the one man he had trusted before and the one he knew he could trust again. Yates would not disappoint Wallace. After all, the man's task was simple, just to stand guard, to keep people away from the getaway door behind the depository while Wallace was inside. The Secret Service credentials would do the job.

As Wallace pulled into a parking space behind the depository, he saw Junior. Yates pulled in behind Wallace. Ten o'clock in the morning was not too early to be seen. The men would be there, recognized as rightfully on the scene to protect the president. If bystanders came too close to their locations, they would be directed to move away. Junior had removed the suit jacket that held his weapons. He looked casual but businesslike, and certainly not a threat to anyone.

Parking the car on the east side of Houston, Wallace got out and the two walked over to talk briefly with Junior. They checked their badges and looked around, saying little. They knew what had to be done. Cigarettes were taken out and lit as they lingered by the car, waiting. As they talked, Wallace casually handed Junior the bullets. The plan was that, with the three men using the same bullets, identifying the shooters' rifles would be harder to do.

At eleven, they quickly reviewed the plans once more. Yates would stand guard at the depository while Wallace was inside, to keep people from entering and to secure the stairwell, keeping it open from noon on. After the assassination, the credentials would give them safe exit.

Junior was the backup sniper, ready to shoot if Wallace failed. He would be in the thick trees along the wooden fence reaching to the triple underpass, on the back side of the wall. Using his fake Secret Service credentials, he would keep bystanders away.

Wallace nodded and the three parted company, Junior to walk up the slope and stand by the pergola, Wallace and Yates to position themselves behind the building. As he walked Wallace kept glancing back at Junior. Then Junior was past the pergola at the top of the grassy knoll, past the wall and out of sight.

Wallace was concerned about one thing. The patsy. Oswald was presumably upstairs at work but even that was not certain. Wallace shrugged. He knew, of course, that no plan was ever perfect. At least the basics were in place. Wallace had decided he only needed one patsy.

Dallas police officer Joe M. Smith arrived at the downtown station early and hurried to his assigned location on the north side of Dealey Plaza. He would be on the street corner in front of the depository. He had to be sure there were barricades in place, then control the crowd before the motorcade arrived, keeping the people back as the limousines went by, and, when the parade was over, be sure the traffic cleared.

The early morning rain had ended and a clear day with a bright sun warmed the cold air. He smiled. An easy day today.

Wallace slipped into the depository from the north side, through the loading platform, into the lower floor. It was about a quarter after eleven. The east elevator was ready and Wallace rode it up to the sixth floor where he left the doors open, locking it off.

Moving cautiously in the large room cluttered with boxes and building materials, he ducked back when he saw the men still working in a nearby area.

Cursing, knowing he had only an hour, he carefully slipped away from the elevator shaft until he was shielded by the stacks of books. As Wallace waited, he assembled his rifle and stayed in place.

Just before noon, Roy Truly, the superintendent, appeared and told the five workers on the sixth floor that they could leave for lunch, giving them time to see the motorcade that was due sometime soon. All but one took off, riding the west elevator down. Oswald stayed behind, telling them to send it back. They did.

When it returned, Oswald locked it off, moving the door so the grate was up, keeping it from moving until released. Locked off, the elevator could be moved only with that lever. One escape route was ready, or so he thought.

The men on the sixth floor were now alone and together. Wallace stepped out from behind the stacks. The two talked briefly, then moved across the floor to get ready. Oswald walked with Wallace to check out the boxes stacked in the southeast corner, to get ready for the shooting. Behind the wall of book boxes, Oswald had placed a carton of books to sit on. He explained to Wallace that the windowsill would be a rest for the rifle. The crowd was already gathered and their voices could be heard through the open window.

Wallace shook his head and moved another carton under the window, in front of the box to use as a seat, in the process leaving his fingerprint. Oswald helped with the other boxes. Two more were stacked, giving him a rest that could not be seen by onlookers in the plaza below.

Oswald retrieved the rifle he had assembled earlier and hidden behind a long stack of cartons. He sat on the box, holding the rifle, looking out. Wallace nodded his approval and walked over to another window, four to the west, to set up his sniper's position.

By noon, the presidential motorcade had just entered the downtown area, many blocks from the waiting men. The sun warmed the occupants as the crowds tried to press forward. The limousine continued down Main, moving slowly, taking in the cheering audience. Only a few minutes elapsed for the drive down Main.

Officer Marrion Baker was grim as he rode motorcycle patrol several vehicles back in the motorcade. He enjoyed the large crowds and the easy work, his mere presence commanding, keeping onlookers from moving past the imaginary line separating the pressing people from the dignitaries. But

the crowds were more than expected, and it was just too busy, too dangerous for his liking.

A professional, he was prepared for anything, but, for the short run from
the airport, this was easy, almost like escorting a funeral procession. He
grinned ever so slightly, impressed by the adoring crowds cheering the president and the first lady.

Junior was in place, acting like a Secret Service agent. He surveyed the
scene and noticed a man in the nearby railroad tower. He also saw one police
officer on the bridge that was the triple underpass, then saw another.
Carefully ignoring them, he walked the distance behind the wall along the
top of the grassy knoll, looking it over for the best location for what he had
to do. His jacket was there on the back side of the wall, folded over. He had
laid it on the ground, rifle inside.

The trees along the wooden fence were thick, so his cover was good. He
walked the distance and, looking back, found the best position for shooting,
looking straight up Elm toward the depository. The fence was long and any
place would give a clear shot, straight ahead to Elm Street, less than one hundred feet, with the needed cover. There, under the trees and bushes at the
east end of the fence he took his location.

Glancing up again, Junior waited as the man in the tower walked around.
Junior caught his eye and held up the badge. Too far for the man to see, he
did not notice what it was. Junior looked for the police officers on the overpass. Neither man could be seen.

He shrugged and walked back to the pergola where he waited. Behind
the structure itself, he watched casually as the crowd assembled. Several people were already there. A man approached the back of the pergola. Junior
showed his badge and told the man he would have to move somewhere else.[4]
The man walked away. There was time to do what he would do, get to his
hidden location under the trees, assemble his rifle, and wait. Twenty seconds
was all he needed.

For Kennedy, the downtown parade was far better than he had expected.
Adlai Stevenson had been in Dallas the month before and had been attacked
at a downtown hotel. Kennedy was concerned. He had seen one of the hate
posters that morning in Fort Worth and had told Jackie, "We are in nut country now." Once in Dallas, however, the motorcade was welcome and he loved
the cheers, the shouts, and the applause. Although a few posters attacked
Kennedy's policies, there was not a single voice of protest.

While the last few months had been very demanding, his confidence was not shaken. Here he was in the heart of the enemy camp, home of the ultra-rightists he had publicly deplored in a recent speech. Despite the best efforts of his opposition, the people still loved him. The outpouring was exceptional. The police escorts were often pushed back. The noisy welcome echoed and drummed between the tall buildings. His driver, Secret Service agent William Greer, had to ride with his door open, to keep the crowd back by just a few inches.

He smiled as he waved, mostly to the right. Jackie was waving to the left. They would glance at each other as the procession went down Main, toward Dealey Plaza.

As the motorcade proceeded through the canyons of tall buildings, the open limousine warmed as the day heated up. Jackie felt she was wilting. The president noticed and smiled grimly. She was truly an asset. Reluctantly, she had agreed to the trip. Kennedy's thoughts wandered. He knew she knew of his many women and she knew he knew. Nothing was said. Both knew better than mention it. The understanding was carefully veiled but that thin line could break easily. He smiled again as he glanced at her and then back to his right, waving, leaning on the car's window jamb, nodding as he made eye contact with people in the crowd. The motorcade was better than expected.

Most important, he knew the Kennedy charm still worked. For all the serious problems he had, none was fatal to his reelection. If the public did not learn the details of his affairs, he was okay. They would not know. The enthusiasm of the crowds proved he was in excellent shape with the American people. His deep and abiding self-confidence was getting a healthy boost. Briefly, he thought ahead to the speech he would give. He was ready.

Shortly after noon Wallace had a problem. One of the workers had returned to the sixth floor. As the man entered from the stairwell, Wallace had ducked in time, staying hidden, waiting. Bonnie Ray Williams looked around, saw no one, and sat down in the snipers' area for lunch. He had walked up to see if there was anyone to watch the parade with him. With no one there, he finished his lunch, then looked out the window and seeing the crowds assembling below, he took the locked elevator down and went down one floor where his co-workers had assembled underneath the killers' windows. One escape route was gone.

It was 12:15. The motorcade was due in ten minutes. Wallace had decided to kill the worker but, in that instance, the man left. Wallace grinned and gripped his rifle, grimacing at his tender fingertips, the ones he had sanded, for a better hold on the trigger, for a fine touch, for fewer fingerprints. The prints would prove to be his only problem. He did not do a good job covering his prints. Fragments would remain on one of the book cartons.

Now, with Bonnie Ray Williams gone, everything was once again back on schedule. The sixth floor was clear now. Wallace walked back to the front window and glanced to his left, giving Oswald one last look. Then he surveyed the open space on the sixth floor and walked across it, to the stairwell at the far northwest corner. There he slid a stack of cartons in front, to block the entrance to the sixth floor, just in case someone else wandered in. The floor was as secure as he could make it.

It was time to get in place.

Again, Wallace walked over to Oswald's position, saw the crowds along the street, and glanced at Oswald. The plan was ready. The two men were to shoot at the president from behind, after his motorcade turned and proceeded down Elm. When it cleared the trees by the sign, shoot. Get them from behind, when they least expected it. Critical moments would pass before they realized what happened, time to escape.

Wallace took up his position at the third window to the southwest and sighted down the street. The shooting zone was laid out before him. Snipers typically operate in pairs, and the two former marines were doing it by the book. There would be a concentration of fire, tightly coordinated. There would be only one shot by each shooter. Wallace knew Junior was above the knoll, behind the fence, ready as backup, for triangulation, and, if needed, to complete the ambush.

Rising applause and cheers could be heard. Oswald leaned forward, looking out. The motorcade had turned off Main and onto Houston, heading directly toward him. He pulled back.

In the motorcade below, as it moved down Houston toward Elm, the governor's wife turned and said, "You can't say Dallas doesn't love you."[5]

Kennedy leaned forward to hear Mrs. Connally.

As the motorcade turned from Houston onto Elm directly beneath the Sixth Floor, the limousine slowed to make the tight turn. A motorcycle had to pull back. The cars moved slowly in front of the depository. The motorcade had lasted forty minutes and everyone was hot.

Officer Smith was in front of the building, watching the crowd, glancing at the motorcade.

Officer Harkness was to Smith's right about one hundred feet down the street. Officer Baker was still on Houston, some two hundred feet from the turn.

Six floors up, above the police, hidden from many by the trees and concealed from others by sun reflecting from the windowpanes, both men were kneeling as they placed rifles to their shoulders, back from the windows, sighting over the branches, past the street sign, onto the street. The wave of applause grew louder as it rippled and then seemed to cascade ever closer, finally reaching a peak beneath them. Glancing up from his scope, Wallace saw the lead car clear the trees.

The presidential limousine was behind it, moving slowly after barely negotiating the sharp turn from Houston onto Elm.

The angle between the two men sighting onto the street resulted in the next mistake. Oswald saw a clear shot and squeezed the trigger. Nothing happened. A spent cartridge was still in the gun. He had forgotten to remove it. He quickly ejected it and moved another cartridge into place. He realized Wallace had not fired, so he waited.

The limousine was still in the trees, still moving slowly. An eternity passed as the vehicle came into full view. Kennedy was a sitting duck, thought Wallace. The setup was perfect.

The crowd was thick both at the turn from Houston onto Elm and in front of the building but it quickly tapered off toward the underpass. The parade was almost over.

Six floors up, almost 150 feet behind the president, Oswald, driven by an unbearable excitement, fired.

The loud report from the rifle shot startled the pigeons roosting on the building and they rose with a loud snapping of their wings. The clock on the Hertz sign above the depository stood at 12:29 in the afternoon, ready to click to 12:30.

Many in the crowd thought of firecrackers. Some thought it was a back-firing motorcycle. Officer Baker heard it. Too loud, he knew from his many years of hunting. The past weekend he had been out in the country, shooting. It was a rifle. Noticing the pigeons, he decided the shot came from the depository.

The first bullet was low and to the right, hitting the pavement in front of and to the right of the Lincoln, then ricocheting into oblivion, never to be seen again.

Wallace cursed. The shots were to have been together. Oswald had lined

Kennedy up beside the street sign but was by seconds ahead of the angle
Wallace had. The first overt step in the assassination and it had gone wrong.
No matter. Wallace was disciplined from his career in the marines, from his
other killings, and from knowing exactly what was to happen next. The
shootings would happen so fast that the small differences would be no difference at all.

Wallace centered on Kennedy's head and fired. The shot went almost two
hundred feet but was barely low and slightly to the right, hitting the president in the back shoulder blade. The bullet was deflected upward ever so
slightly, exiting at the tie knot, the bullet's jacket separating to hit and crack
the windshield, the remaining slug hitting the curbing in front of James
Tague, an onlooker standing in front of the triple underpass on Commerce
Street. The slug knocked cement shards in all directions. A splinter nicked
Tague on the cheek.

Kennedy reacted with a shocked look as his central nervous system
instantly took over. His hands were fists as they went up, elbows out. The
hands never touched his throat. He felt he was choking. He could not say
anything. His head was up, erect, lined up for another shot.

The limousine moved forward a few feet, just past the sign. Barely
three seconds had passed. To the onlookers, it was a moment locked in
eternity.

Oswald knew his first shot was off, way off. In his rush to do his job, he
got off a second shot but was again too excited. The bullet was a little high
and to the right, hitting Connally instead of Kennedy. The bullet entered the
back shoulder, slowed in the soft tissue of the chest, exited below the right
nipple, hit the wrist, and, now deflected, it lodged in the governor's left thigh.

Connally reacted to the overwhelming pain, twisting and falling toward
his wife. "My god, they're going to kill us all," he muttered.[6] Then, slumped
over, now in his wife's arms, he was convinced he was dying.

Five seconds had passed. Many in the crowd now realized what was happening and they reacted. People were turning or falling, instinctively trying
to escape the imagined bullets. The awful sound of the three shots still echoed
in the cup of sloping ground and tall buildings at Dealey Plaza, a natural
echo chamber.

The limousine almost stopped. Kennedy was still erect but leaning
toward Jackie. The limousine started moving again.

"Ready," Wallace murmured to himself, carefully aiming, ready for one
more shot. He remained cool, steady, determined. He would not panic. He

had done this before and he knew what to do. His attention was on his target as he began to squeeze the trigger.

Junior was also ready. In his scope he saw that Kennedy's head was still erect. For him it was a perfect shot. He centered the crosshairs on the president's face, right between the eyes. Carefully squeezing the trigger, his rifle fired the fatal shot, one that went only one hundred fifty feet. In that same instant the bullet hit the president's head, slightly to the left, entering the tightly enclosed brain cavity, producing a cavitation effect that exploded the skull, first backwards, then upwards and sideways, to the right. The force of the explosion threw the president's body hard to its left, into Mrs. Kennedy's arms.

Junior's bullet also fell apart, its fragments going up, around, and away, some scattering inside the limousine, some hitting the pavement and grass outside.

For an instant, the pink spray that was the end of Kennedy's life seemed to hang forever, almost a spirit over the man. Then it was gone. And from that moment Kennedy belonged to the ages. All he would be as a man ended. What he was as president now belonged to history and its inevitable judgments, a process that will not end.

In another instant, the assassination was over.

The limousine was gone.

Less than seven seconds had elapsed between the four shots.

Wallace did not fire his second bullet. He did not need to shoot again. He saw the explosive impact of Junior's one shot. Wallace knew Kennedy was dead.

Wallace also knew all hell was breaking loose.

With that fourth shot, Clark's plan for Johnson to become president was complete. Kennedy was dead, instantly killed by Junior's one shot at the end of the seven seconds required for the murderous barrage.

In that same instant Johnson became president. The formal oath would be on *Air Force One,* but the Constitution does not allow for any delay. The transition of power was immediate. As Kennedy died instantly, it was now *President* Johnson. In the shock that followed in the days to come, he would prove to be untouchable.

Clark heard the official news at his office. He pretended to know nothing, showing great shock. In reality, Clark had done the first half of his job.

So far, so good. Even though the killing had not gone according to plan, now Clark only had to hide what had happened. A coverup was essential to protect the succession and the power he had won

The coverup started with the escape by the two snipers. The murder of Oswald was an essential part of cleaning up the mistakes. The Warren *Report* served to lay a mantle of official approval for the "lone nut" theory of one man determined to bring down a presidency and a nation. The coverup Clark had to control finally ended with the death of Jack Ruby.

In the last analysis, the run for cover took only a few months when the official part of the coverup, the Warren *Report,* was delivered to the president, the top assassin. Uncovering the official coverup would take another forty years.

> Political power grows out of the barrel of a gun.
> —Mao Zedong

> Happiness is a warm gun.
>   —John Lennon

If you wish to make a man noble, your best course is to kill him.
—Alexander Smith

15

Run

At 12:30 on November 22, 1963, as Kennedy died, Wallace had only one objective. He had to run. The success of his escape depended on one thing: while chaos was everywhere in Dealey Plaza, he had to become a Secret Service agent again, back in place where he was before, with Yates. When he saw the president thrown back by Junior's bullet, he did not hesitate. He ran for the stairwell. Pushing the cartons back, he stepped into the stairs and pulled the stack of boxes back in place. If the police did not move fast enough, and every second counted, the blocked stairwell might convince Oswald to stay and shoot it out.

Dissembling his compact rifle as he moved down the stairs, he saw his guard and cover, Yates, on the second floor. Signaling Wallace to move fast, Yates led the way down the one flight of stairs, to the back entrance and outside. By then, Wallace had the rifle in parts and inside his coat. Both men could stop and stand there, acting like they were guarding the building.

Working crowd control in front of the depository, Officer Harkness heard the shots and, as the shock wore off, he reacted quickly.[1] Looking around, he turned and ran along the east side of the building. Stopping and looking to the north and seeing nothing, he came back to the front. In front, there was only confusion, a seemingly endless crowd still running for cover as more people poured into Dealey Plaza, curious to see what had happened. Turning back, he moved further along the east side of the depository, to the northeast corner.

Wallace and Yates were standing there, further back, near the loading dock and railway. Seeing the two men in suits surprised Harkness. He paused. One of the men showed his Secret Service badge. Harkness nodded and moved on, looking in all directions, but never back. In the confusion of the moment, he did not question why they were doing nothing. The Secret Service men were above reproach, unquestioned guardians of the president. Besides, he was only a police officer. On matters of the presidency, the Secret Service was in charge.

As the police officer left, nothing was said between Wallace and Yates. The two men in suits smiled grimly and parted company, each going their separate ways. The suits were an excellent cover. In those chaotic first few minutes, a businessman was not the likely profile for a sniper. Only when a semblance of order for a crime scene was established could everyone become a suspect. As it turned out, Wallace and Yates only had about five minutes. That was all they needed.

The two men quickly parted. Yates walked a distance away from Dealey Plaza and returned to his home in Dallas. Wallace got in his car and drove off, heading for the state line and then back to California, to his waiting wife and daughter, back to his job with Ling and the LTV conglomerate.

Within eight years, Wallace would die, at the time still convinced his most terrible secret was forever hidden. In the course of the assassination, however, he left a few markers, just enough to hang Johnson and Clark. We only had to know where to look and what questions to ask.

Junior also followed the escape plan. Move quickly. Get back in place as a Secret Service agent. Immediately after the shooting, he looked around. No one saw him through the trees and the shade they provided. Before shooting, he had removed his coat and put it on the wet grass; it might have interfered with his shooting. Kneeling, he broke his portable rifle into four parts and concealed them in the pockets on the inside of the suit jacket spread out before him. Slipping back into the jacket, he shrugged it into place and walked toward the pergola, acting like he was looking for someone.

On the southwest corner of the depository, Officer Smith had reacted quickly, checking the movement of the crowd, glancing toward the front of the building. Seeing some people looking up the grassy slope toward the pergola, he ran in that direction.

He was soon behind the wall and in the parking lot area. Pistol drawn, he approached a man in a suit standing at the northerly edge of the pergola.[2]

The man who was Junior smiled grimly and said, "Secret Service."

Feeling foolish, Smith holstered his weapon and moved on, looking around the parking lot, then at the crowds now filling the area. He did not check the credentials at all.

Junior did not linger. He headed for his car, saw Wallace and Yates standing there, and waited. Then, as they moved on, so did he.

Within ten minutes of the assassination, the three conspirators were in their cars and gone from Dealey Plaza, into the deep fog of history, one made all the worse by the investigation that followed.

Oswald had not been told what to do except to hide and be ready to shoot it out. He was ready for it. For a few long moments, he watched from the sixth floor as people flooded Dealey Plaza. When they started looking in his direction, he hurried over to see Wallace. His partner was gone. Oswald looked at the stairwell. Still blocked. Rifle in hand, he surveyed the sixth floor. No one. Oswald may have finally realized what had happened, that he was on his own. A survival instinct must have taken over. He moved the barrier of book cartons, quickly placed his rifle behind a nearby stack of boxes, and ran down the stairs. On the second floor, he headed for the breakroom and some semblance of an excuse to cover what he had done.

"Act normal," he told himself as he walked toward the soda machine. Within ninety seconds of the last shot, Oswald was struggling to relax. His adrenalin, now at a new high, strangely helped calm him. He knew he had to relax. He did.

Officer Baker watched as the limousine disappeared. From his perspective further back in the motorcade, he knew there had been a shooting. The escort part of his job was over. He had to find the shooters. Time to make an arrest.

Surrounded by a crowd flowing around him in all directions, he moved and pushed his motorcycle to the red-brick building. Parking it, he raced toward the depository entrance. He knew the bullets came from there, from up high, and he assumed the shooters were from the top floor or near it because the pigeons had flown from there.

As Baker entered the lobby of the depository, he asked where the stairs or elevators were. A man stepped forward, identifying himself as a building manager and telling Baker to follow him.

The two men went to the freight elevators, found them locked off on other floors, and shouted for them to be sent down.

Baker waited a few moments, then said they should take the stairs. Truly took the lead, going up to the second floor.

Stopping on the second floor Baker saw movement and looked. Through a windowed door, he saw the back of a man in the breakroom.[3]

Moving quickly, gun drawn, Baker went into the room and stopped Oswald. Truly followed. The assassins' patsy was standing before a soft-drink machine. Gesturing with his pistol, Baker asked Truly if he knew the man.

Truly identified Oswald as one of the workers.[4]

Baker glared a moment longer, then turned back to the stairs and resumed his climb, Truly following. They hurried up to the roof. No one was there.

Immediately after Baker and Truly continued up the stairwell, Oswald left the building. He had almost been caught because he had moved slower than Wallace; however, Oswald also got away in the confusion. Once on Elm Street, Oswald took a bus but got off when traffic grid-locked. He walked to a nearby cab stand, and the taxi drove him to an intersection near his boardinghouse in southwest Dallas. Walking the block, he got the pistol he was supposed to have had on the sixth floor, left the house and started walking, apparently with no specific objective. Officer J. D. Tippit was on patrol and stopped Oswald. Almost immediately, he shot and killed the policeman.[5] Still on foot, he escaped to the nearby Texas Theatre. There several policemen moved in to apprehend him. Oswald tried to shoot it out, but Officer M. N. MacDonald grabbed the gun, preventing it from firing.[6] Oswald was arrested and taken to the city jail.

At Clark's law offices, the news of the assassination first reached Lorraine Barr, the receptionist. She started getting an unending stream of calls; soon the switchboard was lit up and busied out. She passed the word around and the lawyers came out of their offices, talking, strangely awed but quietly pleased that Johnson was president. At the heart of the seat of power, the implications for Clark's lawyers were clear.

Clark stayed in his office, talking to partners as they came in, then making the phone calls he needed to make. Mainly, he was waiting, trying to find out what was happening, to be sure the crime was complete and covered up. He was on standby, desperate to know what was happening, but compelled by circumstances to act distressed but calm.

Another participant in the conspiracy blew his carefully planned cover. Johnson had been warned; he had been woodshedded. He knew he had to compartmentalize his feelings. But, at the very same time in that instant of Kennedy's death, he had achieved his lifetime ambition. Now he was president. With that realization, he also experienced an adrenalin rush. Then he remembered he had to express a nation's shock and sorrow. He had to be sad and deadly serious while filled with an overriding thrill of victory.

In the hour that passed while he waited at Parkland and then at *Air Force One*, he could not resist calling Robert Kennedy to ask for a legal opinion on taking the oath. After all, the president's brother was attorney general. There was absolutely no need for such an invasive and direct reminder of the personal loss Robert Kennedy had suffered. After three years of torment from John Kennedy's brother, Johnson had to rub it in.

Johnson did not rest there. When the time for the oath arrived, he insisted the president's widow stand by him. Jackie had just witnessed the unimaginably horrible death of her husband; she was clearly in shock. The only description for her standing by Johnson as he takes over from her husband is an overriding grief and shock far too deep to measure. Now Johnson was Jackie's leader. Again, in terribly boorish and unacceptable poor taste, he insisted she be there beside him.

At that moment, with a crass reminder to the brother of what had happened and a needless and useless show of power to the widow, Johnson made a third mistake. In his ecstatic happiness at becoming the most powerful man in the world and with a sense of absolute power that was gradually taking over, his cover was again blown for a fleeting moment.

On *Air Force One*, Johnson had taken the oath of office from Judge Sarah T. Hughes. The photos clearly show a solemn new president beside the still-shocked widow undertaking his new job with deep regret, all as he should. Then, as he completed the oath and officially assumed the mantle of president, he could not contain himself. The last photo in the series shows him with his face turned, the back left side of his face deeply creased with a big smile, apparently winking at longtime colleague Congressman Albert Thomas, who was there as a witness.[7] The congressman winked back, and Lady Bird smiled. As he would later candidly say, on that day "I never felt better."

By any measure, these reactions were clearly inappropriate. Johnson let his guard down and made it clear that he was overjoyed to have pulled off the succession. The photo was not released for general distribution. Later, however, it was made public and has become an essential part of the assassination history.

A further unnecessary step under the circumstances was to delay the return to Washington. Johnson insisted Kennedy's body fly on *Air Force One* and that Jackie accompany them on the flight. The Kennedy group could have easily flown on the backup plane. Johnson's insistence meant a delay that allowed him to keep full control of Kennedy's body.

Although Clark was also overjoyed to have Johnson president, he had a far more important issue on that day and in the days immediately following the assassination. He had to cover up his plan at the points where it had unraveled.

As *Air Force One* was returning to Washington, the first bad news arrived. The police had arrested Oswald. Clark was livid. Oswald should have been killed in a shootout with the arresting police. He escaped the depository but was almost in a shootout at the Texas Theater. Only the hand of an arresting officer prevented him from firing away. Maybe it would have been better for Wallace to have shot Oswald. Clark shook that thought away. Already fearful of what Oswald might say, when the news reported that the prisoner announced he was a "patsy,"[8] Clark was truly terrified. He had to find a killer for the captured assassin.

While Clark was moving to cover up the mistakes, law enforcement was at work. Dallas district attorney Henry Wade announced that anyone involved in "the conspiracy" deserved the electric chair. Wade received a call soon after from Cliff Carter in the White House and was told there should be no mention of a conspiracy.[9] Wade shut up.

Waggoner Carr, the Texas attorney general and a Clark friend, was also called by the new White House, to be instructed there was no conspiracy.

The coverup for the assassination was moving ahead but there were more problems in the works as Clark was trying to tame a wild horse to bring the chaos under control. So, at the end of the first day, Clark took the time to evaluate his plan and its objectives. Johnson was president but the assassination had not been free of mistakes. In Clark's carefully ordered world, there had been far too many flaws. Oswald was in custody, not dead. Four shots had to be explained instead of just one or two. Johnson's behavior had not been graciously innocent. Now, as the chaos in Dealey Plaza ended and night fell, there was Oswald and there were the bullets. In the two days between the shootings of President Kennedy and Oswald, the entire crime scenario in Dallas had every appearance of a conspiracy. Clark had told Wallace, "There must be no evidence." Contrary to Clark's wishes there was evidence, more than enough. There was a great deal of cleaning up to be done.

The next morning, the immediate, very pressing problem for Clark was how to take care of Oswald for good.

The path taken at this point in the coverup is not clear but the tie lines are. Clark phoned Murchison for help, to tell him that the president did not need a long trial for this assassin. Using weasel words as only he could use them, parsing his phrases as a master, Clark suggested the nation would be served by eliminating Oswald. Murchison understood and the necessary arrangements were quickly completed, probably through H. L. Hunt. Through their friends in the local mob, Jack Ruby, a two-bit crook with a big debt, would take care of the potential witness.

Ruby was enlisted, and Oswald was dead the next day. When the prisoner was being moved to a police vehicle in the basement of the city jail, Ruby moved quickly out of the crowd and fired one bullet into and across Oswald's abdomen. As Ruby expected, the shot was fatal. Oswald died at Parkland Hospital, the same place where Kennedy had been pronounced dead only two days earlier.

Strangely, Johnson called one of the surgeons working on Oswald to see how the patient was doing.[10] When told there was no hope, he instructed the doctors to try to get a deathbed confession. As was his wont to meddle, Johnson was staying on top of key points in the coverup. At the time, it was strange but accepted. Now the reasons for his call are patently clear.

At one time Will Fritz, head of the police homicide bureau, was promising a complete investigation into Oswald and his connections. As soon as Oswald was killed, Johnson himself phoned to tell Fritz to stop talking about a conspiracy.[11] Fritz shut up.

In the basement of the city jail, Ruby was immediately overwhelmed. To all appearances, it was a gangland killing by the mob. After all, the shot was across the abdomen and was sure to kill. All the marks of a professional shooter were there. In a crowded police building, Ruby knew what he was doing.

Only some of the benefits for Ruby are known. In another typical step by Clark and his coverups, Ruby got help. For one, he was provided an attorney. There were probably more benefits, related to help for family members and friends. The record is far from clear and probably lost forever.

Clark was pleased now that Oswald was gone and Ruby was in jail. Clark knew the killing covered him and Johnson. Oswald looked like a disgruntled communist allied with the Soviet Union and Cuba. Ruby looked like a Mafia hitman. If there was to be an investigation, better the suspects be the communists or the mob than them.

Clark also knew he needed more. His standard operating procedure was to have an attorney loyal to him handle the criminal case. Cofer was the best but that would be too obvious. Instead, Clark took care of a defense attorney for Ruby with a call to his former brother-in-law, Joe Tonahill. A prominent trial attorney in Jasper, Texas, Tonahill had divorced Clark's sister, but the men were still good friends. Clark could call on Tonahill as and when needed, and, for Ruby, he called again.

Tonahill took the necessary steps to land Ruby as a client. Ruby clearly understood the message. He accepted Clark's agent as his attorney. Now Clark was back in control. Once again, the attorney-client privilege was in place.

Within four months, Ruby was tried for capital murder, found guilty, and sentenced to death.

The Warren investigation then centered on Ruby. He was the only witness in custody who might know something. Commission chairman Earl Warren even interviewed Ruby personally. On fifteen separate occasions, Ruby begged Warren to take him out of Dallas, to safety elsewhere so that he could tell what he knew. Warren did not give him the safety requested. A polygraph exam was given with mixed results; however, nothing was done to clear up the ambiguous answers Ruby gave.[12] Incredulously, Warren later stated he was satisfied with Ruby's evasive answers, that there was no one else involved.

Ruby appealed the conviction and it was reversed. While awaiting a second trial, Ruby was diagnosed with cancer and he died soon after. Most important, he did not talk.

Reportedly, he sent a message to friends that Johnson was behind the assassination. This allegation was not investigated and became public knowledge only indirectly.[13] As is now clear, his message was correct.

With the assassins out of the way and Ruby under control, Johnson and Clark still had problems. The morning after the assassination, steps were taken to control the necessary investigation.

Because the crime had occurred in Dallas, Texas law applied. Any criminal trial would be in Dallas and would be conducted by the district attorney. Clark also anticipated a Texas Court of Inquiry, a procedure under state law where the attorney general investigates a crime and makes a report. The procedure would be perfect for Clark's system of Texas justice.

Clark had raised the possibility of a Court of Inquiry with the Texas attorney general before the assassination. The question was subtle. Of course, he did not ask Attorney General Waggoner Carr if he would investigate an assassination of John Kennedy. The question was whether Carr knew about a Court of Inquiry and how to appoint one and conduct such an investigation. In short, Carr had been briefed and would respond favorably, almost automatically, to the suggestion. Like any judge prejudiced by Clark, Carr reacted as Clark expected.

On the day after the assassination, Clark also alerted Walter Jenkins, Johnson's chief assistant in the White House, to call Carr and get the Court of Inquiry started.[14] Clark wanted a Texas investigation as the best way to contain the evidence and complete the coverup. The makeup of the Texas investigation was also important. Clark settled that by suggesting the key member should be Leon Jaworski. As Johnson's attorney in the election challenge and as confidant with Clark, he readily agreed to do so. The aging law dean at Southern Methodist University was also named but he was a useless figurehead. Jaworski would be in control. After briefing Carr, the man called to ask Jenkins if the names were okay, and, when told they were, the Texas Court of Inquiry was ready to go. In other words, there was prior approval by the White House, and an attorney of record for Johnson was named to conduct the investigation. If any evidence pointed to Johnson, Jaworski would be bound to keep it secret or resign.

Johnson took one further step. Within three weeks of Oswald's death, he ordered that the presidential limousine be flown to Cincinnati, there to be cleaned up and completely refurbished. Additional important evidence from the crime scene was destroyed. Carter took care of this small matter.

As the days passed and nothing dramatic happened, Clark took great comfort in the investigation. He knew experts would be enlisted and, because he knew there were always experts who would say anything, he was ready. None proved necessary. The notions of "lone nuts" always committing assassinations and of only one person being arrested by the police were all that was needed.[15] A media closely wedded to the presidency and its new occupant readily accepted and promoted the lone gunman idea. A national consensus developed. Surprisingly, the media still defends that original position. Perhaps they are covering up their own failure to dig deeper into the suspicious circumstances.

An important step in the coverup occurred in the White House on November 25, 1963. That Sunday morning FBI director Hoover arrived to brief Johnson on the investigation. Hoover had secretly sent sixty top agents to Dallas, and he reported that they were certain there was only one assassin. He promised Johnson a complete report within a few days. The ensuing Warren investigation would mean nothing because the FBI was designated to handle the investigation, and they had already decided. The Warren Commission was set up to ratify what the FBI had already decided. In effect, Warren and company would approve Hoover's short report from that Sunday morning.

For all practical purposes the coverup was complete. The FBI had spoken. There was only one gunman. There was no need to look further. In fact, however, as the James Hosty case shows, the FBI was also covering up its mistakes before the assassination.

Although FBI agents stayed on the job in Dallas for a month following the assassination, one item was never investigated. No need was seen for the all-important motive, an item at the heart of any investigation. Who stood to gain the most? The question was not asked.

Only one person had an overriding motive. Johnson would be called upon to give a statement, but he only had to sign a short summary of what he had witnessed. No notary, no affidavit, just a signature. The faith placed with the president, one that was a reminder of the lingering notion that the king could do no wrong, effectively blocked any official suspicion of Johnson.

The perfect crime had been committed at the highest levels. Three days after the assassination, the case was over. Further investigations would be made but the final decisions had been reported. They would not be challenged. The assassination was history, at least in the eyes of the conspirators.

Even before the limited investigation had started, Clark sent Don Thomas to Washington. Thomas was to keep an eye on things, much as he had done in Alice, Texas, in 1948. Thomas stayed with Johnson for over a week. There he would learn of new developments, relay them to Clark, and handle any crises that might arise.

Thomas was also another measure of reassurance to a very nervous president. The cover for Thomas was a legal one. Supposedly, with Johnson now president, his business and property rights had to be changed. That little charade was false. The transfers had already been agreed upon when Johnson became vice president.

Thomas was there primarily to stay advised of any developments in the investigation. He was Clark's conduit to the president, to the federal government, and to all the news in Washington.

With Hoover's preliminary report in hand, Johnson was ready to let things rest, as planned. He would stick with the Texas Court of Inquiry. Within a few days, however, pressure for a national commission was too great. In the Congress, a joint congressional committee was proposed to conduct the investigation. Politics would have played a big role, and Republicans would be in a position to pounce on anything they could about Johnson. Not only would that embarrass the new president; it might uncover the facts.

Johnson had no choice. He agreed to name a national panel, one handpicked by him. He could make sure to name members who would keep things quiet. In effect, Johnson would name the judges of what was essentially his case. Headed by Chief Justice Earl Warren, Johnson made sure there were solid conservatives on the commission including his key mentor, Senator Richard Russell of Georgia.

While the commission was getting organized, Texas attorney general Waggoner Carr appeared before them to promote the rights of his Court of Inquiry. He put enough pressure on the Warren members to get his insider involved. As part of the investigation procedure, Jaworski was named to work with the commission's agents as the representative from the state of Texas. He was also designated as the man in charge of the Texas part of the investigation. His role would be that of figurehead because the commission's lawyers did most of the work writing from the affidavits presented to them. Jaworski was in a key position inside the investigation and could keep track of how the interviews were going.

Jaworski would do only two things publicly: stop publicity that might disclose the FBI's shortcomings and coverup and control Ruby.

The first control that was necessary involved the FBI's incompetence. Jaworski took the lead. The FBI had been alerted to Oswald when he had returned to the United States from the Soviet Union. Routine visits were made to assess his danger to the nation. Later, when he returned from Mexico

City, the FBI in Dallas was again alerted. Several days before the assassination, Oswald appeared in the Dallas office of the FBI to demand that his wife be left alone. James P. Hosty, the agent assigned the task of monitoring Oswald, had been absent that morning, so Oswald left a note threatening some kind of action if the alleged harassment continued.[16] After the assassination the note was destroyed. The FBI was making sure that it was not implicated in anything involving Oswald.

This is a very subtle point but a very important one in legal matters. A basic principle of the law is that no person should be the judge of their own case. Here we had written confirmation of the FBI's incompetence. It proceeded to lie, instructing Hosty to destroy the note and deny that it ever existed. The pattern was established early in the investigation. The FBI had to protect itself. It was in charge of the investigation. The protection of its reputation was more important than the facts.

The power to judge one's self played a key role in the investigation itself, of the federal government investigating its own chief, its president. The question lingers. How do you obtain independence in such investigations with their inevitable judgments?

Word got out during the Dallas investigation, however, that Oswald was an agent of the FBI. This bombshell was immediately squashed. The newsman making the report, Alonzo "Lonnie" Hudkins, soon withdrew it because Dallas law enforcement would not confirm the story. During the Warren investigation, the issue came up again. The question was referred to Jaworski and he reported that someone had made the remark but that the reporter could not be found.[17] The matter was quickly, almost too easily dropped. The suggestion that the FBI could have done something before the assassination was ignored. Also killed was any notion of incompetence on the part of the FBI. They stayed in charge of investigating everything, including their own incompetence.

The alternative was for independent investigators to do the work for the Warren Commission. Instead, on the first day, the FBI remained in control, and they defended their initial findings to the end. Interestingly, while the FBI reportedly still carries the Kennedy assassination as an open investigation, the objective is to defend what they did in 1963–1964. Finding out what they are still doing is virtually impossible. Even as late as 1998, the ARRB was unable to get anything resembling even a portion of the key records.[18]

One other problem for Jaworski concerned Ruby. When Tonahill, Ruby's lawyer, threatened to make a circus out of the trial, Jaworski conferred with

Clark and then wrote Tonahill a warning letter.[19] A follow-up call from Clark to Tonahill ended the possibility that Ruby might become a media circus, become overly excited, and perhaps feel a necessity to talk. He just might say something that would lead to more questions. The woodshedding might not work. Ruby was muzzled by his attorney who was, in fact, attorney for Johnson and Clark. The pattern was clear. As Cofer muzzled Johnson in 1948, Wallace in 1952, and Estes in 1962, Tonahill kept Ruby quiet.

A week after the assassination, Clark could rest, satisfied that the loose ends had been tied. There would be no evidence and there was no way to uncover the evidence. In any litigation, civil or criminal, to get the best evidence, investigators have to move quickly. By the time the Warren Commission went to work in January, it was too late. As we have seen, the coverup was within the same *modus operandi* Clark had used since 1948. Nothing new. Just nothing ever investigated. Everyone shut up. No evidence. And it all happened proactively, behind the scenes, by the lawyer acting behind the privilege.

At least some key parts of the record remain.

When the Warren *Report* was issued on September 25, 1964, under pressure for release well before the November presidential elections, the case was considered closed. Most Americans were satisfied. So, too, was the media.

Some Americans were not. Many citizens of other nations were also skeptical. By the time these independent researchers had completed their work, a majority of the Warren Commission no longer believed their own report. The general opinion was there had been a conspiracy. The question was, who was in that conspiracy?

> What happened to Kennedy may well have been divine retribution.
>
> —Lyndon Johnson

> Hell, boys! Don't you know? I am God!
> —Attributed to Johnson

> Everything secret degenerates, even the administration of justice;
> nothing is safe that does not show how it can bear discussion and
> publicity.
> —Lord Acton

16

Bonus

On November 22, 1963, shortly before one o'clock, while completing law school, I was feeding my firstborn son and planning to attend the Democratic parade and fund-raiser for Kennedy's visit to Austin that evening, when my then mother-in-law burst in, tears streaming down. "The president's been shot!" she exclaimed.

Realizing her terrible distress, I paused, and then tried to reassure her. "He'll be all right. Modern medicine works wonders." My response was truly hopeful, a part of the optimism many of us had in the early 1960s. Besides, something so terrible as the killing of President Kennedy was unthinkable. No bullets could be so accurate as to kill a president of the United States.

In the same breath, however, in that same stream of consciousness, I added, "You know who that makes president." I said the words flatly, with a profound sense of both amazement and sadness.

We turned the TV on and, as the tragedy unfolded, I recall my feelings of dedication to Kennedy's ideas, the message that prompted me to take a job in Washington once law school was completed. I realized those ideals were over. I would be ever closer to the raw power Lyndon Johnson represented.

The difference could not have been greater. Having listened to Kennedy's Inaugural Address, I was impressed by his ideas and leadership. More than that, I was entrapped, thoroughly enamored by what he said. I was convinced he was the leader we needed. The Soviets had put Sputnik in orbit. Cuba had fallen to revolutionaries. Blacks were pressing for civil rights. Kennedy seemed most qualified for the Cold War.

Johnson could not have been more different. Many in Austin considered him a joke, but a very serious one. He was feared. For me, the point had been driven home in February 1961, shortly after the inauguration, when he carelessly killed two pilots by ordering them to fly to his ranch in a dense fog. Three days later the wreckage was finally located in the rough hill country. Johnson paid handsomely to cover up the incident, but the family of one of the pilots vividly and dramatically confirmed the awful details. That was but one early and very personal insight I had of Johnson, a man of great power willing to abuse it to the maximum, to the point of taking human life.

Looking back, the sharp division in my thinking has been with me to this day, between the sacred and the profane, between ideals and realities, between principles and raw power. While I kept my plans to serve my country and went to Washington, I changed my motivations. I would go to Washington to learn how power was exercised.

For the next fourteen years, I was torn between my admiration for Kennedy and the progressive things he stood for and my respect for the amoral world Johnson and Clark controlled in the most stark and unprincipled ways imaginable. I should have appreciated the division far more than I did. At first, however, I did not even know what was really happening.

In Washington after completing law school, I was with the National Labor Relations Board for six months and then with the Federal Power Commission for two years as attorney for Larry O'Connor, the so-called Texas member of the Federal Power Commission. While I was there we issued legal opinions and decisions on setting rates for natural gas, certifying new pipelines, and keeping Texas electrics out of the national power grid. As my term was ending, I contacted Clark about joining his firm, was accepted, and started as an associate attorney with Clark in the first week in July 1966. At the time Clark was ambassador to Australia, serving from late 1965 to early 1967, far away from any questions about the assassination.

The day I started, I went to the law offices of Clark, Thomas, Harris, Denius & Winters on the twelfth floor of the old Capital National Bank Building and met Martin Harris, the managing partner. The orientation was brief but thorough. After going over operations and my position, Harris also told me we never talked about Johnson but, he said with a nervous laugh, "Just be careful. He's a strange duck."

I nodded. This contradictory advice would prove to be typical. As superlawyers, we had rules but we did not have to follow them. Besides, we were the president's lawyers. We would follow that line as conservative Democrats struggling to keep from being Republicans. Then, whenever Johnson would promote a progressive agenda, we would be the inside information, that he really didn't believe in all that "liberal stuff."

We discussed a few more points and then walked to the next office, for a look at the Ambassador's suite. The main room was small and dark, highlighted by Vanity Fair's caricatures of lawyers at work.

"Anyone we know?" I asked.

Harris laughed. "He put all of us up there." To the left was a large man, Clark himself. The combative Thomas was next, a bantam rooster with small legs on a compact body. Harris, the lean and hungry one, was followed with an eager, youthful Frank Denius. Last was the tough sophisticate, Sam Winters.

"Impressed?" Harris asked in his mildly cynical way.

"Very nice," I replied with a shrug.

"Let's get to your office," said Harris, and I followed him out, starting the first day of eleven years of very exciting and demanding legal work. Initially centering on lobbying in Washington, with many flights back and forth to cover that world, it expanded to include litigation, oil and gas regulation, and about any type of political or government activity.

There were many contradictions in our practice. Forbidden subjects would come up, and the laws against talking about those subjects would be instantly invoked by the official. "I can't talk about that." Immediately following the denial, of course, we could talk freely. Later, if questioned about any prohibited contacts, we would always say that we said that we could not talk about that. No one asked the follow-up question, "Did you anyway?" If we had been asked, the honest answer would have been, "Yes. Of course." The privilege was the ultimate defense but was never used. It did not have to be used. Everyone knew it was there.

A standard feature was this deniability, this dodging the key issue, this avoiding even an appearance of illegal access. There would be "no evidence" of secret contacts. The law practice with Clark was this bundle of contradictions, conveniently providing the needed cover for illegal activities. All were for one thing, results for the client. In our version of the law, no opponent knew what was really happening. Even clients were kept in the dark. What we did to get results was secret.

I had been with the firm less than two months when Don Thomas had me prepare a brief in a labor dispute Johnson's television station, KTBC, was having with one of its unions. We had to oppose the union and at the same time avoid any hint of prejudice against unions. I prepared a short, to the point, statement. Thomas read it, liked it, and filed it.

The immediate result was an invitation to Johnson's television station for lunch in the first family's private quarters. There I visited with Jesse Kellam, station manager and longtime Johnson confidant. The television station itself was in a windowless building at Brazos and Tenth Streets. The president's Austin home was a penthouse on top, complete with a small garden area.

A short time later, I became moderator for the junior bar's "Law and You" television series on Johnson's station. The program aired weekly, just before the Sunday NFL game of the week. For me as well as the firm, it meant a major exposure to Austin and its surrounding counties. In our power position, we got all the perks on the only television station in Austin.

That fall, it was time to meet Ambassador Edward A. Clark, senior partner and owner of the law firm. He had been in Australia producing no legal business while getting paid back home with lots of "retainer" money, the checks we received for doing essentially nothing.

I was called to meet him so I hurried over, to be introduced to a man about six foot, but very stout, even fat. As one newspaper described him, he was robust and husky. Bushy eyebrows hid dark eyes that were always squinting, slit-like. The first big surprise came when he spoke. He had a lisp. Always outgoing, he was easy with a laugh and could be very loud. He always demanded the utmost respect. Another surprise was when I shook his hand. The two outer digits of his middle fingers were missing. Later, Harris warned me that the cause of their loss was never to be discussed.

"My new lawyer," Clark exclaimed. Harris was standing by the desk.

"Mr. Ambassador," I said. We had been warned to refer to him as "ambassador." That was easy enough. He was one. The desk he stood beside was cluttered. The lights on his office phone were blinking on hold and he was holding his private line, apparently in the middle of a conversation.

"Real pleased to have you." He looked at me closely and smiled. "You take care of things in Washington, you hear?"

"Yes, sir."

Then, to Harris, Clark demanded, "Where is that letter?"

"Right here, Mr. Ambassador." Harris handed it to him.

Clark quickly scanned it while speaking to me. "I need you to write up some speeches on this Vietnam thing," he said.

"Do you need anything special?" I asked.

Clark said nothing.

"Draft up something," Harris interjected. "He wants an idea about how we support the war."

"Take care of this," Clark said, handing the letter to Harris. "Is the car here?" he shouted to Edna O'Donnell, his secretary. "Lyn-don's waiting!"

She hurried in. "Yes, sir," she said. "The chauffeur's in front."

"There is an election coming up," he said to her. "You do know that." Johnson always wanted the fullest show of support from Austin, and, with the Vietnam issue taking over, the elections that year were very important.

"Of course I know," she replied testily. She was among the few who had little respect for Clark. "I know him too well," she would later tell me.

"I have got to get going," said Clark impatiently. "Take care of that, will you," he said to me. He then turned to his crowded desk. "You have to find that invitation," he demanded of O'Donnell, who nodded and began shuffling through the papers.

Harris looked at me and smiled. "Write it up several ways." With a nod of his head, he indicated I should leave. I did.

I prepared three speeches on Vietnam, one taking a strict hawk's approach, another proposing an international police force, and the third suggesting moderation and peace. Clark delivered all three.

The building the law firm leased had been constructed in 1931, and the top floor had been set aside as a penthouse home for the landowners for life. When they died, no one was interested in spacious penthouse rooms atop the old Capital National Bank Building so Clark took the floor to store client records. An inglorious fate for the area but certainly a secure place for the top-secret files.

Soon after joining Clark's firm, I needed some records, so our bookkeeper got the key and escorted me there. We went up two flights of stairs, through a locked door, into the hallway, through another locked door, and then into the storage area. This was the warehouse for the firm's records. The penthouse was large, a series of rooms with high ceilings and tall windows letting ample light enter. Since the space was not regularly cleaned, dust hung lightly in the sunlight, casting visible rays as I looked around. File boxes and cabinets were everywhere, in no particular order.

Half the available space was behind still another barrier and lock. A heavy wooden and mesh fence had been built, and behind it, boxes full of records were piled ever higher and deeper. A locked gate barred entrance. They were Johnson's records, accessible to no one. Even the bookkeeper did not have a key.

I was fascinated. These stacks of boxes were the records of Johnson's relations with Clark, of Clark's handling Johnson's many businesses and political races, and of the high crimes and misdemeanors. I knew the details about Johnson's unsavory activities had to be there. Clark would not even rely on the attorney-client privilege to keep them secret. There were some matters not even the privilege could protect. There were some things no one could know about. A vast record for history, all in writing.

All unavailable.

I found the old file I needed and glanced again at the secret records. Here, an arm's length away, was a storehouse of history.

I left.

Soon after meeting Clark, I learned firsthand the immense power he exercised and how he exercised it.

Gulf+Western, one of the then-popular conglomerates, was going to make a tender offer for Sinclair Refining Company stock. Sinclair was opposed to the takeover and arranged for one of its stockholders, Grogan Lord of nearby Georgetown, Texas, to sue. Lord ran the small business investment company handling some of Johnson's money along with healthy infusions of government funds.

What we had to do was enjoin the offering. The purpose was to make still more money on the stock. The most important immediate objective was to stop the mailing of the prospectus. By the time we got the case, the prospectus was completed and was being prepared for mailing.

We had less than eight hours to stop Gulf+Western.[1] We got the case at nine that morning. The mailing was to go out late that afternoon. Legally, anybody can make a mailing. What is done with the mailing is another thing. In other words let the mailing go but do not let anything be done with the results. It was not even a close case, but what we had to do was show raw power. We had to get a binding order barring the mailing, and we had to do it in secret. We did.

Thomas called me in to prepare the affidavits and get them to the federal court, to Judge Jack Roberts. I had to allege we did not have time to notify one of the biggest companies in the United States. No matter. The papers were filed with the orders ready to be signed by Roberts, all without notice to the other side. Roberts signed. When the order was in effect, the clerk called Gulf+Western and told them to stop the mailing.

Later that afternoon, Thomas and I were ushered into Clark's office for the next critical step. Clark was already at work, sitting at his desk, animatedly talking by phone with Roberts. It seems Gulf+Western's attorneys had called Roberts and they were outraged.

Gesturing for us to sit down, Clark suddenly hollered, "Dammit, Jack. I got to have this one." He then rambled on, as was his style, talking and waving his free hand as he clutched the phone. Constant talking was an important way of life for Clark. By talking, he could keep anyone else from making points. If the judge could not hear from the other side, you win.

Most importantly, of course, this was an ex parte conversation. Gulf+Western knew nothing about it. It was in secret, in what is known as a conspiracy, and this one was within the legal system, deep inside the judge's chambers.

Clark suddenly stood up. "I'll be damned, Jack. I need you in the trenches." He turned red and almost spun around, an amazing feat for such a large man. Looking at Thomas, Clark covered the phone's mouthpiece up and said, "The son-of-a-bitch wants on the Fifth Circuit." Roberts wanted a promotion for what he was about to do. He wanted to be named a judge on the Fifth Circuit Court of Appeals. Roberts knew Clark could get it done through Johnson.

Turning his attention back to the phone, Clark nodded. "That's what I said!" Then he laughed, and, in the same moment, changed his tone completely. "I want that order." He paused again, listening.

Then, with his eyes squinting, he said, "This is a damned close case."

Another pause, then Clark nodded. "I want that order, period." As he again listened, he gradually smiled, winked at Thomas, and sat down, now entangled in the cord. "Thank you, Judge," he continued, then listened a few moments more, and added, "Yeah, sure. I'll be there tonight." Another pause. "Okay."

Hanging up and sitting down, he let out a whoop. "Take him an amended order. He'll sign again."

Thomas turned to me. "We need another order."

I nodded. We had been through two. What's one more?

Looking down at the telephone cord entangling him, Clark laughed and stood up. "This one was tougher than usual. He said there's no way to do it." Turning around and untangling the cord, he mused, "Still, he has to do it." Shaking his head, he added, "I'll see that he wins at poker tonight." Clark's forehead furrowed. "I wonder what ails him."

Saying nothing, Thomas stood and gestured for me to leave. As I walked down the hall to the library, I understood this was part of my apprenticeship into the very real world of the law at work, right on the front lines. Still, I wondered what those lofty phrases and noble intentions in the law books meant. Forget the books. I had just learned how the law really worked.

At the summit of this real world of superlawyers, I was fast becoming part of the good old boys' club. I was in the middle of Texas's famous "Bubba justice." I considered it part of the learning process, getting to know how the law really works. If this is the way it's done, so be it.

Harris and I traveled to Bayview, Texas, on the Gulf Coast that winter to attend a weekend meeting of lobbyists. We drove because airline service to the Texas Valley was always uncertain. Besides, as it turned out, we had many things to talk about. Mostly I listened to Harris.

Johnson's name would come up again and again because we had to talk to the lobbyists about federal and state legislation. We also talked about billing. I asked about the time for the long weekend. Who was paying for my time? Billing was not supposed to be my concern but I wanted my time to show income to the firm. As the years went by, I did more and more to bill and collect. The partners were just too lax about bringing in the fees. While Johnson was president, the money just kept on coming. They were not too concerned. I was. I had a family and needed a good income like my friends in Houston law firms were making.

Harris was nonchalant about the income, assuring me that the partners would collect what was owed. His main point was to put everything in a memo. Do that instead of time billing, he suggested, because who wants to keep up with all that time. He assured me Clark just sets a price for what we've done and the partners collect it.

What they expected from me was five billable hours daily at fifty dollars an hour (this was in 1966). The rest was public service and that meant helping Johnson. Since we were Johnson's men, we were expected to represent him at whatever political events might arise.

Bayview was a resort near Padre Island. Originally built to attract tourists to Texas in the winter, it never had much business. Too cold. That winter of 1966, it was for company business, and specifically "the lobby." They assembled to see what the next session of the Texas Legislature, or "lege," had planned. They also wanted the latest from Washington, to find out what Congress and the president had in store for them. I was the insider reporting the facts. After arming our clients with the latest insider information, steps would be taken to keep changes from happening or to make some changes. We didn't just oppose legislation. We wrote legislation, usually with a twist, sneaking it past the opposition because of the access we had to the back rooms of Congress.

After a brief review of legislation, dealing that year mainly with taxation, there was an open bar and excellent food. Flush with the power of a Texan in the White House, the conference closed on a high note. We headed for Mexico for the traditional drinking and dining, fun and games.

On the drive back Harris took me through Alice, Texas, and the King Ranch. In the middle of a flat, dry prairie, Alice is the county seat for Jim Wells County. Located atop part of the huge King Ranch oil field, the county was famous for that review from August through October 1948 when Johnson stole key votes there.

Harris brought up the unique relation Johnson and Clark had with the King Ranch, telling me how Johnson had been top assistant to Kleberg in Congress. He reminisced on several points of history we had with the King Ranch. I mentioned that they were Republicans and he said that did not matter. Candidates run and some win, some lose. The winners always need money to pay off debt. When we show up with the cash, they are always very grateful and agreeable. Before or after we get access and we get commitments.

The preparation for lobbying was just beginning. Following the Bayview meeting, there was a major meeting a few weeks later. This time all electric, gas, and telephone utility lawyers met at a secluded resort and golf course. Again, the lobbyists reviewed plans for the coming year and heard about the ongoing threats of state and national regulation. The group was so secretive that, when it organized formally several years later, its charter specifically provided that the group would be known as the "Texas Utility Lawyers Association" but that the name would never be used. What you saw was not really there. This paranoia, duplicity, and secrecy were typical of our actions behind the scenes.

A key area of my expertise was oil and gas, and this brought me into my first contact with the east Texas oil field on behalf of Clark.[2] An application had been filed to drill new wells on a T. W. Lee lease, operated by an L&G Oil, a small company in Longview. Seems it had illegal wells on the east edge of the east Texas field. I reviewed the brief application that had been filed, and then met with the client on the hearing date, in Clark's small sitting room next to his office. Lewis, a narrow-shouldered man with a slight, willowy build, was a tight-mouthed management type. Bailey Sheppard was short and rotund, always smiling and talking, a longtime Johnson political supporter in east Texas. An attorney by trade, his main line of business was promoting oil deals and taking care of voters.

The problem for Sheppard and Lewis was twofold: slant holes and lack of money. Clark owned the lease but refused to help in the funding, at least not until he returned from Australia. Now he was back and ready to spend some money. Sheppard and Lewis were ready to help him.

At the hearing Exxon demanded a multiple series of explosions on the drill stem as the well was drilled, to be certain it was not deviated again. The well itself was also opposed, on the grounds that it had always been a deviated tract outside the boundaries of the east Texas field and should have been closed a long time ago. A map was laid out, showing more than thirty illegal wells. In short, Clark and the law firm as owners of the lease were crooks along with L&G. I turned to Lewis, who mumbled that the very expensive multiple drilling tests were acceptable. We agreed with the settlement proposal and left.

Back at the firm, after leaving Sheppard and Lewis to wait for Clark, I went to see Harris. He laughed and explained that hundreds of wells had been deviated and, when the theft was clear, the producers came to see Clark. The recommendation was to plug and abandon, then pour cement down the hole and the illegal slant could never be proven. No evidence, no crime. We would keep a few going and, when things got quiet again, re-drill the rest later.

The cases I handled covered a wide range, from stopping expressways with Mexican dinners flown from San Antonio to Washington for Senator John Tower's birthday to doubling natural gas prices and blowing the lid on federal regulation.[3] The bottom line for the client was an increase in stock value from eight to one hundred forty-five dollars per share over a two-month period. Unions were routinely enjoined to protect big business and I even called in the Texas Rangers when a judge was not available to break up union work stoppages. Utility rates were increased, one time so outrageously that statewide regulation was finally imposed. Parades protesting Vietnam were stopped so Johnson would look good at home. San Antonio and Texas highways were enjoined so a judge's son could get into law school and wealthy Johnson contributors could keep an unrestricted view of parklands. I ended up taking the case into the United States Supreme Court and getting a writ of certiorari that stopped the expressway.[4]

In short, I did what I was supposed to do—get results.

Politics remained vital. After all, that was our *pro bono* work. Support for key candidates was a necessity. That meant fund-raising and that meant I saw how Brazos-Tenth worked. There I saw into the heart of politics at its very worst.

On March 31, 1968, the role of power and politics came home to me. Because we had to keep up with Johnson's policies, I was intently watching his address about the Vietnam War. I was shocked when, near the end, he dolefully announced he would not be a candidate for reelection. In that moment I knew the political power Clark exercised would come to an end. The feeling was the exact opposite of my feelings five years earlier when I learned Kennedy had been shot.

Clark had obtained agreement to be paid over time, much of it in the form of retainers. Those payments were for doing nothing. Then, when Johnson quit after only one term instead of two, Clark was not going to get four more years of work-free income. He wanted something more, perhaps as a bonus. His friends and clients had made a lot of money. He not only wanted more for himself. He needed more.

The stage was set for the additional payoff for the assassination of Kennedy. During my research I was able to follow the money, to find out what had been paid and what was still owed for the assassination.

The first sign of the loss of money came two months after Johnson returned home in January 1969. I was approached by the firm's bookkeeper demanding to know why one of our regular clients, Pacific Lighting, was not sending its monthly retainer. I explained that, with Johnson's departure from office, free income like that was over.

I don't know how many other clients quit paying but there were many. Retainer income fell off disastrously. Panic resulted as the senior partners finally began calculating work hours and amounts owed by clients. We were short of what we needed to keep the firm running. The clients were sophisticated businessmen. They were not good old boys anymore. Most knew that, because Johnson was no longer president, they no longer had to pay any debt for Clark's secret legal services.

Clark was particularly unhappy. He never got all he expected and he felt the past due sums were also owed. So, as income fell, Clark went to work.

He agreed with the partners to a timekeeping system to bill currently. Clark also decreased his capital account below 50 percent. He no longer owned the law firm and its lawyers. He did not accept the change easily. In return, his extralegal income did not go through the firm's accounts. That income was always discretionary with him, paid depending on his tax situation and the law firm's finances. Now he kept it for himself.

When all this was done, there was still not enough money. For Clark, it was an even greater decline. He had a net worth in stocks of about one million dollars. That was three million in assets and two million in debt.[5] This balance sheet was for personal assets, not funds in trusts and for family. He owed too much, and he had nowhere near what Johnson had accumulated. He set out to collect what was owed him. Forget the partners. He wanted to be paid for what he had risked and for what he had done.

I would be attorney of record for Clark in his quest for a payoff for what he had done in the Kennedy assassination. The payoff was a power play, a demand for a bonus at a very high level for benefits conferred in the past. It was typical of the old-style billing. The bonus application was prepared a few months after Johnson's return to Austin. For five years, it would be pending as an unpaid bill.

The logic behind Clark's claim was inescapable. Through Johnson, Clark had saved the oil depletion allowance. It remained unchanged during the Johnson presidency. When he left, it was changed from 27.5 percent to only 15 percent; however, a new intangibles allowance made up for the difference and more. The minimum total net deduction to the oil industry was almost 30 percent. This meant over one hundred million dollars to the oil industry, to Big Oil, and to the majors and independents.

That savings was just one benefit.

For this, Clark expected to be paid. The national political office needed to pull off the power play was gone. He had to use leverage at the state level.

What he did to collect started with a visit to his friends with Big Oil in Dallas. The conversations led to the agreement for a payoff. The basic deal was with Murchison. Murchison had been very pleased with his income during the Johnson presidency and had gone so far as to put Clark on the board of directors of his corporation. Such outsider access in the secretive business of Big Oil was very unusual. Looking ahead, knowing what Johnson's retirement meant, Clark turned to Murchison in February 1969 and received a promise to pay and an unusual suggestion of how to get paid; however, Murchison died June 20, 1969, before Clark could get the payoff underway. The beginning of the payoff plan was delayed for a year.

The deal was that the Big Oil landowners in east Texas, the ones living in Dallas, okayed giving Clark one hundred wells in the east Texas field. He could apply. They would not object. Murchison had warned Clark they could not help with the majors like Exxon and Texaco. Murchison suggested Clark make the request and see what happened. It might be fewer than one hundred wells but, then, a deal was a deal. The oil business was changing and Clark had to take what he could get.

After the basic deal was made, I was called in to handle the application. The details are so convoluted and the basic oil process so complex that few understood what was really going on. Here is what happened.

Exxon was the major producer in the east Texas oil field and, following unitization, was director for production. By unitizing the field, all oil wells were subject to equal production rights. Along with the other major producers, Exxon carefully protected its very large hold on the reservoir, the underground bank. Although the Railroad Commission watched over the production process, the majors and their private enforcers were the only effective way to control the oil thieves, the illegal drillers, and the slant-hole artists. By 1965, after finally plugging most of the illegal wells, the great field was again stable. Except for Clark's T. W. Lee lease, L&G Oil, and a few other deviated wells, illegal activity seemed to be a thing of the past.

After almost forty years of production and development, the black giant was a stable field. There were no more leases to be drilled. All tracts were developed. The field had production stability and, more important, legal and political stability.

Clark's plan was relatively simple. He would claim a vacancy on land in the east Texas field by taking a lease claimed by adverse possession and limitation title. In other words he would take a lease from a man claiming squatters' rights. At one time, small tracts were easy to acquire. There were small tracts, typically owned by the descendants of former slaves. By 1968, however, every possibility for a legal well had already been drilled or had been turned down.

This did not deter Clark. There was no other choice. We had to go with a power play using a fake lease to test the major producers' resolve to fight and to start negotiating the bonus. All we needed was a tract of some kind, any kind, to give us a basis for filing. The tract would be taken to the Railroad Commission where title to land was not decided. If an applicant had a lease that was all we needed to get permission to drill a well.

The lease Clark used was for a tiny tract in Gregg County, in the middle of the east Texas field.[6] The black landowner's claim was based on adverse possession. He would later testify in a separate case that he remembered his father and grandfather had plowed the field over fifty years ago on the other side of the old fence line. We took the lease. There was one big problem. The exact same claim had been made and rejected in 1938, more than thirty years earlier. Clark showed up again with the same claim to the same tract. In law, once a case is decided, the legal issues are over. The law of the case governs. Clark was violating the oil field's legal and political stability.

At this point I became a participant in the assassination payoff. At first, I did not know what was really happening, but I had more than enough suspicions. Later events and admissions made the bonus clear.

The fake well application was the vehicle but some outside help was needed. Clark called on his buddies with L&G Oil. The key man was Bailey Sheppard, the east Texas attorney with a long and successful background as a political supporter in the Johnson-Clark axis. Harry Lewis, partner and manager for L&G Oil, joined him. I had worked with both men before on T. W. Lee lease amendments.

The standard form application was prepared and sent to me for filing. Clark was the operator for the proposed well. He had become an oil producer. He was no longer sharing with his partners. He was now an oilman.

Early in the morning of the hearing date, I went over to Clark's office. Sheppard and Lewis were already there, ready to testify. After telling them we needed no witnesses since this application had already been heard—we were relying on the prior record—I suggested they wait at a coffeeshop near the Railroad Commission. I did not tell them their reputation for slant holes would not help the application, that I did not want them as witnesses. Clark agreed.

The hearing drew a crowd. I explained we relied on the prior record and needed nothing new. There would be no testimony. Exxon was the key opponent but could ask no questions because there were no witnesses. A hearing for a well into the biggest oil field in the country on a proposal for the biggest theft of all passed in front of everyone with barely a whimper. Everyone knew it was a power play. The record or the hearing would not matter. After some objections by the lawyers, the briefing schedule was set.

I left the room and hurried to report to Sheppard and Lewis. The coffeeshop was on Congress Avenue, the main street leading to the Texas capitol. Sheppard and Lewis were there with two other men I assumed were employees or consultants. One was a small redheaded fellow. I do not remember his name so "Rusty" will do. The other was Mac Wallace. I remember his name only because, while Clark's application was pending, a person with the same name but a slightly different spelling was a member of the Railroad Commission. The man was Mack Wallace.

I gave a brief review of the hearing and told them the dates for the closing statements. Rusty remarked, "When we get this one, there's one hundred more ready to go."

Sheppard nodded. "It's true. This one leads to one hundred more."

I smiled, still shaking my head.

Sheppard persisted. "It's the payoff."

I shrugged. "I just gotta keep my client happy."

In the laughter that followed, the subject of the application disappeared from the conversation.

Wallace said nothing.

Back at the office, I told Clark's secretary I needed to see him and went to my office, to complete a summary report and to prepare a closing statement. The immediate need was a closing statement that looked good. There was no way to justify granting what had been denied, so I resorted to a brief with long sentences and no apparent subject or object. When in doubt, confuse. To this day the brief makes no sense.

As I was dictating, the intercom buzzed. Clark was back and needed to see me. Just before seven that evening I entered his office. Only a table lamp was on; the overhead lights were off. The darkened room had an intimacy I knew Clark used when he wanted secrecy. He was sitting in his judge's chair, leaning back, his eyes closed.

"I have this report on the hearing," I said, handing him a one-page summary. For Clark, the rule was inflexible: for him to read something, keep it to one page and easy to read.

Opening his eyes, he reached for the memo, saying nothing, for a long moment studying me through narrowed eyelids. Then he leaned back, put on his half-glasses, and glanced at the single page.

"So it went as you wanted?" he asked.

"Yes, sir. I was surprised . . ."

"About what?" he quietly interrupted.

"The opposition. Exxon had a bunch of executive types there. Otherwise, it was quiet. Too quiet."

He nodded as he put my summary on a cluttered desk. "I need you to handle a few things," he paused, "for me."

"Yes, sir."

"This application is just for me," he continued. "In addition, you will represent just me as my lawyer," he paused, "not for the firm. Understand?"

"You want me to sign just for you?" I was surprised the other partners were excluded.

"You will be my lawyer, not the firm's lawyer." He paused as he grunted and sat up. "This is a very, very important matter." He looked at me. "You do understand that?"

"Mr. Ambassador, for you, yes, of course."

Gesturing to my memo, he continued, "This application means a great deal of money. Some may go to the lawyers here, you know. Most is for me."

Taking off the glasses and leaning back again, he closed his eyes. "Some very large companies owe me a great sum of money."

"Yes, sir," I said.

"There is no room for mistakes," he quietly remarked. "You will give this one application all your attention. You cannot make a mistake." He leaned forward, looking at me.

"I appreciate that," I replied.

Clark leaned back, the tips of his hands together, almost prayerful. "Yes, this is a very important matter," he mused, almost to himself. "This is a payment, a payment to me for services rendered." He glanced at me.

"We are talking about a great deal of money," I commented.

"We are," he agreed. "Yes, we are." He paused. "We are talking about a very great service done for my friends in Dallas." He grinned. "They do not think I know how much I made them. But I know."

Saying nothing, I watched, letting him ramble on. When he started talking, you did not interrupt.

"Yes, I know," he continued, "and now so do you." He glanced at me and then back at his hands. After a long pause, he quietly remarked, "I think that is all." I had expected more but he stopped.

"Yes, sir. I'll have you a draft of the statement in the morning." I stood to leave.

"Yes. You do that." He leaned forward. "Just push this hard. Very hard. You understand?"

"I do."

He kept studying me. "Yes," he finally remarked. "I'm sure you do." Then he added, "There is one more thing. Tell no one about this."

"Yes. Right."

He turned his attention to the cluttered desk, moving paper around aimlessly. I left.

The next day I prepared Clark's statement, signed by me as his attorney. The law firm was not mentioned. What I knew was just between Clark and me.

I personally delivered the statement to the hearing examiner. He assured me he was not saying anything about the case. He was just taking it directly upstairs, to the men who had the power to approve.

The fight now began in earnest. After closing statements by the opposition were filed, word came back from Ben Ramsey that there was no way to get approval from all three members of the Railroad Commission. This was strictly oral advice—not on the record. Exxon never knew. Two members of the commission were ready to vote for Clark but they were not going to act over a dissent by Mack Wallace. Then we got word back on still another decision. Final action on the application was postponed. We had to test the limitation title in district court. A trespass to try title case was filed in Tyler to see if there were any squatter's rights. The application for the bonus well was put on hold at the Railroad Commission. We waited. Even after the Tyler attorneys lost the title case, we waited.

In 1974, the fight for the payoff changed dramatically. Now it was strictly between Exxon and the state's most powerful lobbyist. The negotiating Murchison had warned about was continuing at a very high level, and it would last another year.

The net effect of this effort for Clark's bonus, what I did for Big Oil to deregulate natural gas, and getting the San Antonio highway case in the Supreme Court was to become a partner with him in 1972. I had earned Martindale-Hubbell's highest rating in the shortest possible time. The private rating system for lawyers around the world, it represented a consensus opinion from my peers. It was time to move up.

On getting the news of the partnership, I went to see Thomas to express my appreciation. He was pleasant as always, taking but a brief moment for the congratulations with a warm handshake and a short visit on what being a partner meant to him. Then he took me upstairs to see John Cofer.

Thomas said he wanted a little woodshedding from Cofer for me, on how to deal with criminal activity by clients.

If clients commit crimes, they tell us about them before they happen. We simply let Cofer know so that the crime, if ever committed, will be in a friendly jurisdiction. In short, we helped plan crimes and keep the clients out of trouble. The privilege protected everything, from learning about criminal conduct to learning about plans for crimes and helping commit them.

As I learned later, our criminal policies fit in perfectly with the assassination. Years later, however, I concluded that the attorney-client privilege did not cover the crimes.

The bonus application had lingered for four years. Then, in 1974, the case was finally ready for more action at the Railroad Commission. Clark was going to confront Exxon directly, in a matter involving huge sums of money, far greater than Clark wanted as a bonus. In short, the subtle negotiations in the back rooms and the board rooms were proceeding, changes were happening, and Clark finally had the leverage he needed.

The exercise of influence is something very few ever see. Even chief executives and their top attorneys don't know what really happens. The few that know do not leave a written record. There are no tapes or videos or transcripts of their exercise of influence because there can be no evidence. Superlawyers know incriminating evidence and they know how to avoid it. To another superlawyer, however, there is ample circumstantial evidence. In this one we have the public record plus what happened behind the scenes.

Exxon, it seems, had been talking to the Railroad Commissioners about the King Ranch oil field. This great oil field was being prepared for blowdown. The natural gas in the reservoir had been used to produce oil. By 1975, the oil had been produced and the time had come to start producing the natural gas, literally to "blow down" the field. Ironically, the field was located, in part, under Jim Wells County, which just happened to be the home of Box 13 in the 1948 election fraud.

The huge field was largely on the west half of the King Ranch. The Zone 10-B production area was the first part ready for blowdown. Clark learned of the application from Ben Ramsey, who told him it would require Exxon to file for special production rules. Clark also learned Exxon would have a problem. Under the prevailing law in 1972, the gas would be produced based on a surface acreage allotment, a calculation favoring the small producer.

The problem was that the thickest part of the field was in the center, under land owned by the King Ranch and leased to Exxon. The King Ranch, relying on the terms of its lease to Exxon and the accompanying royalties, was demanding it be paid on the basis of gas in place. There was a compromise calculation called net-acre feet which combined the two formulae.

The differences between the three calculations were immense. Surface acreage meant production was pro rata among the owners of the surface land. Because the gas field was very thick under the land leased to Exxon and very thin on the edges, Exxon would lose a substantial sum. It asked for net-acre feet only as a compromise. The King Ranch insisted on gas in place for a much larger royalty payment to them.

The Railroad Commission considered the case and, consistent with the law and Clark's silent pressure, ordered production based on surface acreage. The cost to Exxon would be enormous.

Exxon had no choice but to go to court. While Exxon was one of the toughest guys on the block, it was also a realist. They finally realized a deal with Clark had to be made.

As soon as Clark knew he had the leverage, we went to pursue a little more influence with the Railroad Commission. In May of 1974, while the

Exxon case was pending in the courthouse and while the Clark Rule 37 application was still pending after four years, we paid another visit to the members of the Railroad Commission.

Again, everything was off the record.

Clark and I entered railroad commissioner Jim Langdon's office without benefit of prior appointment and were quickly ushered into a large, cluttered office. We gave Langdon another copy of the brief for the bonus well. We made prohibited secret communications in the style and manner of the good old boys' circuit. Promises of benefits were readily offered. Off-the-record conversations had dominated Texas courthouse politics from the beginning of time but the law had started to change, to prohibit secret meetings between judges and applicants. No problem for Clark.

Because there was no effective penalty on the official or on the lawyer, there was no real way to control these discussions. After all, they are secret. No evidence.

Langdon had a request for better season tickets to University of Texas football games. I presented our case briefly. There was no need. Langdon was in favor of the well application. After only a few minutes, having gotten agreement from Langdon, Clark glanced at his watch and we left.

Clark had all he needed—a vote for his bonus well. Langdon had all he wanted—better football tickets.

We walked down the hall to Ben Ramsey's offices. Clark just walked in unannounced and perfunctorily handed Ramsey the application, saying nothing. Clark did not need to say anything. Both men knew what was happening. They had been talking.

We reviewed what needed to be done with the third commissioner. Ramsey said he would talk to Mack Wallace but promised nothing. He also told Clark to visit the third commissioner.

We abruptly left, and, to my surprise, Clark gestured down the hallway, to the offices of Mack Wallace and said, "We don't need to see him." Clark abruptly turned his back to me and headed for the elevator.

Once outside, we walked the two blocks to the bank where he called for his car at the parking ramp.

"You've done all you can," he said with a grim smile.

As we waited, Clark continued, "It's all about money. That's all."

"A whole lot of money," said I.

He nodded. "Yes, it is. Yes, it is. Just remember, no matter what else, this is all about money." He paused, then angrily added, "They owe it to me, by God. They owe it!" He jabbed his finger at me. "They owe me. Don't ever forget that."

Taken aback, I said nothing. His car drove up, he tipped the attendant, and turned to me. "Just remember, it's the payoff."

Millions of dollars in "payoff!" In my determination to learn why things were happening, the only certain conclusion was that this was a very big deal. My mind clicked over the real reasons that just might lurk behind this strange application.

This time, he did not mention Dallas.

As we parted company at the building's motor ramp, Clark barely fitting his obese self into a yellow Mustang, I knew the only possible connection was the assassination. That would be the closest Clark came to telling me what was really happening. Only later would Thomas confirm my suspicions.

I watched as Clark drove away. He said he needed the money and that he was owed it. His Town Car had been replaced with a Mustang. I later learned his huge debts caught up with him. That afternoon, I was already in too deep for his bonus oil well to worry about his finances. Not my problem. I shrugged and went back to my office.

What happened behind the scenes was that Clark put together one of the most clever and totally fraudulently cases ever run through the courthouse. Clark arranged for the Exxon case to be assigned to Judge Herman Jones, a district judge committed to Clark.[7] Mobil Oil was enlisted to oppose Exxon in court. Then Clark arranged for Thomas and me to represent Mobil but to be sure Exxon won. The public appearance would be a major lawsuit between two very large oil companies, fighting with all their resources to protect their best interests. Surely there was nothing improper.

In fact, Thomas and I were instructed to present a poor case. Thomas put it bluntly, "We're supposed to lose this one." He added, "That damned Clark. Never seen anything like it. He wants so much money."

With those comments, I knew the case had a new face, that of a money-maker.

Sure enough, Jones ruled for Exxon. With Mobil barely putting on a case, it was not too difficult; however, the cover was perfect. When Jones signed the order, the Railroad Commission immediately gave notice of a direct appeal. In Texas, the importance of Railroad Commission orders allowed the state to take a direct appeal to the Supreme Court, avoiding the delay of intermediate appeals. To all appearances, it was a slugfest between heavyweights.

Before the direct appeal could be completed, however, the Railroad

Commission had a new order, favoring Exxon by giving it more than it wanted. Exxon could produce on the basis of gas in place. There were no further objections. The direct appeal was canceled.

During the time between the first order by the Railroad Commission giving Exxon nothing and the final Railroad Commission order giving Exxon all that it could hope for, Clark had collected his bonus of two million dollars net after taxes.[8]

The case had never been a "case" at all. Courts do not decide questions just because someone wants to know what they think. There has to be a real dispute. A real controversy was faked for Exxon to win and for Clark to get his payoff. What we did is fraud on the court. When the courthouse belongs to you, however, there is no fraud. Who can complain? The lawyers for the clients? The judges? The clients? Important new rules are obviously needed for this abuse to end.

There was one final note on the assassination and payoff. At a statewide bar association meeting that year, I met Warren Ellis, an attorney from Tyler who had assisted with the lawsuit between the landowner and Exxon. On instructions from Ramsey to prove up title, Clark's payoff application had been tried in the heart of east Texas.

"That case we had for Clark?" he asked in the smoke-filled ballroom.

I nodded.

"We put that old man up there [on the witness stand], had to you know, and he up and said there were all kinds of leases on that land." Ellis laughed. "We counted twelve."

"So Clark never had anything?"

"Nothing." He took a sip from his drink and, with that confidence lawyers working together have, added, "You know that yahoo giving Clark all the trouble?"[9]

I didn't know but I nodded.

"Harry took care of him, simple as that, and for good." He was referring to Harry Lewis, manager for L&G.

"How'd he figure in the matter?"

"Yeah." Ellis smiled. "For good." He suddenly frowned and looked at me suspiciously. "You didn't know?"

"Give me a clue."

Ellis looked at his cigarette, took a puff, and exhaled a cloud of dirty smoke. "I wish I knew," he said, then took a drink from his glass and walked away. He never mentioned Mac Wallace's name but I know that Wallace was the yahoo. Wallace the assassin had been killed.

Clark never got his one hundred wells because the majors and Big Oil were in the midst of a big change. He did get two million dollars in a final settlement involving future production from the black giant. The details are buried in Clark's financial statements but show a net improvement, after taxes, in that total amount.

Two million dollars cash, net after taxes.

Clark was paid. His partners were not. The final legal services for the assassination of the president were paid and the case was closed. Only twelve years were needed to complete the coverup.

Wallace's end was near. He showed up for the bonus application in 1970 and was working with Harry Lewis and L&G Oil while he waited, along with Clark, for more money. Wallace's fortunes had ended in California with a divorce and a return to Dallas. After pushing Clark for more money, he was told of the bonus well and became a party to the expected money. When payment was delayed, he had to be taken care of "for good." He had to be eliminated. After driving to see his daughter in Troup, Texas, he went by L&G's offices in Longview, Texas. There his exhaust was rigged for part of it to flow into his car.

After dark on January 7, 1971, as he was driving into Pittsburg, Texas, near his birthplace at Mount Pleasant, he drifted off the road and died of massive head injuries. An empty bottle for his medication for narcolepsy was found in the wreckage. Combined with the carbon monoxide, sleep resulted.[10]

So, in a final measure of justice, Wallace died of carbon monoxide poisoning and massive head injuries, just as many of his victims had been killed.

The stage was set for Jaworski and my final conflict of interest with Clark. Again, the fight involved competing interests and several lawsuits.

In the complex maneuvering between oilmen in their effort to raise prices, the increases in natural gas had resulted in oil prices going up. By 1971, Texas was no longer holding back production. Allowables were set at 100 percent. Shortages were coming to Texas and that was the new problem. Cutbacks were necessary.

In Texas, Lo-Vaca Gathering Company had entered into long-term contracts to supply natural gas to most of the central and southern parts of the state. As prices went up, Lo-Vaca could not buy new gas at its fixed prices. It could no longer operate "on the come," gambling on new money to cover debts. During a major ice storm in Texas, Lo-Vaca cut back on supplies. Emergency orders were required to keep gas flowing. Only key industries and homes were supplied. Lawsuits were filed everywhere. The Railroad Commission was asked to review the fixed prices and set new prices. That meant setting aside the contracts, something the commissioners were very reluctant to do.

An old case set the rule that contracts were not to be set aside. To test that rule, Clark enlisted Sam Ballen, the geologist in Dallas who had put him in touch with Oswald, to ask the Railroad Commission to set aside his contracts. Ballen had tried several years earlier and had lost. Clark planned to work his magic, knowing the commission would help Ballen and then help Lo-Vaca. I represented Ballen and got him some rate relief.

At the same time I represented most companies doing business with Lo-Vaca. In other words I was opposing Lo-Vaca. Clark kept asking my opinion on the case, and I kept sending him memos suggesting how the case might be settled. I should have guessed Clark had a connection to Lo-Vaca. We were doing too much that helped Lo-Vaca to be opposed to them. I soon found out, to my still further surprise, that Clark was working with Lo-Vaca, and he was doing it through Leon Jaworski.

The revelation came in an interesting, very personal way. I was in my corner office when Hazel Arnold, secretary to Thomas, entered and handed me a petition to sign. She simply opened it to the signature page, my name typed there. Apparently, I was only to sign, not even look at it. I did one thing: took the petition and turned to its cover. It was an answer to a lawsuit against Lo-Vaca by the Lower Colorado River Authority. I returned to the signature page. Clark and Thomas had already signed it. So, too, had Tracy DuBose, counsel for Coastal States, the parent company for Lo-Vaca.

I told Hazel I wouldn't sign. She looked at me in amazement and left. Within two minutes, DuBose strode into my office, demanding I sign. When I refused, the stocky, black-suited man looked at me in disbelief, then turned and left.

Within another minute, I was called into Thomas's office to explain why I wouldn't sign. I told Thomas we couldn't because we represented every company opposing Lo-Vaca in the courthouse. Thomas was genuinely worried and called the managing partner who quickly joined the conference. Again, we discussed the conflict, getting nowhere. There was another break while Thomas left his office, this time walking down the hall to meet directly with Clark.

When Thomas returned, I was told the law firm could never refuse a request from Leon Jaworski considering all that he had done for Johnson and Clark. At this point it was no longer just a conflict of interest. For me, it was also personal. There was no way I could face the many lawyers I had worked with to oppose Lo-Vaca. In matters of high politics, things do get personal. I flat refused to sign. Forget conflict of interest, forget legal ethics, and forget power politics. I could never sign on behalf of Lo-Vaca.

Finally, Thomas conceded and gestured for me to leave. I walked out of his office, still shocked that Clark would abandon Central Power and Light, the company that paid his bills when he opened in 1939 and that he would go against the Texas Utilities' systems to go with Lo-Vaca.

From that point on, I knew my days with Clark were numbered.

What I tried to understand was what Jaworski had done for Johnson that made Clark believe he could never refuse whatever Jaworski wanted. I knew Jaworksi helped Johnson run for both vice president and the Senate in 1960 by representing him in litigation but that had been a cakewalk. The only other thing I knew for sure was what I learned later, about Jaworski and Jack Ruby's attorney and Clark's brother-in-law Joe Tonahill. Jaworski had helped Johnson and Clark cover up the assassination.

Clark was irrevocably committed to Jaworski so our law firm violated all the rules of conflict of interest among clients. Jaworski came out on top.

Within a few months, in a dispute over a small lawsuit I handled, I left. After the Lo-Vaca confrontation, I knew the next excuse would be all that was necessary. When it happened, I resigned.

> [Superlawyers'] very profession is at stake.... a quotation from Dick the Butcher in Shakespeare's Henry VI [is]: "The first thing we do, let's kill all the lawyers." The public opinion of Washington lawyers [superlawyers] has not reached that point. Not yet, anyway.
> —Stephen Goulden

> You must base your decision on the greater weight of the evidence
> or the evidence that is more credible and convincing. You are to
> decide by what is more probable than not.
> —Standard jury instruction, civil case

17

Jury

Having seen what happened on the available record, insight into the depth of the conspiracy is still needed. In order to see the most likely scenarios for the key steps in the development of the plot, we need to consider the connection between this known record and what happened in Dealey Plaza on November 22, 1963.

When lawyers connive with clients as parties to what is essentially a criminal conspiracy known as racketeering, no one truly understands the details except the participants. Behind the scenes and off the record, however, what happened should be reviewed to show how it most likely happened. From my perspective, I am in a position to bring to life the key steps in the conspiracy.

I emphasize there is no public record; however, the tradition is clear and the term used in writing is "faction" or the journalistic novel. I do not know exactly what happened, but, because I knew the conspirators and worked closely with them, I know how they thought, and I am able to get right next to the conspiracy.

In addition, for purposes of trial, I can tell you what happened in that final argument to a jury with a look into the heart of the conspiracy. I will show you from the greater weight of the credible, believable evidence what happened behind the scenes, how LBJ killed JFK. All we need to do is connect the dots, take the known evidence, and understand what happened.

With that caution, this is what went on behind closed doors, in that time between Kennedy's inauguration and Johnson's becoming president.

Desperation

In a wicked twist, Kennedy's inaugural was also the start for Johnson's inaugural. Ambition without end was always there for Johnson, and the loss of power was a great emptiness for him. A motivation that was just as great, if not greater, also moved him forward. Fear was present, that fear of a loss of everything. The dual motivation of ambition and fear could not have been stronger.

The fear rested with Estes and his problems. His empire was collapsing, and Johnson's participation stood a good chance of bringing him down also. When Johnson met with Cliff Carter and Estes inaugural week, steps were started that only worsened. At that meeting, the only thing decided was to see if the USDA investigator Henry Marshall could be persuaded to call off the dogs. Wallace was to be enlisted.

The situation worsened and, within a month, Estes insisted on another meeting. At the time Johnson was back in Texas, and he agreed to fly to Pecos. Early in the morning of February 19, 1961, Johnson called for his airplane. The day was heavily overcast, not safe for flying.

"God damn it to hell!" Johnson shouted into the phone. "I am leaving at dawn." Ed Clark was in Johnson's office at the ranch, listening as the vice president glared at him and then at the phone. "We have to leave right away," Johnson bellowed. The meeting with Estes could not wait.

Suddenly, Johnson handed the phone to Clark and stalked away. "You tell him. I leave this morning." Johnson turned in his huge ranch office and shouted, "He wanted to stay in Austin last night. I warned him we had to fly today. I want that son-of-a-bitch here, right now."

"The vice president does not give a damn about your fucking fog," Clark shouted into the phone, mimicking his favorite client. "He has to be in Pecos, in two hours, this morning."

Another pause and Clark shouted, "Then get your replacement here." Clark nodded as he listened, then smiled and turned to Johnson. "They're leaving."

"Okay!" Johnson shouted.

"He says the fog and rain is . . ."

"I don't give a good goddamn," Johnson muttered as he sat on the nearby big desk.

Clark walked over to the big man.

"What am I going to do?" Johnson asked, more to himself than Clark.

"We just need time." Clark lisped, then stepped back, sitting on the nearby couch. "I need time."

"They're moving too fast, Ed-ward." Johnson emphasized each word as he spoke. "They are going to get me."

"Not a chance," Clark assured him. "You're covered."

"That goddamned peckerwood," muttered Johnson, referring to Estes. "Wallace has got to . . ."

"Already started." Clark's finger went to his mouth and he whispered. "You remember now. This is out of your hands." In the silence that followed, Clark grunted as he stood up, walked to the bar, and poured a shot of whiskey.

Johnson looked up. "We gotta do something."

"Do not even think about it," Clark said, firmly adding, "I got it handled." His voice trailed off. He did not have it handled, but steps were being taken. He just needed a break, several breaks in fact. He knew that, if you keep plugging away, something good happens.

As it turned out, he had over a year before the scandal made the headlines.

As the two men spoke, the pilots left Austin on their last flight, one that killed them and resulted in very favorable settlements to their families. This first act of desperation should have exposed the underlying problems but did not. For now, when the pressure was great enough, Johnson would do anything.

Within four months, Marshall was dead, brutally murdered by Wallace when the investigator refused to pull back. Clark, alerted by Carter, had the necessary steps in place to assure a verdict of suicide. The Department of Agriculture was not about to let one of their personnel die under mysterious circumstances and then drop the investigation already underway.

Early in August, Johnson was notified that the USDA would soon schedule another meeting. Estes still had serious problems, this time involving murder.

Help!

The key decision was made soon after the murder of Henry Marshall by Mac Wallace. Johnson summoned Clark to the ranch. The two men had to be alone, with no witnesses. This was more difficult because Kennedy had ordered Secret Service protection for his vice president. When Clark arrived that afternoon, Johnson immediately took him for a ride across that wide expanse of barren, rocky hills west of Johnson City to a place next to the Pedernales River, to a place where they had met in the past, assured of complete privacy.

Little was said as the men drove off. The day was already hot and dry. There was no wind and even the cicadas were silent. *All the better for what I have to do today,* the tall, lanky politician thought as he accelerated his Lincoln convertible across the rock-hard ground. With the ruts for the hunting road his only guide, the rattling and shaking of the rough ride tossed him and his sole passenger rudely about.

The freedom to speed was one of the few pleasures left to him, and he was often criticized for his recklessness. He simply ignored the critics. Today, under the worst of circumstances, he was like a juvenile new to the wheel. He had to have speed. A driven man of intense energy, Johnson thrived on danger. In anticipation of a very risky undertaking, his adrenaline was at its maximum. Johnson grinned as he glanced at the speedometer. Whether consciously or subconsciously, he wanted that sense of careless abandon, that sense of danger that was only too appropriate on that fateful morning. If he died, that was life.

For today, a most important and delicate subject had to be discussed with the only person available to discuss any subject at any time, where no holds were barred. Clark was always at his beck and call to share those deepest hopes and fears. Today, without his friend having any idea about the fateful consequences soon to be discussed, Johnson was going to settle the course of his future and the remainder of his life.

He was comfortable about what he planned to do. The two "good old boys" had weathered many a storm. Once again, Johnson knew something had to be done.

As the Lincoln hit another hard bump, the usually talkative Clark finally said, "Hadn't you best slow down, Lyn-don?" Clark had never seen his most important client in such a hurry, acting with such disregard for his life. Grasping the panel before him in those pre-seatbelt, pre-airbags days, Clark did not enjoy the thrills Johnson liked. This time, Clark, drawing on his ability to read men, and particularly this man, sensed fear. Glancing again at Johnson, Clark could tell from the lines around the eyes and forehead that something big was up. *Interesting,* he thought, recalling prior discussions.

The car was designed for hunting and Johnson would use it whenever he wanted to shoot. On his ranch, he did not worry about hunting season. If he wanted to shoot a deer, he would. If he just needed to kill something, there were baited places for shooting the graceful animals. For night shooting, spotlights were placed to blind the prey and set them up for the rifle. Today, Clark had noticed, there were no weapons in the car.

Johnson glanced at Clark and laughed. "This time, Ed-ward," he said, "you trust me." He made a sharp turn, leaving the thin, dry dust hanging behind as he bounced the vehicle roughly onto a rock outcropping beside the river.

"We got something to talk about," Johnson added. "Alone."

As the car stopped, Clark lamely replied, "Well, now, Lyn-don, we can talk anytime, anywhere. You know that."

"Come on," Johnson ordered, stepping out. The area was barren except for a few patches of mesquite bushes scattered here and there without pattern. There was no sound; just a heavy, very dry heat that stilled the senses.

Clark hesitated, opened his door and, lifting his heavy body with a pull on the top of the front frame, muttered, "Right behind you."

They walked over to a few scraggly mesquite bushes, ringed with dried-out cacti, decayed yellow flower pods still holding on. The ground produced little—never had, never would. Clark was uncomfortable in his suit coat, mismatched tie, and unbuttoned vest. Officially, Clark was an attorney but he was primarily a power broker, a man who sold access to power for a price, for things that happened "out of sight."

Johnson stooped to pick up a flat rock and skate it across the Pedernales, the small river glimmering in the heat, slowly moving between the low cliff and flat pasture on the other side. The rock skipped a few ripples, then sank. He turned to Clark. "Something's gotta give."

Clark nodded. The Estes scandal had quieted down with the Marshall death but something new was surely underway. He knew Johnson must have heard something about developments in Washington. Something was very wrong.

Wallace had made mistakes with the Marshall killing. There had never been direct orders to murder, only to talk to the investigator and intimidate him into agreeing. The meeting took a bad turn, Wallace lost his temper, and Marshall was killed. Still, the crime was covered up. Nothing more needed to be done. Let that sleeping dog lie, Clark reasoned.

Standing only a few feet from his attorney, Johnson paused, not looking at him, not even threatening the famous LBJ treatment, a combination of alternately fond and excruciating embraces, full-body style, as he physically worked a senator over to get their agreement. Johnson had never used "the treatment" with Clark and never would.

"Can Mac handle something else?" Johnson asked.

Clark grunted. "He makes mistakes."

"Yeah. Found that out." He spoke flatly, his mind far away, racing. The killing had been a mistake but now he was deeply implicated. If Estes or Wallace talked, his political life was over and he was in prison.

The vice president suddenly drooped, and Clark looked at a man who became in an instant very sad, forlorn, and wasted, showing all the signs of hopelessness and desperation.

"I don't know about the Bobby deal," Clark said, speaking slowly, quietly. By mentioning names like Bobby Baker, he hoped to get more information from his client.

Johnson's rugged face looked up, surprised. "Ed-ward, it ain't that Bobby," he said. "It's the other one." His big hands went together, rubbing each other.

Clark hesitated. He recalled the Democratic convention in Los Angeles the previous year, of their trying unsuccessfully to dig up enough votes to win. He knew but asked anyway. "You talking about baby boy Kennedy?"

"Yes." Johnson looked at Clark, his eyes now intense, mean. "Plain and simple, that asshole is out to gut me."

Clark looked away. Johnson was always a bully to his closest associates, and, for his sworn enemies, was too often vindictive. In moments of success, Johnson could be the most grateful and generous of men; however, in his moments of black terror and fear, Johnson was the meanest man alive. Ever a good judge of men, Clark recognized the classic pattern of judging others' intentions by the same motivations Johnson had. Whenever he was in deep trouble, Johnson always feared that his enemies would do to him what he wanted to do to them. Then his fears could rise to monstrous anxieties, too often feeding on each other. He thought of every bad thing that could happen and, like a coyote on the run, he only saw danger everywhere.

"Ed-ward!" Johnson commanded, his voice low, furious. "Look at me. I'm telling you." Then Johnson emphasized each word. "Bobby Boy will put me under."

"Lyn-don," Clark said soothingly, slowly, his brow furrowed. "I, uh, don't believe he'll change the president's mind."

Johnson leaned close to Clark. "Bobby is pushing hard. He wants to know everything about the Marshall killing." He threw his arms up. "I am telling you, it's gonna explode."

Stepping back, looking away, Clark just shook his head.

Johnson's voice trembled as he added, "I'm telling you, right here and now, both are after me."

Clark said nothing, wanting his client to talk, to pour his heart out.

"Here's the worst," Johnson continued. "He warned me!"

Clark watched quietly as Johnson stepped away and bent over, dry heaving. Clark had seen this physical anxiety many times. Johnson appeared to be a strong man but, inside, he was constantly churning, a terrible bundle of nerves. Clark looked away.

"I got to do something," Johnson whimpered as he spit, then wiped his mouth. "We gotta do something." He suddenly lunged forward, grabbing Clark's shoulders. "We got to get them before they get me."

Inwardly, Clark winced at the foul breath but he stared back, realizing Johnson's frenzy would not go away. Clark moved his arm to Johnson's back, turning him, to embrace the man's shoulders. "Go easy, Lyn-don," he soothingly remarked as he waited, keeping a firm hand in place, controlling the situation as it developed.

Clark knew he had power behind him. He also knew to move first, to be the aggressor. Most important, he knew how to bait people, how to set them up to get them to do what he wanted. To top it off, he had Johnson. In that symbiotic relationship, the two men dominated Texas politics. Whatever either wanted, they got. If both men wanted it, it was a cakewalk.

Johnson stepped away, wiping his mouth on his sleeve, spitting, walking back to the car. Turning suddenly, he spoke in a strangely hoarse voice. "I am one heartbeat from the presidency and I am about to be crucified." Clenching his hands, stretching them before him, then throwing his arms up, he breathed deep and slumped. "God damn it, Ed-ward," he blurted, "I'm going to jail."

Silence. In that subconscious communication that existed between them, Clark suddenly realized what Johnson was talking about. He wanted John Kennedy out of the way for good. There was a long silence. Johnson glanced at Clark, saying nothing, his eyes pleading, *"What do we do?"*

Clark's eyes narrowed as he looked at the tall man in a rancher's khaki fatigues. "We can't touch the president," he said.

Johnson was stunned. At first, he seemed not to have heard Clark. Then the words sank in and he looked around, then back, suddenly bristling with anger. "Ed-ward! Think of me, man." He strode over, confronting the lawyer. "Put yourself right here, where I am! Damn it! It's clear! Clear as day!" He stared at Clark, his face jammed against Clark's, an inch away, searching the lawyer's dark eyes, now narrowed to slits in the bright sun. "There is only one way."

Clark said nothing. He knew what Johnson wanted.

Johnson abruptly turned away, pacing back and forth. "We know what to do to make me president," Johnson said quietly, his face locked into a scowl, now glaring into Clark. "Legally," he added. "You know you can do it."

Clark pondered the only option placed before him. Then, stepping away from the car, toward the edge of the low cliff, he paused. "There are ways," he said slowly, his lisp more pronounced than ever, "to do a job where there is no evidence." Clark straightened as he rose to the challenge. "No evidence," he repeated, as if to convince himself.

Johnson smiled inwardly as he listened, appreciating his lawyer's assured, comforting response.

Then Clark turned and walked away, his head down, talking quietly, almost to himself, saying, "I will have to give this some thought." Clark waved his arms helplessly, the enormity of the request still sinking in. "I, uh, just don't know, Lyn-don."

"Yes, Ed-ward. Yes, you do." Johnson stepped over, to stand by his lifetime friend and partner in crime. "You never let me down. You can't let me down."

Clark slowly nodded, shifted nervously and, almost in a daze, stepped away.

"Ed-ward! Don't you see?"

Clark looked at Johnson, suddenly angered. Johnson was that way, always looking at everything, fearing any and every possibility, making things a lot worse than they were, and always wanting Clark to handle it. Clark knew the risks better than anyone else but he had to worry about one thing, the result. Was there anything he could do that would work?

Johnson stared at Clark, then nodded and, with a trace of sarcasm, said, "Okay. You think about it. And keep a close eye on these things they're hitting me with." He stood by Clark, and, placing an arm across his shoulders, pulled the man to him. "Just think about it. It'll make the papers. You'll see. And it's gonna be awful, just awful."

Clark looked at Johnson, their faces almost touching. With a blank expression, he nodded and turned away.

Johnson suddenly let Clark go. "That envelope in the car," he said quietly, almost an afterthought. "It's yours." Stepping toward the car, he muttered, "Put it to good use." He turned, putting his arms across Clark's shoulders and, pulling him along, the two walked to the convertible.

As they drove back to the ranch, Clark opened the envelope. It contained the policy manual for protection of the president.

On that hot day in a barren land, the most monstrous of crimes was born. The evil word was never mentioned; too dreadful even for the perpetrator, both men knew Kennedy's death was the only way Johnson could be president. Outwardly passive as he looked across the dry land, Clark knew the fear Johnson had. As he felt it, he realized that Johnson's fear had become *his* fear.

Memo

Early that Saturday morning in September 1961, Clark faced the very difficult problem of serving Johnson's request. Clark was in his office, listening to his trusted partner and legal technician Martin Harris.

"He's well protected," Harris continued. "No one could touch him . . ." He was referring to his memo on security for Lyndon Johnson as vice president.

Not looking up, apparently studying the memo Harris had prepared, Clark interrupted, "Except maybe from a high building . . ."

"Yes, sir," said Harris, shrugging, giving his trademark nervous laugh. "That's about the only loophole." He paused, shrugged again, adding, "Not much danger." Harris shrugged nervously. "He'll be safe."

"Very interesting," Clark said. Leaning forward, he rolled out of his high-backed judge's chair and stood.

"I mean . . . ," Harris continued.

Clark waved him away. "I will assure the powers that be. Our client is well protected."

"The agents just need to keep an eye out."

Clark looked at the man over his half-glasses, then lisped gruffly, "Yes. I see that. I'll take care of it." He sensed Harris may be grasping what was really involved.

"You need more of them, too. They gotta be on the ground. Everywhere."

Clark nodded, his attention seemingly elsewhere.

"No one would ever get away," Harris continued.

Clark looked away as he replied, "Keep this top secret."

Harris nodded. He was temporarily speechless as he suddenly realized the implications of his memo.

Clark stepped into his secretary's office, and his attorney followed, still stunned. Harris was an excellent attorney, and his ability to look at both sides, at all sides, had given him the insight to realize what was really going on. Almost innocently, he asked, "How do I charge my time?"

"Hum, well, I think, uh, charge it to the firm," Clark said, standing by his secretary's desk, going through the stack of mail that had been delivered by the clerks. "Yes, okay," he muttered as he flipped envelopes here and there.

Harris just stood there, still confused and upset, just watching. Clark looked up, and for a moment stared at Harris, then asked, "Anything else?"

"Uh, no, sir," the younger man replied as he looked at his senior partner, his boss, the man he called his "owner" when Clark could not hear it said. Harris's eyes narrowed, still wondering.

Clark noticed, stared at his partner for a moment, then looked away, adding, "Kennedy's insisting on protection for Johnson. Lyn-don's against it. You see why?"

Harris, nodded, shrugged, and quickly left.

The Harris memo on the security of the vice president would never see the light of day. Stored away safely in the top-secret penthouse records, the first plans for a monstrous crime were protected as if placed in a safe and welded shut

The Wall

Late that Friday afternoon toward the end of October 1961 Clark left his offices to see a felon at the law offices of John Cofer, his criminal attorney.

By 1961, Cofer was an experienced lawyer; he had the ability to say little in public but do a lot in private. Enlist the relative of a jury member to show up on behalf of his client. Drop an important news item in the jury room. Let the jury read articles slanting the case toward his client's defense. Sometimes, let them read about articles harmful to his client. Always fall back on Clark's special access to the judge.

As Clark rode up the elevator to see Cofer, he was still struggling, trying to figure the "no evidence" angle. How could he arrange an assassination and leave no evidence? How could he be certain that Johnson would not be implicated? Could he develop a plan so that the risks were minimized to the point where they were acceptable? Somehow, Clark had to set up a plan that would work, and, in return, pay him millions of dollars.

As if the offices were his, Clark did not hesitate as he entered; he just walked past the receptionist and went directly into John Cofer's office. She smiled and waved him through.

Cofer's inner sanctum was large, extending across the west side of the building. In the distance, the beautiful downtown lake was a silver ribbon in the late afternoon sun.

"We're all here," Clark said as he entered.

Two men were already there, waiting. Cofer was behind the desk, leaning back in a judge's chair. The other man perched on the edge of a chair before the desk, almost leaning on the desk, plaintive. The two started to stand but Clark ordered as he sat down, "No, no, no; stay where you are."

Cofer was a tall man with a fatherly demeanor, a man you could trust, in a way almost Lincolnesque. He was always pleasant, ready to smile, his pallid skin almost translucent. The other man was dark and heavyset, with thick, black-rimmed glasses and a surly appearance. He was younger than Clark by fifteen years. At that moment, three criminals were together in the room. Two were protected by their unique position as officers of the court. The third man was a convicted felon, a murderer, and soon to be a fugitive.

Within two years, he would be an assassin.

The three men looked at each other for a brief, awkward moment, then, gesturing with his hand, Clark said, "I do not like what I hear, Mac."

Mac Wallace was the convicted murderer who had been saved by John Cofer nine years earlier. Now he was being saved again because he held the key to the exploding Billy Sol Estes scandal. He was the man who killed Henry Marshall, and that murder was causing Johnson all kinds of trouble.

"From the facts I have been given," Cofer interjected, speaking slowly with his surprisingly high but soft voice, "our friend here," he gestured to Wallace, "has covered his tracks while leaving one hell of a lot of evidence." Cofer smiled awkwardly. "Open-ended evidence."

Clark saw nothing pleasant in the situation. "God be damned," he exploded at Wallace. "What were you doing?"

Wallace drew back from the assault. Clark had criticized him so many times and he so hated the personal attacks, but what could he do? He was a murderer, now several times over. He had been rewarded with good work and steady pay, and his family had been taken care of. There was always the promise of more. Now, there was no turning back. The decision to kill for Clark had been made long ago. He gave Clark his full attention.

Clark's voice was harsh, "How for damned long have you been with us?" Not waiting for an answer, he turned to Cofer. "John, damn it, we save his worthless skin, we tell him what to do, and he still don't know squat."

Cofer nodded and leaned back. "Now, Mr. Clark, Mac's not done so bad."

"He ain't worth shit," Clark shot back. "I'm playing hell getting the locals to stay with suicide." He turned back to Wallace. "Judge Cofer here may enjoy tough cases. I don't." Clark knew that, if anything broke in Washington, the

Texas authorities would also push hard. After all, next year was 1962, an election year for statewide candidates.

"Yes, sir," Wallace whispered respectfully.

"With me, you get it exactly right," Clark bristled. "Do you understand that?"

Wallace drew back. "Yes, sir." He had been summoned for today's meeting. Clark called his number in Dallas, still in service even though he was living in California, and left word. Wallace showed up.

"For Christ's sake, Mac!" said Clark. "You gotta do it right."

"I made one mistake," Wallace interjected. "I shoulda just up and shot Marshall, but Carter wanted me to talk to him."

"So you did."

Wallace looked at Cofer, then back to Clark, then out the window. "Things just went from bad to worse. He was trying to cooperate. Then he made a move. He was scared. I hit him, and, well, . . ."

Acting surprised, Clark said, "This Estes thing's not going to just dry up and blow away." He paused. "It's gonna get a whole lot damned worse."

Wallace had a lot of questions but he knew better than ask. With Clark, just get the damned job done; that's all.

Clark turned to Cofer. "John," he asked, "what do we do?"

Cofer smiled and shrugged. "Nothing."

"Another grand jury?" Clark asked.

"Well now, they may just try to set aside the suicide ruling." He leaned back in the chair, fingertips together, looking at Wallace. "For now, we just rest." Cofer was playing the Wall, this time against Clark, trying to keep everyone calm. He was a solid barrier against information but knew little about developing a major political case, especially this case. He just knew you said nothing and reacted very, very carefully.

Clark turned to Wallace again. "You get directions at a filling station and then go back?"

Wallace smiled nervously. "Trying to cover my tracks."

"So, you made another mistake," Cofer interjected.

"Yessir," Wallace said. *Just do what he says,* he reminded himself quietly.

"Leave no tracks. The law cannot convict." Clark looked out the window, toward the evening sunset as it reflected across the lake. "The law can do nothing."

"The perfect crime," Cofer agreed.

Wallace nodded.

"You were a marine?" Clark suddenly asked.

"Yeah," Wallace said, surprised. "Why?"

"Thank you, John," said Clark. "Let me know anything you hear." He looked at Wallace who awkwardly stood. "Let's go," Clark said, nodding to the door, waving his hand as he walked out of the room. Wallace glanced hopelessly at Cofer, who gestured for him to follow.

Control

The process of enlisting a shooter for an assassination was underway. At this point Clark was far from certain what to do. He knew he needed personnel and Wallace was a natural. He made mistakes but he learned. He was proven, not unknown. All things considered, he was closest to what Clark needed, at least for now.

So, outside Cofer's office in the hall by the elevator, the two key men in the Kennedy assassination were together in private. Clark had one objective, to get Wallace thinking about another killing. Not the president. Not yet. He would reveal that key target only when he had to and only if he could see a way to do it. Clark knew the killing of a president was not a federal crime. Any resulting murder would be tried in Texas. That law gave him comfort. He wanted any trial under his control.

Clark also realized all national law enforcement offices would be at his disposal. The success of his legal steps would be in the hands of the immediate successor to President Kennedy. Johnson would direct any criminal investigation. *All the makings of a perfect crime,* he thought. He had control of the investigators. But, he cautioned, *there is no perfect crime.* Some are harder to cover than others, but that came later, if at all.

The only thing he needed right now was a sniper. Wallace was one of his candidates. He had to see if the man could do the job. He would give Wallace his own treatment, the one that got a witness ready to testify, the one that made a person do what he was told to do. Wallace had to be under control. Clark would take his time. This "case" could not be rushed.

As the two men paused, Clark suddenly turned, grabbing Wallace by the shirt, sticking his face into the younger man's face, whispering. "With me, you never make a mistake. Understand?" Rage flared across his pudgy features. "We think of everything!" Clark was lifting him from the floor. "The plans are perfect. They always are. Then you do it, without mistake."

Wallace could only nod.

"Say it," Clark's icy voice insisted. "Do you understand?"

Wallace nodded again as Clark stared at him. Then, lowering the man to the floor, letting him go, Clark pushed the down button for the elevator.

Brushing his shirt, Wallace cleared his throat. "The Marshall deal may have been a mess," he said, "but it was done. No one'll ever know."

Clark nodded. "If you did it right, there'd never have been another question."

The Marshall killing was over, thought Wallace. Suddenly, he realized Clark was thinking about something else.

The elevator door opened. The two entered and Clark pressed the down button.

"I'm sure you understand," Clark said in a voice so low Wallace had to lean forward to listen. "I have another problem. I may need your special attention." He pressed the down button again and they started moving.

Straightening, Wallace replied, "Yes, sir."

"What did you do in the marines?" asked Clark. He knew but he was using it as a reminder to get to thinking on shooting.

"Just a soldier," he replied. "Got hurt, got out."

"Yes, I know," Clark said as he stepped onto the elevator, Wallace following. "Were you a good marine?"

"I could march, shoot, fight. All that crap you get in training." The elevator stopped on the fifth floor and three of Clark's associates stepped aboard.

"Good evening, Mr. Clark," one young attorney said as the others crowded in.

Clark glanced at his watch. "Heading back to the office?"

"No, sir," another responded. "We're heading for the library." The others laughed nervously at the standard after-hours excuse to get a beer.

As the elevator closed and descended, Clark snorted. "I tried that," he said. "Didn't work." He surveyed his employee-lawyers. "Won't work with me either." The men shifted nervously and rode the rest of the way in silence. As the elevator opened on the ground floor, the young lawyers quickly left. Clark and Wallace followed.

Enlistment

In the fading afternoon sunset Clark stopped, watching his lawyers walk away, holding Wallace back. Austin did not have rush-hour traffic in 1961. At closing time, everyone downtown went home quickly, and, by six, Colorado Street was vacant. In that quiet afternoon with the sun now out of sight, the street cold and dark, Clark brought Wallace still deeper into the plan.

"We need you for another killing," he said.

Wallace nodded as his eyes darted around, looking up and down the street, scanning the sidewalks, looking anywhere but at Clark.

"Probably be a time before anything happens," Clark continued. "Let this Estes thing die out. For now, we just need to look for some help."

Wallace stood silent, listening.

"This time, I need a long shot." Clark paused. "A sniper."

Wallace narrowed his eyes.

"What you have to do on this one," Clark said slowly, "has to be done precisely. Things will happen quickly. There will be no room for mistake." Clark paused, looking the stocky man over. "You must do things automatically."

Wallace said nothing.

"For this one, the perfect cover will also be necessary."

"Yes, sir," said Wallace.

"The plan must govern whatever you do," Clark added. "I will set out the plan, down to the smallest detail. You must follow it."

"Yes, sir." Wallace shivered at the intensity of Clark's remark.

"For now, we need only one thing." He paused. There was not a trace of his lisp as he spoke. "Find some shooters."

Wallace was surprised. "How do I do that?"

"You bait 'em," Clark said. "You bait 'em."

"What?" He asked, bewildered.

"Find me some sharpshooters," Clark said. "Look for troublemakers needing money. Tell them you have a political cause. Promise them anything. Get them interested, then get to know them. Then, test 'em." Clark studied Wallace. "Whatever it takes," he added.

"I don't understand," said Wallace. "Just see who wants to shoot someone?"

Anger flared briefly on Clark's face. "No. Look for men with nothing to lose. Ask around. You just want someone good with a rifle. Someone with a grudge against the world. Not to shoot someone. Just a good shooter."

"Okay," Wallace said. "Let me work on it."

"Think about it." Clark reached into his coat pocket and handed a folded paper to Wallace. "I have some names."

"Names?" Wallace was suddenly overcome with emotion. As he looked at the paper, the plan suddenly became very concrete. A killing was going to happen. He glanced at the list.

"Names of radicals," Clark continued. "Militants. Criminals. They'll do anything."

"Do what? I mean, what've they gotta do?"

"Check 'em out. See if they can shoot. Tell them they're working on some secret mission or another. Keep it quiet. Just tell them you need someone who can shoot over a distance, say, uhh, over five hundred feet. Good shots."

Wallace looked at the list. There were names and addresses for seven men in three cities: Houston, San Antonio, and Dallas. "What is going on?" he asked.

"Maybe nothing. For now, just find me some snipers."

"I don't know."

"Yes, you do," Clark interrupted. "We have a good job for you, for now. When this one is over, we have business for you and your family; the usual. You'll be okay."

"How much?" Wallace asked.

Visibly angered again, Clark replied carefully, "Do not ever push me, Mac. This one takes care of you. Your family comes out okay. Just like we've been doing. For now, that's it."

Wallace hated Clark's games. "When?" Wallace asked.

"I don't know. Maybe soon."

A new awareness came over Wallace. "You want me to kill some big shot?"

"I don't know yet," Clark said as he vaguely waved his hand. "In due course. You will find out, in due course."

Wallace nodded.

Clark looked away, irritated, cursing under his breath. "I know what I am doing. You will need cover. For now, we take one step at a time."

"Okay. Yes, sir."

Clark looked him over, now whispering a threat. "You damned well gotta do better than you have."

Wallace nodded, his resolve returning. After all, it was just a plan. Nothing had to be done. Nothing might come of the whole thing.

"For now, just go on," Clark said, gesturing. "Get to it. I'll call you when I need you." Turning abruptly, Clark walked away, toward the Driskill Hotel, toward its private club.

Wallace stood, watching the man, seeing if he would glance back. Clark did not.

On that cool evening in downtown Austin, Wallace lingered where he stood. Clark once told him killers had no rights. Now, for the first time, he knew what Clark meant.

Wallace would not know the details for two more years. He was called within the month, to go to Sam Rayburn's funeral, to look around and see what security was like. He was assured that the main interest was to be sure the vice president was well protected.

At about the same time he began efforts to recruit shooters from Clark's list. He did it slowly and, after a year, had no one recruited.

Bait

The following spring 1962, the Estes case broke wide open. Estes was indicted and Johnson figured prominently in the media. Clark would be tested as never before. First, some key witnesses and participants had to be silenced. Wallace had to do the job. For almost an entire year, from November 1961 to the following November, Estes dominated Clark's free time, his *pro bono* work.

As the crisis died down, Clark turned to the assassination plan again, this time directing his attention to getting paid. As usual, he would tempt his supporters without letting them know a single thing about the conspiracy. In short, he would bait them. Not the same way Wallace would bait snipers but still a trap for the willing unwary.

The downtown club was majestic even before it moved to spatial quarters in the new building towering over Dallas. Small tables widely separated, fresh flowers, servers in tuxedoes, and secluded alcoves to the sides for the big deals. For business purposes, it had one very valuable advantage—privacy.

That November 1962, Clark, acting counselor and paid adviser to Delhi Petroleum, a flagship company for Clint Murchison Sr., was dining with the owner of the company, a large man with a jovial, whiskey-red face. One was the chief spokesman for Big Oil. The other was the chief spokesman for Lyndon Johnson. Both had power, one for the political system of the state of Texas, and the other for cash, lots of cash, measured in the billions.

Both were trying to understand each other and cut a deal. As they carefully circled the unstated issues of assassination and payment, they were as two scorpions in a bottle—fully respecting each other and mutually deadly.

Still, they spoke with the utmost respect for each other. They needed each other and they knew it.

"You will be served," Clark lisped, "that I can assure you. Yes, you will be *well served.*" Clark's words told the equally sophisticated Murchison that what Clark had in mind would cost and would be worth it.

Murchison laughed grimly. "I split the blanket with Kennedy way ahead of the election." His equivocal statement may have meant he knew what was happening or it may have meant he did not want to deal with Clark.

"I know that, Clint," Clark replied. "Hell, man, we all know that." Clark had been treasurer for the Kennedy-Johnson ticket in Texas and had raised money by turning it into a Johnson ticket, assuring donors that the election of Johnson was an important step up. Kennedy was barely mentioned. Reading the 1960 letter had given the distinct impression Johnson would be the next president.

Murchison shrugged as he lifted his drink. Sophisticated in the ways of money and of power, he knew he had to pay for what he got. Because Johnson had helped him in many ways over the years, Murchison stayed with him. They communicated regularly.

"We all did," Clark said, laughing again. "Yessir, we all stuck with him. And it has paid off."

Murchison nodded. "You know I helped our man," he said, then added, "Didn't like it but I did it." Murchison was a solid conservative and did not like any liberal programs.

"I gotta handle on your problems," Clark said quietly, confidently. Clark was talking about oil problems, about depletion and imports, about production and protection. "There will be, uh, some major developments assuring you of that fact."

"Depletion?"

"Not so," Clark assured the oilman. "Not so because we are going to eliminate the source for changes."

Murchison studied the big man. He knew what Clark said was gospel. He did not know what the "source" was. "You will have to show me that," he commented over the rim of his glass as he lifted it to his lips.

Clark absently stirred his coffee. "I will do that," said Clark. "Yes. I will do that." Smiling, shaking his head, he added, "All in due time."

The waiters hovering nearby stepped forward as one, placing new forks beside each man, putting a dessert before them.

Murchison smiled. "Amos, a refill."

"Yes, suh," the waiter said.

Putting the napkin into the front of his shirt, Clark forked up a huge mouthful of cake, and then said, as he chewed, "I am telling you one thing." He paused and looked at Murchison. "There will be no problems for anyone."

"Now, Ed," Murchison asked, "are you promising me something?"

Clark nodded.

"Now you've been dancing 'round all morning, Ed. What's on your mind?" Murchison had worked around vague proposals for many years. Something alerted him. Perhaps Clark was too mysterious. He wanted to know more.

"I will tell you what," Clark replied, his eyes scanning the room. "Yes. I will do that. But only to the best I can. Not everything is possible, not now." He lifted his napkin to his mouth and continued. "We are in a position to assure you that you will not suffer in your business. In fact, you will prosper. And be assured your friends will be served well." As was Clark's habit, once he got to the heart of his subject, he kept talking, leaving no opening for Murchison. "Lyn-don will protect you fully, completely. Only Lyn-don can do it. You will be pleased." Clark paused only long enough to glance at the man, to let the assurances sink in.

"You do not need to do anything for now," Clark continued. "You will be taken care of." Clark smiled. "That I can assure you." The words were very final and very authoritative. "Two years ago I told you getting Lyn-don elected was a move up." He glanced at Murchison. "It was." Clark looked around. "And it still is." A waiter moved toward him. He gestured the man away. "And that is all I can tell you." He looked again at Murchison, laughed and added, "I got a dog that hunts." An old east Texas saying both understood, Clark was telling his client that a plan was underway that would work.

Murchison grinned easily, then leaned back and said very slowly, "I hear you, I hear you, and . . ." Murchison was making his standard reply to any proposal. The question anyone dealing with him had was what words he would use to reply, to close the deal, or to let it go.

Clark waited, to see if Murchison would add his patented, "I don't hear you," rejecting the proposal. Clark knew the proposal was vague. It had to be.

Murchison smiled broadly. "I hear you." With those words, both men knew the deal was cut. Murchison had noticed Clark's deep concern and understood something very big was underway. "I will watch," he added, "and you show me, all later."

Realizing the deal was made, Clark smiled, then laughed, and kept laughing, that loud, whooping series of laughs only he could do. For now, all he had to do was keep his end of the bargain. He had to deliver. He had to get Murchison results. He knew he would do it, and now he knew he would be paid.

Not a word was said about crimes. The code was clear. The more obscure and clouded a gentleman's proposal was, the more terrible the plan. Murchison knew that. He knew no one could be incriminated. He knew he would hear more, later, about the delivery of the goods. He knew a payoff would be expected.

For now, that otherwise meaningless agreement was all Clark needed. The gentleman's way of setting up lawsuits and agreeing to pay for them was complete. In those days in Texas in the early 1960s, there were no time sheets and very few retainers for Clark and his attorneys. The very powerful knew superlawyers had to be paid and that payment would be after the fact, based solely on results.

The proposal had been very discreet, very protective of both parties, and very subtle. Many times in the past, Clark had been in a position to alert clients to benefits soon to happen. He had insider information on converting the oil pipelines to natural gas and alerted his clients. He knew of the forthcoming slant hole investigations and could propose moneymaking solutions. In the case of Big Oil, it was usually to protect the depletion allowance, to keep regulation away from natural gas, and to restrict oil imports, all intended to keep the price up and to protect the income flow, to make more money. In addition, it was to satisfy the billionaires in their right-wing view of the world, to halt change and set in stone what they had and what they knew in 1960 and before. They lived in what they considered to be a perfect world. There was no need for progress and change in that world.

Patsy

In December 1962, just before Christmas, Lee Harvey Oswald was any one of several contacts Wallace was pursuing. Clark had an oil client who had said in passing that word was out in the Russian community about a radical Marxist recently returned from the Soviet Union. Sam Ballen was the man giving the information. In one of those strange turn of events where two things happen at the same time, Clark also learned of the same militant from friends in Georgetown, Texas. In still another coincidence, Joe Schott may have been involved. Schott was Wallace's college friend, a confidant prior to the Kinser murder, and a character witness at the trial. Schott was also with the FBI in Fort Worth, the office responsible for Oswald when he returned from the Soviet Union.

The way Wallace and Oswald met is not known, but they did meet and were together on the sixth floor of the Texas School Book Depository when Kennedy was shot. The first contact would have been the most important, one to instill trust and appeal to Oswald's basic instincts. The most likely scenario can be constructed.

As Wallace watched, the potential patsy walked out of the printing shop. He recalled the little he knew about the slender, wiry man, that he had no phone, that he had a wife and child, that he was sometimes living in Dallas, and that he needed money. Wallace had an easy way to relate because Oswald was also a Marxist.

Wallace would have approached Oswald and tried to make a connection. "Got a minute?" asked Wallace.

Oswald looked at Wallace, strangely identifying with the man in a thin jacket and khaki pants, a cigarette dangling from his lips. Unshaven like Oswald, he could have been a regular companion, one of the outsiders who never had enough money and had no attachments to anyone or anything. To any police officer, Wallace and Oswald would look suspicious, fitting the unwritten profile for troublemakers. Oswald liked what he saw in Wallace.

"What?" Oswald asked flatly, glancing suspiciously at the horn-rimmed glasses Wallace wore.

"Understand you been to the Soviets?"

Oswald was suddenly on guard. "You, uh, FBI?"

Wallace chortled. "Heard you just got back," he commented, changing the subject.

"Yeah?" said Oswald. "So?" He started to walk away.

"You still in the cause?" Wallace asked as he caught up with Oswald.

"So what?" Oswald repeated.

"I, uh, used to be a marine."

With a brusque nod, Oswald mumbled, "Yeah."

Wallace laughed. "Didn't take me long to get out."

Oswald kept walking. He had to get to the bus. "Where'd they send you?" he asked.

Wallace laughed derisively. "Boot camp," he said, "Then Pearl. I got out quick."

"Look, mister," Oswald said, turning to face Wallace. "I don't want trouble." He looked down the street. No bus in sight. "I'm getting on the bus and going home."

"Okay," Wallace said amicably. "Sure. I just heard you were still, uh, with us."

"There's nothing to fight for," Oswald said quietly. "Why do you think I left Russia?" Oswald looked down. "They're's bad as here."

"I know, man." Wallace hesitated, then said quietly, "But we can change that."

Oswald sized Wallace up again. "You a communist?"

"Hell, no, man," Wallace said, pausing to flick the butt away. "I gave up on the bastards."

"Don't tell me that," he said, adding, "You gotta be FBI."

"Fuck 'em," Wallace said, spitting the words.

Oswald remained uncertain but intrigued.

"Thought you might join us," Wallace continued, paused and added, "We're helping Cuba." The Cuban Missile Crisis was still in the news.

Oswald's interest returned. Suspicion. Intrigue. He needed acceptance in a hostile world, one he would never understand. "What can we do?" he asked, then shrugged. "Nothing."

The bus pulled up. "Ride with you?" asked Wallace.

Oswald stepped on. "It's a free country." He laughed.

Wallace followed and the two went to the back. Few people were on the bus, its Christmas decorations strangely out of place.

"Cigarette?" Wallace asked.

Oswald shook his head. "No thanks."

"Got a light?"

Oswald shook his head. Wallace reached in his pocket for a matchbook and lit up.

"Just not many of us left, are there?" Wallace mused as he blew smoke away from Oswald.

Looking out into the darkness, Oswald nodded.

Wallace took a drag on the cigarette and exhaled. "We just gotta let 'em know."

"Yeah, sure," Oswald cautiously agreed, apparently wanting to hear more.

"You interested?" asked Wallace.

Oswald glanced at Wallace, then turned back to the cold night outside. "What are we for?" he suddenly asked, still looking out the window.

"A better world," replied Wallace, his voice sincere. He studied Oswald, then continued, "From each by ability, to each . . ."

Oswald interrupted. ". . . by need."

"Yeah," Wallace said quietly.

"Yeah," Oswald facetiously agreed.

"It's gonna happen." Wallace was reading his man, baiting him like Clark wanted. Don't push too hard, he cautioned himself. We got time.

"Like when?" asked Oswald.

"War, revolution, it's gonna happen," Wallace continued. "Things gotta change." He paused. "Maybe, you know, some big event, . . ." The words trailed off.

Oswald still had his doubts. "Yeah," he said. "Right."

"We got a meeting, outside the Y, next week."

Oswald stood. "I'm getting off, next stop."

Wallace stood aside. "We need men like you."

Men like me, Oswald thought. After a moment's reflection, he asked, "Where?"

"Downtown 'Y.' Thursday. Six."

"Bye."

As Oswald walked sullenly away, Wallace knew he would not be disappointed. He knew Oswald would be there.

For the next few weeks, he was busy working with Junior, his new ally and backup.

Test

After the December meeting, Oswald was busy, ordering weapons, getting ready to be a sniper, a rifle for long shots, a pistol for personal protection. Soon after, Wallace decided on a test shot by Oswald. The target would be real, a part of the still-evolving plan. Edwin Walker, former army major general who had resigned following remarks critical of Kennedy's policies, was the target. For Oswald, a Marxist who hated America, if he shot Walker and escaped, his later participation would be perfect. Kennedy would be killed, not by Johnson's right-wing friends but by dangerous, left-wing zealots.

The political angle was Wallace's idea. He and Junior were cooperating. Junior had been sent to him by Clark. As complete opposites, they got along just fine. Wallace was the Marxist arguing with a right-winger who was also ready to attack the government. Both agreed the current political system had to be destroyed. Both agreed to bring that government down and then to fight over the remains. To the victor went the power. The debate was not unlike the communists against the Nazis in the 1930s in Germany. Once the Weimar Republic that was ruling Germany was brought down, the two extremist groups fought it out. Hitler won. The same dispute determined the course of Soviet Russia. When the Russian Empire collapsed, the Whites and the Reds fought it out. Unlike Germany where the fascists won, in Russia Lenin and his Bolsheviks took over, paving the way for Stalin and his communists. Similarly, Wallace and Junior were together, united because they were so far apart.

After checking out the neighborhood, Wallace returned with Oswald two days later. Could he persuade the man to kill? The attack on Walker would be the acid test. As a fellow Marxist, Wallace had convinced Oswald of the benefit of killing a right-wing politician. Could Oswald be convinced to shoot? Anyone could agree to anything, Clark had pointed out. Were they able to do it?

Wallace glanced down the dark alley, its muted light and darkness making it hard for him to see. Sitting in the getaway car, Wallace saw the vague shape of his sniper. Oswald aimed his rifle over a wooden fence toward a lighted window in a home typical of the upper-middle-class Turtle Creek neighborhood. The rifle seemed suspended for too long when Wallace's anticipation was suddenly shattered by the shot, a sharp crack resounding down the alley, echoing for a moment, then quickly muted by the surrounding trees and just as quickly fading away.

Come on, Wallace thought as he watched Oswald staring toward the window. Another eternity passed and Wallace could wait no longer. Speed was essential. There was only a short period for surprise and confusion. Time to act was measured in seconds. Quietly, Wallace engaged the gears and started moving. Oswald, hearing the sound in the deep quiet after the shot, crouched and ran toward him.

"Damn it, hurry!" Wallace cursed.

Oswald drew back, offended. "You don't like it?"

Wallace shook his head. Oswald could not take criticism. He was thin-shelled, too easy to anger. Wallace had decided it would probably help for the shooting. The plan included the patsy or patsies getting cornered, firing back, and getting killed. No witnesses. Oswald would do. His anger would kill him.

"Get in!" Wallace ordered, nervously looking down the alley. "We gotta move fast."

Oswald looked inside, opened the door and tossed the rifle into the back seat. He slid quickly into the front seat.

"We gotta get out of here," Wallace muttered as the door closed. He let the car idle down the alley, onto the lighted street and then he accelerated. The car screeched forward.

"Get him?" Wallace asked.

Oswald paused for an instant. "Yeah." He stared ahead, ignoring his partner, still angry.

Wallace sighed a breath of relief. "What happened?"

Oswald shrugged. "He was right there, dead in my sight. I fired. He dropped." Oswald paused as Wallace stopped the vehicle by a nearby church. "I waited a minute. Nothing moved."

Wallace smiled grimly. "One more fascist out of the way." He paused. "One more to go."

"Who's next?" Oswald asked.

"I don't know. I'm waiting to hear."

Oswald smiled inwardly. He liked the idea of killing and he liked the idea of getting publicity, headlines, and fame. And he liked the intrigue. Oswald had hesitated at first, but then agreed to get the rifle and pistol. Tonight, he found he enjoyed it.

Wallace smiled grimly as he gestured for Oswald to get out. "I'll keep the rifle," said Wallace. "Get it to you later."

Oswald nodded, opened the door, and stepped out.

"Be back to you," Wallace said as he glanced around. Oswald stepped out, and the station wagon jolted forward.

As Wallace drove away, Oswald stared after the car, then walked toward the waiting bus. Their timing for the entire project had been good.

The next day, Oswald learned Walker had not been injured. Two weeks later, disappointed in everything, he left for New Orleans.

Wallace, angered by the bad news, decided the erratic Oswald would not be useful as a shooter. Six months later, after Oswald had gone to New Orleans and then Mexico City only to return without what he wanted, a passage to Cuba, planning had advanced. Once again, Wallace needed Oswald.

Fees

Less than an hour's drive from John Kennedy's overnight hotel in Fort Worth, at Clint Murchison Jr.'s estate on Turtle Creek Drive in Dallas, a meeting was underway. Described as an after-hours party, it was in fact a smoker, a time for men to relax, have a few drinks, and a good smoke. They would also take care of some business. And then they could enjoy the fun and games. A good time for the good old boys was guaranteed.

The huge reception room had many friends in attendance. The conservatives that were Big Oil were there, all wealthy and very secretive, out of sight from the rest of the world. They had been told that the Kennedy visit to Dallas the next morning would be discussed. Two posters attacking Kennedy were to be distributed the next morning, to "welcome" him. Those posters were displayed to cheers.

Clark was there. He had insisted and Murchison had agreed that the standard pitch should be made, the bait should be played. With the drinks flowing freely and the air clouded with the steel gray of tobacco smoke, Murchison started the business at hand, talking loudly as only he could. Clark was asked to say a few words.

"Men," Clark shouted over the din in his falsetto voice. "We have been misled the past three years."

The crowd suddenly fell silent.

"We believed the reasonable and friendly government President Eisenhower gave us." After a long pause, he continued. "We do not have a reasonable and friendly government."

A murmur of agreement moved through the crowd.

"Something has to be done," said Clark. "We cannot keep going this way." Not a sound was heard. The men waited to hear what was to be done.

"I assure you," Clark added, his lisp now more pronounced, "that the solution is at hand. Under the sound leadership of Lyn-don Johnson, we will turn this nation back on the path of prosperity and greatness."

There was a moment of silence as the men considered and then realized what Clark had said. They responded with loud cheers.

Then, waving his hand aimlessly, Clark concluded, "You can rest easy tonight. Our Republic will soon be safe from its enemies."

His closing words were barely heard as the crowd laughed, cheered, applauded, and shouted their support. For the next few minutes the discussion Clark had started kept moving through the crowd. Then the party turned to other things.

Cash

Clark watched Wallace carefully as they sat in the black Town Car, the morning still dark, sunlight barely lighting the horizon. A light rain was falling. The time had come and Clark was impressed.

Listening carefully to Clark over the past month, Wallace had reviewed the plan that would kill the president, allow both him and Junior to escape, and leave his "helper" dead. Oswald was set up to shoot at Kennedy, then resist the police, fight back, and be killed. So far as history would ever record, at least with a controlled investigation, he would be the assassin.

"Here is one more item you need," Clark said, handing Wallace an envelope.

"What . . ." asked Wallace as he opened the envelope. There was money, a stack of one hundred dollar bills.

Wallace looked up, smiling.

"What else do you need?"

Wallace shrugged. "That's it. We're ready." He looked out the window into the skyline, just starting to light in the sun. "Just between us, you are one hell of a smart man."

Strangely angered at the familiarity Wallace expressed, Clark looked away, letting the man know his place. This killing was not to his liking. Never had been. Right now, he was too deeply involved and so was the vice president. So far, the breaks had gone his way and what was soon to happen was the best he could do. Shaking off any doubts, he knew that, no matter what the consequences, it was going to happen. Johnson had to be president. That decided, you take your chances.

"We only judge a smart man by results," Clark said quietly. "You do it right and get rich or you screw up and become the greatest villain of all times." In a strange moment of compassion, in a sharing of the terrible crime between the men, Clark reached over and grasped Wallace's shoulder. "Just that one thing, Mac. Do it right. Exactly like we talked. Follow the plan every step of the way."

Wallace glanced at the hand on his shoulder, and, with a grim smile, asked, "Gun and run?"

Clark nodded. "That is most important. Run. Get the hell out of there. You have only a minute, probably less." He let his arm fall and turned to look at the freeway, at the few cars speeding by. "Move very quickly," he said quietly.

Then, gesturing for Wallace to leave, he said, "Don't contact me. I'll get to you." He stared at Wallace through the dull light. "No contact. After, maybe a year or so." His voice drifted off. "Give things time to get quiet."

Wallace nodded, opened the door, and left, stepping again into the windy, drizzling cold, and into some of history's darkest pages. Clark had set the stage and his snipers were moving into place.

The rest would belong to history.

The pattern for the conspiracy is clear. The characters involved are known and the assassination scene is reasonably well understood. The various steps taken by Clark included responding to Johnson's pressing needs for ultimate power and for avoidance of his crimes. There was the need to recruit shooters and to have the necessary cover, that of a patsy or two as the fall guys, so the shooters could escape. Testing the recruits had to be done. The objective of the conspiracy could not be disclosed until it was too late to turn back. Payments had to be arranged. The plan had to be developed for the assassination itself, complete with the getaway. The plan depended on changing developments, where the president would be, who was there, what could be done, what needed to be done.

By November 1963, the necessary steps had been taken and the plans for the assassination were ready.

We can work forward from the start of the conspiracy, why it was necessary for Johnson to kill Kennedy, and see how the conspirators put their plan together. We can work backward from the crime scene itself and fit any loose pieces together. Knowing the criminals, where they were, and how they acted, we can pull the facts together and present a full case to the jury, to the American people.

For we are not here to praise Lyndon Johnson but to bury him. There are those seeking to raise him from the dead just because he was a president. The redemption of any president must be based on whether that person led us so that we achieved what is best for America. By any measure of the available evidence, Johnson did very little, if anything, for the United States. And he did a great deal that would condemn any citizen to prison and perdition.

And, so, ladies and gentlemen of the jury, based on the evidence presented, you must find by the greater weight of the credible evidence that LBJ killed JFK.

And we will bring an end, a sunset, to the darkness planted on our history by Lyndon Johnson.

> Ladies and gentlemen of the jury, what say you?
> —Question for the verdict (archaic)

Cui bono? —To whose advantage?
—Basic legal principle

18

Sunset

Having seen what Johnson did and how he did it, acting through his key conspirators Ed Clark and Mac Wallace, we come again to the end. How did Johnson carry this terrible crime on his shoulders? Was he ever driven to a sense of guilt? In the final year of his life, he had intense sessions with his psychiatrist gave him relief from his "demons."

When Johnson was undergoing this deep psychotherapy, his lawyers looked into the question of whether what he told his psychiatrist would be admissible in court. Did what he said need to be protected by the attorney-client privilege? The consensus we reached was that the psychiatrist could tell all so the standard trust arrangement was negotiated. These steps were a serious indication that Johnson had something to hide, something big. He had promised full disclosure when his library was dedicated. Clearly more was involved than what his public archives revealed.

Following Johnson's death, Thomas let me know that the psychiatrist had "gotten rid of the demons" and that Johnson was "cured." He also told me that what had been disclosed was not to be told to anyone until after Johnson's wife had died. Finally, I learned there was still more. There was. The assassination of John Kennedy. While no one was there to record the discussion between Johnson and Thomas, what follows is a scenario as close to the facts as we will ever have.

The Johnson Freeway from Austin to Johnson's ranch was a vast improvement over the old days, Don Thomas thought as he reached the intersection with the highway to San Antonio. Because Lyndon Johnson liked speed and took far too many risks, the highway department had upgraded the little-used road to a four-lane freeway. In Clark's Texas, some people were far more equal than others.

Thomas turned his black Lincoln Town Car right, heading into the little town of Johnson City and then west to see the man he owed everything. Going past Hye to just east of Stonewall, he turned onto Ranch Road One, ill-named because there was no ranch. The large tract of land was hardly a farm, but "ranch" reflected the ego of the former president. Thomas grinned. If Johnson owned a farm but wanted a ranch, then, what the hell, call it a ranch. Thomas knew what later politicians would call "spin." After all, Thomas had edited political statements for Johnson and his opponents for many years.

The car crossed the low-water bridge and dam holding back a dark green creek, then over the cattle guard and past the oak trees of the family cemetery to arrive at the former Texas White House. The afternoon sun brightened the two-story building's white sides, leaving them glittering on that otherwise cold and windy afternoon, just before Christmas 1972.

Thomas, a stocky five foot ten in a business suit, thin tie barely reaching a rounded waist, walked quickly to the front door, down the long hallway, and into the bedroom where his client was sleeping. The room seemed small, crowded as it was with a bed, furniture, and television. A portable oxygen tank was in the far corner by the bed.

From the window Thomas knew there was a panoramic view of the swimming pool and the long runway for *Air Force One*, one that reflected the spectacular setting sun, now a deep orange; but that outside world was shut away, leaving the room shadowed and hazy, filled with vague memories from a history already past and gone. The former president was dozing, mouth open, head back, a low sound escaping from his throat as he labored to breathe.

Knowing he could not awaken Lyndon Johnson from his important afternoon nap, Thomas sat down to wait in the armchair on the far side of the room. Soon enough, Johnson was aroused. His eyes opened and he looked around.

Since appearing on a closed circuit broadcast at his LBJ Library just ten days earlier, the man had changed for the worse. His pallor was a dark gray, his long hair unkempt, and a ragged beard sprouted loose hair in every direction. Thomas knew Johnson had simply quit grooming. During the past year only his wife had been able to keep him shaved and clean and then only if guests were coming. Following the December 12 appearance, she had simply given up, letting him decline into a mere apparition of his former glory.

"Don," the president said quietly. "Glad you made it." Grunting, he twisted to sit up.

"Comfortable?" Thomas asked.

Waving a gnarled hand, its fingers curving down, Johnson nodded dejectedly, "Now, Lawyer Thomas, don't you worry none about me." He then smiled and reached for his longtime friend and confidant. They shook hands ever so briefly, and Johnson moved his hand back to his forehead, then down the grimy face, and, by long habit, to his ear lobe, now drooping more than ever.

"This is pure damned hell," Johnson grumbled as he looked around. Gesturing to the nearby oxygen, he ordered, "Hand me some of that." He took it himself and gulped a few deep breaths. "Now," he continued, "that's better." He took another deep breath and looked at his lawyer. "Don, just how damned long have you been saving my ass?"

Thomas smiled and shrugged. "'Bout thirty years, Mr. President."

Johnson chuckled. "Couldn't of done it without you." His face seemed to fall as a wave of sadness swept him. "You gotta do it again."

As a trial attorney Thomas could read people. He instinctively noted the sadness and assumed the dark depression that had fallen over Johnson since leaving office had returned. Supposedly it had been cured by the high-priced shrink, but, maybe not. "Do you want me to tell the ambassador?" Thomas asked, referring to Clark.

Johnson suddenly brightened. "Dear Ed-ward," he said, mimicking the power broker's lisp. "He served me well."

"Still serving you," Thomas said quietly.

Clark had called Thomas early that morning because their chief client needed help on some "important matter, probably the damned shrink." He sent Thomas to visit Johnson. After completing a management meeting at the television station early that afternoon, Thomas hurried to the ranch.

"Yeah," muttered Johnson. "Then, why the hell'd he stay home?"

Thomas expected an outburst from the old man. Of late Clark had kept a distance, almost, Thomas thought, as if the two men were too close. Thomas also knew Clark needed money, lots of it, and was trying to get a bonus from the same oilmen that Johnson had saved so many times. Like any power broker, Clark's eye was on the next client, the new money, the bigger case. In the high-powered law Clark practiced, friends came and went with hardly a welcome and goodbye. Dollars did the talking.

"You know him better than me," Thomas replied grimly, recalling the many times both Johnson and Clark had viciously attacked him, had kept him working from before dawn to well past midnight, had stretched him to the breaking point more than once. "He's mean to the bone," added Thomas, "like you."

Johnson smiled. He knew why the senior lawyer stayed away. "That dear old Ed-ward is a son-of-a-bitch," he lisped, again mimicking Clark. "Just think. At one time, he was ready to ride 'ol' Sparky' for me." Johnson was referring to the electric chair at the state prison. "Hell of a man," he continued. "Willing to give all for me. You just gotta admire that." His pink-rimmed eyes, now bloodshot and teary, bored into Thomas. "Yessir. That man's got balls!"

"No, sir," Thomas agreed. "You were just too damned close, a little too much alike. Mr. President, a little distance's good for you."

Johnson glanced over, and a gnarled finger jabbed the air. "Next god-damned time, you tell him to get his fat ass up here when I call." The president smiled and leaned back for his oxygen, taking three more deep breaths, his swollen chest heaving. Then, the mixed fear and anger gone, he looked back at Thomas and gently said, in that shift of moods that only he could manage, "No, don't you say that. Just tell him I'd like to see him. Just once more."

Thomas nodded. "Okay." He had never heard such a final thought from Johnson. He wondered if telling Clark would do anything. Clark did what he damned well pleased. When Johnson was president, Clark would have brayed to the moon. No more.

Suddenly, Johnson slid off the bed, then struggled to stand. Thomas moved beside him, offering a hand, then a shoulder. "I need to walk around a little," Johnson muttered. "Damned doctor's damned orders." Up close, the man reeked of old age, of a heavy musk, sweaty and dusty, like old furniture too long in an attic. The dying man, now stooped but still tall, leaned an arm on the smaller man's shoulder, took some baby steps as he shuffled a few feet, and then, stepping backward, turned and leaned against his bed. "That's damned well enough for the pill-pushers," he muttered. "Here, help me get back." Thomas lifted gently under the shoulder, helping deposit the wasted skin and bones back on the bed.

"Now," continued Johnson, "I got something important." He again used the oxygen.

Thomas nodded. "I know. Right now, that damned minder-bender can tell anyone anything you told him; anything he wants to."

"Not that," Johnson said.

"Our investigators checked him out," Thomas continued, catching Johnson's interest in something else but ignoring it. "He's about as professional as they come."

Johnson shook his head. "Not that. For what I told him. You set up a damned trust for him?"

Thomas nodded.

"Still got plenty of cash, don't we?"

Thomas was administrator for the former president's businesses. "You damned well got that right," he emphasized, smiling. "Over ten million in ready cash. Same amount invested, you know, here and there." He did not tell him Brazos-Tenth had been shut down. They had plenty of money in the trusts.

Johnson grinned wryly. "Just unbelievable. Back then, Don, who'd ever thought?"

Thomas knew that was true. Extra cash had flowed freely well before the start of Johnson's 1954 Senate reelection campaign, and so much had been raised that every potential opponent had been scared away. That meant no campaign expenses so the huge sums of leftover money had to be put somewhere. In anticipation, Clark had Thomas set up the "corporation," and it "handled," or in modern terms, "laundered" the huge sums. The money faucet flowed again in 1960, in 1964, and even in the lead-up to the aborted 1968 campaign.

Between the campaigns, donations to the lawyers were accepted to avoid any appearance of bribing Johnson. Thomas invested the money in land and in banks, two solid and very safe assets. "Looking back," he replied, shaking his head and grinning, running a hand across his balding head, "we just got rich."

"Give the good doctor the money," Johnson ordered with a wave of his hand. "Set him up a trust, you know, like we always do." Thomas had million-dollar funds to be paid over time for several potential or actual threats, for witnesses who knew damaging facts. One trust fund had gone to a mistress, another to a judge, still more to lesser officials. Typically, the money went to an attorney and then to the key witness or to a family member of a potential witness. Payments to his or her family always kept the witness quiet. The money was never paid directly and was never traceable because it, too, was behind the attorney-client privilege.

The money would flow to the potential witness "as long as the peace was kept"; that is, so long as they kept their mouths shut. Break the silence and lose the money. Of course, nothing was ever said explicitly; that was never necessary. The process was simple: "We've set up a trust for you." And the reply, "You shouldn't have done that but thank you so very much." No one had ever taken the risk of blowing the cover.

"I'll get on it tomorrow," Thomas said cautiously, not telling him the trust was already set up. Always concerned about saving his client money while insulating him from any criticism, two key protections Clark always demanded for Johnson, Thomas had been shielding the client since 1944 when he reviewed political statements for libel, making changes as needed but always keeping the gist of the story favorable to Johnson. The censorship was very effective. After all, what were essentially political controls had been done in the name of the law.

"Just get it done," said Johnson.

Thomas looked at his client and suddenly realized the former president looked like a hippie, like one of those many protestors he and the law firm had worked so hard to keep silent, blocking them from the news through control of the radio and television stations, stopping their parades in Austin, and through a loyal college administration keeping the peace at the University of Texas campus. Just as suddenly, he realized something far more important: that Johnson had undergone a very real change of heart.

"You've no idea what all I told him," Johnson quietly continued. "Had to, Don, to get out of that black hole I was in. Let me tell you something— it worked."

Reeling emotionally from his unexpected insight, Thomas studied Johnson. The former president, now silent and relaxed, stared back. "So, do you need to tell me something else?" Thomas asked. His instincts now recharged, he knew Johnson had insisted on seeing his lawyer for something far more significant, something that could not be handled by phone.

Johnson nodded and turned away, a stooped figure now looking very lonely at the bed's side. "Where to start?" he wondered out loud. After a long pause, he quietly continued. "The damned military was just flat wrong," he said, in carefully measured words. "We had so many damned options back in '64, '65." Turning to Thomas, he almost pleaded, "Don, you want to know something?"

Thomas nodded. "You better tell me." He shrugged and was surprised to find his shirt soaked with sweat. His mind was racing, trying to protect Johnson but all the time knowing he could no longer save his client from himself. *What should he do?* he wondered. *What could he do?*

"We did not have to fight on the ground." Johnson shook his head. "Those sons-of-bitches!" He slumped even further and was silent again as he stared at the floor.

Now tuned into the unexpected direction of the conversation, Thomas digested what Johnson was saying. In that code two lifelong friends can use, Thomas realized Johnson was making a critical admission, that the Pentagon had been flat wrong, or, more appropriately, *dead wrong.* "I always say, Mr. President, 'Forget the law, give me the facts.'" The comment was weak but true. He was agreeing with Johnson that reliable facts had to be disclosed for solid decision making, whether by a juror or a president.

Johnson smiled weakly. "You said that more than once." He reached again for the mask and breathed deeply. "I know what you're saying. I never had the facts. What I needed was them talking to me straight."

"Yes, sir."

"But, you know and I know everyone was lying, big time, all the time."

Thomas could only nod, recalling the many lies he had told on behalf of Johnson.

"Any hew, that's what I learned with that damned shrink." Johnson breathed again from the mask and then seemed to slump even lower. Through the mask he mumbled, "He made me say it."

"I don't understand," said Thomas, confused.

"Hell, yes, you do!" the old man shouted, the mask still in place. "We hid as much as the military did. Even the damned civilians were on their side, not mine." Turning ever more pallid, Johnson continued, "That was the big problem. Everyone was lying." His sunken eyes again glared at the lawyer. "And here's the damned rub. That included me. Don't you see? Me! Me, worse than anyone else!" His voice was a desperate whimper.

Thomas realized what was happening. "You told the shrink, uh, everything?"

Johnson looked hard at Thomas, then looked away. "You know, two years back, I was going to an early grave. Things just got terrible. There was nothing else to do." Grasping Thomas's forearm, he pulled himself closer and continued, his eyes narrowed, "He told me to talk about it, you know, to 'fess up." He kept intense eyes on his lawyer. "But now I just need to tell someone, someone else, you know." He paused, and then added, "You see, I told him and he showed me something else." Johnson relaxed, then almost shamefully added, "That's what I gotta tell someone, . . . was gonna be Clark, . . . now you're the one."

Thomas grasped the point. "About admitting to the doctor?"

"Yessir," Johnson replied, looking up, his eyes scanning Thomas's face. "That's what I gotta do." Tensing, he added. "So, I just did. I told you." Johnson seemed more relaxed now that the facts were making their way out.

"I guessed you had something important," Thomas remarked, stepping back from the edge of the bed. With a hand to his chin, he asked, "Did you tell . . ."

Johnson interrupted with a nod, then, with mask in place, he lay back on the pillows. "I told him about the killings."

Although expecting the ultimate confession but at the same time fearing it deeply, Thomas reeled at the words. At first, Clark had done most of the dirty work on his own, keeping Thomas "out of the loop." When he had to act, it was through trusted relatives or compromised public officials to protect Johnson from any involvement in the necessary crimes. In the 1948 election, Clark had to enlist Thomas. No one else could add the needed votes. Then, in the early fifties, Clark had drawn Thomas deeper into the web, making him the chief contact with John Cofer, the firm's attorney for criminal matters.

"Oh my god, man," Thomas heard himself explode. "Damn it!" Never a man to use profanity and never one to turn on this president, Thomas knew instantly what had been done and what it meant. Had every crime they'd committed been disclosed? While the doctor would likely never tell, the political considerations were overwhelming. He just might talk. Something had to be done.

"You can't . . ." Thomas hesitated as his voice broke. When arguing to jurors, that voice inflection was always very convincing because it seemed to reveal his inner soul, to show he was speaking from the heart. Feeling his chest heave, feeling pain shoot through his shoulders, feeling his flushed face drain, Thomas did something he had learned to do when surprised before a jury—he deliberately relaxed. Slumping beside Johnson, he quietly remarked, "You damned sure gave him plenty to talk about." Knowing most of the details of the enormities Johnson had admitted, Thomas added, "I'll get right on top of this payment."

In his heart, he knew the most terrible of all crimes had likely been told. The assassination of a president simply could not be "contained." If the doctor knew, that was it. The word would be out. Thomas was sure the doctor knew because, being the outstanding psychiatrist he was, the patient was the only concern. He had to find out what troubled Johnson. The killing of John

Kennedy was, he was sure, the primary cause of Johnson's paranoia. That was followed by Vietnam and its paranoia with even more depression. Together, they led to the collapse of his presidency.

Grimacing in pain as he sat up and extended an arm, Johnson reached over to Thomas. The lawyer turned and looked at the man, and, to confirm his worst fears, asked, "Did you tell him about, uh, Dallas?"

Johnson looked at him wanly with raised brows and eyes that would have filled with tears, Thomas knew, if the man had any emotional energy, any feelings left. Johnson nodded. "Yes." The two men were silent. Then Johnson added, "Don't you see, Don? I had to! Hell! You know that!"

Thomas did not know all the details. Clark had handled the Dallas planning and had kept it very close to the vest. The fewer the participants and potential witnesses, the better. Any good lawyer knows that, if there's crime to be committed, do it alone. Illegal ballots are best cast under cover of darkness by one man and one man should destroy IRS records that implicate a client. "Just between us boys," said Thomas quietly, "I didn't know, . . . not until later." He shrugged. "Clark was a one man show . . . on that . . . day."

Johnson nodded. "There was no damned choice." He suddenly let go. "You know full well what was happening back then. They were closing in." He was still speaking in that code longtime friends use. Both knew what he meant but they also knew not to say it. No one, not even the assassins, could ever be direct about something so viciously unthinkable, the most terrible of crimes.

"You know who 'they' were," Thomas cautioned.

"Yeah," he replied. "Us."

"Okay. So you're the one that's got to tell me."

"Don't play those damned games with me," Johnson replied loudly, then lowered his voice to say, "You know what was going on. Investigations everywhere. Hearings all over the damned hill." He was referring to Congress.

How well Thomas knew. He had been subpoenaed about their "corporation" and had provided solid coverup at the deposition, including a well-timed interruption. His deposition had never been rescheduled.

"And every day I was getting hate mail!" Johnson continued. "Hate mail from my money men." His eyes glared. "You know just how damned awful that is! I'll be damned. You just gotta listen to them!" His head slumped. "It was holy hell."

Thomas said nothing. You cannot push Johnson because his paranoia would kick in and he would shut up. But, once he started talking, it was sermon time. No telling what you'd hear. A nudge here, a question there, and you would learn everything.

"You remember all that hell I was catching!" Johnson continued, jabbing his arm. "You know about the damned killings. Hell, Don, we had to do it." Referring to Kennedy, he added, "That damned Bobby boy. He was stirring everything, and I damned well mean everything!" His arm swept up and around. "And I could not do a damned thing!" His fist hit the pillow. "Except that one thing," he added with a grim smile. "There was one thing. When you are surrounded and about to get killed, what do you do?" He was shaking all over. "Shoot back!"

"So, you told Clark, 'Kill the president'?" asked Thomas.

"Now, just a second," Johnson shot back, his tone both defensive and condescending. "You know better than that." He relaxed, his voice steady. "When he said 'we gotta move,' I just agreed. That's all. Did not have another damned thing to do with Ed-ward's damned plan."

"Protected by your man?"

"Just this one thing," Johnson said, his words barely heard through the mask. "Keep it from Bird. Lord only knows that woman's stood with me." The gnarled hand again grabbed Thomas's forearm. "For god's sake, keep it secret from her. You know that!"

Thomas nodded. "No one's gonna know." He would take care of the wife he knew would soon be a widow.

Johnson moved the mask from his face, his head suddenly shaking furiously. "Don, we gotta let folks know," he said quietly but once again with his old authority. "That's the whole problem. We just gotta have it out in the open." He turned, trying to rise on one arm. Thomas helped him. With a renewed passion, Johnson said, "So, you see what you gotta do?"

"You want me to tell . . ." The question drifted off into silence.

"I damned sure do," said Johnson. "Be sure word gets out." Johnson stared at Thomas. "You hear me?"

Staring back, searching his client's eyes, looking into his soul, a thousand thoughts filling his mind, Thomas finally nodded. "I know what you need done. We'll see to it."

Thomas paused and Johnson studied him, then asserted, "Even Dallas," said Johnson. "Even Dallas."

The lawyer could only nod.

Johnson grimaced. "We gotta! We just gotta!" As he fell back, bringing the mask to his face, he muttered quietly, "That's what finished me and that's why I'm dying now."

Thomas underwent another awakening. Johnson's abject paranoia compelled him to decide on the assassination. That same paranoia, projected by Johnson, was used by the military ever so subtly to hide the real war from him. Realizing Johnson's presidency was born of lies and died from lies, Thomas asked, "Mr. President, what you're suggesting, . . . I mean, the presidency will never be the same."

"No," he said quietly but firmly. "But my damned epitaph ain't getting no damned worse. You know that." Both men knew the polls. The American public rated Johnson so low that he was below even the standard margin of error of 5 percent. In 1964, when Johnson was elected to the presidency, he had achieved the greatest majority ever received by a candidate. Today, it could not be lower. None of his predecessors had ever risen so high or fallen so low.

"So we destroy your presidency?" Thomas asked, quietly persisting.

Shaking his head, Johnson said, "Don't you see, Don? That's just best. I know that now." His voice broke. "My damned legacy just might improve if the facts come out, just like it was . . . if I told it."

Thomas pondered the remark. He always told his partners and associates, *"When you make a mistake, just take off your hat, lower your head before the judge, and admit it. Go ahead and take your licks. Get it over 'cause its just gonna sit there and fester till you do."* But what Johnson wanted was too big for any simple advice. Thomas shook his head, "Mr. President, I just don't know."

Johnson seemed to have a strange peace. "We the people really and truly just gotta know what happened, what's happening." He looked away. "Hell! Might just improve my reputation, you know." He chuckled grimly. "Can't get lower." Johnson knew. No man watched the polls more closely. Johnson bowed his head and his shoulders shook.

Embarrassed, Thomas looked away. He noticed the room was darker, lit only by the bed lamp. The sun had set. Night was falling. Shadows crossed the room.

Again, Johnson slammed his arm on the bed. "What in the name of hell! Do you know what I coulda done had I gotten the facts?"

Thomas shook his head. "You don't have to say a word."

"Okay! You're right." Johnson was angered. "Just keep it up. You never let me say a damned thing. But I've given one hell of a headache to it, and everything's really clear, . . . like this morning. You know, it was colder than a witch's tit when they wheeled me out there." He smiled weakly. "And now I'm coming in from that damned hate. Do you have any idea how bad hate gets?" The man shuddered again.

The hate had been terrible. *MacBird* had been a play based on Shakespeare's *MacBeth* where the king was killed; *MacBird* featured Johnson and his wife killing Kennedy. And he had heard the chant from the White House, "Hey! Hey! LBJ! How many kids did you kill today!" Thomas ignored the question, demanding, "You're ready to lose it all?"

Ignoring Thomas, Johnson continued, "I never had much faith, but if that hell is waiting, I need my best foot going first." He smiled. "And I know this one damned thing if I know anything, that I feel a damned sight better than I've done in years."

Thomas realized Johnson had unburdened his soul and was ready to face death.

"Okay, then, Don," Johnson said quietly, more a command than a question. "Do you understand!"

Thomas finally nodded. "Yes, sir, I do. Your way's the way. I'll tell 'em."

Johnson looked away, then back at Thomas. "Yeah. We'll survive it. Always do. Nation's so damned strong."

"Okay," said Thomas quietly.

"What I did, . . ." Johnson paused to correct himself, "What I let Clark do, that was wrong . . ." His hands reached out, grasping, and then fell back. In a whisper, he added, "Yessir, I knew it was there so I took it 'cause I had to." Then he twisted in the bed, arms to his chest, grimacing.

"You need the doctor?" Thomas asked. With mixed emotions still overwhelming him, Thomas waited.

Johnson shook his head, "Yessir. I'm dying. But I'm ready. For nothing else, that damned shrink got me seeing straight again." He glanced over at Thomas and, with eyebrows raised, appealed, "Now, my dear old friend, take care of it." Again he extended a hand. "You're the only one I got left."

The hand fell as Johnson did something Thomas had never seen before. The big man started crying. His shoulders slumped and his chest heaved. The sobs started slowly and then rose. Head down, he cried, shaking all over. Then his head leaned back and he cried, louder this time, with his whole frame shaking as he seemed to throw off years of evil.

There was a knock on the door. "Is everything all right?" a voice asked.

Johnson continued sobbing as Thomas walked over and opened the door. "It's okay," he told the housekeeper and she nodded and left. Closing the door, Thomas returned to the bedside and waited.

The old man shuddered and sobbed until he seemed to have exhausted himself. Teary eyes looked up at Thomas. Johnson shook his head. "Supposed to be good for me," he said, back in control of his voice.

Thomas nodded.

"Go on," Johnson ordered. "I'm okay now."

"You sure?"

"Just do what I told you."

"I will," Thomas said quietly, knowing it would be a long time before he would ever let the facts go public.

Johnson studied the lawyer, trying to read his mind, then concluded that Thomas would do as he asked and that it would be done right, carefully and with grace. "Now, go on," Johnson replied, leaning back, relaxing, the mask again in place. He was satisfied because he knew the enormity of the crime was just too great. He also knew it was now, forever, out of his hands. He had told all he needed to tell and the problem was no longer his. Whoever knew had to tell someone else. But he was ready for the word to be out, and, if it happened before Lady Bird died, then so be it. He smiled inwardly. She probably knew anyway.

Thomas studied the former president and, as the eyes closed, the man fell instantly into a deep sleep. Thomas took the withered hand, squeezed it and, looking away, muttered lamely, "I will."

In the quiet that followed, Thomas let his mind wander freely as he considered what could be done. He knew the secret could not be kept. One thing he had to do was force the psychiatrist to tell him how much Johnson told him about "the event," "the killing," "that day." That alone would take pressure off any moral compulsion the psychiatrist might feel to tell someone, anyone. To get it off his chest and his conscience, the doctor would have to tell him.

Clark would never know what Johnson had said that late afternoon. The power broker was simply too deeply implicated in everything and would forever fear disclosure. Since there was no statute of limitations on murder, Clark would have to carry his secrets to his death. Thomas grinned inwardly. Only Clark was tough enough. Even Johnson had succumbed. Clark was so damned bad, Thomas knew, that he would not need to tell anyone. Clark had no soul to unburden, Thomas knew, as he wondered who craved power more, Johnson or Clark.

Thomas decided he would never tell Lady Bird. She had suffered enough, living with a husband that was as mean to her as he was to anyone. Thomas had often heard Johnson rant at her, belittle her, attack her whenever he could. She always stood by him, and she was always supportive of whatever he stood for at the moment. Only in public, however, when the press was around, had he ever backed her. Among friends, she was just another nuisance, not pretty enough and not young enough for him.

Finally satisfied with the course of action he would take, Thomas left the room and strode down the hall, stopping momentarily to tell the housekeeper he was leaving and that they needed to keep an eye on the president. She nodded, saying she would check on him right away. Thomas said nothing else. He headed for the door, his mind too burdened for additional conversation. His emotions were shot.

Quickly outside, the cold air hit him, and he again noticed his shirt was soaked. Shivering as he pulled his suit coat together, he got into his Town Car and headed for Austin, knowing just one thing, he needed a drink. And that inward compulsion to tell someone began to gnaw at him. He wondered how long he could keep things to himself.

The car was soon back on the highway and, as it cruised smoothly toward town, the city limit marker for Hye flashed into his vision. Thomas was instantly reminded of that friendly wave, that little "Hi" drivers give everyone on the rural roads of Texas. Laid back little Luckenbach was nearby, just down the road, even then a favorite watering hole. And he remembered the tiny hamlet named Stonewall, recalling how appropriate the name was.

He grinned as he peered into the dark, knowing that contrast and conflict were the essence of the Texas hill country, a beautiful inhospitality, a harsh place ready to kill in an instant but at the same time inspiring a cherished love for life. "A savage splendor," just like Johnson. No matter what the crime, Thomas still cherished the old man. It was a personal thing that is perhaps the essence of politics, at its heart still person to person.

The next morning Thomas paid a quick visit to the psychiatrist, giving him the "gift." Nothing was said about keeping quiet. A million dollars in trust generating regular monthly payments was all it took.

On January 22, 1972, a month after Thomas left the ranch, Johnson died of a failed heart. After all, he was ready. When he cleared his mind and his soul to Thomas, his therapy was over. Leaving Thomas to tell what had happened, Johnson was focused on that last refuge he had, his home and his family. The afternoon that he died, as the pain awoke him from his afternoon

nap, in a last-minute panic changing his mind, he called for the Secret Service
agent's help as he reached for the oxygen. This time, nothing could save him,
not his doctors, not his lawyers, not the politicians, not history. The agents
found him on the floor.

Lyndon Johnson had reached the end that he himself had made. As
Thomas loved to argue to a jury, the man "shot himself in the foot." In his
case, Johnson's many fears compelled him to kill. Others embraced that same
paranoia, and their paranoia brought them down.

The legacy hangs as a darkness over America. As Johnson met his sunset and disclosed all, the time is right to end that darkness, finally to bring
that sunset and darkness to a close.

> *Qui sentit commodum sentire debet et onus*—
> He who derives the advantage ought to sustain the burden.
> —*Broomi Legal Maxims*

Just do the right thing. Everyone knows what it is. Do it.
—a father's advice

19

Fight

Clark's standard operating procedure with his partners and associates was simple: you were for him or against him. More precisely, you were 100 percent for him or you were against him. Anything less than 100 percent for him was against him. The reason was simple. Once you knew the keys to his kingdom of political control, of his controls of access to lawmakers and his commitment from them to decide in his favor, you could use the tools only for him, never against him.

Once you left, you were assumed to be against him. Like all his attorneys who left, I became a target the day I resigned and walked out. Looking back, I became a future target when I joined him, and I certainly was a target when I became a partner and represented him. The target was simple. You were marked for reward if you were 100 percent with him, and you were marked for exile from the Austin and even the Texas power system if you were for him only 99 percent or anything less.

As I was leaving the firm, Clark offered me the position of university attorney. This offer was easy for him because he was on the Board of Regents at the University of Texas. The job would be easier; at least no more twenty-four hours, seven days a week. This special arrangement had happened before with his former attorneys, usually to corporate positions but some to the courthouse. The reason for the job was simple. Give the departing attorney enough income to get by, in this case a $50,000 annual annuity, while keeping them ingratiated to you. Even if you don't get their loyalty, you kept the peace with them. A subtle offer of a deal helped many former attorneys keep their mouths shut.

For me, the break from the partnership was a welcome relief. I had poured my life into the partnership with Clark and I was exhausted.[1] I took the job offer simply because I looked forward to a sabbatical, to take some time to find out what had happened and to take a new direction with my life. I needed some time to rest, take some personal insights, and recover.

That was not to happen. The time with the university was not personally rewarding, I was in a deep personal swamp at home, and the opportunities were inviting in the legal arena. For these reasons I returned to the very fulfilling private practice of law.

Perhaps the advice I received while in Washington was at work. The former chairman of the FPC had told me that government work was the most fulfilling because there was a star to guide you, that of the public interest declared for the agency. I disagreed. The real world also had its guidelines, and I knew they were not what Clark practiced. I firmly believed I could follow those guidelines of doing the right thing with my own law practice.

So, after a year at the university, I left to open my law firm. I was doing what plaintiff's attorneys refer to as "getting religion." You are not practicing church law. You are simply determined to do the right thing, and that is one of the great and enduring beauties of the law, helping the average citizen, the little guy, by protecting them from the powers that be. As a practical matter, when you are not in the ranks of powerful "suits," you have to be a lawyer fighting for the underdog. More important, you have rededicated yourself to carefully enforce the law as written with all the opportunities it provides. You also get the twenty-four and seven routine.

I knew what I was getting into and I knew whom I would be facing. I found out in a very blunt way. When I decided to return to the private world, the real world, I made a courtesy call on my old partners. After all, I had taken a secure job with their help. Instead of courtesies, I was given an implicit warning that I should not expect to come to them needing money and begging for help. In that measure of confidence I had, I ignored the threat and went to work.

Again, subtle steps were necessary. As a measure of my determination in that spring of 1978, I arranged a line of credit with Clark's Capital National, his flagship bank. After all, attorneys could routinely open a $100,000 line of credit. A few months later, I learned what Clark thought of my credit line. It was canceled. I changed banks, going with the Travis Bank. I later found out Clark had an interest in that bank, too, and that he had a law firm office at that bank building. In effect, it was just another of his many banks.

By that fall in 1978, the clients were coming in. Most were individuals or small businesses throughout Austin. The personal satisfaction was immense. I was trying cases. I was doing what trial lawyers do. I was pursing what to me was righting the wrongs. For the next four years, my private practice was very enjoyable, and, at a personal level, very rewarding.

The cases covered many areas of the law. Communication clients subject to utility regulation were seeking mobile phone licenses. I got their work. A group of electric contractors found themselves in a pitched battle with a union. I restored a contractor's permit rights and commenced litigation against the union for damages. The contractors were very appreciative and referred several other lawsuits to me. I had the basic business needed to keep the office open.

I also started some contingent cases. One was an exploding Ford Pinto case. I took it after no attorney in Houston was interested in a relatively minor lawsuit. My client had suffered minimal burns, so her claims were relatively small. Ford refused to settle. We went to court and she finally got paid. I took on a case involving the negligent granting of credit to a fraudulent business promoting patently defective microchips for sub-metering devices. The case went to jury trial and a favorable judgment. A firefighter had been kicked out of the city's fire department and needed help on sexual discrimination and harassment charges. In a word, she was fired for her gender. A small businessman whose mobile home fell apart set the stage for another jury trial, one that brought Clark's old firm into the picture. After a particularly vicious trial before a hostile judge, I got a small judgment from the jury. I filed a claim against the Veterans Administration for allowing and even encouraging my client to smoke. Within a few months of his admission to the VA hospital, he developed lung cancer and died soon after. This *pro bono* claim, attempted at a soft underside of the tobacco business for health-care costs, could not be pursued beyond the administrative appeal. An old friend of the family called for help with his estate, and I handled it to a satisfactory completion.

One of Lyndon Johnson's old confidants came to me. Buck Hood needed help on an estate. In travels with Hood to Chicago on estate matters, we became good friends and he would tell me, "Terrible things happened during the Johnson administration." Hood had been managing editor of the Austin newspaper during the 1950s, and, after the assassination, had gone to Washington, to be on Johnson's personal staff. He would later tell me an important measure of Johnson's crimes.

In short, after a year in business, I had a good variety of cases and good income. With business income over $100,000, I had it made—or so I thought.

Then, in April 1981, cracks began to appear in my legal mortar. I went to Travis Bank to renew security on my assignment of receivables totaling several hundred thousand dollars. Assured all was well there, I tendered payment ten days later of almost $20,000. Suddenly, the bank called the note and demanded payment in full. In addition, they filed criminal charges, alleging a forged deed of trust. I was allowed time, "several days," to pay almost $35,000. This apparent act of grace, in fact an attempted extortion, quickly changed. Within two days, the charges were filed, charge and countercharge were made, and three lawsuits were fought to the bitter end.

The criminal trial went first. After delays of almost eighteen months and then a jump ahead of other priority cases, I finally went to trial. The judge refused the standard recusal that was granted all other attorneys facing charges in the county, we had a jury trial, and the verdict was guilty. In reality, the bank's case was deemed so weak my attorney assured me I did not need to testify.

The first trial lasted a week and involved numerous issues, including bank testimony that an alleged missing deed of trust had, in fact, been delivered and was not a forgery; that no money had been taken; and that the alleged forged documents included documents available only to the bank, not to me. The verdict, however, was guilty and judgment was probation and reimbursement of $35,000.[2] As a separate requirement, I was forced to cease the practice of law. Instead, I resigned, knowing that further practice was impossible until the verdict was reversed. I would then reapply and get back to work.

One thing became apparent. The powers that be wanted me out of Austin. I knew this fact even before the trial. I had been offered a job in Dallas and, when the criminal case came up, my attorney recommended getting a lawyer from out of town. The power of Clark was well recognized.

Once the surprising verdict was reached, the appeal process began. While the cases were pending, I moved to Houston and started a practice. After I resigned from the Bar, I was in the communications business there with my second wife, Cecile.

Clark and the Travis Bank were not through. The same claim involved in the criminal case was filed against me as a civil case.[3] I responded with a counterclaim for damages in excess of one million dollars. During discovery in the civil case, the bank resisted all efforts to disclose, including a refusal even to accept service of process for a deposition and a refusal to produce documents. A familiar process of stonewalling started. The bank also failed to appear at depositions scheduled for a key witness. The civil case was then put on hold, to await the result of a separate appeal in the criminal case. My counterclaim for damages and penalties had to wait.

During the appeal, with mixed feelings of anger and disgust, I prepared a full response to Clark's case and laid out the basics of what I knew about Clark's corruption and his Bubba justice system.[4] I repeated under oath what Thomas had told me when he framed the crimes of the Johnson years, of his taking care of things at Box 13 and of Clark being the person who took care of things in Dallas, of the assassination. I only laid out the basics of the crimes and the payoff. The details would have to wait for further disclosures and, as it turned out, some deep research. My affidavit was filed with the district attorney as a public record for everyone to know what was happening.

Until that point, I had carefully protected what I had learned with Clark. In April 1984 I still believed the information was privileged but, for me, it no longer mattered. I told what I knew. A year later I reviewed the law of privilege and learned that, under new theories, there was no privilege for crimes that were being planned to be committed.[5] This meant that any coverup was not protected and that any application for payment for a crime could be made public. Now I could tell it like it happened.

I revealed what John Coates, an associate attorney, told me, "If the truth be told, Clark arranged the assassination of Kennedy." I set out what Don Thomas, Clark's senior partner and Johnson's personal attorney, told me, that he was the only person who knew what happened at Box 13 but that "Clark took care of things in Dallas." I explained the application for oil wells in the east Texas field, to get a payoff bonus for Clark for arranging the assassination.

The affidavit was filed in the trial and appellate courts, and, on a special motion, would be filed in the Texas Supreme Court. In short, my position was stated to every court in Texas.

Clark knew what I was doing. After the conviction, one of my former clients was taken over by Clark's law firm, primarily because he owed one of Clark's banks a substantial debt. To make the transfer, I accompanied the client to a meeting with Don Thomas, who denied only one thing I had revealed, that Judge Roberts had become unfriendly to me personally because his son had not been admitted to law school by my then father-in-law, the dean there. Clark knew what I was saying in court. The opportunity was there to deny the allegations. Clark stayed silent.

During the appeals, I also proposed a book on the assassination. At a writing conference in Houston, I suggested the story to a literary agent. He told me to hire an investigator. At that time, with the Texas economy in a complete bust, there was no way for me to hire researchers. When the litigation ended over a decade later, I could get an investigator. In fact, to complete the research needed, I worked with many researchers.

By 1989, the various lawsuits were ending. First, the Federal Deposit Insurance Corporation had taken over Travis Bank. My counterclaim would never be paid because there was nothing left and the FDIC had nothing that could be foreclosed. Arbitration of the case was ordered. During the hearing, the FDIC agreed to drop their claims and I agreed to drop my claims provided all criminal charges were dismissed. They agreed to support the dismissal. On September 16, 1992, while I was pursuing final termination of the charges, Clark died. During this same period of appeals, Thomas died on November 11, 1994, following two strokes and a long illness. At that point, with a combination of no money available for me to recover from FDIC, the FDIC dropping all claims against me, Clark's death, Thomas' passing, and the FDIC helping get the criminal case over, a complete dismissal was ordered. A minor technical point: The dismissal was well before the probationary term had ended.

The final order dismissed everything. There never was a criminal charge, there was no jury trial, and the verdict was dismissed in its entirety. The public record shows that no crime was committed at all.

This personal review shows the power Clark exercised over the Austin and Texas judiciary. He had done the same thing to Frank Scofield. By the late 1980s, however, that power was largely gone and did not extend to Houston. After his death, it ended in Austin.

What happened to me is long, involved, and complex but it happened. Most of the persecution is still on the public record, a complete nullity. The technicalities of the law must be appreciated to see the depth of the persecution. For purposes of understanding the power of the Clark with the Texas political and legal system, the conspiracy against me personally reveals what could happen and what did happen in Dallas.

In 1994 with the persecution behind me, I could begin my investigation into the far greater reach of Clark's conspiratorial system. I could find the supporting details of what I knew happened on November 22, 1963.

The private investigation included many experts and much digging at the National Archives, the Texas State Library, the LBJ Library, and the Southwestern University Library. The LBJ Library proved surprisingly helpful. The most important discovery was the Clark Collection at Southwestern

University in Georgetown, Texas. Those private records, including diaries and notes, had not been sanitized by his estate. The boxes of records were just delivered. The librarians had organized most files but some records involving personal intimacies were initially withheld. The collection reference system was being reorganized at the time. Most of the Clark story is there or in the penthouse records.

In completing my research numerous books were studied, and many supplemental exhibits were obtained to verify persons, events, and dates. The Warren Commission *Report* was reviewed again. The original affidavits of the witnesses were accepted as the best evidence available from that investigation. Numerous genealogies of participants or suspects were checked to see how the key participants tied together.

Then a few unexpected breaks came my way. Books were published detailing what Johnson had done as viewed by the media and then by an attorney. While many of the stories were not accurate, there was a measure of fact in each. Madeleine Duncan Brown published her story, *Texas in the Morning.* I obtained the corroborating details for the meeting at Murchison's estate the night before the assassination. The Clark records were a true discovery detailing all that happened around the assassination and showing the connection with Leon Jaworski. The review permitted me to understand some of what I had learned with Clark and Thomas, particularly showing Wallace had the key role, that he had pushed Clark too far, and that he, too, had to be killed. The deep background for Clark's early years also showed up, enabling me to present in writing what I had heard. The old problem of one person's testimony against another was over. We had solid supporting evidence to go with the direct evidence.

The most telling evidence, when considered with all the other evidence, was the fingerprint match.[6] I reviewed the print evidence relied upon by the Warren Commission and concluded an independent review was needed. For that, I began the search for an expert. With the help of J. Harrison, a researcher in Austin, we engaged the services of A. Nathan Darby, an independent and certified print examiner with the highest credentials. To avoid any prejudice, we asked Mr. Darby if he would do a "blind" examination; that is, he would not know who the suspect was and he would not know what crime was involved. He agreed, and provided his services at no charge.

After intensive study and several reviews, he issued his report. My researcher called to tell me, "We have a match!" I was not excited because I knew we would find the corroboration we needed, we already had a solid case, and the print match served as the final step. An affidavit of what had been done was prepared.

Before any other communication was made to anyone, I provided this information to Senator Edward Kennedy for his family.

Because the assassination remains an open case at the Department of Justice, we submitted the evidence to that agency. At the time the Assassination Records Review Board was completing its work, and the affidavit was also filed with them. A formal petition was filed that also disclosed the bonus well application. Apparently because the ARRB was completing its work, the petition could not be included in the final report; however, it was forwarded to the Department of Justice. That agency disagreed with the print match but provided no supporting explanation.

The report in the Appendix reviews the Darby affidavit and what happened after it was filed. Several experts disagreed, one agreed, and I realized that the politics involved in the assassination could not be escaped. The solution was to seek review outside the United States. French print examiners made their review and concluded there was a match.

With the prints and a complete record of the Johnson-Clark conspiracy in hand, we had a case based on independent evidence, of Wallace and the 1984 indictments for the murder of Henry Marshall, of the affair with Madeleine Duncan Brown and her insights, and of the inside workings between Johnson and Clark and of Clark and Jaworski.

I had gone from a top partner with Clark to the depths of persecution. Fighting back all the way, I finally prevailed. The case was made. The court ruling that there was no crime was one bonus. Then, with the print identification, I had another bonus. With it answers were provided for an assassination investigation that has lingered far too long.

Further work needs to be done. There is a very large source for records that must be considered. The penthouse records must be disclosed. In addition, some important reforms are needed. For that we turn to the problems with the investigation of the Kennedy assassination and to a concluding look at the solutions to the problems of power and its abuse.

I am not a politician and my other habits are good.
—Artemus Ward

Remember, democracy never lasts long. It soon wastes, exhausts,
and murders itself.
—John Adams

20

Renewal

The massive abuse of power that surrounded the assassination of President
Kennedy demands correction. Abuses occurred both before November 22,
1963, in planning and carrying out the crime, and then afterward, in failing
to uncover what happened. Disclosure alone will not provide the justice owed
to John Kennedy. We need to relegate Johnson to the position he deserves,
we need to control the superlawyers, and we need better controls on government conspiracies.

Problems remain. What are the solutions?

As my investigation was drawing to a close, one fact became ever clearer.
The conclusions of the Warren Commission would have been the judgment
of history had it not been for the determined efforts of countless private
citizens.

Consider the difficulties of a public investigation by private individuals.
None have the power of the district attorney or the United States attorney.
The researchers had no subpoena or other investigative or enforcement powers. The privacy protections given individuals also barred what was too often
a very private investigation. Yet the search was kept alive.

Investing heavily of their time and money, determined individuals and
associations of researchers rejected the lone nut and anarchist theories. The
scene of the crime in Dallas as it unfolded over two days, between the shooting of the president and the shooting of the alleged assassin, just looked,
sounded, and smelled like a conspiracy.

The private citizens who believed there was a conspiracy are right. These
researchers are an independent group, and many are pursuing difficult theories, sometimes with questionable facts and objectives. Because of a necessary streak of independence, they tend to disagree among themselves as much

as they disagree with the Warren Commission and its apologists. Because of their efforts, however, the conspiracy is exposed. New depths remain to be uncovered but at the heart of the conspiracy there was sniper Mac Wallace acting at the direction of power broker Ed Clark, who was fulfilling Lyndon Johnson's wishes.

The more than two thousand books on the Kennedy assassination are compelling in their own way, and there is no way to do justice for the combined efforts of the many researchers. Most are well written in the sense that they marshal the facts and assumptions to support their theses. Countless manuscripts have been prepared taking the details of the assassination apart. A vast wealth of material is available on the Internet. All have common defects: they did not know what went on behind the attorney-client privilege; none followed the money trail; and most tend to ignore Johnson, perhaps with that subconscious respect or fear we carry for our presidents.

More fundamentally, even while showing the probability of a massive conspiracy, few researchers have suggestions about what needs to be done apart from full disclosure. The drive to disclose has been a major achievement.[1] Even the ARRB, however, did not produce what was needed. Some say there is no hope of changing government, that improvements are not possible. We shall see there is one important change, a fundamental one reaching to the heart of our democracy.

As time has passed, many important witnesses and participants have died. Indeed, it is generally accepted that many have been killed. At the same time, however, many have come forward or have left their testimonials.

Jack Ruby wrote a long note from jail saying that the killings of Kennedy and Oswald had been by Johnson. Soon after, under strange circumstances of suddenly contracting cancer, he died.[2]

Madeleine Duncan Brown was on record that Johnson was behind the killing of Kennedy and of several other men. Brown has a bound manuscript and a book on the subject but has been largely disregarded.[3] She passed away on June 22, 2002. Again, her story was extended beyond its original basics, a problem for many in the wake of the assassination.

Billy Sol Estes convinced a Texas grand jury about what he knew.[4] A skeptical media ignored him as a big talker. No mention was made of Texas Ranger Clint Peoples's contribution to that same grand jury. Estes has told much more but, as the salesman he is, he tends to take anything too far. Not so with Ranger Peoples. What he said and did is gospel.[5]

George de Mohrenschildt, the Russian émigré and friend to Jackie Kennedy, befriended Oswald in 1962 in Dallas and introduced him around. He was convinced Oswald could not have done it alone. He died under strange circumstances just before he was to tell investigators what he knew.

Dallas police chief Jesse Curry originally agreed with the Warren Commission but later concluded there had been a conspiracy.[6] His views were set forth in a book which was withdrawn from distribution. Limited copies remain available.

Robert Caro set the stage for Johnson as an assassin by showing a careful measure of the man through 1948.[7] His more recent book concentrates on the activity of the Senate, not the crimes. Perhaps that will be revealed in his story of the vice presidency and the presidency. To date, certainly, his analysis of Johnson's character is not inconsistent with an assassin of the president.

Ronnie Dugger concluded Johnson was a man without moral principle or compass, a man capable of murder and assassination.[8] While editor of the *Texas Observer*, he closely followed the developments in the Warren investigation, and the newsweekly regularly reported on progress. In perhaps the closest he got to the conspiracy was noting recognition between Oswald and Ruby just before the fatal shot.

In 1979, the House Select Committee on Assassination concluded there had been a "probable" conspiracy.[9]

Within ten years of the Warren Report, a majority of the commission had expressed serious doubts about their conclusions.[10] Richard Russell, Johnson's mentor in the Senate, believed from the beginning that there was more than one "magic" bullet so there had to be more than one sniper. Joining the doubters were commission members John Sherman Cooper and Hale Boggs. John J. McCloy admitted there was no credible evidence that there was not a conspiracy. Finally, even Earl Warren said new investigations were needed.

Texas governor John Connally was certain there were two separate shots, not one magic bullet.[11] While he stated he did not believe there was a conspiracy, his firm belief about the shots means there had to be at least two snipers.

Johnson knew there was a conspiracy, at different times suggesting the Cubans and organized crime were behind it.[12] He did nothing about this expressed belief, simply saying the incredible, that he couldn't get the Department of Justice to do anything.

Robert Kennedy planned to disclose what he believed about the Warren Commission after the 1968 election. Supposedly he was suspicious of organized crime and of the CIA.[13]

Jackie Kennedy did not believe the Warren Commission report and supposedly authorized the French secret service to conduct an investigation.[14] The book, *Farewell America*, says Big Oil did it. According to the ARRB, Mrs. Kennedy's conclusions, if any, remain sealed for many more years.

William Manchester studied the assassination events and remains open, apparently, to a conspiracy.[15] His papers were not given to the ARRB and remain private. This is significant because he spoke to many individuals *before* the Warren investigators did.

In still another book involving the people most deeply involved, Seymour Hirsch notes that the Kennedy family still has its doubts.[16]

Oliver Stone provided the most publicized and dramatic response with his movie *JFK*.[17] The debate he triggered led to further research, and, in some cases, to still more inconclusive and incomplete disclosures.

Nigel Turner did outstanding research. Based in Great Britain, he started a television series titled *The Men Who Killed Kennedy*.[18] His documentaries were an important inspiration to Oliver Stone.

Failure Analysis produced an excellent study of the crime scene, and its video was used at a mock trial during the American Bar Association meeting in 1991.[19] The jury split on what happened, essentially a hung jury on Oswald's guilt.

Yet the accepted wisdom is (1) one lone nut—despite the presence of at least two "lone nuts"; (2) anyone who supports a conspiracy is clinically paranoid—not unlike Johnson; and (3) there are no conspiracies anywhere—unless you have it on video.

Johnson also has his apologists. The leading group is the LBJ Library itself. A continuing series of books respond to anything derogatory of the former president.[20] Instant responses are provided to key accusations.

Several authors similarly respond quickly, fully defending a man they do not respect.

Robert Dallek praises Johnson with the back of his hand and concludes Johnson did not assassinate Kennedy.[21] Dallek cites nothing to support his conclusion.

Doris Kearns Goodwin takes a fascinating insider's view that is generally sympathetic to Johnson.[22] Supposedly very close to him in his last years, she leaves unmentioned his psychiatric treatment. Johnson's ability to compartmentalize and Clark's ability to coverup worked.

Over the years many professional writers and journalists have expressed their opinions about Johnson's role. As may be apparent, their opinions will not easily change.

Finally, the Department of Justice reportedly has an active group reviewing the assassination. They refused to release any internal information on their investigation to the ARRB. Their files will apparently remain sealed forever. The ARRB sent the Wallace print evidence to the Department of Justice but never received a full report. Our researchers requested all files on Wallace, and received one set of reports—FBI surveillance of Wallace as a communist during the early 1950s. Presumably there is nothing else.

Looking back, the circumstantial evidence was so strong that the crime scene literally cried out "conspiracy." The only thing missing was what went on behind the conspirators' shields, those of government secrecy, presidential privilege, the attorney-client privilege, and the corporate veil.

The final barrier for all the investigators, both public and private, was the attorney-client privilege, created by the courts and sanctioned by the lawmakers. Only an insider can breach that privilege. That has now been done.

The criminal process then goes to work. When an insider discloses a conspiracy, the conspirators are required to come forward and show the evidence, if any, that there was no conspiracy. The entirety of the secret penthouse records must be disclosed forthwith.

The massive LBJ Library in Austin is adjacent to Interstate 35 and cannot be missed. Dedicated within three years of Johnson's retirement, the structure is a huge monument to an assassin. Johnson was not expected home until January 1973 after serving two full terms so his library had to be completed on an expedited schedule. Some shortcuts were taken and a lot of extra money was spent to satisfy his pride.

The library is beautiful. A replica of the oval office tops the ten floors. Surprisingly, Johnson agreed the oval could be ever so slightly smaller than the White House version. Containing 35 million documents, the library covers the record of the Johnson years from the early 1930s through 1968. Administered by the National Archives system, Johnson's presidential monument is the largest of the nine now completed.

Dedicated on May 22, 1971, amid considerable celebration, dignitaries from around the world attended. I was responsible for escorting Jerry Brown, then California's secretary of state. The festivities covered several days and climaxed that evening with a party attended by hundreds of well-wishers. Stretching up the main stairs, crowds struggled for refreshments and a chance to see Johnson.

Johnson's remarks on declaring his monument ready for the public became the high point in the dedication. Significantly, he said:

> This Library does not say, "This is how I saw it," but "this is how the documents show it was."

> There is no record of a mistake, nothing critical, ugly, or unpleasant that is not included in the files here. We have papers from my 40 years of public service in one place, for friend and foe to judge, to approve or disapprove.

> I do not know how this period will be regarded in years to come. But that is not the point. This Library will show the facts—not just the joys and triumphs, but the sorrows and failures, too.[23]

Not so.

The burden is now on the conspirators. Their crimes are recorded in the penthouse records. The records must be released totally, completely, and promptly. There is no one left to send to prison. Johnson said he wanted the facts. The facts should be disclosed.

Clark never gave an oral history for the LBJ Library. Thomas did but, in advance, he limited his recollections to the business, mainly the radio-television station, and not to all the land and banking. He carefully guarded the investment transaction by Brazos-Tenth Street. There was no mention of the 1948 election or any other crime. Those matters were specifically excluded before the oral history even started.[24]

Consider a historian's recommendation:

> . . . the mute witnesses must be asked the reasons for their silence, for the piece of evidence that is missing from where one might reasonably expect to find it is, after all, a form of evidence in itself.[25]

Recall, too, that I made the accusation in court proceedings and under oath. Clark followed the proceedings carefully. He knew what I was saying. Consider Clark's silence with another practical feature of the law:

> The failure of a party to deny statements in documents or writings

may sometimes be received as an admission where it is shown that the document was brought to his attention and the circumstances were such as to call for a reply.[26]

Let the lawyers argue whether there was a duty to respond.

The Johnson Estate should authorize the disclosures. In fact, Johnson may have authorized a waiver of the privilege when he dedicated the LBJ Library. The penthouse records will go a long way to filling in the blanks and adding the details. They must be released.

Any disclosure must be done quickly. Legal records have a tendency to be "vacuumed" to remove the dirt. From this day forward, the longer Johnson's lawyers, his estate, and his library continue to hide the records, the less reliable they will be for research. The disclosures must include the psychiatrist's files as well.

Any defensive responses should be treated with the same skepticism that has been leveled at the researchers. Do not simply take the word of the Johnson apologist. Everyone attacked Estes when Wallace's murder of Marshall was revealed and the grand jury acted. None mentioned Texas Ranger Clint Peoples. There was more evidence than just what Estes said. If the skeptics had been more aggressive then, the assassination might have been solved much sooner. Indeed, had the investigators done their job in 1948 or 1951 or 1961 or 1962, there would have been no assassination.

There is more to the government's inaction. An unwritten determination to absolve the presidency or any branch of the government of any crime was present. Johnson headed the investigation and provided only a written statement to the Warren Commission. The basic legal principle of the common law was violated, that "No person may be the judge of his or her own case."

Today the defensiveness has only worsened. Now the government, and particularly the Department of Justice and the FBI, defend their prior determinations of no evidence and conceal everything.

With good reason, Texas justice is infamous. The legend of Judge Roy Bean and his law West of the Pecos is a measure of that raw Western justice still practiced there. There have been many more examples since the turn of the last century. When John Kennedy flew into Texas, he was immediately entrapped in that system.

Many have worked to reform the Texas courts but have been largely unsuccessful because of the politics involved. Only a few judges and lawyers are in need of reform; however, the corruption of those few contaminates the rest. Fundamental change is needed to assure the independence of the courts.

Secret, *ex parte* contacts must be outlawed. The prohibition must include all employees of the court. Heavy criminal penalties should apply to such comments, both to the judge and the lawyer. Everything communicated must be in writing and disclosed to all parties.

Lawyers are officers of the court and must be barred from abuse of their rights. The attorney-client privilege is at the heart of that abuse.

A little history is needed to understand this rule of law, of secrecy. The privilege was first adopted to protect the attorney's honor. The idea was that, for an attorney to disclose what his client had told him would be to suggest the attorney was less than honest. Needless to say, this justification was soon abandoned; however, the rule based on that reason continued.

The privilege should not cover acts intended to commit crimes. The planning of criminal acts should not be privileged. Any ambiguity in the current state of the law regarding crimes must be corrected.

Consider the current justification for the privilege:

> The "Ethical Rules" require disclosure by an attorney only where necessary to avoid assisting a client's criminal or fraudulent act in proceedings before a tribunal.[27]

When the client chooses to testify falsely or when the client provides the attorney false information for use at trial, the attorney must resist presenting that evidence. The attorney is no longer muzzled by the privilege.

The same rule goes further:

> Lawyers may, but need not, reveal confidences in only two other circumstances: to prevent crimes likely to result in imminent death or substantial bodily harm, or to assert their own claims in a controversy with a client.

The first instance involves an attorney knowing a crime is about to be committed and knowing an innocent third person will face "imminent death or substantial bodily injury." By implication, any other crime is okay. This very limited exception does not go far enough. If an attorney learns their client plans to commit any crime, then it must be disclosed. If not, the attorney becomes a party to the crime and should be subject to the criminal processes.

The second exception to the privilege only underscores the greed built into the system on behalf of attorneys. If a client refuses to pay, the attorney may disclose any confidences of the client that are necessary to collect. A client is not well served by this form of extortion. Clearly it should be abandoned. If the privilege is absolute for the attorney, then the client should also benefit.

Interestingly, the privilege represents, in part, an American tradition against the tattler. This is a separate consideration from protecting a client's confidences within the attorney-client privilege. We need the tattler and we need the whistle-blower when crimes are planned.

The following is perhaps the best solution:

> When self-interest is not at issue, many professionals, including lawyers, have concluded that "the uncertain and conjectural charac-ter" of threats to client confidence should not take precedence over concrete risks to innocent third party victims.[28]

When there is any threat of crime, there should be no privilege. When lawyers plan the crime, there should be no privilege.

This reform is not just for Texas. It should apply to all attorneys. The American Bar Association rationalizes that, "official ideology not only per-mits but may require counsel to remain a silent witness to highly asocial con-duct." The ABA's "highly asocial conduct" apparently includes murder.

Surely this kind of conduct cannot continue. Any "asocial" acts should not be privileged whether in criminal or civil courts. To return to the assas-sination, had Clark reason to fear disclosure of what he knew, he just might have been far more cautious and far less willing to do what Johnson needed. Unfortunately, by the time Johnson had to have the assassination, Clark was too brazen to have any fear of his legal system.

If there were no privilege, surely some of the Warren Commission's attor-neys and investigators would have been more aggressive. Perhaps they would have been encouraged to consider the key element in any crime—the motive—and then they might have dredged up the obvious suspicions against Johnson and his lawyers.

The privilege must be restricted to very limited exceptions. Then, per-haps, it will disappear . . .

. . . along with the superlawyers.

There is one additional solution. Our democratic system of government needs reform at the very heart of the problem that compelled Johnson and

Clark to assassinate President Kennedy. Simply stated, unlimited ambition was at the heart of that most horrific abuse of our political system. This unlimited greed for power is at the heart of most political problems.

The attitude of most citizen voters toward our government is a good-natured skepticism coupled with a proud sense of civic responsibility. We willingly elect individuals who are true characters in the dramatic sense. They usually have been egocentric, loving of the extremes, and almost pathological. This type of personality is too often without a strong sense of right and wrong. The law may apply to everyone else, they believe, but it does not apply to me.

While we may welcome this aggressive personality, the more fundamental fact remains that this type of character cannot be trusted, not completely. We have to keep a close hand on our leaders. Elections every two or four or six years are simply not good enough. Specific issues arise that require unique correction. The effort by researchers to compel disclosure is one example. One lesson from the Warren investigation is that government cannot be the judge of its own case. Here the expressed concern was not to become another banana republic. The irony was, we did just that.

To make that correction, we need to reassess the system that has been with us since the original Constitutional convention. Do we trust the people or the politicians? We need more trust to the people and empower them accordingly. We need to take the next reasonable step in the evolution of our Constitution by trusting the voters even more.

Individuals are not perfect, and they are capable of corruption. Society is similarly not perfect and is capable of corruption. Power does tend to corrupt. Patrick Henry recognized this fact in opposing the Constitution. Lord Acton recognized it in very clear terms. Henry Kissinger commented on power as a great aphrodisiac. Any government representative has power, is not perfect, and is subject to corruption.

During the Constitutional debates, there was a fear of this self-enrichment:

> Federalists and anti-federalists both agreed that man in his deepest nature was selfish and corrupt; that blind ambition most often overcomes even the most clear-eyed rationality; and that the lust for power was so overwhelming that no one should ever be entrusted with unqualified authority.[29]

Despite these fears, James Madison argued, clearly too optimistically, that "I go with this great republican principle, that the people will have the virtue and intelligence to select men of virtue and wisdom."[30]

Consider in the context of the assassination conspiracy what the men of "virtue and wisdom" did. Perhaps then we can see what needs to be done.

We need two quick changes. One way to limit corruption by coverup is to require full disclosure. What our public officials are doing must be disclosed to us, in detail and completely. Knowing their records will be disclosed may just prompt our representatives to be honest and trustworthy.

Second, resolve the ongoing debate in this country about telling the truth. Some argue there is no place for a lie. In government, that must be the law. We need laws mandating that government representatives cannot lie to the public just like there are laws prohibiting the people from lying to government.[31] Our elected representatives must be held to the same standard we are.

Sissela Bok is an outstanding philosopher on lying. Relating the issue of truth in government directly to Johnson, she said:

> Believing they were voting for the candidate of peace, American citizens were, within months, deeply embroiled in one of the cruelest wars in their history. Deception of this kind strikes at the very essence of democratic government.[32]

In addition, a new limit on government is needed. Prompt and effective accountability is essential. At this time, there are three main threads to self-government: First, from the beginnings in our Constitution, we have been called upon to trust the government. As will be seen, this call for trust was originally based on the belief that the people were not to be trusted. The balance of trust between the government and the governed has changed dramatically over the past two hundred years. We have gradually placed more and more trust in the voters. Now, to a very significant extent, more trust must be taken from the politicians and returned to the people.

We as a democratic people cannot blindly trust our representatives. We can trust ourselves. If someone's vote is to be bought, let it be ours. If someone is to be wined and dined, let it be we the people. If corruption is inherent in humans, let us share fully in the corruption.

So, to return to the question, who bests runs our government?

> The question of popular elections was indeed at the heart of republican government—a test of how far men trusted their fellows, how much power they dared grant to the people.[33]

This was the question during the Constitutional convention in 1787: How much power to the people? The leaders held the power. How much would they give back?

Until then, the rulers held the power. Thomas Paine argued representative government was the way to run a nation:

> The nation is essentially the source of all sovereignty; nor can any individual, or any body of men, be entitled to any authority which is not expressly derived from it.[34]

During the writing of our Constitution, the issue of whether to trust the "common man" was fiercely debated in *The Federalist*. Basically, the founders compromised, in favor of representative government but with only a few people empowered to select the leaders. Only members of the House of Representatives were elected directly by the people.

The Constitution provided an electoral college to elect the president, to prevent possible abuses of government by "the multi-odored many" and the "great unwashed masses." In addition, the people did not elect senators at all; they were selected by state legislatures.

When the Constitution was adopted, most people were not even allowed to vote. In many states, only white men could vote. In some elections, owning property was essential, if not to voting, then to serving in office. Women were denied voting power. In the slave states, persons held in bondage could not vote. A vast electorate was purposely disenfranchised because they were not to be trusted with political power.

Over the past two hundred years, many of these limits have changed. Now almost all people are entitled to vote. We have gradually become a much more direct democracy. The people have become the rulers to an ever-greater extent.

Consider Thomas Jefferson's idea:

> Sometimes it is said that man cannot be trusted with the government of himself. Can he, then, be trusted with the government of others? Or have we found angels in the form of kings to govern him? Let history answer this question.[35]

Second, communications have improved to the extent that the Internet makes interactive voting possible. With the ever-increasing pressure of daily life, there is a need for more convenience to the voting process. Some states allow Election Day to extend over a week. With absentee balloting it extends over thirty days and even longer. The voting must also be easier, perhaps like Congress votes, by signing in and recording electronically. The Internet is the current means, and most websites offer voting on specific issues. The e-vote will happen, and soon.

There is a third thread to popular democracy. A common feature of the populist revolution late in the nineteenth century was local power through direct democracy. The modern pioneers of democracy appear to be from Switzerland who insisted on returning government to the people. The referendum became an important part of government there. The referendum idea grew in America with the populists in the 1890s. Starting in the west, cities, counties, states, and school boards became subject to direct vote. During the twentieth century, the idea continued to grow and expand.

Today, the people have been empowered in many states and cities to initiate laws, to recall leaders, and to vote on controversial ideas. This is another line of change giving the power of direct democracy to the people. Half the states now have some form of referendum. Most local governments not only allow it; quite wisely, they encourage it.

A far more compelling case is to involve the entire electorate in the process. As we have seen, for many years Johnson and Clark worked with a very restricted electorate, basically white, Anglo-Saxon Protestant males. Even today, with very limited voter turnout, elections are decided by minorities of the people. All must be involved and direct democracy on issues as well as candidates will best accomplish that result.

Thus, we have three converging trends. (1) more voting rights to the people; (2) initiative, referendum, and recall; and (3) Internet connectivity and active voting.

When all these trends are pulled together, the solution is direct democracy; our needs are initiative, referendum, and recall on a national basis.

We have trusted our leaders for over two centuries while gradually reclaiming that trust. The time has come for direct democracy on an even greater scale.[36]

Consider just one change. A referendum system might have approved a law requiring full disclosure of the assassination in 1964 rather than the long wait. When so much time passes, witnesses are dead, evidence is destroyed, and memories are weaker. The time to solve crime is promptly. Government inaction has postponed what was needed for almost forty years. Even in 1998, the Department of Justice, the FBI, and the CIA successfully stonewalled the ARRB. A national vote requiring full disclosure is needed.

There are many more examples in all areas of government and politics. We need voter participation on the issues, not just the candidates.

John Kennedy praised senators who had the courage to vote their convictions even though they knew their voters would be against them.

[*Profiles in Courage*] is about the most admirable of human virtues—
courage. "Grace under pressure," Ernest Hemingway defined it.[37]

While giving the examples of nine Senators who stood against their voters and voted what they believed right, he emphasized that he was not critical of democracy and popular rule. He emphasized that we can improve,
that "The true democracy, living and growing and inspiring, puts its faith in
the people."[38]

The American experience has shown a remarkable strength of character
in many of our leaders and in ourselves. The examples are everywhere. So,
too, are the issues. For now, the entire subject of direct democracy is left for
another book.[39]

John Kennedy stated:

A man does what he must—in spite of personal consequences, in
spite of obstacles and dangers and pressures—and that is the basis of
human morality.[40]

The American people have shown that basic morality over and over. Now we
are in a new millennium. The time has come not only to bring closure to the
Kennedy assassination, but to reform our government. The failures just in
his case are so obvious that we could use that example to open up our government by renewing it, by giving still more trust back to the people.

There is an individual whose rights have not been served. John Kennedy
demands justice.

Kennedy said that his generation represented a new torch, a symbol of
the change that his administration undertook. When he spoke, the prior
decade had been the silent generation. The decades following his remarks
have witnessed change in a big way. By direct democracy, we will be ever more
likely to have change as an accepted part of government. We are supposed to
be a government of and by and for the people. We should go ahead and place
trust where it belongs, with the people, where it cannot be compromised,
except by the people themselves.

Every citizen a senator and, if there is to be corruption, so be it; enrich
us.

Lincoln said it best:

No man is good enough to govern another man without that other's
consent.[41]

Finally, for our present purposes, consider the remark in the book that was released with Stone's *JFK*:

Et tu, Lyndon.[42]

This is one of the paradoxes of the democratic movement—that it loves a crowd and fears the individuals who compose it—that the religion of humanity should have no faith in human beings.
—Walter Lippman

> Man's capacity for justice makes democracy possible, but man's
> inclination to injustice makes democracy necessary.
> —Reinhold Neibuhr

Conclusion

The last time I saw Johnson was late in the evening after the dedication of his library. He was standing with Clark near the outside fountain on a warm, still night.

I walked over to congratulate him but we did not shake hands. I knew his hand was hurting from the well-wishers he had visited.

Johnson was already stooped and his eyes tired and hollowed. He was in the beginnings of that deep depression that would reach into his heart and slowly kill him. He had less than two years. At the time I did not know the depths of his crimes so I could only wish him well.

Clark stayed silent during this brief visit. The party was over and it was time to go home. Johnson was back in Austin for good and would soon begin that deep psychiatric insight necessary to bring him out of the debilitating effects of his depression.

As we have seen his catharsis would serve him well.

For too long many researchers have known Johnson was behind the conspiracy. No one has been able to say it.

Stated simply, LBJ killed JFK.

The crime opens, once again, the need for government action. The Dallas Police Department still carries the assassination as an open crime. The Department of Justice has an open file on the case, and the FBI routinely reviews new disclosures. Congress has committees with responsibilities. Each needs to take steps to clear the record. We need to start with the Department of Justice and the FBI disclosing to the Senate and House Judiciary Committees what they kept from the Assassination Records Review Board.[1]

But there is more. Benjamin Cardozo, a former Supreme Court justice, recognized a subconscious determinant in the judicial mind that controlled decisions on innocence and guilt. He suggested the judges themselves needed to be aware of this unknown quality to their decisions and act accordingly.

We remove the bias by denying to any person the right to be the judge of his or her own case.

Perhaps, as we render a collective judgment on this horrific event, we need see both this subconscious determinant in ourselves and the need for independent judges.

More in point, in Shakespeare's *Hamlet*, actors and audiences are always left wondering why Hamlet delayed so long in seeking the justice he knew he would have to find. A subconscious reluctance to upset the government may have been one consideration. After all, in the final act all the key players are dead. Perhaps Hamlet delayed because he knew his necessary actions would destroy not only his family, but also his nation.

We as a nation may have a similar reluctance to face the fact of the conspiracy just because we know what it means to our republic. We still do not want to be a banana republic.

Perhaps the final decision each of us will make will be based on this subconscious determinant in the judicial process. If we recognize that fact and then decide, we can face what happened and accept the idea of trusting the political system to survive and grow. We can experience a catharsis in this great drama and high tragedy that is John Kennedy and Lyndon Johnson. Aristotle believed that this catharsis, this cleansing of the emotions, is the effect of great tragedy. The result is a restoration of the spirit.

Most important, if we face up to what happened, we are very clearly reaffirming the spirit of our democracy. In so doing, we strengthen our government and ourselves in ways yet to be seen. In that same faith in our nation we know it will be for the better. With closure, we will be stronger.

Decision time brings to mind the famous Hamlet quote, "To be or not to be; that is the question."

The new paradigm or system of direct democracy would not only apply to the process but to the reasoning behind the process. We would be in charge, empowered ourselves to take the steps needed for a better democracy.

The words emblazoned on the main building at the University of Texas are, "Ye shall know the truth and the truth shall make you free." The way is available for us to be ever more free, to be in charge of our lives both individually and as a great nation, to face what is before us and do what we have to do.

The cure for the evils of democracy is more democracy.
　　　—H.L. Mencken

Then will I confess unto thee that thine own right hand can save thee.
　　　—*Acts 40:14 (KJV)*

Appendix

Overview: Photos and Documents

The Conspirators

1—Lyndon B. Johnson (restrained by JFK)
On the 1960 campaign trail, Johnson reacts angrily to a heckler while a worried Kennedy tries to restrain his running mate. Johnson did not take criticism easily and always acted to avoid embarrassment. He was a violent man.

2—Edward A. Clark
This photo is from the files of the Texas Bar Association. Clark was the power broker and superlawyer for Texas in the Johnson years. When those years ended, so did his power. His final big play: the bonus from Big Oil.

3—Malcolm Everett Mac Wallace
Wallace at the peak of his political career. This photo from the University of Texas yearbook is just after Wallace was student body president and led a remarkable march on the Texas capitol to protest the firing of the university's president. As his political future waned, he became more and more the radical Marxist and murderer-assassin.

4—Donald S. Thomas
The ever-friendly Thomas, always quick to smile and very understanding, was completely different from Clark. Following his fraudulent votes in 1948's Box 13, he became Clark's right hand as well as business attorney to Johnson and his family. An excellent trial attorney, he was only reluctantly involved in the crimes of the Johnson era.

Big Oil for Big D

5—The "black giant"—East Texas Oil Field
This oil-field giant, the only one in the lower forty-eight states, was the source of wealth for the Dallas billionaires known as Big Oil. Clark fought Exxon

over oil rights in this field to collect his bonus for the Kennedy assassination. With help from the King Ranch, he collected two million dollars.

6—Big Oil hunting—Murchison, Cain, Richardson
Three of the seven key members of Big Oil, all multi-millionaires, on the hunt. Sid Richardson, Wofford Cain, and Clint Murchison were all friends of Johnson and Clark. Murchison was the political leader and helped set up the bonus for Clark. He was also behind the recruitment of Jack Ruby.

7—D. H. Byrd on an oil well
A member of Big Oil in Dallas, Byrd was interested in rockets and helped set up the military-industrial complex in the Metroplex. Called "Dry Hole" because of a string of unsuccessful oil wells, when the great east Texas oil field was discovered, he got wealthy. Byrd owned the Texas School Book Depository at the time of the assassination.

Clark—The Early Years

8—Campaign poster
After finishing law school, Clark was elected county attorney in San Augustine in 1930. When he ran for district attorney, he was defeated. He never ran for public office again, preferring to work behind the scenes.

9—Clark for FDR
Clark started in Austin politics as a liberal and a Democrat. Here he plays the "no bull" routine, to support FDR's reelection. Clark was chief administrator for the last liberal governor of Texas (until Ann Richards was elected). Clark quickly changed colors, becoming a dedicated conservative who disliked intellectuals, had no use for liberals, and supported John Tower avidly.

10—Clark, LBJ, Stevenson, and Nimitz
This remarkable photo after World War II ended shows the key opponents in the 1948 election together. Clark is speaking while Johnson looks on admiringly. Stevenson will fight all the way to the Supreme Court in 1948 and still see his victory stolen by Johnson.

11—Clark, Ramsey, Tower, and Anne Clark

Ramsey was a childhood friend who exercised power for Clark during the 1950s and 1960s. This ceremony honored Tower, with the lead taken by Clark. Anne Clark is also present.

12—A tradition for violence

A horrific photo of a lynching in Sabine County, next to Clark's home county, was kept by Clark with a connection to his grandfather. The depths of violence these men were capable of had no limits. (Photo blurred intentionally.)

13—Clark discharged from the army

Clark was a captain in the quartermaster corps of the army during World War II and was involved in the theft of two vehicles. To end the proceedings, charges were reduced to the disappearance of funds and a summary discharge from the service. His wife was also required to testify, to be certain he never received any benefits as a veteran.

The Corruption of Power

14—Clark breaks the law for Johnson

As an attorney, Clark used the privilege to cover for crimes. Here he advises that a donor is taken care of for good and that he has arranged a new loan under suspicious circumstances. The basic working arrangement between Johnson and Clark is in place. The conspiracy protected by the privilege is working in 1949 and will stay in place until Johnson's death.

15—Johnson agrees to protect "the patsy"

Replying to Clark's memo, Johnson acknowledges the legal dangers the lawyer faced and promises to help. If all failed, however, Clark was the fall guy. The working arrangement is defined in these two documents by the conspirators.

16—Wallace sentenced for murder

Following the murder of Doug Kinser, Wallace was tried and convicted. The jury split on life imprisonment or the death penalty. The judge ordered a five-year sentence and surprisingly suspended the imprisonment despite the cold-blooded killing. Wallace later worked with Clark to carry out the assassination.

Johnson's Dark Side—The Senate Years

17—Billy Sol Estes by his airplane

Estes built a farming empire in west Texas but financing problems caught up with him in 1960. Estes was recognized as an "interest" for Johnson as early as 1958; however, when criminal charges were filed, Johnson denied knowing him. Estes was protected by Johnson and Johnson was protected by Estes. Johnson would not be dropped by John Kennedy and then indicted by Robert Kennedy.

18—Bobby Baker with Johnson

The two men had a very close working relationship in the Senate. Together they took care of the business of that most exclusive men's club in the world. Johnson considered Baker to be the same as a son. When Baker had to resign, Johnson promptly denied any close connections.

19—Madeleine Duncan Brown

Madeleine was one of Johnson's lovers during his Senate career and later. She had a son by Johnson and was paid through Brazos-Tenth, the money-laundering corporation.

20—Ellen Rometsch

An East German, she was married to a West German army officer and was a call girl to Kennedy and others. When the relationship was about to be exposed, she was deported.

21—Johnson has an interest in Estes

When the Estes scandal went public in April 1962, Johnson denied any contacts. This memo shows Johnson was "very interested" in the wonder boy from Pecos, Texas. Those many contacts led to fraud, murder, and coverup, and then almost engulfed Johnson.

22—Naval Intelligence tracks Wallace

When Wallace was given a safe job with the military-industrial complex for Big Oil, security clearance was required. Wallace's background as a murderer, a Marxist, and an abusive husband led to the recommendation he get no clearance. He was still cleared as ONI monitored him for "higher-ups."

Clark's Power Plays

23—Clark's "round table" runs Texas
The top government leaders of Texas are on Clark's list, and he is in charge. Clark was on top in Texas politics as "boss of Texas," a title originally given him by *Reader's Digest* in 1951.

24—Johnson indebted to Clark
More than any other document, this letter expresses the close relationship between the two men.

25—Clark—money for Johnson's greatest opportunity
This revealing letter raising money for Johnson during the 1960 campaign emphasizes the future power for Johnson while downplaying any role for Kennedy. Both Johnson and Clark knew the vice presidency was essentially worthless.

Assassin Mac Wallace in Trouble

26—Johnson by plane crash
While the Estes scandal was still developing, Johnson had arranged a meeting to keep Estes quiet and cut off any investigation. Despite terrible flying conditions, Johnson ordered the two pilots to fly to the ranch. They were killed when they could not locate Johnson's personal landing strip in the thick fog.

27—Senator with suicide rifle
Wallace murdered USDA investigator Henry Marshall in June 1961, following an agreement between Johnson and Estes that the investigation had to be stopped. Here Senator McClellan shows that the rifle could not have been used for suicide. In 1984, another grand jury changed the ruling to murder and would have indicted Johnson had he been alive.

28—Wallace photo, about 1960
This photo shows Wallace about the time of the Marshall murder. Compare it to the composite for a fugitive being sought in that case (compare to next photo).

29—Police composite for fugitive, 1962
The day Marshall was killed, a man asked a filling station attendant how to get to Marshall's ranch. The next day the same man returned to say he had not needed the directions. A year after the murder, the Texas Department of Public Safety prepared this composite of the missing man (compare to preceding photo).

30—Johnson subject to indictment for murder
Thirteen years after Marshall's vicious murder, the grand jury again reviewed the case and concluded it was not suicide but murder. Estes and Texas Ranger Clint Peoples provided the key evidence. Johnson could not be indicted because he was dead. Cliff Carter and Mac Wallace also escaped indictment because they, too, were dead.

Assassination in Dallas

31—Kennedy's last speech
In Fort Worth on the morning of November 22, 1963, Kennedy delivers his last speech. Johnson looks on with a pained expression. He had promised his mistress that Kennedy would never embarrass him again.

32—Dealey Plaza
The scene of the assassination. The motorcade came down Main and went right on Houston. Turning left on Elm the president's limousine was directly in front of the depository. Wallace and Oswald were on the sixth floor and Junior was in the trees beside the pergola.

33—Sixth floor of the depository
The layout of the sixth floor is shown with limited detail. Basically an open area for storing books in cartons, the clutter of book cartons provided cover. Wallace and Oswald were on the lower side and escaped down the stairwell on the northwest corner.

34—Kennedy's view of the grassy knoll
This street level view of the pergola and grassy knoll area shows what Kennedy would have seen. The triple underpass is in the background. Junior was in the tree cover straight ahead. Kennedy did not have a chance.

The Coverup

35—Johnson grins on *Air Force One*
Clark had tried to be sure Johnson was properly remorseful and concerned. Here the new president drops his cover for an instant as Congressman Thomas winks and Lady Bird grins. A distraught Jackie Kennedy was compelled to stand there, still in shock.

36—Court of Inquiry under Johnson's control
Johnson carefully controlled the investigation from the start. He preferred a Texas group operating in close connection with him.

37—Jaworski covers for the FBI
The FBI had been warned about Oswald in advance but had ignored a note from him. The note had been destroyed after Oswald was arrested, but a reporter heard there was some connection. Any inquiry might have opened the inquiry up, but Jaworski carefully killed the idea.

38—Jaworski muzzles Ruby
Ruby wanted an expanded trial with television coverage. Since that might open up all kinds of questions. Jaworski sent this letter to Joe Tonahill, who was Ruby's attorney and Clark's brother-in-law. Clark's notes indicate he would help muzzle Ruby.

39—Brazos-Tenth is closed
The money-laundering corporation was set up in 1954 to funnel the large campaign donations into investments for Johnson. Thomas ran the company for Johnson. Some money went for elections but most was invested in land and banks for Johnson.

40—Final order for the payoff
Following settlement of this lawsuit, Exxon ceased all objections to the bonus payment for Clark. He was paid two million dollars by "Big Oil."

41—Clark's bonus well
The original application for a bonus for the assassination was with this proposed well location in the east Texas oil field. When Exxon opposed him, over

the wishes of Big Oil, Clark used the same application five years later to work a deal with Exxon.

42—The penthouse files

Clark's offices were in the old Capital National Bank Building, the tall, white structure to the left. The main offices were on the twelfth floor and criminal attorney John Cofer was one floor up. The top penthouse was where the secret records were stored. The present location of the records is not known.

The Fingerprint Identification

Fingerprints are one of the best forms of hard evidence.[1] Understanding how the Warren Commission handled the limited print evidence it recovered is necessary to appreciating how experts make their analysis and to see how our research produced the identification of a second sniper on the sixth floor of the Texas School Book Depository. The critical discussion that followed our identification affirms what we did, and it shows how to evaluate contested expert evidence.

1. Warren Commission Prints

The Warren Commission recovered thirty-seven prints from the four boxes used as a sniper's nest on the sixth floor of the Texas School Book Depository.[2] Exhibit A is a photo of the sniper's nest showing the four boxes. The prints presented to the commission were 23 marked exhibits showing twenty-four fingerprints and thirteen palm prints.[3] Exhibit B is the initial summary of these prints by Arthur Mandella, a noted expert with the New York Police Department. Exhibit C is Warren print 29 with notations retyped at the bottom of the page.[4] This is a key print.

During testimony before the commission, FBI expert S. F. Latona matched two palm prints and one fingerprint on the boxes to Oswald.[5] For comparison purposes, one of the commission's print matches for Oswald is attached Exhibit D. The fragmentary nature of the prints relied upon by the FBI is also shown by the identification of a smudge on the gun barrel as Oswald's palm print. Although a cursory effort was made initially to identify the rest of the prints,[6] they were quickly ignored. The main objective in April 1964 was to show Oswald had been there.

On August 28, 1964, as the commission was completing its report, an emergency request for identification of the remaining prints was made by the Commission to the FBI. Exhibit E. The commission was concerned that the unidentified prints would lead to speculation that there had been a conspiracy. Within a week, the remaining prints, with the exception of one palm print, had been identified as belonging to two law enforcement officials, Robert Studebaker with the Dallas Police Department and Forest Lucy with the FBI. Exhibit F. Unlike the earlier procedure where an outside expert was used to review the print identifications, this time the FBI relied solely on its own resources.

The FBI was requested to prepare a chart for the commission, showing the identification of each specific print. Exhibit E. The chart is not in the public record available at the JFK Archives and apparently was never prepared.[7] The commission's conclusion as to the specific latent prints matching the card prints is not known. Because of the FBI's limited disclosure, our independent evaluation was more difficult.

2. Summary Review of Print Evidence

Fingerprints are unique. The odds of another person having the same prints have been placed at one in sixteen billion or higher.[8] Many experts reject any number, simply accepting the proposition that no two prints are alike.

Inked prints are prints placed on cards designed for that purpose. The inked prints are carefully taken by trained personnel. Prints recovered from crime scenes are not as reliable as inked prints. These latent or hidden prints are usually incomplete and may be subject to extensive interpretation.[9]

Although the identification process is subject to careful protocols, some judgment is necessary. Latent prints may be changed by (1) pressure; (2) twisting; and (3) external additions or contaminations. These circumstances require an expert's judgment to distinguish between similarities and distortions.[10] In addition to careful review, considerable judgment is required. Experts meeting FBI standards must have extensive experience. Perhaps the most important ethical consideration is to be certain an innocent person is not implicated.

Comparisons between original prints and latent prints are possible because of the unique nature of the ridges.[11] These distinct lines are classified into three main groups based on their pattern: loops, whorls, and arches. Additional refinements result in eight subcategories and, finally, in 1,024 distinct groups.[12] Prints have a core or center and at least one delta or the point where the ridges diverge. This process of identification locates the center of the print. Once these key features are identified, many latents are eliminated on sight.

The next indispensable step in the identification process is to consider the types of ridges.[13] Ridges come in many sizes and shapes. These very specific details, called minutiae, are of seven main types: bifurcations, ridge endings, short ridges, enclosures (or islands), dots, trifurcations, and ridge crossings.[14] A final, perhaps most critical step is to be certain the relation between minutiae is close enough.[15] The overall review objective is to determine the match points between the inked and the latent prints.

In the United States, the FBI position is that there is no minimum requirement for such match points, but it suggests eight matches.[16] Many foreign jurisdictions require at least nine match points for a latent print to be admissible in court. Great Britain requires at least sixteen match points, and France requires twelve. In those countries, very few latent prints are used in trials.

In the United States the FBI position is not to question the judgment of its experts. This does not mean those experts are infallible as several recent studies have disclosed. Finally, an analytical consideration for an expert is to be able to explain and justify to another expert the reasons for an identification or elimination of a suspect's prints.

One English analyst has observed that, had print testimony been developed under current courtroom tests for admissibility, there would be no print evidence.[17] It is also noteworthy that the standards for print identification in 1963–64 were not as rigorous as they are now.

David Stoney, a forensic chemist with the McCrone Research Institute in Chicago, has questioned the science that backs up print identification.[18] Admitting that the ridges and whorls "can be pretty convincing," he asks whether there is enough information "when an identification is based on partial or degraded prints." Acknowledging the problems "in mathematically quantifying the endless variations of shape," Mr. Stoney concludes that, "since the experts cannot quantify their opinions, they must rely on their experience to render an expert opinion."

In other words Mr. Stoney is restating the FBI position that, if your expert reaches a conclusion, that judgment is enough.

A further consideration is probability. Most print experts will deny there is any guessing; they assert the latent and the inked prints match or they do not match. The current debate among jurisdictions, however, shows that counting the number of match points is a mathematical measure of the certainty to attach to an identification. The fewer the match points, the less likely the identification will be correct.

Many print experts today will deny there is any weight given probability because, in criminal proceedings, scientific evidence must be certain beyond a reasonable doubt. A latent is either a match or it is not a match. On the other hand, some scientists recommend probabilities be used. The expert should be permitted to give a probability that the scientific evidence is valid.[19] Their print experts suggest that a weighing of the probabilities is an important part of print identification.

These probabilities played a key role in the FBI's investigation for the Warren Commission. This is apparent from the match to Oswald based on a poor latent print. See Exhibit D. In 1963, this was acceptable.

In developing a match, an accepted practice by some experts is to make a tracing of the latent print and overlay the tracing on the card print. As the FBI Manual cautions, however, do not rely on the tracing or overlay evidence because ridges and minutiae may be distorted from pressure and twisting.[20] For present purposes, tracings of the attached Warren latent and Wallace card prints indicate important similarities.

3. Darby Identification of Wallace Prints

We contacted A. Nathan Darby for his review of the Warren prints with the print card for M. E. Wallace. Mr. Darby had directed the city of Austin's police identification unit, had set up the print system used by the Philippines, and had assisted Kodak in developing its camera techniques for fingerprints. Certified by the International Association for Identification, Mr. Darby had testified on numerous occasions and his opinions had never been reversed. We were convinced he was independent of any government agency and that he would not have any predisposition one way or the other because of the crime involved.

In order to assure complete independence, in January 1998, on our request, Mr. Darby agreed to a blind submission of the prints and commenced his extensive review extending over several weeks. He did not know where they were from or what crime, if any, was involved.

Mr. Darby concluded that there was a match between the Wallace inked print and Warren Commission print 29. We then disclosed to him that his identification involved the Kennedy assassination. Fully apprised of the consequences of his identification, he nevertheless agreed to support his match. An affidavit was prepared and submitted to the proper authorities. Exhibit G.

Mr. Darby's affidavit describing his match is Exhibit G. The affidavit was filed with the Dallas Police Department, who forwarded it to the FBI. The match was then filed with the Assassination Records Review Board, who also forwarded it to the FBI. Although advising that the FBI opinion was no match was shown, the supporting analysis has not been made public.

4. Comparison of the Print Matches

An important initial consideration is to review Mr. Darby's work with the identifications by the Warren Commission. From the Warren record, its print 29 may have originally been deemed too fragmentary for identification; however, in a blanket statement, the FBI may have suggested the identification was to Dallas police officer R. L. Studebaker. We have accordingly made the assumption this was the possible identification. The purpose is to compare Mr. Darby's identification to the work of the Warren Commission on its print 29.

The comparison of latent commission print 29 to inked prints from Studebaker and Wallace shows, at best, that there are only two matches between Studebaker and Warren print 29. In addition, the Studebaker print has a core and delta that is noticeably wider than the latent. If the match is to Studebaker, it is not correct.

More likely, the FBI made no decision for a match on Warren's latent print 29. It apparently considered the latent to be too fragmentary; however, it originally noted the latent "may" be identifiable. This problem of including or excluding latent prints as smudges or questionable may apply to other print identifications. The difficulty also highlights the problems encountered in reviewing the Warren Commission's work. Details of how the FBI made its emergency identification in September 1964 are not available despite the commission's request to provide those details.

5. Debating the Wallace Identification

When we released the Darby identification, considerable interest was generated among conspiracy researchers.[21]

First, two San Bernadino, California, law enforcement personnel were called upon by other researchers to see if the Warren latent prints matched Wallace's inked prints.[22] They reviewed Darby's identification and concluded that they agreed on twelve of the fourteen match points; however, they said there were two dissimilarities. Their process did not consider the fact that latent prints are subject to contaminations. In addition, these two experts provided no written support for their conclusions and are not active in the review because they obtained Wallace's prints under improper procedures.

The next expert to offer an opinion was Mr. Ed German, a special agent with the Army Crime Lab at Fort Gillem, Georgia.[23] Launching a spirited advocacy, he found allegedly inexplicable differences, none of which he even attempted to discuss with Mr. Darby. Mr. German also said there was an intervening ridge between Darby's points four and six. Mr. Darby explained this was a defect in the latent copy. Mr. German also objected to a difference in ridge lengths between Darby's points six and seven. Mr. Darby explained the difference to be in the sizes of the photos.

Significantly, Mr. German threatened Mr. Darby with proceedings to revoke his certification.[24] Mr. German made these statements and threats without knowing anything about Mr. Darby's qualifications. We note that Mr. German teaches a print identification course that relies on the Warren Commission's procedures.

Mr. Al Johnson was another expert, and he decided the latent was an entirely different print classification.[25] No other experts had a problem with the classification. Mr. Johnson also asserted there was no pressure involved; however, the carton that was part of the sniper's nest was packed with books. There was pressure of at least seventy pounds. Finally, he said there was no ridge on the known print. This conclusion is based on a bad reproduction.

At the conclusion review, Mr. Darby considered the questions and concluded one of his match points was incorrect; however, he also decided there were two additional match points. Finally, he noted there was still another match point between the latent and the second digit of the Wallace print.[26]

In the course of conducting the necessary peer review and in preparing our results, we contacted another print expert. Mr. E. H. Hoffmeister, an expert with the Texas Department of Public Safety for many years and now retired, concluded the identification by Mr. Darby was correct. Exhibit H. As was done with Mr. Darby, we made a blind submission of the prints to Mr. Hoffmeister for purposes of eliminating any bias. When informed that the assassination was involved, however, Mr. Hoffmeister reconsidered and quite frankly expressed a fear for his safety. He then wrote that his identification was tentative only, depending on a review of the originals at the Kennedy Archives.

Because of the importance of the identification, still another review was requested. Senior print examiners for Interpol, located in Paris, France, reviewed and confirmed the Darby match.

Three years later, after analyzing the prints again, Mr. Darby reaffirmed and expanded his identification. Attached is his print match showing thirty-two points in common. His identification was completed September 20, 2001. Exhibit I.

There is one further step in our identification process. Mr. Darby is prepared to explain and justify his identification to any other expert. This essential part of any review of an identification is available on request.

6. Conclusion

For these reasons, we are convinced that the identification by Mr. Darby is correct. The process of his review and analysis is disclosed on the public record. The necessary conclusion is that Mac Wallace was on the sixth floor of the Texas School Book Depository at the time of the assassination.

Expert testimony in the Kennedy investigation is too often at odds. Independent judgment is required. Make the tracings. Consider the probabilities. Weigh the greater preponderance of the fingerprint evidence. Compare the Warren Commission's match prints to those of Wallace. Is it more likely or less likely that the prints are from Wallace? Compare the validity of the differences between the experts. Review the background of each expert. Then make your conclusions.

This review highlights the importance of the expert's opinion. Mr. Darby's qualifications are certainly far greater than those of any of his critics. Unlike the often emotional review by his critics of poor reproductions, Mr. Darby's opinion is based on a blind review independent of defending any government agency and has none of the emotions generated by the assassination.

Finally, Mr. Darby adheres strictly to the ethical standard that an innocent man must not be condemned. In addition to Mr. Darby's careful work, his excellent qualifications, and his commitment to ethical standards, he has a devout faith. He would never bear false witness against anyone.

The *Modern Researcher,* a standard text used by historians, states:

> The mystery of human personality remains. And in any case—which means in every case—explanations by means of a single cause, hidden, startling, "scientific," is to be distrusted, if not on the face of it disallowed. The concatenation of acts, motives, and results can only be understood and described by the intuitive skill of the historian as an artist.[27]

Stated otherwise, when experts disagree, you be the judge.

Notes

1.   For many years fingerprint evidence was literally impregnable and defense attorneys simply did not challenge an examiner's identification. Recently, the criminal bar has mounted better defenses. Some expert identifications are very difficult to justify but, when considered with other evidence, an accused will usually have very little evidence to avoid conviction. Our identification is based on standards in effect in 1963–1964 as well as currently effective standards.

2.   The commission's experts recognized only the prints or smudges they deemed "identifiable." Their total number of prints varied from thirty-three to thirty-six and then to twenty-five. In some cases, they used prints they originally concluded could not be identified and rejected others they had considered identifiable. The FBI did not reveal the precise steps it took so what it did cannot be followed or duplicated.

3.   Ten print photos that were in the numbering sequence at one time are not included in the public record.

4.   The entire record of the fingerprint evidence is available from the JFK Archives in College Park, Maryland.

5.   Latona's testimony appears in the Warren Commission Proceedings for April 2, 1964, starting at p. 32.

6.   The only indication of additional prints being taken before the April 1964 testimony was the effort to print the workers on the sixth floor. See Latona testimony, p. 42.

7.   The JFK Archives advises the chart is not available.

8.   Richard Saperstein, *Criminalistics: An Introduction to Forensic Science,* 5th ed. (Englewood Cliffs, N.J.: Prentice Hall, 1995), at p. 415, mentions one in 64 billion; however, the text goes on to state the number is not mathematically reliable.

9.   "Due to the fragmentary nature of most latent prints, it is not possible to derive a classification which makes a file search practicable. A latent impression may be identified, however, by comparison with the prints of a particular subject." *FBI Manual: The Science of Fingerprints* (Washington, D.C.: U.S. Government Printing Office, Rev. 12-84), p. 171.

10.   A discussion of analysis standards in fingerprint identification is reviewed in the *FBI Law Enforcement Bulletin* (June 1972).

11.   A standard manual states: "A latent fingerprint is best described as a combination of chemicals which is exuded by the pores on the surface of

the skin. These chemicals consist of perspiration, which contains water, oils, amino acids and salts. The moisture exuded is deposited along the surface of the friction ridges found on the palm side of the hands and soles of the feet." Sirchie Finger Print Laboratories, Inc., *Technical Information: Latent Fingerprint Field Kits* (Raleigh, N.C.: Sirchie, 1991), p. 2.

12.   Saperstein, at p. 421.

13.   "The one-to-one identification of fingertips is made by direct comparison of details of ridge endings, bifurcations, and other small features of the print on a submillimeter scale. A number of such points must be found to agree in topology and direction, although not in measurement, before an identity is firm." Charles E. O'Hara et al., *Fundamentals of Criminal Investigation*, 6th ed. (Springfield, Ill.: Thomas Books, 1994), 707.

14.   Saperstein, at 415; Anne Wingate, *Scene of the Crime* (Cincinnati, Ohio: Writer's Digest Books, 1992), p. 109.

15.   Saperstein, at p. 415: "The individuality of a fingerprint is not determined by its general shape or pattern but by a careful study of its ridge characteristics (also known as minutiae). It is the identity, number, and relative location of characteristics ... that impart individuality to a fingerprint." The *FBI Manual states*, at p. 195: "Individual ridge characteristics may vary slightly in actual shape or physical position due to twisting, pressure, incomplete inking, condition of latent print when developed, powder adhering to the background, etc. Identifications are based on a number of characteristics viewed in a unit relationship and not on the microscopic appearances of single characteristics."

16.   In testimony before the Warren Commission, Latona stated, "We have confidence in our experts to the extent that regardless of the number of points, if the expert ... gives us an opinion, we will not question the number of points." Warren, at pp. 13–14. Latona later testified that he would use a minimum of four. Warren, at p. 14.

17.   Tony Vignaux, Professor of Operations Research, Victoria University, Wellington, New Zealand and barrister Bernard Robertson, *Interpreting Evidence—Evaluating Forensic Evidence in the Courtroom*, a John Wiley & Sons publication.

18.   Statement at genetic_foren.html.

19.   Professor Vignaux' comments are at www.acsp.uic.edu. (1997).

20.   The *FBI Manual* states, at p. 195: "Methods involving superimposition of the prints is not recommended because such a procedure is possible in only a very few instances, due to the distortion of ridges in most prints

through pressure and twisting." The *Manual* adds, at pp. 194–195: "All the ridge characteristics in the prints need not be charted. Twelve characteristics are ample to illustrate an identification, but it is not claimed nor implied that this number is required."

21.   Assassination researchers are constantly seeking a solution to the crime. When word is out that a major breakthrough will be announced, the competition to be first is often intense. These criticisms have to be included in the analysis to be made by any interested citizen. A key site is net.conspiracy.jfk.

22.   At sixthfloor.earthlink.net.

23.   Mr. German commences his attack on Mr. Darby by suggesting it is a joke that the Warren Commission and the FBI could be wrong. He also faults persons trying to enrich themselves by offering solutions to the crime. This bias is apparently inherent in the review undertaken by many experts. Mr. Darby made his match points and final decision based on blind submission to him of the prints. He was independent of any government agency with an interest in disproving any suggestion of a conspiracy. Finally, he refused to accept any compensation.

24.   Mr. German's attack is another measure of the emotions generated—even among experts—by research into the assassination. What Mr. German should have done as a matter of fairness would be to determine Mr. Darby's qualifications and then discuss the identification with Mr. Darby.

25.   At home.earthlink.net/~sixthfloor/.

26.   Additional excellent reviews are available by Walt Brown in *Deep Politics Quarterly* at njmetronet.com/jfkdpq and by Richard Bartholomew at bart/inetport.com.

27.   *The Modern Researcher* (Houghton Mifflin), p. 165.

Exhibits, Pictures
and Documents

Calling whole thing this Confidential to you — I strongly
recommend all going along and
making monthly payments — I hope
everybody will be happy

Always your friend

1) JFK restrains LBJ

2) Edward A. Clark

3) Mac Wallace, c. 1945

4) Don Thomas

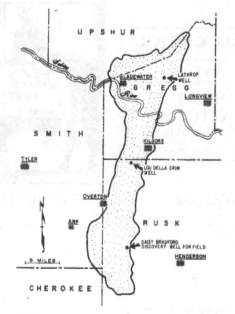

5) The "black giant"

6) Big Oil for Big D

7) "Dry Hole" Byrd & oil well

8) Clark campaign poster

9) Clark for FDR

10) Clark talks, LBJ listens

11) Clark, Ramsey, Tower

SCENE IN SABINE COUNTY, TEXAS, JUNE 15, 1908.

The Dogwood Tree.

This is only the branch of the Dogwood tree;
　An emblem of WHITE SUPREMACY.
A lesson once taught in the Pioneer's school,
　That this is a land of WHITE MAN'S RULE.
The Red Man once in an early day,
　Was told by the Whites to mend his way.

The negro, now, by eternal grace,
　Must learn to stay in the negro's place.
In the Sunny South, the Land of the Free,
　Let the WHITE SUPREME forever be.
Let this a warning to all negroes be,
　Or they'll suffer the fate of the DOGWOOD TREE

　　　　　—Pub. by Harkrider Drug Co. Center, T

12) Lynching by Clark's uncle while sheriff

Camp Blanding, Florida
January 16, 1943.

123.5

SUBJECT: Approved Recommendations of a Board of Officers.

TO: Captain Edward A. Clark, Brown Building, Austin, Texas.

1. The recommendations of the board of officers appointed to investigate and report upon the loss of funds pertaining to the Company Fund of Company "D", 111th Quartermaster Regiment, and redesignated as Company "A", 111th Quartermaster Battalion, 36th Division, covering the period from November, 1940 to February, 1942, to fix the responsibility for the loss and to make appropriate recommendations, have been returned to this headquarters disapproved by higher authorities.

2. Inclosed is a copy of the recommendations contained in a copy of the supplemental report of a Board of Officers.

3. If you desire to file any further evidence or make exceptions, it is requested that you do so within the next fifteen days. Otherwise, the Board of Officers will be compelled to forward the proceedings to higher authority without your reply.

For the Commanding General:

C. F. DERRICK,
Major, Infantry,
Assistant to Chief,
Judge Advocate's Branch.

1 Incl.
Cpy Recommendations
of B/O

13) Army proceedings to discharge Clark for theft.

MEMO

ED CLARK

To Lyndon B. Johnson

Enjoyed talking with you today — Brown immediately called Houston and told Woolsey to take care of Lucas' friend for good, Bank matter all ~~straighten~~ fixed up — tho just in time for Walter to retrieve letter from his mail calling whole thing this Confidential to you — I Strongly recommend all going along and making monthly payments — Hope everybody will be happy

Always your friend

Ed

14) Clark memo - conspiracy starts, 1949

March 7, 1949

Dear Ed:

I am grateful for your wire, and thanks much for your memorandum re Brown calling Woolsey and the letter that Walter Bremond
was about to send. You may be sure that I deeply appreciate your
own personal attitude toward your individual situation. I shall see
that you are thoroughly protected and taken care of when we get the
picture worked out. Very shortly our friends here will communicate
with Walter and I will keep you informed.

Certainly hope you will take such time as is necessary to
look after our interests in the Longoria matter. If you have a chance
to see our friend Abe Lincoln, Jr. soon, I hope you will get him to
re-wire (even if I have to pay for the wire) all the County Clerks
and get the complete vote in each county ~~and each precinct~~ and Senator
in the general election. I believe that this will show that I got
the largest majority of any one of the thirty-two Senators who took
the oath this year. It will also reduce the lead Mr. Truman now has
over me. It will be essential that we have this information to present
to Chairman Myers.

Thanks again and hurry up to see us.

Sincerely

Lyndon B. Johnson

Honorable Edward Clark
Brown Building
Austin, Texas

P. S. Ask Lela if she has forgotten that she is supposed to come up
and spend some time with us in June.

lbj dj
gen.corr.-clark,edward

15) Johnson thanks Clark for being the patsy

IN THE 98TH DISTRICT COURT OF TRAVIS COUNTY, TEXAS.

February 27, 1952

NO. 27,419

THE STATE OF TEXAS   VS.   MALCOLM E. WALLACE

SENTENCE OF THE COURT

On this the 27th day of February, 1952, this cause being again called, the State of Texas appeared by her District Attorney, and the Defendant, Malcolm E. Wallace, having waived time and being in open court in charge of the Sheriff of Travis County, Texas, for the purpose of having the sentence of the law pronounced against him in accordance with the finding of the jury and the judgment of the court heretofore entered in this cause, and the defendant being asked by the court if he had any sufficient reason why the sentence of this court should not be pronounced against him failed to give such reason.

IT IS THEREFORE CONSIDERED BY THE COURT that the defendant Malcolm E. Wallace is adjudged to be guilty of the offense of Murder with Malice so found by the jury, and that he be punished as has been determined by the jury by confinement in the penitentiary for Five years, and that the State of Texas to have and recover of the said defendant all costs in this prosecution expended; and it is further ordered by the court that sentence of the judgment of court herein shall be and the same is hereby suspended during the good behavior of the defendant, and that the said defendant be released from custody upon his personal recognizance in the sum of $1,000.00 conditioned as the law requires for his good behavior during said period of time.

_____
J U D G E

_____
APPROVED AS TO FORM

16) Wallace sentence for murder of Doug Kinser

17) Estes by his airplane

18) LBJ with Bobby Baker

19) Madeleine Duncan Brown

20) Ellen Rometsch

May 1, 1958

Mexican labor

MEMORANDUM:

TO: Senator Johnson

FROM: Lloyd Hand

RE: Pecos Labor Problem

Cliff Carter called last night (11:00 P. M.) strongly urging that you attend the conference this morning between Secretary Mitchell and representatives of the Texas farmers to urge his consideration of their problem which stems from the minimum wage ceiling imposed by Secretary Mitchell.

Cliff states Yarborough will be present and the farmers in that area with whom Cliff has been talking the past two days are desperately concerned. He has visited Plainview, Ralls and other areas and states the problem is not confined to just the Pecos area.

I explained the delicacy of this problem. Cliff's judgment is to favor the growers and users over organized labor, if necessary. He states as an example Billy Sol Estes, in whom we are very interested. He has 26,000 acres of crops and stands to lose $250,000 if labor is not available for harvesting. Two farmers, L. D. McNeel and W. J. Worsham, are enroute to D. C. for this meeting. Others are already here. Cliff called from Bill Jackson's home in Lubbock.

21) Johnson interest in Estes

SEP 27 1962

MEMORANDUM FOR THE DIRECTOR, OIPAAR

FROM: SCREENING BOARD, PANEL NO. 1

SUBJECT: WALLACE, Malcolm E.   62-340

1. Applicant has been employed by Ling Electronics Division, Ling Temco Electronics, Inc., Anaheim, California as a control supervisor since February 1961.

2. Extant access authorization of applicant as set forth by the file: Secret. Requested: Secret. Service recommendation: revoke and deny.

3. All members of the Panel have read and evaluated the complete contents of the case file attached hereto. Pertinent information in the file regarding applicant includes the following:

a. Applicant was investigated and tried for the fatal shooting of John Douglas Kinser, a golf professional, on October 22, 1951 in Travis County, Texas. He was found guilty of murder with malice by a jury on February 28, 1952, and awarded a five year suspended sentence as provided by Texas law.

No motive for the crime was ever developed and applicant stood mute during the trial and investigation. Homosexuality and sexual perversion was thought by some close to the situation to have been the motive as applicant's wife, an admitted sex pervert, alleged that during her marriage with applicant they both practised sex perversion. There were indications in the States Attorney's investigative file that applicant's wife was a lesbian. One informant stated that it was rumored that applicant's wife and the man applicant murdered had participated in unnatural sex acts and was killed as a result. Applicant's former wife in a written statement executed in 1962 stated that applicant was very possessive of her and did not want her to have social contact with anyone. She also stated that she and applicant, at applicant's request engaged in unnatural perverted sex acts covering a period of ten or twelve years and she was of the opinion that he was a sexual pervert and an unstable person. She also stated that at times applicant beat her, suggested joint suicide pacts and on about 100 occasions suggested that she participate in a sex act with another man while he remained a spectator.

Captain Clinton T. Peoples, Texas Rangers, Waco, Texas, who is familiar with applicant's trial and conviction for murder stated he considered applicant a bad security risk and would not trust him in any capacity. He characterized applicant as a pervert.

21

b. The file indicates that applicant had incestuous relations with his nine year old daughter in 1959.

c. Applicant was arrested on February 2, 1961 on a drunk and disorderly charge in Dallas, Texas. He was fined $5.00. Applicant was "staggering eastward on public sidewalk in 6400 block Gaston Ave. and found to be intoxicated to a degree whereas - he found difficulty extreme difficulty in walking - his breath was strong of alcohol - his speech slow and uneven."

The foregoing arrest was not listed on applicant's Personnel Security Questionnaire nor was an arrest of 11/15/52 because applicant was drunk in a Judge's office in Williamson County, Texas. He was fined $15.00 on this charge.

4. Rationale:
This case needs little rationalizing. Applicant's conviction of murder with malice; his abnormal sexual behavior and his omissions on his current Personnel Security Questionnaire indicate that the granting of access authorization is not in the national interest.

5. On the basis of all the information available to it the Screening Board determines as follows:

a. A favorable finding as to granting of access authorization is not warranted.

b. Neither further investigation nor written interrogatory, nor personal interview is needed or considered appropriate.

c. A Statement of Reasons, enclosed herewith, should be issued.

d. Any existing authorization which grants applicant access to Army, Navy, or Air Force classified information should be suspended.

John Owen, Capt USN, Chairman

Harris J. North, Lt Col, USA

David H. Maretta, USAF Member

22) Continued *(page 2 of 2)*

January 28, 1959

Lt. Governor Ben Ramsey
State Capitol
Austin, Texas

Dear Ben:

Due to a conflict with a party previously
arranged, I am changing the date of our session of
the Order of the Round Table from Tuesday, February
10, 1959, to Wednesday, February 11, 1959. I trust
that you can be with us at the later date. Again
the call to order will be at 4 p.m.

With kindest regards, I am

Sincerely yours,

EC:jca

Senator R. A. Weinert

Senator Bruce Reagan

Senator Jimmy Phillips

Senator Johnie B. Rogers

Senator Ottis E. Lock.

Governor Allan Shivers

Mr. Gus S. Wortham

23) Clark runs the Texas round table

United States Senate
Office of the Democratic Leader
Washington, D. C.

August 6, 1960

Dear Ed:

When the good Lord made us friends, he must have
known that I was getting the best end of the deal.
More than once your great talents have been my
means of salvation -- and never more so than in the
past few days. It would be impossible for me to thank
you with words that would really express my gratitude.
Please know that I hold no one in higher esteem nor do
I feel more indebted to another man on earth than I do
to you.

Warmest regards.

Sincerely,

Lyndon B. Johnson

Honorable Edward Clark
Brown Building
Austin, Texas

24) Johnson letter to Clark

LAW OFFICES

GLARE, MATHEWS, THOMAS, HARRIS & DENIUS

BROWN BUILDING

AUSTIN, TEXAS

P. O. Box 888
(GREENWOOD 8-0691)

August 29, 1960

Mr. Arthur Temple, Jr.
Diboll, Texas

Dear Arthur:

You are aware, I know, of the big job ahead of us this fall.

The Republicans are amassing a huge campaign to try to defeat Senator Kennedy and Lyndon Johnson in Texas.

You fully understand, Arthur, why we cannot allow this to happen. Lyndon Johnson's greatest opportunity to serve our state and nation is now before him and we must make certain that he and our state are not stripped of this great advantage. John Kennedy is a capable, popular leader, and he and Johnson will make a great team.

I have been asked to serve as chairman of the finance committee for the Kennedy-Johnson campaign in Texas, and I must--very earnestly--ask your help. The Republicans are sparing no expense. Already they have huge allotments of billboards and daily radio programs under contract. It is going to be expensive to offset their immense propaganda campaign, but we can do it.

Right now, we need funds, quickly and in generous amounts. Won't you please let me know--with your check--that we can count you with us all the way.

Very truly yours,

Edward Clark

25) Clark raises money for Johnson

26) Johnson by plane wreckage

27) Senator with suicide rifle

28) Wallace 1960s

29) Composite of fugitive

The opinion of the previous grand jury was that "the evidence is inconclusive to substantiate a definite decision at this time or to overrule any decision heretofore made." Based on the testimony presented today, which was not presented to the previous grand jury, it is the decision of this grand jury, that Henry H. Marshall's death was a homicide, not a suicide. That the parties named as participants in the offense are deceased, and therefore it is not possible for the grand jury to return an indictment.

Signed this the ___20th___ day of ___MARCH___, A.D. 1984.

Norman Koch	John Sifuentes
Lois McGaughey	Jackie Gibson
Melba Luster	Willis Dixon, Jr.
Leslie Wilson	Wendell C. Hall
F. B. Elliott, Jr.	George F. Ashley
Jim Gray, Sr.	Kenneth W. Swick

30) Grand jury action on Johnson

31) Kennedy's last speech

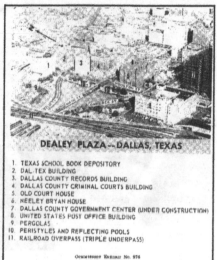

DEALEY PLAZA -- DALLAS, TEXAS

1. TEXAS SCHOOL BOOK DEPOSITORY
2. DAL-TEX BUILDING
3. DALLAS COUNTY RECORDS BUILDING
4. DALLAS COUNTY CRIMINAL COURTS BUILDING
5. OLD COURT HOUSE
6. NEELEY BRYAN HOUSE
7. DALLAS COUNTY GOVERNMENT CENTER (UNDER CONSTRUCTION)
8. UNITED STATES POST OFFICE BUILDING
9. PERGOLAS
10. PERISTYLES AND REFLECTING POOLS
11. RAILROAD OVERPASS (TRIPLE UNDERPASS)

Commission Exhibit No. 876

32) Dealey Plaza

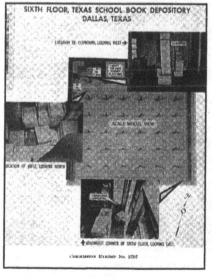

33) Sixth floor layout

34) "Grassy Knoll" area

Pictures and Documents: 31-34

35) Johnson sworn in aboard Air Force One

What is the reaction of the White House to the appointment of Abner McCall, President, Baylor University and President of the Texas Baptist Convention, to serve as one of the two outstanding attorneys as co-counsel in the Court of Inquiry. Is the Baptist angle hurtful? No approach has been made to him.

I have approached Leon Jaworski, who is agreeable to serve if I want him. I understand from our past conversation he is acceptable. *No announcement will be made for a while.*

We are getting some doubts expressed of us about Robert Storey. These doubts may be classified into two categories:

One, the question of whether we should have anyone from Dallas; and

Two, doubt has been expressed due to his elderly age and a tendency lately to lack patience with confining assignments as well as a tendency to "pop off" when not necessary to do so.

Do you have any thoughts about this that you wish to express?

I want to conduct myself strictly in accordance with your organization. Am I to restrict my calls to Mr. Fortas, even when I need an opinion from the White House itself, such as now? I will be happy to abide by your desires once I understand them.

Although we are working diligently to reach decisions on such matters as this, we are publicly only cooperating with the FBI whenever needed in the making of the Presidential Report and after the report is made we will then proceed to announce details of the Court of Inquiry.

Walter, I do hope that the FBI Report can be sent to us directly from either the White House or the Department of Justice so that we may continue to demonstrate to the public that the State of Texas and the Federal Government are working as partners, each in its own field of responsibility and each supplementing the efforts of the other, for only in a Court of Inquiry, as authorized by Texas law, can be the plain facts be developed and publicly shown through a judicial process of record.

36) Texas Court of Inquiry

FULBRIGHT, CROCKER, FREEMAN, BATES & JAWORSKI

ATTORNEYS AT LAW
BANK OF THE SOUTHWEST BUILDING
HOUSTON 2, TEXAS 77002

May 8, 1964

bcc: Honorable Waggoner Carr
Honorable Robert G. Storey

CONFIDENTIAL

Honorable J. Lee Rankin
General Counsel
President's Commission
200 Maryland Avenue, N. E.
Washington, D. C. 20002

Dear Lee:

Upon my return to Houston I advised Waggoner Carr of our conversation, and then I talked with W. P. Hobby, Jr., executive vice president and executive editor of the Houston Post, yesterday for the purpose of discussing with him the obtaining of an affidavit from Lonnie Hudkins, or in the alternative having him appear before the Commission in line with our discussion. Hobby informs me that Hudkins left the employ of the Houston Post over a month ago. He does not know where he is now employed; in fact he does not even know whether he is in Houston. He had offered, however, to locate him if you so desire.

Following my conversation with him I turned to my file to reread the story in question. Inasmuch as you have the testimony of the FBI agents as well as that of Marguerite Oswald, I am wondering if it is really worth your effort to follow up on Hudkins.

Hudkins' story does not say that Oswald was an informant, including that of Bill Alexander, assistant to Henry Wade, who pointed out that Oswald had Ruby's telephone and car license numbers, and on Mrs. Paine's statements as to the interview the agents had with her.

I should add that Bill Hobby volunteered to carry a story in the Houston Post to the effect that Oswald was not in the employ of any federal government agency if the testimony by competent federal authorities to the Commission so showed. Inasmuch as this would involve disclosing testimony given before the Commission, I doubt that you would want to avail yourself of his

---

CONFIDENTIAL

Honorable J. Lee Rankin
May 8, 1964
Page 2

offer. I did not undertake to discuss this offer with him, simply stating that I would convey it to you.

Please let me know whether you want to pursue the matter further; and if so, I shall be glad to follow whatever course you suggest.

With every good wish and kindest regards, I am

Sincerely yours,
Original Signed By
Leon Jaworski

Leon Jaworski

LJ:bs

Enclosure

P.S. Not knowing whether you have a complete copy available, I am sending you Xerox copy of the Hudkins' article which appeared in the Houston Post on Wednesday, January 1, 1964.

L.J.

---

37) Jaworski provides cover for FBI

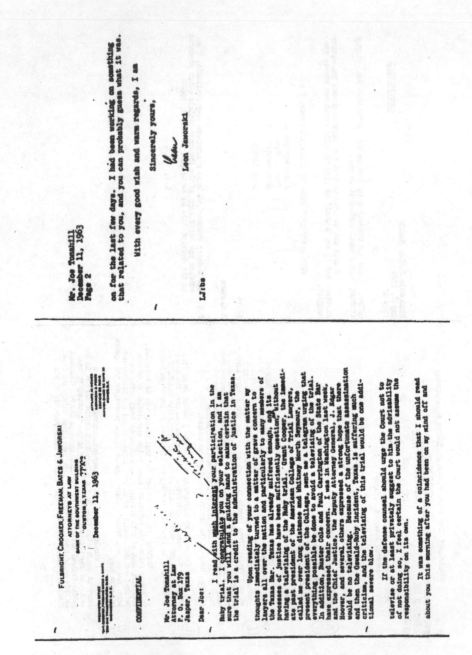

38) Jaworski muzzles Ruby

ARTICLES OF DISSOLUTION

Pursuant to the provisions of Article 6.06 of the Texas Business Corporation Act, the undersigned corporation adopts the following Articles of Dissolution for the purpose of dissolving:

1. The name of the corporation is BRAZOS-TENTH STREET CO.

2. The name and respective addresses of its officers are:

Name	Office	Address
Donald G. Thomas	President	1300 Capital National Bank Building, Austin, Texas
Jane Wpit Thomas	Vice President	2901 Oakmont Austin, Texas
Hazel Arnold	Secretary Treasurer	2905 Little John Lane Austin, Texas

3. The name and respective addresses of the directors are:

Name	Address
Donald G. Thomas	1300 Capital National Bank Building, Austin, Texas
Jane Wpit Thomas	2901 Oakmont Austin, Texas
Hazel Arnold	2905 Little John Lane Austin, Texas

4. A written consent to dissolve, a copy of which is attached, has been signed by all shareholders of the corporation or in their behalf by their duly authorized attorney.

5. All debts, obligations and liabilities of the corporation have been paid, discharged, or adequate provision has been made therefor.

6. All remaining property and assets of the corporation have been distributed among its shareholders in accordance with their respective rights and interests.

7. There are no suits pending against the corporation in any court.

Dated this the 22nd day of November, 1971.

BRAZOS-TENTH STREET CO.

By: _____
    Its President

By: _____
    Its Secretary

THE STATE OF TEXAS   )
COUNTY OF TRAVIS   )

Before me, the undersigned authority, on this the 22d day of November, 1971, personally appeared Donald G. Thomas and Hazel Arnold, known to me to be the persons and officers whose names are subscribed to the foregoing instrument, and acknowledged to me that they executed the same for the purposes and consideration therein expressed, and that the statements therein are true and correct.

_____
Notary Public in and for Travis County, Texas

39) End for Brazos-10th corporation

40) Final order for the payoff

NO. 214,930

EXXON CORPORATION,
PLAINTIFF,

VS.

RAILROAD COMMISSION OF
TEXAS, ET AL.,
Defendants

IN THE DISTRICT COURT

OF TRAVIS COUNTY, TEXAS

201st JUDICIAL DISTRICT

FINAL JUDGMENT

On the 11th day of March, 1974, came on to be heard the above entitled and numbered cause, wherein Exxon Corporation is plaintiff; the Railroad Commission of Texas and the members thereof, Jim C. Langdon, Ben Ramsey and Mack Wallace, are defendants; and Mobil Oil Corporation is intervenor defendant.

And came all of the parties, plaintiff, defendants and intervenor defendant by their attorneys of record and all parties announced ready for trial and the Court having first ruled as shown by its order of March 12, 1974, setting forth that the Court had already sustained plaintiff's special exceptions and that all matters of fact as well as of law were submitted to the Court without the intervention of a jury; and the pleadings, the evidence and the argument of counsel having been heard and fully understood, and it appearing to the Court that the law and the facts are with the plaintiff and the Court having found that there is no evidence that the gas allocation formula of 1891 productive percentage adopted in the Railroad Commission rulings of November 18, 1972 and December 18, 1973, affords each producer in the field an opportunity to produce its fair share of the gas from the Eveligoon (Zone 21-9) Field, and that said gas allocation formula is not reasonably supported by substantial evidence and is therefore arbitrary, unreasonable, capricious and confiscatory and should be set aside and the plaintiff should have the relief for which it prayed,

It is therefore ORDERED, ADJUDGED and DECREED by the Court that the gas allocation formula of 1891 productive acres set forth in the Railroad Commission's letter of November 28, 1972 and December 18, 1973, for the Eveligoon (Zone 21-9) Field be adjudged and is wholly null and void and is hereby set aside and cancelled.

It is further ORDERED, ADJUDGED and DECREED by the Court that the defendant Railroad Commission of Texas, its members, agents, servants, employees and anyone else acting for it, be and they are hereby permanently enjoined from enforcing or attempting to enforce the gas allocation formula of 1891 productive acreage as set forth in the Railroad Commission letters of November 28, 1972 and December 18, 1973, for the Eveligoon (Zone 21-9) Field; provided nothing herein is intended to or shall inquire with or restrict the Railroad Commission in hereafter exercising its valid powers under the conservation statutes of the State of Texas with respect to the matters here in issue.

It is further ORDERED, ADJUDGED and DECREED that intervenor defendant take nothing by its intervention.

To its further ORDERED, ADJUDGED and DECREED that plaintiff do have and recover from defendant and intervenor defendant herein, all sums of suit, for each let execution issue.

To all of which action the defendant Railroad Commission of Texas and the intervenor defendant duly excepted in open court and gave notice of appeal to the Supreme Court of Texas.

Signed, rendered and entered this 22th day of March, 1974.

Judge, 201st District Court
of Travis County, Texas

APPROVED AS TO FORM:

RAILROAD COMMISSION OF TEXAS

JOHN L. HILL, ATTORNEY GENERAL OF TEXAS

By:
Linward Shivers
Assistant Attorney General

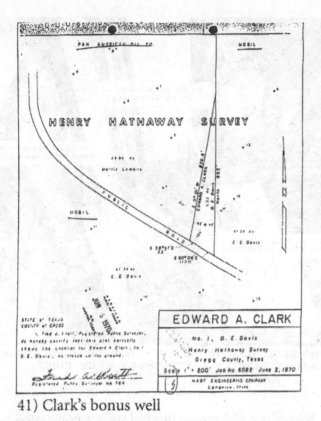

41) Clark's bonus well

42) Penthouse - top floor, building on left

RIGHT PALM PRINT—
HAND POINTING WEST

LEFT PALM PRINT—
HAND POINTING SOUTHWEST

RIGHT INDEX FINGERPRINT—
FINGER POINTING SOUTHWEST

SOUTHEAST CORNER OF SIXTH FLOOR SHOWING ARRANGEMENT
OF CARTONS SHORTLY AFTER SHOTS WERE FIRED.

Commission Exhibit No. 1301

Exhibit A - Snipers' nest with cartons that had Wallace' print. Latent print examiner Nathan Darby matched the Wallace print card to a latent print recovered from one of the snipers' nest. The prints were recovered from the four cartons shown, each filled with books. The location is the southeast window of the sixth floor.

Exhibit A

Exhibit B - Base print identification by Mandella (NYPD print examiner): This list of prints recovered from the sixth floor was the first step in determining who left the prints. The examiner then tries to identify them.

Exhibit B

```
Warren analysis:
1. Possibly same as 21, 24, 26, 32/Insufficient Charac-
   terisitics (back - 11/63)
2. Part value/unidentified (4/64)
3. Studebaker (or Lucy) (9/64) [use Studebaker]

─────────────────────
Notes (for Exhibits C, D, E):
11/63 - original notations on exhibits
4/64 - Mandella notes
9/64 - Final FBI Report
```

Exhibit C - The key print identified by Nathan Darby: The key latent print left on one of the cartons of books is at the bottom center. This print by Wallace was matched to his print card from the Kinser murder in 1951.

Exhibit C

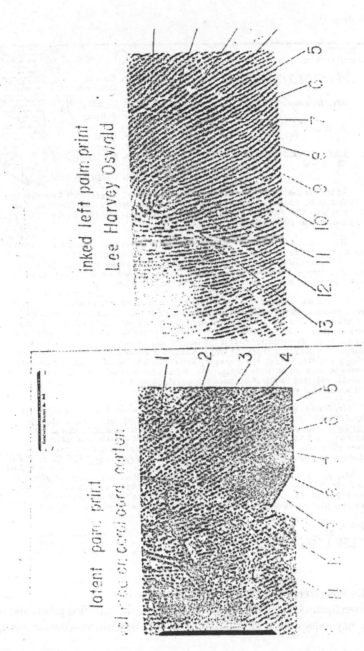

Exhibit D - Warren identification of one Oswald print: This match between a latent and an inked card print shows the methods used and the problems with matching Oswald's prints to latent prints recovered on the sixth floor.

Memorandum

TO : Mr. Belmont

FROM : A. Rosen

SUBJECT: LEE HARVEY OSWALD, aka.
IS - R - C

1 - Mr. Conrad
1 - Mr. DeLoach
DATE: August 28, 1964
1 - Mr. Sullivan
1 - Mr. Trotter
1 - Mr. Belmont
1 - Mr. Rosen
1 - Mr. Malley
1 - Mr. Shroder
1 - Mr. Rogge

At the request of J. Lee Rankin, General Counsel, President's Commission, Mr. Sebastian F. Latona, Latent Fingerprint Section, Identification Division, and Malley met with Mr. Rankin, Mr. James Wesley Liebeler and Mr. Burt Griffin at the Commission office today.

Mr. Rankin advised that the members of the President's Commission were rather anxious to try to resolve a question that existed relative to the palm prints and latent fingerprints that had been developed on four cartons that were located on the sixth floor of the Texas School Book Depository Building in the area of the window from which it is believed Oswald shot President Kennedy.

from the Bureau
Mr. Rankin advised that the Commission had received/a number of pieces of correspondence concerning this matter wherein it was set forth that Oswald's prints had been found among the latent fingerprints and palm prints located on the cartons, but they were concerned over the identity of the latent prints which had not been identified. He commented that the Bureau had obtained prints for elimination purposes from the employees of the Texas School Book Depository Building which Mr. Truly, the manager, believed might logically have a reason to have been in the area of these boxes. Mr. Rankin commented that Truly had strenuously objected to all of his personnel being printed at that time due to the loss of work being sustained by his company.

Mr. Rankin stated that the situation now exists where the Commission has not resolved the identity of these prints and it leaves room for the allegation and speculation that Oswald had a co-conspirator in killing President Kennedy. For this reason Mr. Rankin desired the Bureau to attempt to resolve this issue by whatever additional investigation was necessary, fully realizing the scope of the investigation that might be necessary.   REC 12   *105 - 82555 - 4814*

Mr. Rankin stated that he would appreciate the Bureau's making an effort to obtain Mr. Truly's permission to print all of the employees of his company for elimination purposes. He advised that in the event there were any objections on Mr. Truly's part he would appreciate being told so that either he, Mr. Rankin,

JRM:Job   XEROX
(10)   SEP 1
67 SEP 17 1964

CONTINUED - OVER

PY SENT TO MR. TOLSON

Exhibit E - Warren request to identify all latent prints:
Warren investigators realized the problem with the unidentified prints and made an emergency request for a prompt review to eliminate any co-conspirator. *(page 1 of 3)*

or Chief Justice Warren could contact Mr. Truly to advise him of the importance of this matter to the Commission in order to obtain his full cooperation.

A detailed letter is being prepared by Mr. Rankin's office outlining the investigation that is desired and will be sent to the Bureau as soon as it is ready. In the meantime, the Dallas Office has been filled in concerning the request of the President's Commission in order that they could get started on this rather large request for additional investigation.

In addition to the foregoing, Mr. Rankin requested relative to the latent fingerprint and palm print impressions that a chart be made visually demonstrating the location of the latent fingerprints and palm prints developed on the four cartons. He stated that he would appreciate it if this chart would show the latent finger and palm prints that actually belonged to Oswald as well as the other impressions that were developed and remain unidentified. He stated he would appreciate these being numbered in such a manner that it would be easy for the Commission members or anyone else reviewing this matter at a subsequent date to follow the complete picture relating to these latent prints. Mr. Latona is proceeding with the preparation of the chart as requested.

Request for Additional Data Re Palm Print on Barrel of Assassination Rifle

Mr. Rankin advised several questions had been raised relative to the palm print found on the barrel of the assassination rifle located on the portion of the barrel which was attached to the wooden foregrip of the rifle. Mr. Rankin stated as he understood the matter the palm print located on the rifle barrel had been located by Lieutenant Day of the Dallas Police Department and had been lifted from the rifle by Lieutenant Day. He noted that the Dallas Police Department made no mention of this latent palm print for a number of days following the assassination. He commented that on November 23, the day following the assassination, Chief of Police Curry, when questioned by news media, answered that fingerprints had been found and when asked further questions about identification stated the rifle had been forwarded to the FBI Laboratory. On Sunday, November 24, District Attorney Henry Wade, when questioned before news media, made the statement that a palm print had been found. Mr. Rankin states that based on the information made available to the Commission the existence of this palm print was not volunteered to the Bureau until a specific request was made of the Dallas Police Department.

- 2 -

Exhibit E - *(page 2 of 3)*

Mr. Rankin further advised that when Lieutenant Day testified before the President's Commission he stated on finding the print he considered photographing it and had intended to do so and then lifted the latent palm impression. The Commission testimony does not show whether Lieutenant Day did or did not photograph the palm impression that he located prior to lifting the palm print impression.

In view of the foregoing, Mr. Rankin desired that Lieutenant Day of the Dallas Police Department be contacted to ascertain from him whether or not he did or did not make photographs of the latent palm impression that he found on the rifle barrel and if he did, in fact, make photographs to obtain such photographs and make them available to the President's Commission.

Mr. Rankin advised because of the circumstances that now exist there was a serious question in the minds of the Commission as to whether or not the palm impression that has been obtained from the Dallas Police Department is a legitimate latent palm impression removed from the rifle barrel or whether it was obtained from some other source and that for this reason this matter needs to be resolved.

During this discussion about the location of this latent palm impression there was considerable conversation about the use of fingerprint dusting powder, the procedure used by Mr. Latona in his examination of the rifle, and Mr. Rankin requested that an examination be made even at this late date to determine if any trace of a dusting powder other than that used by Mr. Latona could be located on the wooden foregrip of the assassination rifle. The Laboratory has been advised and is handling the requested examination.

Submitted for information.

- 3 -

Exhibit E - *(page 3 of 3)*

On September 4, 1964, the fingerprints and palm prints of the following named Dallas Police Officers connected with the Crime Laboratory of the Dallas Police Department were submitted to the Latent Fingerprint Section of the Identification Division of the FBI for comparison with the identifiable latent fingerprints and palm prints on the four cardboard cartons:

>   Captain George M. Doughty
>   Lieutenant J. Carl Day
>   Detective Richard W. Livingston
>   Detective Robert Lee Studebaker

On September 8, 1964, the fingerprints and palm prints of Detective Bobby Gene Brown of the Crime Laboratory, Dallas Police Department, were submitted to the Latent Fingerprint Section of the Identification Division of the FBI for comparison with the identifiable latent fingerprints and palm prints on the four cardboard cartons.

The 19 identifiable latent fingerprints and six identifiable latent palm prints on the four cardboard cartons, which are exclusive of the one palm print of Lee Harvey Oswald found on Box "A", were identified as follows:

19 Latent Fingerprints

> 8   latent fingerprints of Detective Robert Lee Studebaker, Dallas Police Department, on Box "A".
> 5   latent fingerprints of Detective Robert Lee Studebaker, Dallas Police Department, on Box "B".
> 1   latent fingerprint of Detective Studebaker on Box "C".
> 2   latent fingerprints of FBI Clerk Forest L. Lucy on Box "B".
> 1   latent fingerprint of FBI Clerk Forest L. Lucy on Box "C".
> 2   latent fingerprints of FBI Clerk Forest L. Lucy on Box "D".
> 19 Total

COMMISSION EXHIBIT No. 3131—Continued

Exhibit F - Rush identification of unknown prints: The FBI found two officers whose prints were matched to the unidentified prints. The exact latents matched to the two officers is not known. *(page 1 of 2)*

LEE HARVEY OSWALD

6 Latent Palm Prints

2 latent palm prints of Detective Robert Lee
    Studebaker, Dallas Police Department, on
    Box "A".
1 latent palm print of Detective Studebaker on
    Box "B".
1 latent palm print of Detective Studebaker on
    Box "C".
1 latent palm print of FBI Clerk Forest L. Lucy
    on Box "A".
5 Total

From the above tabulation, it should be noted that
there is one latent palm print remaining unidentified, and
investigation is continuing in an effort to identify same.

- 18 -

COMMISSION EXHIBIT No. 3131—Continued

Exhibit F - *(page 2 of 2)*

9 March 1998

THE STATE OF TEXAS)

)   Affidavit

County of Travis   )

1) My name is A. Nathan Darby. I am a resident of Austin, Texas, and I am fully competent to make this affidavit.

2) I have been active in law enforcement for many years, starting with the Texas Department of Public Safety as a State Trooper in 1938. I then served with the Austin, Texas Police Department from October 1940, and including my military service, I was with the Austin Police Department until my retirement in August 1979. During that period of service I rose to the rank of Lieutenant-Commander. I am presently an expert in fingerprint identification, and I hold the designation of Certified Latent Fingerprint Examiner (#78-468), which is issued by the International Association for Identification, pursuant to the attached Exhibit DAN #1.

3) I first became interested in fingerprint work in 1942. My direct work in fingerprint identification began soon after, during my military service. I joined the U. S. Army in October 1943 and graduated from Officer Candidate School as a lieutenant in February 1945. I was immediately put in charge of preparing a fingerprint identification system for the Philippine Commonwealth. For my work of setting up their Central

Page 1 of 5

Exhibit G - Darby affidavit with match to Wallace: The match between the Wallace print card and Warren print 29 is made by certified print examiner A. Nathan Darby. The affidavit also shows the examiner's qualifications and the procedures he used. *(page 1 of 10)*

Fingerprint Bureau, I was awarded the Philippine Military Merit Medal, the Philippine Commonwealth's highest non-combat award for foreign military personnel. The United States Army also awarded me the Army Commendation Medal. This achievement was further recognized in the 1946 textbook, "Lectures in Fingerprints" by Fred C. Luchico, then Chief of the Identification Division with the Department of Justice, where he states that I "provided a modern, current, and complete fingerprint file for the Philippine Commonwealth." By 1946 I had risen to the rank of Captain. When my tour of Duty was completed in the Philippines, I returned to the Austin Police Department in November 1946.

4) On 1 January 1948 I was promoted to sergeant and assigned to the Identification Section of the Austin Police Department. On 7 July 1953 I was promoted to lieutenant. In 1956, I was made supervisor of the four employees of Identification and Criminal Records Section of the Austin Police Department. At this time I handled the classification of 176,000 cards and expanded the section to fourteen employees, training and supervising all personnel. In 1970, I worked on advanced record-keeping with the Kodak Miracode system and developed the fingerprint and photograph coding method for the system.

During this time I also served on the board of directors of the Texas Division of the International Association for Identification. I hold an Advanced Certificate in Law Enforcement and an Instructor Certificate

Page 2 of 5

from the Texas Commission on Law Enforcement. I have been a member of the Texas Division of the International Association for Identification since November 1946.

5) Since 1949, I have testified in numerous cases in the State and Federal Courts about fingerprint identification. This testimony included the preparation of latent charts as exhibits. There was never a mistrial or appeal based on my testimony. Attached is Exhibit DAN #2. This exhibit shows the opinions of two District Judges, Travis County, Texas regarding my testimony experience.

6) Fingerprints are an important part of law enforcement because no two prints are alike. Although no person has been able to calculate the likelihood of a mismatch with statistical certainty, the courts accept the admissibility of evidence from fingerprints. Human fingerprints are from unique ridges, which are useful for gripping and holding. An inked fingerprint is the reproduction of the ridges of the finger. An inked fingerprint is provided by putting black ink on the finger and then placing the finger on a suitable contrasting background surface, such as white paper. A latent fingerprint is the production of the ridges when the finger has been placed on a surface. The ridges of the finger leave a residue, body fluids, and chemicals on the surface touched. The latent prints are recovered and compared to the inked prints.

Page 3 of 5

Exhibit G - *(page 3 of 10)*

Exhibit G - *(page 3 of 10)*

For an expert to identify a latent print with and inked print, matching formations must be found on both prints. The ridge lines between the matched formation are then counted. This ridge count must be the same count for both the latent and the ink print. There is no fixed documented limit on how many matching points must be made. The identifying marks on the ink print and on the latent print are then marked and numbered. A conclusion and identification is then made based on the location of the characters on the prints, their formation, and the ridge count between them.

7) Recently I received a photocopy of an inked print along with a photocopy of a latent print from Mr. J. Harrison of Austin, Texas. After careful and extended examination of the inked print photocopy and the latent print photocopy given to me, I have their identifying characteristics marked and numbered. The inked print is Exhibit DAN #3, and the latent Print is Exhibit DAN #4.

8) In addition to exhibit DAN#3 and exhibit DAN #4, Mr. J. Harrison gave me a photocopy of a standard form fingerprint card. This is exhibit DAN #5. Exhibit DAN #5 is from an unknown source and has fingerprints of an unknown person to me. The space #10 on exhibit DAN #5 is the same inked print as DAN #3. Space #10 on exhibit DAN #5 is the space used for the left little finger. There are other indications that the print in space #10 on exhibit DAN #5 is the left little finger.

4 of 5

a. n. w

9) Based on my comparison, I conclude that the unknown person to me who produced the inked fingerprint Exhibit DAN #3 produced the latent print Exhibit DAN #4, and produced the print in space #10 on exhibit DAN #5.

A. Nathan Darby

Subscribed and sworn to before me this *22* day of March, 1998.

Notary Public for Texas

Page 5 of 5

G. N. ω

LATENT PRINT CERTIFICATION BOARD
International Association for Identification

Chairman
ROBERT L. JOHNSON
4203 Whitebre Road
Fairfax, Virginia 22032
Office: (202) 634-5530
Home: (703) 323-1494

Secretary-Treasurer
GEORGE J. BONEBRAKE
Post Office Box 146
Damascus, Maryland 20750
Home: (301) 942-2672

Board Members
MICHAEL J. FITZPATRICK
Route 2, Box 17, Riverview Estates
Cedar Hill, Missouri 63016
Office: (314) 889-3048
Home: (314) 285-3830

DOUGLAS M. MONSOOR
44 Union Boulevard
Lakewood, Colorado 80228
Office: (303) 234-8530
Home: (303) 986-4718

SINGLETON C. TAYLOR, JR.
2911 Bonnie View Road
Shreveport, Louisiana 71119
Office: (318) 226-6061
Home: (318) 635-2928

JOHN W. TYLER
Route 1, Box 444
Rockville, Virginia 23146
Office: (804) 746-4706
Home: (804) 749-3763

SPIRO P. VASOS
1075 Lake Glen Way
Sacramento, California 95822
Office: (916) 445-8902
Home: (916) 422-7941

November 6, 1978

Lt. A. Nathan Darby
Austin Police Dept.
700 E. 7th St.
Austin, Texas   78701

Dear Lt. Darby:

EXHIBIT
DAN #)
a. 1. ᵭ.

    I am most pleased, on behalf of the
International Association for Identification
Latent Print Certification Board, to extend to
you hearty congratulations on your certification
as a latent print examiner.

    This certification program is certainly a
milestone in the fields of forensic science.
It is an accomplishment that individuals of
your integrity and ability may now be recognized
as outstanding members by their associates.
Through this process, the fingerprint field will
be better qualified and deserve even more respect.

    It is with complete confidence that this
certificate is awarded, and again I would like to
extend the congratulations of Mr. Johnson and
all the Board members and express our gratitude
for your input in the professionalization of the
latent print field.

Sincerely,

George J. Bonebrake

George J. Bonebrake
Secretary-Treasurer

Certificate
#78-468

If you are interested in Scientific Identification and Investigation, you should be affiliated with the International Association for Identification.
Information and applications may be obtained by contacting the office of the Secretary-Treasurer.

MACE B. THURMAN, JR.
DISTRICT JUDGE
147TH JUDICIAL DISTRICT COURT

County of
TRAVIS
STATE OF TEXAS

COUNTY
COURTHOUSE
AUSTIN, TEXAS

May 26, 1978

Mr. George J. Bonebrake
Secretary-Treasurer
Latent Print Certification
    Board, I.A.I.
Damascus, Maryland   20750

Dear Mr. Bonebrake:

　　I highly recommend to you Lt. A. Nathan Darby, who
has applied for certification as a fingerprint expert.

　　Lt. Darby has testified in the District Court over
which I preside on numerous occasions. With his vast
experience in fingerprints, there has never been a question
as to whether he could qualify to testify as an expert.
His conduct and appearance in court is excellent and I
firmly believe that his testimony as a fingerprint expert
is the best that I have heard in my 20 years experience as
a District Judge.

　　I sincerely feel that he should be certified as a
fingerprint expert and that he will prove to be a distinct
asset to your organization.

　　　　　　　　　　　　Sincerely yours,

　　　　　　　　　　　　MACE B. THURMAN, JR.
　　　　　　　　　　　　Judge, 147th District Court
　　　　　　　　　　　　Travis County, Texas

　　　　　　　　　　　　TOM BLACKWELL
　　　　　　　　　　　　Judge, 167th District Court
　　　　　　　　　　　　Travis County, Texas

3/12/98
4/31/01

/dk

Exhibit G - *(page 7 of 10)*

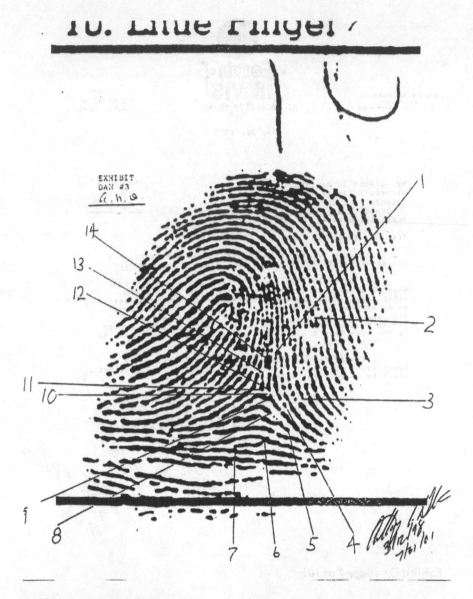

Exhibit G - *(page 8 of 10)*

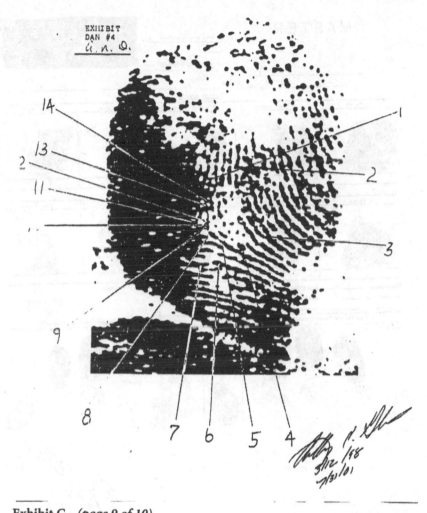

Exhibit G - *(page 9 of 10)*

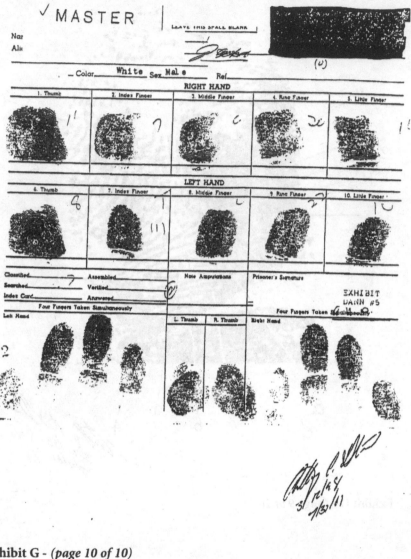

Exhibit G - *(page 10 of 10)*

E. HAROLD HOFFMEISTER
FINGERPRINT CONSULTANT
CERTIFIED LATENT PRINT EXAMINER
INTERNATIONAL ASSOCIATION FOR IDENTIFICATION

1685 DEXTER
AUSTIN, TEXAS 78704-2102

(512) 442-6460 Austin
(512) 875-3830 Luling

4-15-98

Mr. J. Harrison

It is my opinion that a unknown latent print I compared with the inked fingerprint impression of a subject unknown to me at this time matches the left little fingerprint of this subject.

I concur with the marked exhibits of a latent print + rolled fingerprint given to me. And done by an unknown CLPE.

E. H. Hoffmeister

I have examined the rolled inked impressions of malcolm Everett Wallace + they match the rolled inked impressions I compared with the latent print

E. H. Hoffmeister

Exhibit H - Hoffmeister agrees with Darby match: A second print examiner agrees with the match by Darby. Hoffmeister later amended his match to await comparison with original prints.

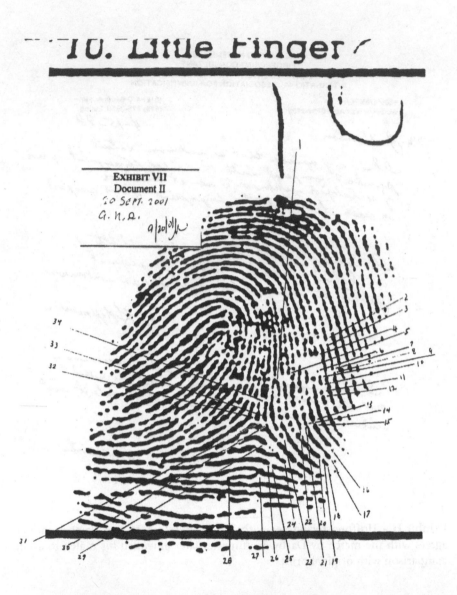

EXHIBIT VII
Document II
20 SEPT. 2001
G. N. D.
9/20/01

Exhibit I - Darby amended match points for Wallace to Warren latent: Darby reconsidered his first affidavit and identified many additional match points between Wallace's print card and the Warren latent from the snipers' carton. *(page 1 of 2)*

Exhibit I (1 of 2)

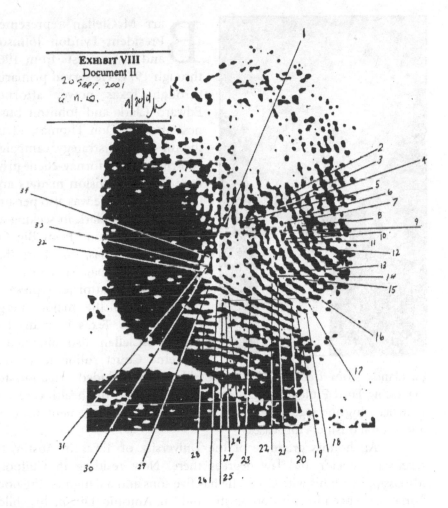

Exhibit I - *(page 2 of 2)*

Exhibit I (2 of 2)

B arr McClellan represented President Lyndon Johnson and his interests from 1966 through 1971. He served primarily through Texas power attorney Edward Clark and Johnson business attorney Don Thomas, advising on political strategy, campaign contributions, attorney-client privilege issues, television matters and labor disputes. He was also personal attorney for Clark in seeking an assassination bonus from Big Oil interests in Dallas, an effort that resulted in two major lawsuits.

A practicing attorney representing several of the major energy companies in Texas in many key cases, McClellan also obtained a Supreme Court ruling to protect parklands from freeways. Other notable cases included litigation for exploding Ford Pintos, tobacco-caused expenses on the health care system, licensing and regulation of cell phones, union-management disputes, and several business tort cases.

An honors graduate of the University of Texas in Austin, he received bachelor and law degrees there. Now residing in Gulfport, Mississippi with his wife Cecile, he has five sons and a daughter. Previous homes have been in Houston, Austin and San Antonio. During his childhood, Barr lived in Maracaibo, Venezuela and is conversant in Spanish.

A one-time TV narrator, he is now completing two additional books on his experiences while serving Johnson. He is also active in investments and serves as a business consultant to several companies in the Gulf Coast area.

Visit the author at www.BarrMcClellan.com.

Sources

The sources for this book include many people involved in Lyndon Johnson's life. Most of what I know is based on personal friendships and associations I developed over forty-five years as well as serving as an attorney and a partner with Clark's law firm for twelve years, from 1966 through 1977.

On looking back, a major problem has been the vagaries of memory, both for me and for my friends and associates. This circumstance alone meant corroboration was required. In every case possible, I searched for documents, and between the documents, the recollections of others, and just plain recall, I found the facts I needed. The relevant documents were in many of the usual as well as unusual places including such locations as old personal files, news articles, books, diaries, and other similar sources. Three key areas were Southwestern University's Clark Collection in Georgetown, Texas; Johnson's Library in Austin, Texas; and the Kennedy Assassination records at the National Archives in Bethesda, Maryland. The Texas State Archives held information from the Court of Inquiry.

The individuals I knew and contacted included old and new friends; people I would socialize with and invite into my home; and people I would travel with, covering long flights to and from Washington or long drives across those famous "vast expanses" of Texas. On those occasions deep secrets would often be shared and that is basically how I know what happened in Dallas. I seldom pushed for this information. I just listened and let them tell me, sometimes keeping the line of conversation going, perhaps nudging them a little to add a little more, but usually just letting them talk.

My main sources, of course, were Ed Clark and Don Thomas, my law partners. Johnson was always well protected by those two attorneys, and there never were any direct admissions by Clark of the many crimes. Thomas was far more open. Both lawyers were deeply involved and, just for reasons of personal liability, were limited in what they could tell me; however, in working so closely with them, I had to know many details just to get our cases prepared, tried, and completed. Much of the incriminating conversation was in the professional code of attorneys, but it always had a clear meaning.

I had few contacts with Clark alone but those I had were both highly confidential and very revealing. He did not waste time, and, when so moved, he could say what he wanted. He could also be as vague as the weather and when the conversation was obviously going that mysterious way, it was always a sign to look, not for innocence but for guilt. Code words were not used to protect the innocent. My main occasion to talk with Clark was during the payoff application with its different forms and mutations over a five-year period. In addition, we had informal conferences, partnership meetings, and dinners together.

Thomas and I spent many hours working for clients and traveling across the state, just talking. The cases included labor matters with Johnson's radio/TV station, enjoining a stock issue by conglomerate Gulf+Western with a weekend appeal to Houston, stopping a highway through a major parkland in San Antonio, working with one of the Big Oil companies in Dallas, and presenting the Exxon-Mobil case involving the King Ranch oil to gas field.

Much of what I knew came to me directly. I helped Johnson while he was president. Once he was back in Austin, there were close contacts through Thomas, particularly for the library dedication, then while he was in deep analysis and when he died. Once I was a partner, the ever-changing circumstances and litigation warranted far more of this personal information so I could do what had to be done. For example, in speaking with Clark, I knew he was admitting to the payoff for the assassination even though he never said he received a payoff for assassinating Kennedy and that the total was two million dollars cash.

When I joined the law firm as an associate, my first mentor was Martin Harris, with whom I spent many hours working cases or driving to or from meetings with the Texas lobby. He was very open and helpful to me. Many other partners and associates contributed to the understandings I developed about the business of representing Lyndon Johnson and his interests. The rule was not to speak about him, even among one another; however, once the rule was broken—and it always was—the conversations were wide open and surprisingly disrespectful. Part of that was the lawyer's "ethos"; nothing was sacred and there was dark humor everywhere. Johnson's ruthless side was both candidly and starkly revealed in the place where he was best known, among his lawyers.

Our law firm had many bookkeepers, secretaries, and clerks who also helped me know the attitudes, activities, and ideas of the lawyers they worked for. Particularly helpful were Edna O'Donnell, who was Clark's secretary for many years; Hazel Arnold, who had always been with Thomas and with the money-laundering corporation; Frances Colby with Martin Harris; and receptionist Loraine Barr. They knew the comings and goings and would often set the stage for the circumstantial evidence I needed to focus my attention and understand what was going on so I could do my job.

Contacts with the political powers were also open and freewheeling. I enjoyed many contacts with Democratic senator Ralph Yarborough and Republican senator John Tower including such times as flying between Austin and Washington and celebrating their birthdays as well as working with them in the Senate. I also had many contacts with Democratic congressman Jake Pickle. The assistants to these men were also important sources for what was going on and what had happened. These men included George Phoenix, Tony Profitt, Lloyd Hatcher, Leonard Killgore, and many others on the congressional staffs. Much dark information emerged from that nether world of deep politics behind the men making the news. Far too often, the real reasons for the news about legislative actions taken had nothing to do with what was recorded on the public record.

On the state level, I knew Preston Smith and dined in the Governor's Mansion. I also knew Attorney General Waggoner Carr and campaigned for him. Attorney General Crawford Martin was a neighbor to my former in-laws. In addition, their legal teams provided insights about Johnson. Linward Shivers was particularly knowledgeable about what was happening in the oil and gas business and at the Railroad Commission. My contacts with other state officials, both active and retired, were extensive, covering the entirety of the Johnson era. This included the key staff members of the Railroad Commission.

The city of Austin was another unique place in the life of Johnson. All elected officials serving in Austin had their stories about him. I knew the city well and represented many clients there. My first wife served as mayor of the city for several years. A further important insight into the middle of Austin and Texas politics came through my former father-in-law who was the long-term and highly respected dean of the University of Texas Law School. I served on several key committees for the city.

In the course of several local elections and in what was just everyday life, I knew the citizens of Austin only too well. Without my even asking, close Johnson associates would make statements that assumed I knew Johnson well. Of continuing interest was this constant dealing with men and women who had fought with and against Johnson over the years. The stories they told were sometimes rumors, but there was always a kernel of truth to what they said. Sometimes there were whole harvests of facts behind seemingly simple statements.

For Johnson's childhood and some of what he experienced in his growing years, I had dinner conversations with Emmette Redford, one of
Johnson's boyhood friends. I had numerous contacts with District Judge Jack
Roberts, who was Clark's first "bought judge." District Judge Herman Jones
was full of insights from his position as district judge. I knew him through
the University Methodist Church as well as at the courthouse.

I got to know Buck Hood as a client. Buck had been managing editor of
the *Austin Statesman* during the fifties and knew many stories that had been
"killed." In 1963, following the assassination, he went with Johnson in the
White House as a "personal arranger."

Many local contacts in my neighborhood were full of insights. State senator Charles Herring was the United States attorney who persecuted Scofield.
Another neighbor was Fagan Dickson, who opposed Johnson's Vietnam policies in the 1966 congressional election in Austin. They were allied with me
when I represented them and many more in litigation against a neighborhood club founded by some of Austin's wealthiest citizens. You learn a great
deal when you take on that group. Interestingly, many facts are revealed in
the deed records.

For the bridge between Wallace and Oswald, I represented Sam Ballen,
a Dallas geologist who met Oswald and later testified before the Warren
Commission. I also spoke with Sam some ten years later about what he
recalled. I had helped him, and he did not hesitate to help me.

For east Texas, there were several key sources, including Harry Lewis, the
office manager for L&G Oil. Together, we handled several oil applications
during the sixties and early seventies. Along with Martin Harris, he gave me
valuable insights into how the east Texas oil field was operated, both legally
and illegally. Attorney Bailey Sheppard was another person with interesting
insights into the oil field and Johnson's elections.

I spent countless hours with Quilman Davis, president of Aztec Oil &
Gas, dining at the Dallas Petroleum Club, pursuing rate increases, traveling
to Washington, Denver, Santa Fe, and many other points on the corporate
jet. With Quilman, we talked about his background with Aztec Oil & Gas,
owned by Wofford Cain, one of the Athens, Texas, residents who became a
millionaire following the development of the east Texas field. Cain was a
member of Dallas' "Big Oil." Through them, I met H. L. Hunt although ever
so briefly. I also learned of Clint Murchison's many meetings with Johnson
and Clark. Clark would have the high honor of serving on Murchison's corporate board of directors. Harris Fender, one of the last of the Texas wild-

catters, had several petitions to be handled at the Railroad Commission, and he had many colorful stories about Clark.

For insights into Johnson's early Texas politics, I had unique discussions with rancher and building contractor R. W. Briggs, who always gave me an earful when we reviewed the expressway litigation. Spending time with San Antonio stockbroker Hal Dewar also added to my personal knowledge of Johnson's campaign financing. With them, I pursued an expressway-parklands case into the Supreme Court in a fascinating look inside that great institution.

On a more personal note, I was born in Texas and lived in Austin from 1957 through 1981. My father's family was from Santa Anna, Texas, about one hundred barren miles west of Johnson City. My uncle, S. E. Damon, was an attorney for Humble who worked the east Texas field for vacancies, for land not leased to any other oil company. He died before I really knew him; however, I still have his law books and his wife, my aunt Addie, could tell many tales about those early days of the wildcatters. She left me, along with my cousins, an inheritance that included royalties in the east Texas field.

After a few years in Maracaibo, Venezuela, as a child, including travels into the swamps with geologists, learning Spanish as a second language, and surviving a commercial airplane crash in Mexico City, I attended public schools in Bellflower, California, and then in San Antonio. High school at Jefferson was a rewarding experience. I graduated from the University of Texas Undergraduate School and Law School in Austin, in both cases with very satisfying results.

This entire experience, and much additional research, are the bases for what I have related in the text, all part of the Johnson years. From my unique position I learned of his darkest sides, came to know his "sordid" friends only too well, and understood the broad outlines of his plans to assassinate Kennedy and cover it up. With this background information, I knew where to look to find the documents showing Johnson to be the assassin of President Kennedy. Perhaps just as important, I also had the extensive circumstantial evidence that compelled Johnson to become an assassin.

For my personal investigation I was assisted at the outset by Sam Castorani, a longtime friend and business associate. Sam and his partner, Cam Crowley, provided the initial background information I needed. For other research, I called on several history students including David Vasquez in Austin; David Weinstein (then a student, now a history professor) at College Park, Maryland, near the JFK Archives; and Rob McCoy at the

University of California in Riverside for Wallace information. Others included Bill Pugsley in Austin, whose Texas Information Network provided powerful insights, and genealogist Warren Ford in Fort Worth.

Through these contacts, I was put in touch with outstanding deep researchers on the assassination including J. Harrison of Austin, who owns one of the most complete libraries on the assassination. He enlisted Nathan Darby, a certified latent print examiner, who made the important match. He also introduced me to other key researchers, many with works in progress. Most were willing to share their efforts with me, complementing what I knew with often extraordinary insights into the assassination and the ties between individuals and Dallas on November 22, 1963.

Walt Brown was another outstanding contact; he was also an editor. Thoroughly versed in the assassination and its many researchers and writers, he was always helpful. More specifically, he provided excellent support in presenting the print evidence to the AARB and to the public. As my manuscript neared completion, he provided important fact checking as well as an overview that was so essential to my personal insights. Throughout, he was always there as a friend and adviser.

Billy Sol Estes's attorney Doug Caddy was very helpful in his legal analyses and comments. I had many contacts with him in Houston and e-mailed him as needed.

Another excellent source for the Johnson story was the *Texas Observer*, an independent weekly in Texas that had the courage to oppose Johnson in the 1950s and to document its position over fierce opposition and constant financial problems. That weekly newspaper plus the investigative skills of former editor Ronnie Dugger make the files of the *Texas Observer* invaluable for understanding Texas politics during the Johnson era. I obtained copies of most of the key articles on Johnson. Interestingly, Dugger kept an open mind on the assassination, and apparently believed there was a connection between Oswald, Ruby, and others.

The Clark Collection at the Southwestern University library was truly a bonus. I would never have expected Clark to leave everything in his personal files but he did. His estate administrators probably decided not to spend the time needed to "vacuum" those papers. The files were still being organized when I first researched there, and some changes have been made to the original system. All records should be easily traceable. In assembling the information Kathryn Stallard and Sheron Johle were most helpful. Knowing how Clark worked so surreptiously, I also know a great deal of personal information is still buried there in his files.

There was one other key source. Since "deep throats" and "undisclosed sources" are routinely used, I will keep one person secret for now and that person will understand. The details relate almost exclusively to the Wallace-Kinser-Josefa problem.

Important review for literary purposes was necessary in developing the book. Excellent support came through Mark Sullivan of New York and his associates. I worked particularly closely with David Branyan of New York, who provided continuing advice both in editing and developing several key parts for the book. For both Mark and David I extend a deep-felt thank you.

This background forms an essential part of my personal investigation, enabling me to find the documents and references to show LBJ killed JFK. The memory banks could be jogged to permit me to draw the understandings I had and still have. Simply stated, trying to grasp the complex activity of a man who was already a legend is not an easy task; however, the facts are there, and I am comfortable in setting forth what I know happened.

When all is said, of course, the final manuscript is mine, solely and alone. I take full responsibility for the conclusions drawn from the facts and advice available to me from these many sources.

Notes

Introduction

1. Appendix 32.

2. Appendix 33.

3. Appendix 34.

4. Mills, *Causes of World War III* (Ballantine) 1958 was typical of this "attitude."

5. Hepburn, *Farewell America* (Frontier, 1968).

6. *The Warren Commission Report* (GPO, 1964) is dated September 24, 1964 [*Warren* or *Report*]. Print or CD versions are available through private publishers.

7. William Manchester provides a deeply felt and excellent statement of the national grief, a sense that prevails to the present day. *The Death of a President* (Harper, 1967). He apparently leaves open the possibility of a conspiracy. Interestingly, an earlier version of his manuscript was reportedly brutal to Johnson.

8. In a very moving account, Schlesinger details the terrible grief suffered by RFK. *Robert F. Kennedy and His Times* (Random, 1996) [Schlesinger]. Schlesinger is apparently awaiting further evidence while for now accepting the Warren *Report's* conclusions.

9. Jackie Kennedy reportedly commissioned a book that concluded Big Oil was involved. See Hepburn, above. Her personal records remain sealed. See Assassination Records Review Board [ARRB], fas.org/advisory/arrb98.

10. Manchester discussed this unacceptable dichotomy between a president and an assassin. Reason required a conspiracy, not an accident. *Death of a President* at p. 627.

11. See Patrick Henry's speech, Virginia Convention, cited in Bailyn, *Ideological Origins of the American Revolution* (Belknap, 1967) at pp. 345–347. We return to the subject in the final chapter.

12. Internet Report on sixth floor tours; Sixth Floor Museum, Dallas, Texas. See online at JFK.org.

13. Of many biographers, those referenced most often appear to be Robert Caro, completing volume four of a projected five volume series: *The Years of Lyndon Johnson: (Path to Power, 1982; Means of Ascent, 1990; Master of the Senate, 2002;* all *Knopf)* [*Path, Means,* and *Master,* respectively]; Robert Dallek, with two volumes: *Lone Star Rising* (Oxford, 1991) and *Flawed Giant*

(Oxford, 1998) [*Rising* and *Flawed,* respectively]; Doris Kearns Goodwin, *Lyndon Johnson and the American Dream* (St. Martins, 1976) [*Dream*]; and Ronnie Dugger's *The Politician* (Norton, 1982) [*Politician*].

14.   The term is from Steve Goulden's *Superlawyers* (1971).

15.   The LBJ Library maintains an excellent staff to answer questions and to provide analysis. Robert Divine, a former professor of mine (he supervised my tutorial), heads the continuing studies section to provide current reports and special studies in book format. Bill Livingston, another former professor of mine, also has important responsibilities. For the LBJ Library Online, see lbjlib.utexas.edu/Johnson/archives.hom/ oralhistory.hom. [LBJ Library].

16.   Even the ARRB could not get information from the government. Particularly critical investigations at the Department of Justice, the FBI, and the CIA are not available. See ARRB Final Report.

17.   The term resulted from Truman Capote's *In Cold Blood* (Random, 1994). The details are helpful to appreciate what happened between the conspirators and are presented as such. Those details are based on my personal knowledge and understanding of what happened and of the characters involved. For the conspiracy in Dealey Plaza and Johnson's role in it, see chapter 17, "Jury," for what happened. I also draw on final argument by an attorney to a jury to present eleven key scenarios in the conspiracy.

18.   The complete fingerprint identification and report is in the Appendix. Certified Latent Print Examiner A. Nathan Darby's affidavit is exhibit G.

1—Epiphany

1.   Several historian-biographers have noted Johnson's mental condition. See, e.g., *Flawed,* p. 605.

2.   Kenneth P. O'Donnell was chief White House aide to Kennedy and served Johnson for a short period following the assassination. For the quote at the beginning of this chapter, see his oral history, LBJ Library.

3.   Flawed, at p. 605. Goodwin is concerned primarily with psychoanalytical problems in childhood, and assigns the paranoia (more as a sense of mistrust) to a later period in this presidency. O'Donnell noted it started almost from the beginning of Johnson's presidency.

4.   See *Flawed,* p. 605.

5.   The book plans apparently began the process, with a start into self-analysis that quickly needed professional help. The relation between childhood problems and the paranoia is not clear.

6.   The problem was, basically, heart failure. Unlike the careful steps Johnson took in 1955 to recover, he did little to improve his health after he returned to Austin in 1969. Psychoanalysis was deemed to be the primary health care needed.

7.   Bob Hardesty, in *Flawed*, p. 607.

8.   The intervention of a private psychiatrist is not mentioned by any biographer. The psychiatrist's name is not verifiable because he was in a group and that group has changed its name over the years. Additional disclosures are needed.

9.   The trust device was routinely used. See Brown, *Texas in the Morning* (Conservatory, 1995) [*Morning*] where she presents some details of the trust for the son she had with Johnson.

10.   The general legal question was researched by three attorneys, and Clark decided the best course of action. This practice is typical in major law firms. The documents are in the penthouse records of the law firm.

11.   The details appeared on the books for the Brazos-Tenth Street Co. kept by Hazel Arnold, secretary to Don Thomas.

12.   Johnson's religion is virtually an unmentionable in most popular histories. He belonged to a church near the ranch but seldom attended. In Washington he attended whatever was politically available. Until his old age, he was not a religious man.

13.   This standard priority list was known at the law firm.

14.   Accounts of Johnson's last hour are generally agreed among historians.

15.   Faction originated with Truman Capote's *In Cold Blood* (1965) and is also known as the nonfiction novel or the journalistic novel. See *Encyclopedia Britannica*. The key people are permitted to tell the facts but without distortion by or intervention of the author's point of view. Within the new journalism, objectivity is required but interpretive material is used.

2—Privilege

1.   Most polls agree on this rating. See gallup.com (membership fee required).

2.   *Flawed*, p. 49.

3.   Important researchers on Johnson's role include J. Evetts Haley, *A Texan Looks at Lyndon* (Palo Duro, 1964) [*Lyndon*]; Craig Zirbel, *The Texas Connection* (self-published, 1991); and Noel Twynman, *Bloody Treason* (Laurel, 1997) [*Treason*]. Most conspiracy researchers conclude Johnson had something to do with the plot.

4. The full reach of the privilege is disputed. Some view it an absolute bar. Others argue it should not include crimes. There is a further discussion with references in chapter 20.

5. Affidavit filed in legal proceedings in Austin, Texas, in 1984. *McClellan v. State,* No. 63,685, 299th District Court, Travis County, Texas.

6. *Id.*

7. Appendix 2, 3, 4.

8. Appendix 6.

9. Appendix 7.

10. The power of the Railroad Commission from 1940 through 1975 is generally acknowledged. "The most powerful government agency in the world." *Government Control of the Economy* (1957). From 1947 through 1975, most ministers and operators with the Organization of Petroleum Exporting Countries (OPEC) received their basic education at the commission.

11. This characterization is by Caro, *Means,* p. 177.

12. The spin that historians give their subjects is shown in the treatment of this election. Some say Johnson won a majority. *Dream,* p. 88. In fact, he barely won a plurality. Others acknowledge the vote was hardly a majority but argue it was across the board in all counties and was substantially more than any one other candidate received. *Flawed,* p. 155. Apparently part of an ongoing effort to rehabilitate Johnson, the fact is that he was fortunate there was no runoff.

13. Appendix 23.

14. See Appendix, fingerprint evidence, exhibit G, Darby affidavit.

15. Reports on-line, Sixth Floor Museum, jfk.org, and LBJ Library, 1999.

3—Roots

1. *Texas Handbook Online* is a standard resource for basic Texas history. Encyclopedic in format, the original three volumes are now on the Net. See tsha.utexas.edu/ handbook/online [*Handbook*].

2. *Handbook,* "Regulator Moderator War."

3. *Id.* Violence was almost inbred and continued for many years.

4. Monogram history by Edward Clark. The short paper is included in the Clark Collection, Southwestern University Library, Georgetown, Texas, Box 2, File 59. [Clark Collection]. Reference is to the file box and then the biographical file number. The collection has been reorganized and references may have to be traced from the original "biographical list" to the new list.

5. Slavery statistics for this early period are difficult to obtain. Illegal

Klan activity was conducted in secret for a reason. Recent studies on lynching show the role of a deep-seated violence against former slaves. See on-line book by Mark Gabo, *Lynching in America,* crimelibrary.com/classics2. San Augustine and most of east Texas led the effort by extremists to continue slavery for blacks.

6.   Appendix 12.

7.   *Handbook,* "Lynching."

8.   Ken Anderson, "You Can't Do That, Dan Moody," 1996; *Texas Alumnae Magazine.*

9.   Appendix 8.

10.   For a history of the East Texas Field, see Clark and Halbouty, *The Last Boom* (Shearer, 1972).

11.   Many Johnson biographers ignore this incident. One treats is as an accident; *Dream,* p. 67. Another says Johnson only expressed regret when confronted by his father. Paul Henggeler, *In His Steps* (Wicker, 1991), p. 41.

12.   This second known killing was related to me by Emmette Redford, a childhood friend of Johnson. Redford had anticipated a good job with Johnson and did not get it. He may have revealed this unthinkable event because of his resentment to what he considered unfair treatment from Johnson.

13.   *New Harvard Guide to Psychiatry* (Harvard, 1988); psychotic disorders, p. 341.

14.   See *Handbook,* "Lynching, San Saba."

15.   See *Path,* p. 214.

16.   U. E. Baughman, *Secret Service Chief* (Harper, 1962). The former Secret Service chief discussed assassination in America as anarchists at work. The book downplayed the conspiracy in the Lincoln assassination and did not mention the attempt on Truman. See also North, *Act of Treason* (Carroll and Graf, 1992) [North], p. 120.

17.   See online report, Roger Norton, home.att.net/ ~rjnorton/ Lincoln for current views on the Lincoln assassination.

18.   *Time,* January 12, 1933. See also the letter by novelist Elizabeth Gaskell: ". . . we could think of nothing else, . . . [a] sense of a great shock and grief."

19.   Another interesting vice president was Aaron Burr, who accepted the vice presidency, then enlisted friends and turned on the early United States. Clark was a member of the modern Aaron Burr Society. See Clark Collection, Box 10, Files 205–213.

20.   Carl Oglesby, *Yankee and the Cowboy Wars* (Berkeley, 1977). See also Peter Dale Scott, *Deep Politics and the Death of JFK* (Calif., 1996). Both have explored the real backgrounds to power and its abuse. The abuse of power I participated in is essential to understanding how Clark thought about problems and how he "took care of" the problems "for good."

4—The Friendly City

1.   Key historians acknowledge Clark's role as a power broker but know very little about him, because they have the Washington history but not the Texas history. Caro visited often with Clark for *Means* but was cut off following its publication. See Clark Collection, Box 34, File 76. Clark's detailed history is important to see his analytical approach to the practice of law and to "life itself."

2.   Many men in Texas started early with Johnson and were with him or in private power positions for many years; examples are Jack Valenti, Warren Woodward, Robert Anderson, Donald Cook, Jesse Kellam, Clifton Carter, and Walter Jenkins.

3.   According to an old Texas tradition, the only gifts at Christmas were hard candy. This impoverishment is an important part of the underlying motivations for Johnson, both by him for the public and from the public to him.

4.   Lawyers are not supposed to discuss this fact about judges. After all, it suggests contempt for the court; however, "owning" a judge is a key for any lawyer.

5.   Chariton, *Unsolved Texas Mysteries* (Woodware, 1991).

6.   During most of his legal career Clark kept a diary. Clark Collection, Boxes 99–100, Files 48–59. Short on detail, they provide an excellent source for what he was doing and where he was. Those records warrant considerable additional study and will play a key role in my forthcoming book on Texas justice.

7.   The actual quote was that the vice presidency "was not worth a warm bucket of piss." Later, when he was vice president, Johnson would remark, "I ain't worth piss."

8.   See oral history, LBJ Library where one precinct chairman admits he simply delivered his votes to whoever wanted them. LBJ Library, Oral History, Precinct Chairman.

9.   *Master*, pages 403–413, emphasizes the donations but does not make a money trail. Compare *Path*, p. 162.

10.   LBJ library report to Bill Pugsley, Texas Information Network (TIN); written report to me.

11.   This hotly disputed military award is apparently resolved by most historians in Johnson's favor: he did get fired at; however, the award itself was little more than politics. The word at Clark's firm was that Johnson never went near combat. In addition, private conversations by airmen on the mission give Johnson very little credit or credibility.

12.   Appendix 30. The entire file was originally sealed by the chief librarian at Southwestern. She later wrote that the letter from the Clark estate said to disclose everything. The original file showed theft of vehicles, reduced to theft of funds, and then discharge. When opened, some of the original documents were missing. Box 17, File 388.

13.   Box 17, File 388. The envelope at the Clark Collection includes his wife's testimony. The army made it clear that Clark could never claim veteran's benefits.

14.   Again, historians differ on this important point. No doubt FDR killed the IRS criminal investigation. The record should speak for itself. Johnson was saved by raw political power exercised at the highest level, and he learned how power works: to the victors go the spoils.

15.   LBJ Library, letter report to Bill Pugsley, Texas Information Network (TIN), request for Murchison documents.

16.   A nonlawyer ("layman" or "civilian" in lawyer talk) may have difficulty appreciating what is meant by a "close case." All cases can be maneuvered to have at least two sides. Clark then made sure the case went his way. As we shall see, even that little difference did not matter. If the judge saw the case open and shut with no room for argument, Clark still had the right to call it a "close case" and get the result he wanted.

17.   LBJ Library, "Scofield." Austin Public Library Newspaper Archives, *American-Statesman*, February 1951, April 1956 (several articles in both time periods).

5—Assassin

1.   The age difference between Clark and Wallace was almost a generation. In those days, change was slow, and both men had similar cultural influences during their childhoods. Both were in that generation between the Gay Nineties and the Roaring Twenties. The major differences between Johnson, Clark, and Wallace were small town versus big city.

2.   *Handbook,* "Ku Klux Klan"; see also "Lynching."

3.   This remark was typical of Clark's attitude toward social change and civil rights. Although he was chief administrative aide to the last liberal governor of Texas, he had little use for national Democrats and eventually became a John Tower Republican. See Appendix 9. As early as 1941 he delivered a speech on *not* being a liberal. Clark Collection, Box 62, File 1109. In another, he attacked "intellectuals." Box 3, File 66.

4.   The old traditions never really disappeared. The Texas Legislature always had its share of characters, too often armed. There were spittoons into the 1960s when I was a legislative aide there.

5.   The yearbooks of Woodrow Wilson High School in Dallas provide most of the information on the period 1934 to 1939. Research by J. Harrison, Austin genealogist.

6.   The Office of Naval Intelligence [ONI] began a security review on Wallace in 1961. The extensive record is available on request or as a Freedom of Information filing. Based on the extensive reports during that review, much information on Wallace has been compiled. Other sources include J. Harrison, Texas Ranger Clint Peoples, and several police reports, also available on request. Peoples's investigations are also in James M. Day, *Captain Clint Peoples Texas Ranger* (Texian, 1980) [*Peoples*]. Wallace's entire FBI file was also obtained under the Freedom of Information Act [FOIA]. The FBI showed only an investigation in 1949 into his Marxist beliefs.

7.   The record at the University of Texas in Austin is based on his academic record and yearbooks during his enrollment, compiled by J. Harrison.

8.   Appendix 3.

9.   The first name appears on a memo that year. The LBJ Library cannot identify the full name of the employee; however, on an ONI report and on one police report, Wallace is reported to be working with Johnson in these early years.

10.   *Handbook,* "University of Texas" and my personal experience as university attorney in 1978.

11.   Political control of the academic president was exercised by the board of regents and the governor who appointed the members. This control extended into the 1960s and Vietnam protests by keeping strict controls on campus activity by students and even tighter controls on the faculty and staff.

12.   Austin *American-Statesman,* "March on the Capitol," October 1944; Newspaper Archives, Austin Public Library.

13.   At one time, the organization was very secretive. Now it is available

online at utexas.edu/students/friars. I was selected to membership in 1960.

14. The Wallace grade transcript has been obtained by researchers and shows a record of mixed grades and often-changing career objectives.

15. The information on the Wallace's college years and following is based on several reports. My conclusions are drawn from those reports as a compilation to show what happened. I also rely on a "deep throat" source that must remain anonymous for many more years.

16. ONI reports, 1957–1963, available on request.

17. This scandal lingered in Austin for many years. I heard details from friends as late as 1957. Most historians acknowledge the scandal.

18. The allegations were in the nature of "he said, she said" with little outside proof. ONI was unable to resolve the various charges. In consideration of the complete Wallace records as well as the court records, violent abuse was involved. This conclusion is corroborated by his relations with a second wife (fourth marriage) while in California. See Case No. D32250, Wallace and Wallace, Orange County Courthouse, California (1969).

19. The divorce petitions are public records. Today, the charge and counter-charge between husband and wife are mainly the boilerplate of "irreconcilable differences" standard in no-fault divorce. In those days, however, there was no such thing as no-fault divorce. Details of the cause or causes could be alleged and they were.

20. This is the date Wallace was employed at the United States Department of Agriculture (USDA). The connection to Johnson is also in Chariton, *Unsolved Texas Mysteries* (Woodware, 1991), pp. 114–116.

21. The practice was common with the federal government as late as the 1960s. Employees at regular "civil service" government jobs, usually holding the position because of political connections in the first place, would be allowed to work for their elected political sponsors on constituent matters while being paid by the department or agency, in spite of the Hatch Act prohibiting politicking by government employees. When election time came up, these employees were granted paid leave from their government job to work at campaign headquarters.

6—Lyin' Lyndon

1. *Reader's Digest*, "Secret Boss of Texas" (February 1953); Clark Collection, Box 17, File 392. For a Dallas *Morning News* article on the same subject, Box 17, File 401.

2.   The information came in many ways. Over drinks after work, during the firm parties, at early Saturday morning coffee, and just the daily office talk.

3.   The appeal was to local Austin judge Roy Archer. At the time the legal team included Clark's partner Everett Looney, a skilled technician in the law. Also on the team was Willard Wirtz, one of Johnson's key legal advisers. For many years, Clark competed with Wirtz for all of Johnson's law business. When Wirtz died of a heart attack during a Texas football game in 1951, Clark took over.

4.   Appendix 8. Clark lost his only elected office through some political maneuvering. His position was combined with the same one in adjacent Shelby County. He had fewer votes in that county so he lost. He never ran again.

5.   For a photo of "Mr. Texas," see *Means*, ff. p. 158.

6.   LBJ Library records show ballot theft was a common practice. Stuffing the votes was clearly the case in 1948; however, when fraud occurs after the election has closed, it was clearly illegal and unacceptable. In the Box 13 case, it was illegal, period. Stevenson had a solid basis for his litigation. He never said that everyone did it, and I doubt he would have tolerated the theft, even before the polls closed. Undoubtedly his supporters bought votes.

7.   As an example, the practice was common in east Austin where minority voters there were paid to cover the costs of getting out the vote. Usually a token payment was enough. This was occurring as late as 1979.

8.   This description comes from our clients in San Antonio who helped Johnson in 1948. Cattleman R. W. Briggs and stock broker Hal Dewar were two such fund-raisers.

9.   There are several biographies about Parr, some directly related to the 1948 election theft. *Handbook*, "George Parr."

10.   Clark may or may not have earned full degrees; however, there is some question whether he graduated from Tulane and from the law school at Texas University. In 1928 law school was not required. Attorneys could study with a lawyer, "read law," and be recognized. In later years, Clark even listed an honorary degree as a full degree.

11.   Salas told his story in a statement provided to Caro. *Means* at pp. 391–397. Salas was mistaken on two points. Johnson was not in Alice. Thomas was there as Johnson's man, and Salas may have been misled as to who he was. Also, Salas recalled two men. Thomas said he was the only one there. Another Clark lawyer may have been there, with Thomas declining to implicate him. When Thomas told me he was the only man living who knew what had happened, he did not know Salas was still around.

12.   Johnson later exhibited this same type of silent humor and pride. He showed Ronnie Dugger the photo of the "padrones" for Box 13, never denying he knew about the theft and how it was done. I doubt that he knew the details. If he had to testify, he could deny knowing anything. The meeting was typical of the "code talk" we used.

13.   This man is not Don Thomas, attorney. The similarity in names caused a small problem later, when Thomas Donald headed for the Rio Grande River for sanctuary in Mexico.

14.   *Means,* pp. 391–394.

15.   Historians do not seem to appreciate the fact that what happened with Black and Fortas was illegal. None have been able to discover what the deal was. The story told by Thomas keys perfectly with the missing secret conversations. Fortas talked directly to Black, and convinced him without allowing Stevenson's team of lawyers to say anything.

16.   An interesting detail: Thomas would help get the record to Washington by flying it there in terrible weather. He refused to fly again, saying the experience ruined him. As a result we spent many hours driving across Texas in his Town Cars.

17.   The difference is the far greater vote for the Democratic candidate for governor.

18.   Statement by Warren Commission member John McCloy, quoted in Marr, *Crossfire* (Carroll and Graff, 1989), p. 465.

7—Murders

1.   This statement was attributed to Johnson by my partners at the law firm.

2.   Clark often used what are known as "East Texas sayings." Some are akin to code talk.

3.   Opening statement from *Morning.* While referring to Johnson's problems with the Kennedys in 1963, the demand to be above scandal and criticism was also an overriding concern in 1949.

4.   Appendix 14 and 15. From LBJ Library.

5.   The LBJ Library has denied any knowledge of what the transactions involved. Interestingly, the Clark Collection does not include the memo and letter. As client records, they are probably in the penthouse files. Clark's other documents and his diary entries at the Clark Collection reveal the fundamental system of crime and coveup set out in the memo and letter.

6.   A member of the Texas Senate said Clark threatened to kill him if he did not support the escheat bill. *Texas Observer,* March 28, 1962. The weekly

newspaper reported Clark was not in Austin when the remark was allegedly made.

7.   For a copy of the original, see Appendix 14.

8.   For a copy of the original, see Appendix 15.

9.   *Handbook;* news reports on "Smithwick death." See Clark Collection, Box 63, File 1093.

10.   *Handbook,* "Ferguson."

11.   Genealogy report, J. Harrison, Austin, Texas.

12.   News reports covered the death on April 16, 1952. See Clark Collection, Box 24, File 596; Box 97, File 1323.

13.   Research by J. Harrison; ONI reports; *Mysteries; Peoples;* FBI reports under FOIA request. In *Master* at p. 433, Caro notes Josefa was loose, wild, and an alcoholic. He makes no mention of Kinser. He also ignores Estes and some of the other scandals that started in the 1950s.

14.   Appendix 22 is one summary ONI Report. There are several reports under the FOIA request.

15.   LBJ Library, Oral history, "Bob Long."

16.   Key Johnson aide Horace Busby says Wallace dated Josefa. *Mysteries,* p. 115. Both were members of the then-secret Friars Society.

17.   The contact is not in writing but appears as a telephone call in the Clark records. Clark Collection, Box 99, File 1332. Wallace may be related to Clark through Mary André and the DuBose line. Three genealogists in San Augustine refused to provide any information on the subject.

18.   The pistol would figure in several crimes committed by Wallace. Ranger Peoples kept an eye on Wallace for many years and was particularly interested in finding a .25-caliber pistol. That caliber slug was involved in the Kinser and Marshall cases, and was the same caliber as a slug fired into Estes's home.

19.   *Mysteries,* p. 122; *Peoples,* p. 229 The problem with insurance was mentioned in the discussion at the Broken Spoke in Austin, but there was a deeper significance involving money: Kinser's need for cash and Wallace's insistence on being paid.

20.   Austin police report, Officer Marion Lee, October 22, 1951.

21.   Peoples, p. 19. Peoples book covered several important cases that he handled. One was the Kinser murder. The book was published four years before the Marshall murder was taken to a grand jury for the third time.

22.   LBJ Library, Oral History, "Bob Long."

23.   Buck Hood, an LBJ aide, was at the newspaper at the time, and he related some of these facts to me when I was his lawyer in 1980–82.

24. Appendix 16.

25. ONI reports state Wallace's job was economist and then control supervisor. His California family states he was seldom at work. His supervisor could not account for his actions in November 1963. The company refused subpoenas for his employment records in 1984.

26. Estes used the term to describe Wallace. See Department of Justice Report on 1987 investigation into Estes. The investigation was halted when Estes refused to cooperate unless granted full immunity. Report from Estes attorney Doug Caddy.

27. George Reedy, *Lyndon B. Johnson: A Memoir* (Anders McMeek, 1982).

8—Cash

1. Michael J. Apter, *The Dangerous Edge: The Psychology of Excitement* (Free Press, 1992) reviews the driven nature of such personalities and how they enjoy the thrill.

2. Johnson and Clark both left substantial estates. With the spouse's community property excluded and trusts ignored, each had about ten million dollars personally. Johnson died twenty years before Clark. Comparisons are very difficult, however, because of trusts the two made. Tracing the money is also difficult because substantial sums were expensed even though invested. The penthouse records hold the details. See also, Clark Collection, Box 88, File 1371; Box 90, File 1373.

3. Appendix 25. The 1960 fund-raising letter states the basic approach: give us money and we get you benefits. Letters had to be followed with at least a telephone call and perhaps a personal visit to the big donors.

4. LBJ Library, oral communication to Pugsley, TIN; reported to me by letter from Pugsley.

5. In *An Economic Interpretation of the Constitution* (Free Press, 1986), the Beards stressed understanding the economy to understanding history. Money and wealth must be explained for politics, influence, and power to be understood. As was also the case with Watergate, "follow the money" remains the best approach.

6. Notably, *Warren* incorrectly stated that the government owned the building rather than considering a possible lead. Note how these points of contact are the reverse of alibis showing a person is not involved. The full extent of Byrd and the assassination are not known; however, he ties directly into Big Oil and the important coverup.

7. Before the 1964 general election, the *Wall Street Journal* had a series

on Johnson's wealth. Clark Collection, Box 34, File 737. See also *Texan* where rancher and historian J. Evetts Haley reviewed some of the prominent scandals involving Johnson before 1963.

8.   Appendix 17.

9.   The Estes story is related in his daughter's book. Pam Estes, *Billie Sol: King of Texas Wheeler-Dealers* (Noble Craft, 1983) [*Estes*]. She tells about her father's accomplishments but omits details of the trials and convictions except to set out Cofer's actions representing her father. Doug Caddy later represented Estes with the Department of Justice inquiry. Two Department of Justice attorneys were scheduled to meet Estes; however, state immunity was declined at the last minute, and Estes refused to participate.

10.   Private office memo uses the term "interest." See Appendix 21.

11.   This amount was presented in testimony before the Senate Committee on Government Operations. North, p. 124.

12.   Baker told his story in a book with Larry L. King, *Wheeling and Dealing* (Norton, 1980). This summary account discloses what Johnson knew and did.

13.   This information was provided by legislative assistants in conversations during the 1960s and 1970s when I was actively lobbying in Washington.

14.   Term "hand-off" also implied in *Master*, p. 393.

15.   Appendix 39; research report by J. Harrison.

16.   Thomas told me this fact when he dissolved the corporation in 1971. Appendix 439.

17.   Several instances of problems Johnson had with banks made the news. None could show any Johnson connection except to mention rumors that Johnson was an owner. Letters from Clark to Johnson show Johnson was an owner. Clark Collection, Box 737.

18.   Letter, Clark to Johnson, Clark Collection, Box 871.

19.   See *Dream*, p. 99. There is no statement about the amounts except the *Wall Street Journal* articles in 1964. The totals do not include other income and, because of the IRS, are not likely to be accurate. In *Master*, Caro mentions huge sums for elections but nothing about personal income to Johnson. Dallek refers to money problems that Johnson mentioned on the phone but, knowing the conversation was recorded, he refused to discuss the matter. *Flawed*, p. 40. Johnson guarded his financial records very carefully. His promise when dedicating the LBJ Library to show all excluded the extensive financial records. His personal, business, and legal life in Texas were, for the most part, excluded.

20.   From 1979 to 1981, I had a working business relationship with

Scofield. Another source in the IRS had to alert Clark to what was happening. Clark then tried to get the IRS, probably through Scofield, to halt the audit. When the audit continued, according to law partner Sam Winters, Clark had Scofield indicted. Scofield probably knew nothing about this activity behind his back.

21.   News reports covered the fires. The police were unable to find the culprit. Austin *American-Statesman*, June 16, 1953, Austin Public Library Archives.

22.   Brown, *Texas in the Morning*. Recently one researcher has taken a serious interest in her inside knowledge and her deep politics. *Treason*, pp. 844–862. A mistress learns a great deal about a man and what she has to say should be considered carefully. Similarly, Seymour Hirsch reviewed Kennedy's sexual activities in *The Dark Side of Camelot* (Little Brown, 1997) [Hirsch hereinafter]. Brown also reviews the payment arrangements made through an attorney and the later abuse of her son by the navy.

23.   Dallek says Johnson had many affairs. *Flawed*, pp. 186–187. Caro mentions the subject in passing. *Master*, pp. 653–654.

24.   Hirsch, p. 112.

9—High-Low

1.   Caro promotes the "master" theory that Johnson was a powerful leader. This *de facto* leadership is disputed by some writers who point to conflicts with national Democrats in 1959–1960.

2.   Clark Collection, Box 17, File 401.

3.   There were no oil interests directly allied with Johnson until Murchison in 1946 and Cain in 1947. The money in Texas was available from many sources including banking, insurance, and construction. Interestingly, Johnson carefully protected Big Oil while pursuing policies considered treason by the same group. Johnson and Big Oil coexisted with each other, according to some, "like two scorpions in a bottle."

4.   Many historians are not critical of Johnson's treatment of Leland Olds; however, the grilling was terribly unfair, and led to McCarthy's rampages.

5.   The bribe by Patman was disclosed to me by Martin Harris when Patman opposed a client I represented at an oil and gas hearing.

6.   *Rising* at p. 499. Clark was furious and never forgave Patman.

7.   This was universally agreed. Until Johnson was president, he "lay low" on civil rights issues. As leader, he was perfect for the silent generation of the 1950s.

8.   See *Rising,* p. 178.

9.   The McCarthy delays are well documented and occurred while Johnson was a leader for the Senate Democrats.

10.   See Clark Collection, Box 99, File 1332, for SEC help.

11.   *Master,* p. 840; cf. Dallek, *Rising,* p. 468.

12.   This was big news in the *Texas Observer,* July 1955.

13.   *Rising,* p. 469.

14.   The problem prompted Clark to prepare a list of "progressive" legislation by Johnson. On hindsight, it is very humorous.

15.   *Texas Observer,* January 1959.

16.   Appendix 23.

17.   Clark had his way in the Texas Legislature, working the floor like he owned it. *Texas Observer,* March 1961.

18.   This matter sets the stage in dramatic fashion. While Russell had to draw back from the presidency, Johnson saw the way to the top. Russell remained one of Johnson's strongest backers and later agreed to serve on the Warren Commission. He disagreed on the magic bullet but went along when the facts were watered down.

19.   Clark Collection, Box 99, File 1333; Box 103, File 1334.

20.   This "deal" was advertised to clients on several occasions.

21.   *Dream.*

22.   Appendix 1.

23.   Jaworski, *Confession and Avoidance* (Anchor, 1979).

24.   North, at p. 78, also covers this budding problem.

25.   Appendix 24.

26.   Appendix 25.

27.   This remark was mentioned among Clark's law partners.

10—Inaugurals

1.   For a thorough list of USDA actions against Estes, see North, above, for corroboration of activity behind closed doors.

2.   Clark Collection, Box 17, File 388.

3.   The Freeman letter to Johnson resulted in a letter back from Johnson to Estes about their friendship and how they would be meeting soon. LBJ Library document, available on request.

4.   The only information about this fatal plane crash at the LBJ Library was an oral history by one of the Ranch foremen.

5.   Appendix 26.

6.   *Texan,* p. 98; Sherrill, *Accidental President* (Pyramid, 1967), p. 76 [*Accidental*].

7.   The scene of the murder is recreated from facts reported from the crime scene investigation. The account is standard for an attorney's argument to a jury. The Houston medical examiner's report dated May 22, 1962, was filed August 17, 1962. The Texas Department of Safety reported its conclusions on July 18, 1962, and included a report from Ranger Peoples dated June 7, 1962. Peoples also testified in *Marshall v. Health Department,* Travis Courthouse, No. 377,991, 52nd District, to change the death certificate from suicide to homicide. The crime is also discussed at length in *Mysteries* and *Peoples.*

8.   Appendix 30.

9.   Report by Doug Caddy, attorney for Billy Sol Estes.

10.   The official line is that such policies are never reduced to writing. Martin Harris told me he made a review of the statement in a memo.

11.   Appendix 42. Clark moved to a new bank building in 1981. The former offices during the Johnson years are now in the renamed Norwood Building.

11—Funerals

1.   Clark Collection, Box 39, File 775; report from researcher in Bonham, Texas. *Mysteries,* p. 211.

2.   There were many strange deaths, and they take on a new reality, that of being necessary for Johnson's political future. They fit together to explain what happened behind the scenes during the Johnson years. A list Estes said came from Cliff Carter included eleven; my information confirms eleven with nine more possible.

12—Bait

1.   North, p. 138.

2.   According to North, Estes mentioned the Marshall murder.

3.   The Dunn reports are available on request.

4.   The fact of the three calls to Carter is in North, p. 201. The content of the conversations is not known.

5.   Johnson denied any contact.

6.   Although the connections are not fully disclosed, the deaths occurred. Strictly speaking, the conspirators must now show no connection. Similarly, deaths continued following the assassination, giving rise to a

generalized fear of knowing anything about the crime. This fear is part of the mystery surrounding Kennedy's death, and, interestingly, impacted our research. One print expert made a match, then expressed serious doubts about participating at all and restricted his opinion. Appendix, fingerprint identification, Exhibit H.

7.   Appendix 29; compare to appendix 28, a contemporary photo of Estes.

8.   This series of investigative reports is available on request.

9.   Within a year, a key member of the inquiry was appointed to a postal director position. Austin researcher J. Harrison.

10.   LBJ Library, Estes Documents, Deposition of Donald S. Thomas.

11.   Appendix 27.

12.   Despite several solid leads and close ties to Clark, the better course for the present is to withhold judgment pending further research and strong corroborating evidence. At this time our leads are through Jaworski and Coffield, and our key suspects fit into the Clark *modus operandi*. The accomplices may never be identified with certainty.

13.   As noted in note 12, above, the man cannot be sufficiently identified to place him with the conspiracy; more information is needed, and solid corroborating evidence is required.

14.   *Estes*, above, p. 212.

15.   Rometsch had compelling information that was not disclosed to the public. North, p. 320; Hirsch, p. 371. She may also be a common bond between Johnson and Kennedy.

15.   North, p. 271.

16.   *Handbook*, "Clint Murchison." There are several biographies. Clark Collection.

17.   Appendix 25.

18.   Ballen was a witness at the Warren Commission. See affidavit of Sam Ballen, *Warren*.

13—Details

1.   North, p. 265.

2.   Hirsch, p. 402.

3.   Peoples kept looking for bullets from a .25 caliber gun. Peoples's personal records after his book was published are not available. He was killed in a one-car accident.

4.   North, p. 260.

5.   Vice president's daily calendar. Supposedly a record of travels and contacts, the calendars were sketchy, at best, per advice from LBJ Library.

6.   *Handbook,* "Sons of San Jacinto."

7.   Clark diaries, 1948–1959, Clark Collection, Boxes 99–100, Files 1329–1340.

8.   Oswald's activity is based on *Warren.*

9.   See Texas Archives for the complete police record. The Kennedy Assassination is part of the Court of Inquiry review.

10.   Johnson hated the Kennedys. He once said he enjoyed the vice presidency but later admitted they were the worst days of his life. Likewise, Robert Kennedy was after Johnson, and he had good grounds with the Estes and Baker cases.

11.   North, p. 233.

12.   *Accidental,* p. 197.

13.   The Profumo incident was top news in June 1963 and is covered in most histories.

14.   Appendix 20.

15.   Hirsch, p. 291.

16.   Brown also benefited from the trust system with payments to her from a lawyer in Dallas. *Morning,* p. 214. The same payments were set up for Estes. The penthouse records would disclose these records.

17.   John Kennedy's remarks about Johnson were verified by Robert Kennedy in a conversation with Schlesinger and are generally accepted. See ARRB report.

18.   The question of dropping Johnson was apparently settled in his favor; he was not going to be dropped; however, there are many lingering uncertainties. Hirsch, p. 408. Two books by the secretary to John Kennedy. None of their opinions matter. Johnson thought he would be dropped.

14—Assassination

1.   Starting with *Warren,* most assassination books cover the motorcade in detail. Because of the vast research and the practical limits on size, readers are assumed to be reasonably familiar with the tragedy and to appreciate the long dispute over the coverup.

2.   There is considerable dispute over Oswald's travels between the bus

and his boarding room. Many alternatives have been suggested, including one that has Wallace giving Oswald a ride to his boarding room.

3.   This man has not been identified. He was there as a cover for Wallace. For now he is "Bill Yates."

4.   This was the first recorded contact with the Secret Service men. Cf. Brown, *The Warren Omission* (Delmax, 1996), pp. 18–19.

5.   Several books mention this remark. *Warren*, p. 136.

6.   Most histories include this remark. *Warren*, p. 76. Connally repeated the statement in the emergency room at Parkland Hospital.

15—Run

1.   The report of Secret Service members in Dealey Plaza immediately after the shooting was carefully downplayed in *Warren*, p. 136. The conclusion was that no Secret Service men were there (except Sorrells later; *Warren*, p. 156), and the reports were deemed to be errors in identifying other federal law enforcement personnel as Secret Service. *Warren*, p. 212. False identifications were made to Dallas law enforcement, and the testimony of the Dallas police officers on what was said to them is correct.

2.   The significance of men having Secret Service credentials has not been fully explored. Brown, *Warren Omission*. The only source for the badges was an insider at the White House. The imposters may have used so-called "pocket credentials."

3.   Many researchers are convinced there was a second Oswald, and that the Oswald apprehended by the police was the wrong man. Others question the travel pattern laid out by the Warren Commission, saying the evidence he rode the bus is good but that the taxi ride is questionable. Roger Craig, a sheriff's deputy, believed he saw Oswald leave the depository and get in a station wagon. There is a photo of a man resembling Oswald getting in a station wagon and driving away. He would then have gone to his boardinghouse room. Wallace could have seen Oswald after the assassination and taken him to the boardinghouse. Some allege a station wagon was involved. Wallace had a station wagon, and there was a station wagon parked on Houston Street just north of the depository. The record does not permit a firm judgment on this point beyond that necessary judgment in courtroom trials: what is the more likely result.

4.   In addition to two Oswald theories, some researchers are convinced Oswald was not involved. Based on my information and understanding from Sam Ballen, Oswald was one of two shooters on the sixth floor.

5.   Questions have been raised about Oswald and Tippitt. It may be that

Oswald shot Tippitt because he had been programmed to shoot to kill, to go down fighting. If so, he would have shot Tippitt in cold blood. When Oswald was arrested in the Texas Theater, he tried again to shoot it out. To all appearances, Oswald was following the Clark plan, that of shooting back, of not being captured.

6. Officer MacDonald suffered a wound to his hand and thumb. *Warren*, p. 171. The point is that Oswald was trying to shoot it out, even though clearly surrounded and in no position to escape.

7. Appendix 35.

8. This remark after the assassination was widely reported. *Warren*, p. 203. No one knows the exact answers Oswald gave while in custody. The interview sessions were not recorded. *Warren*, page 199.

9. Shortly after Wade made the remark, he was called by the new White House according to Cliff Carter.

10. One of the attending surgeons, Dr. Crenshaw, took the call from Johnson.

11. Fritz received a call from the new White House per remarks to his detectives.

12. The Warren Report on the Ruby polygraph exam states answers "were suggestive of deception." *Warren*, p. 814. Warren himself gave an oral history and concluded the test showed Ruby was telling the truth. LBJ Library, oral history, "Earl Warren" (1971) where he says, at page 15, "... [Ruby] cleared it all right."

13. The note is in H. C. Nash, *Citizen's Arrest* (Latitudes, 1977), pp. 46–47.

14. Appendix 36. From the records of the Court of Inquiry at the State Archives in Austin, Texas, the memo shows Jenkins looking for the proposal from Carr. Carr stated Jaworski had agreed to serve and wanted to know if this met Johnson's approval. As noted, Johnson wanted to name the investigators, in effect to name the judges to judge him.

15. The idea was promoted from the beginning of the Warren investigation. U. E. Baughman was a former Secret Service chief whose book on lone nuts killing presidents was released in December 1961. *Secret Service Chief*, above. Former CIA director Allen Dulles used the book at the opening session of the Warren Commission, and the notion of a lone nut anarchist was set in the commission's mind from that point on. Note that the effect of such a statement is not unlike Clark's off-the-record remarks to decision makers. Playing on the mind's tendency to habituate, it makes the original "spin" very important.

16.   Hosty, *Assignment Oswald* (Arcade, 1996).

17.   Appendix 37.

18.   ARRB never received the information requested from the FBI and Justice. See online report.

19.   Appendix 38.

16—Bonus

1.   There is no published record of the case in the court reports. The docket is at the federal court in Austin. An appeal to the Fifth Circuit was decided over the weekend in a rare Saturday morning session without the usual formalities of oral argument. The handwritten order was filed in the archives in the original, very rough version.

2.   The application is docketed at the Railroad Commission under L&G Oil.

3.   The FPC docket was RI71-144. The record was destroyed in routine action at the agency. Report on inquiry under FOIA.

4.   The Supreme Court action is 400 US 939 (1972). No other lawyer with Clark took a case to the U.S. Supreme Court.

5.   Clark's complete tax records have not been released. Two key 1040s are available. Clark Collection, Box 88, File 1371.

6.   The application is Case No. 65,447, Railroad Commission, Oil and Gas Division. Appendix 41 is the lease.

· 7.   *Exxon v. Railroad Commission,* No. 214,030, Travis Courthouse, 201st District. The final decision is appendix 40, initialed by me for Thomas.

8.   There was no check for two million dollars with a notation, "bonus for assassination of Kennedy." The difference showing a net of two million dollars after taxes is from the Clark financial statements and tax returns. See Clark Collection, Box 88, File 1371.

9.   The term "yahoo" was another east Texas phrase referring to a troublemaker. The word originally came from *Gulliver's Travels,* in the story about the wiser houyhnhnms (horses) and the contemptible Yahoos (brutish men). Ellis was referring to Wallace.

10.   The medical report shows extensive physical injuries that are not consistent with the damages to the auto.

19—Fight

1.   The battle between conscience and power or ego was debilitating to me. By 1976, I had tension headaches that required medication. My personal conflict then was between admiring Kennedy and the brute power and fiat

exercised by Clark. In my way of thinking, the law was nothing more than an arbitrary decree if its plain words were not followed. The law that I found was not blind justice; the law was whatever Clark said it was, and I could not rationalize that system, either consciously or subconsciously. Looking back, it was probably a severe case of denial.

2. There were extensive appeals. See, e.g., *McClellan v. State*, 312 S.W.2d 411 (Tex.Ct.App. 1984), review granted, Tex.Ct.Cr.App., opinion issued 1986 (not published); cert.den. 1987.

3. *McClellan v. Travis Bank*, Case No. 164,077, 93rd District Court, Travis County Courthouse. As part of the settlement with FDIC, the entire case was dismissed.

4. Note 5, Privilege, above.

5. The citations are from discussions current at the time of my initial research.

6. See appendix, print evidence, exhibit G, Darby affidavit.

20—Renewal

1. The disclosures are not complete, either to the House committee that concluded there was a conspiracy and a shot from the grassy slope, House Select Committee on Assassinations, Report to the House of Representatives, 95th Congress, March 29, 1979, or to ARRB, Report online, above.

2. The Ruby notes are referred to in H. C. Nash, *Citizen's Arrest* (Latitudes, 1977).

3. *Morning*, above. An earlier bound manuscript is also available.

4. *Estes*.

5. *Peoples*.

6. Curry, *JFK Assassination File* (American Poster, 1971).

7. In *Path*, Caro made the case for Johnson as a man capable of assassinating an opponent.

8. *Politician*.

9. The House Select Committee report is cited above.

10. Warren expressed doubts, at least to the extent of wanting more evidence. He reluctantly agreed to serve and later regretted his service on the commission. LBJ Library, Oral History, Earl Warren.

11. James Reston Jr., *The Lone Star: The Life of John Connally* (Burlingame, 1989), p. 620, ". . . an entirely separate shot struck me." (per Connally).

12. *Treason*, pp. 790–831. Twyman concludes: ". . . [Would Johnson]

become the first elected official in the history of the United States who conspired to assassinate his president? If this is true, and I believe that the evidence shows that it is, Johnson's story is an extraordinary American tragedy."

13.   This is at least implied by Schlesinger, in *Robert Kennedy*, above, p. 391.

14.   ARRB could get nothing from Jackie Kennedy, and her records are sealed for many more years. With Kennedy's death, she left Washington behind and did not look back.

15.   William Manchester, *The Death of a President* (Harper, 1967). He notes that "The absurdity of this [use of plural to describe the Kennedy shooting] does not, of course, preclude a plural responsibility for the tragedy."

16.   Hirsch, at p. 472, apparently leaves unanswered the issue of whether there was a conspiracy. Dallek's *An Unfinished Life* (Little Brown, 2003), at pp. 698–699, reaffirms his opinion that Oswald acted alone. He cites no facts but relies on Gerald Posner's *Case Closed* (Random, 1993), which has been thoroughly discredited by several studies.

17.   Oliver Stone's movie that made the case for the conspiracy. He reached too far, finding a vast number of participants and shooters. If so, surely some of the conspirators would have been disclosed and some of the money would have been found. As we have seen, the conspiracy was a very tight plan involving very few people (and fewer witnesses). Only those needing to know had any idea of what was happening, and they only learned at the last minute. After the fact, those who knew but were beholden to Johnson and rewarded by him, said nothing.

18.   In the 1980s, Nigel Turner started the television series, *The Men Who Killed Kennedy*, now in its seventh edition.

19.   Failure Associates has the video, first used for a mock trial of Oswald at the American Bar Association meeting in San Francisco, 1991.

20.   *The Johnson Years* (Kansas, 1994), edited by Robert Divine, is one volume in the series.

21.   Dallek finds no conspiracy and exonerates Johnson. See *Flawed*, p. 21.

22.   *Dream* does not even mention any suggestion that Johnson was involved in the assassination.

23.   LBJ Library Online, Dedication.

24.   LBJ Library, Oral History, Don Thomas.

25.   Winks, *The Historian as Detective*, xvii.

26.   Ray, *Texas Evidence* (1980), at p. 312. Because of continuing changes in the law, only the standards in effect at the time of the assassination are cited.

27.   Rhode, *Stanford Law Review* (1985), at p. 612.

28.   *Readings on Adversarial Justice* (1988), p. 213.

29.   The constitutional debate was carried into the *Federalist.*

30.   Madison, *Federalist* (Chicago, 1952), Number 39, p. 125, and following.

31.   23 United States Code Section 1001.

32.   Bok, *Lying* (Knopf, 1999), at p. 172.

33.   Catherine Drinker Bowen, *Miracle at Philadelphia* (Little Brown, 1986).

34.   Paine's *Common Sense and The Rights of Man* (Oxford, 1998).

35.   First Inaugural Address, *Writings of Thomas Jefferson* (Easton Press, 1967), at p. 273.

36.   Broder, *Democracy Derailed* (Harcourt, 2000).

37.   *Profiles in Courage,* p. 1.

38.   *Profiles in Courage,* p. 256.

39.   The working title is "Direct Democracy."

40.   *Profiles in Courage,* p. 258.

41.   Lincoln speech, October 16, 1854 (quoted in several books on the Lincoln Douglas debates).

42.   Marrs, *Crossfire,* above, was one of several sources for Oliver Stone's JFK movie. Another was the careful research by Nigel Turner in his continuing television and video series, *The Men Who Killed Kennedy.* [I have been taped to appear in that series in November 2003].

Conclusion

1.   Because a crime is involved, the impact of these disclosures goes a long way. Since the first persons needing to know are the Kennedy family, I sent Senator Edward Kennedy a letter advising him of the fingerprint evidence before our report was submitted to the ARRB in May 1998.

Index